HOW TO SCORE HIGH ON THE

Law School Admission Test

by EDWARD C. GRUBER

arco

219 Park Avenue South, New York, N.Y. 10003

Second Edition
First Printing 1966

CONTENTS

HOW TO USE THIS INDEX
Slightly bend the right-hand edge of the book. This will expose the corresponding Parts which match the index, below.

Part

1

2

3

4

5

. . . continued on next page

CONTENTS
continued

PART THREE

PINPOINT PRACTICE TO RAISE YOUR MARK

PART FOUR

LAW SCHOOL ADMISSION TEST [B]
(Sample)

PART FIVE

SUPPLEMENTARY PRACTICE AND STUDY
MATERIAL FOR THE LSAT

. . . continued on next page

CONTENTS
continued

Part

1

2

3

4

5

How This Book Will Help You

If you are planning to take the Law School Admission Test, this book is indispensable to help you score high.

You are well aware of the importance to your career of the LSAT. It will determine in great measure whether you will be admitted to the graduate school of your choice. There simply are not enough places in the better law schools to accommodate all applicants, worthy as they may be. Your future may depend on how well you do on the test.

This book is designed to familiarize you with the forms in which the questions will be presented . . . to give you valuable practice material to organize what you have learned in undergraduate school . . . to sharpen your ability to perform the intellectual tasks on which the questions are based.

Our assertion that you will get a higher score by the diligent use of this book has psychological as well as educational validity.

1. You will get the *feel* of the examination. This book contains those question-types which you will encounter in the actual examination.

2. You will know what to study by reviewing many typical questions.

3. You will discover what your weaknesses are and so will be able to make a special effort where it will do the most good.

4. You will add to your knowledge. In going over the practice questions, you will not be satisfied merely with the answer to a particular question. You will want to do additional research on the other choices of the same question. In this way you will broaden your background and be better prepared for the examination to come, for it is quite possible that a question on the actual test may require that you know the meaning of one of these other choices.

5. You will be more confident and feel more relaxed on test day because you will have had experience with the form of the examination.

LSAT

PART ONE

The Facts About

The Law School Admission Test

What You Should Know About The Test

THE PURPOSE

The Law School Admission Test (often referred to as the LSAT) is used by:

1. LAW SCHOOLS—to appraise applicants for entrance.

2. COLLEGE STUDENTS AND GRADUATES—to evaluate their fitness for a law career.

3. SCHOLARSHIP COMMITTEES—to select students seeking scholarship grants.

The initiative which led to the development of the Law School Admission Test came from a group of prominent American law schools. A number of them had for years been using their own independent tests, and they all shared the belief that a single uniform admission test, made available several times a year on a national and international scale, would help to ensure the fairness and effectiveness of their admissions procedures. Early in 1947 representatives of these law schools consulted with test specialists regarding the development of a suitable test. After a period of extensive experimentation conducted by Educational Testing Service (ETS) to discover the materials which would do the best possible job, a prototype test was produced. Later research led to the improved form of the test which is now in use.

Two of the guiding principles followed when the LSAT was being developed were, first, to find out from representatives of the law schools themselves what mental qualities are desirable for the study of law and, second, to find out what kind of test material worked best by trying it out on law students and law school applicants. Decisions as to the mental abilities which should be tested were made by the Law School Admission Test Policy Committee. It was the function of ETS, then, to suggest or develop kinds of questions which it believed would test adequately these abilities. Before the content of the test was finally determined, many different types of questions were tried out on law students and their scores were compared with their performance in law courses. The LSAT includes those types of questions which proved most useful in predicting which law students would do well in their studies.

HOW IMPORTANT IS THE LSAT IN GAINING ADMISSION TO A LAW SCHOOL?

Since the test scores provide valuable information about fitness for the study of law, many law schools give preference to applicants who have relatively high scores. It should be emphasized, however, that no law school admits students solely on the basis of test scores, nor does ETS recommend that they do. Consideration is always given to other sources of information about applicants, such as undergraduate record, law school application forms, the results of interviews, letters of recommendation, and so forth.

The test scores have two very important characteristics. 1) They are a dependable measure of certain mental abilities which have been found to be important in the study of law. 2) The scores are based on the same standard for all candidates, regardless of when they take the test. This uniformity of standards differentiates the scores from undergraduate averages, the meaning of which varies markedly depending on the grading standards of the institution from which they come. By virtue of these two characteristics LSAT scores provide law schools with a means of increasing the accuracy of comparisons made among applicants. Thus the use of the test scores as a criterion for admission can help a law school to select from among its applicants those who are most likely to do well in their studies.

From the applicant's point of view, the use of the test scores makes it more likely that his abilities will be fairly evaluated. Thus an applicant with only a moderately high undergraduate record from a college with high grading standards is not so likely to lose out when compared with an applicant having a high record from a college where grading standards are relatively low.

Some people look with suspicion on the LSAT, viewing it as an obstacle intended to make it more difficult for them to reach a desired goal. This is understandable among law school applicants who have been rejected partly on the basis of test scores or among candidates for the test who fear that this might happen. However, such an attitude toward the test is based on a misinterpretation of its purpose and function. Properly used, it can bring about a large saving in time, money and energy both for the law school and for the applicant who may not be adequately equipped to pursue the study of law with profit. It is much better that an applicant be forewarned of probable difficulty in a law school he has applied to than to struggle through his first year only to fail at the end of it.

NATURE OF THE TEST *

MORNING SESSION: The five discrete tests in this battery consist of:

1. Reading Comprehension
2. Nonverbal Reasoning
3. Remembering Main Ideas
4. Law Interpretation
5. Graphs, Charts, and Tables

AFTERNOON SESSION. *The Writing Ability Test:* The three tests in this group are in:

1. Recognizing Common Errors
2. Organizing Ideas
3. Editing Ability

The Cultural Background Test: The three tests in this group are in:

1. Humanities (Literature, Art, Music)
2. Science
3. Social Science

*Subject to change.

HOW QUESTIONS ARE TO BE ANSWERED

All questions are of the objective type; that is, you will be given several lettered answers to a question and from these you are to choose the *one* you think is best. (When you have tried the practice questions, check your answers against the list of correct answers.) In the test itself you will have a separate answer sheet on which you will indicate your answers to all questions. All directions for the sample questions are worded as if a separate answer sheet were provided, so that you will become familiar with directions of this type in advance of the test. The following example will illustrate how the answers are to be indicated on the answer sheet you will use in the test:

15. Chicago is a

(A) state
(B) city
(C) country
(D) town
(E) village.

Sample Answer Spaces:

```
     A   B   C   D   E
15   0   ▮   0   0   0
```

Note that the letters of the suggested answers appear on the answer sheet and that *you are to blacken the space beneath the letter of the answer you wish to give.*

The Arco Practice Answer Sheet, which you will find before each test, is provided to accustom you to the conditions for recording answers.

HOW TO PREPARE FOR THE LSAT

Let us sound a warning at the very start of this discussion of "How to Prepare for the LSAT." Do not wait till a week or even a month before the examination in starting your preparation for it. Cramming will do little for you.

Be systematic. First, take the LSAT Trial Examination that begins on page 17. Analyze the results. You should, thereby, get a fairly good idea of your areas of strength and your areas of weakness. Then concentrate on fortifying yourself where you are weak. Work hard with questions in those fields where the Trial Test has spotlighted initial "softness." Work, work, work in these areas. *You will fare considerably better in the LSAT by following this simple procedure.*

HOW TO TAKE THE LSAT

Arrange to be at the examination center about fifteen minutes before the scheduled starting time. You will start better if you are accustomed to the room.

The test will be held only on the day and at the time scheduled. Under no circumstances will supervisors honor requests for a change in schedule. You will not be permitted to continue the test or any part of it beyond the established time limit. You should bring a watch.

No books, slide rules, dictionaries or papers of any kind may be taken into the examination room; you are urged not to bring them to the center at all. Anyone who is found to have such materials with him will not be permitted to continue the test.

Scratchwork may be done in the margins of the testbooks. Scratch paper is not permitted.

Candidates should bring with them 3 or 4 sharpened No. 2 pencils or a mechanical pencil with soft lead and an eraser. No pencils will be furnished at the center.

You must turn in all testbooks and answer sheets at the close of the examination period. No test materials, documents, or memoranda of any sort are to be taken from the room. Disregard of this rule will be considered as serious an offense as cheating.

If you wish to leave the room during a rest period

or while a test is in progress, you must secure permission from the supervisor.

Every effort is made to assure equally favorable conditions at all centers, with freedom from noise and other disturbance. Visitors are excluded. You can help by refraining from disturbing your fellow candidates.

When you are taking the test, read the directions for each section with care. If you skip over instructions too hastily, you may miss a main idea and thus lose credit for an entire section.

Although the test stresses accuracy more than speed, it is important for you to use your time as economically as possible. Work steadily and as rapidly as you can without becoming careless. Take the questions in order, but do not waste time in pondering over questions which contain extremely difficult or unfamiliar material. The test is so designed that the average person taking it will answer correctly only about two-thirds of the questions. No one is expected to get a perfect score and there is no established passing or failing grade.

In the test you will have a separate answer sheet on which you are to indicate your answers to all questions and on which you will be asked to "grid" your Examination Number. You will find your Examination Number on that part of the application that will be returned to you with your ticket of admission. On the answer sheet you will find a row of six large boxes in which you are to copy your number, one number to a box. Each box has a column of small boxes under it, each with a number from 1 to 0. Go down the column under each box, find the small box with the corresponding number, and blacken the space. Be sure to indicate your number accurately. Please note that zeros are treated as numbers. If your Examination No. were 013065, your gridded number would look like the sample below.

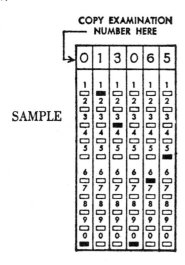

COPY EXAMINATION
NUMBER HERE

SAMPLE

Should You Guess?

Many candidates wonder whether or not to mark the answers to questions about which they are not certain. Your score will be based on the number of questions you answer correctly. No deduction will be made for wrong answers. You are advised to use your time effectively and to mark the best answer you can to every question, regardless of how sure you are of the answer you mark. However, do not waste your time on questions that are too difficult for you. Go on to the other questions and come back to the difficult ones later if you have time.

THE MEANING OF THE MORNING SESSION SCORES

What The Test Measures

As with any test, the score on the morning session of the Law School Admission Test can be best understood by thinking of the purpose for which the test was designed and for which the scores are used. Many faulty interpretations of test scores can be traced to a misunderstanding of the job the test is supposed to do. As has been mentioned earlier, the test was designed primarily to predict success in law schools. The test has been judged successful in performing its job because it has been found that the higher a student scores, the better are his chances of succeeding in law school.

How The Scores Are Interpreted

ETS does not set a passing or failing score on the test. Each school evaluates the scores in its own way. Of course, a score of 700 would be considered high at any school and a score of 300 would be low, but there is a wide range of scores around 500 which cannot be considered high or low in any absolute sense. Different schools judge the scores by different standards and what may be considered a mediocre score at one school may be considered quite satisfactory at another.

In a few cases, there may be special circumstances which the admissions officer will want to keep in mind when considering a test score. He knows that familiarity with the test may improve the second of two scores, and in instances where a candidate has repeated the test he will probably assume that a score somewhere between the two gives a fairer estimate of the candidate's ability. Again, he may give weight to special conditions, such as illness at the time of taking the test, which may have handicapped a candidate.

Obviously you cannot expect to be told your chances of succeeding at every law school in the country. One important practical implication does follow, however, from this discussion. You should apply to several schools. It is an unfortunate mistake to give up when a law school turns you down because your score is too low. The school that turns you down may have had an unusually large number of applicants, or it may place more weight on the score than do other schools. It is a common occurrence for students rejected by some schools to be accepted by others. Your pre-law advisor may be very helpful in this connection. Possibly on the basis of his experience he may be able to suggest schools to which it would be most suitable for you to apply.

THE MEANING OF THE AFTERNOON SESSION SCORES

The afternoon session of the Law School Admission Test includes a test of writing ability and a test of general background. The first of these was introduced into the test because the student of law and the lawyer must be able to communicate effectively in writing as well as by the spoken word. Since there is no time in law school for formal training in the techniques of correct and effective writing, the law schools wish to ensure so far as possible that their entering students are reasonably competent in writing skills. The inclusion of the test of general background results from the conviction of the law schools that a lawyer should be more than a mere technician ignorant of the cultural and historical context within which the law functions. To take his proper place in the community, the lawyer should have an informed awareness of the world around him and its relation to the past. Again, the law schools wish to ensure that their students have something of this quality upon admission.

SAMPLE TEST QUESTIONS

You will find a complete treatment of the sections that make up the Morning and Afternoon Session Tests in Part Two and Part Three of this book. In these pages you have many examples of each of the types of LSAT questions which are given on the actual test. Answer keys are provided in every case.

Samples of some of the questions that customarily appear in the LSAT are illustrated below.

MORNING SESSION *

Remembering Main Ideas

DIRECTIONS: The reading passage given below is followed by questions based on its content. After reading the passage, choose the best answer to each question and blacken the space beneath the appropriate letter on the answer sheet. The questions are to be answered on the basis of what is *stated* or *implied* in the passage.

(NOTE: In one section of the test you are allowed to refer to the reading passages when answering the questions. In another section, you will be given a certain length of time to study the passages in advance, and then you will be asked to answer the questions without looking back at the passages. In such cases, the questions are intended to test your ability to remember the main points of what you have read. You will be told in advance when the questions on the passages you study are to be answered from memory.)

Soon after the First World War began, public attention was concentrated on the spectacular activities of the submarine, and the question was raised more pointedly than ever whether or not the day of the battleship had ended. Naval men conceded the importance of the U-boat and recognized the need for defense against it, but they still placed their confidence in big guns and big ships. The German naval victory at Coronel, off Chile, and the British victories at the Falkland Islands and in the North Sea convinced the experts that fortune still favored superior guns (even though speed played an important part in these battles); and, as long as British dreadnoughts kept the German High Seas Fleet immobilized, the battleship remained in the eyes of naval men the key to naval power.

1. Public attention was focused on the submarine because
   (A) it had immobilized the German High Seas Fleet
   (B) it had played a major role in the British victories at the Falkland Islands and in the North Sea
   (C) it had taken the place of the battleship
   (D) of its spectacular activities
   (E) of its superior speed.

2. Naval victories on both sides led naval authorities to
   (A) disregard speed
   (B) retain their belief in heavy armament
   (C) consider the submarine the key member of the fleet
   (D) minimize the achievements of the submarine
   (E) revise their concept of naval strategy.

---

* The allocation of questions for the MORNING TEST and for the AFTERNOON TEST is not to be taken strictly. For example, English Expression may be given in the Morning Test and/or the Afternoon Test.

3. Naval men acknowledged that the submarine was
   - (A) a factor which would revolutionize marine warfare
   - (B) superior to the battleship in combat
   - (C) more formidable than the other types of ships which composed the fleet
   - (D) the successor to the surface raider
   - (E) a strong weapon against which adequate defense would have to be provided.

4. Naval men were not in accord with the champions of the submarine because
   - (A) they thought that the advantages of the submarine did not equal those of the battleship
   - (B) they believed the submarine victories to be mere chance
   - (C) the battleship was faster
   - (D) the submarine was defenseless except when submerged
   - (E) submarines could not escape a battleship blockade.

Law Interpretation

DIRECTIONS: This group of questions consists of the list of law cases in the left-hand column and the list of legal principles in the right-hand column; these principles may be either real or imaginary, but for purposes of this test you are to assume them to be valid. For each case you are to select the legal principle from the right-hand column which is *most applicable* to the case. To indicate your answer blacken the space beneath the letter on the answer sheet which corresponds to the letter of the legal principle you select.

These questions do not presuppose any specific legal knowledge on your part; you are to base your answers entirely on the ordinary process of logical reasoning.

CASES

5. Mrs. B orders a piano from the Piano Company. It is agreed in writing that if the piano is not satisfactory Mrs. B can return it within ten days and have her money refunded. On the day after the piano is delivered, the piano is damaged by an earthquake. Mrs. B wants to return what is left of the piano and get her money back.

6. B goes to S's music store and selects a certain piano; however, he feels that it will not fit into the color scheme of his home, and so he requests S to have it refinished in a darker color. That night the store and the piano are burned. S wishes to collect from B the price of the piano.

7. B arranged with dealer S to buy a new car from S and to turn in his old car as part of the purchase price. S delivered the new car to B on Monday. On Wednesday B was to give S the used car and pay the difference between the purchase price and the trade-in allowance. On Tuesday B had an accident in which the new car was wrecked. B now claims that the car was S's property and that S should bear the loss.

8. B visited S's orchard. He liked the ripe apples which were ready to be removed from the trees, and so he agreed with S to buy all the apples in the orchard. S was to deliver the apples to B's warehouse. That night the apples were ruined by a severe frost. S now seeks to collect the purchase price from B.

9. B agreed with S to take all the potatoes of No. 1 quality which S could obtain during a specified two-week period. S procured a large quantity of potatoes, but before he could grade them the potatoes were destroyed in a fire which burned down the warehouse in which they were stored. S seeks payment of the contract price from B.

10. B browses around in S's book shop and finally selects and pays for a first edition of George Ade's *Fables in Slang*. As he is carrying the book home, it starts to rain and the book becomes water soaked. B wants to return the book and get a refund.

PRINCIPLES

(A) Where there is a sale of goods and no obligations remain to be fulfilled, and where the goods are identified as the particular goods about which the parties bargain, the ownership interest in the goods, unless a different intention appears, is presumably intended to pass at once to the buyer.

(B) Where there is a contract to sell goods that are identified as the particular goods about which the parties bargain, and where the seller is bound to do something to the goods to put them in a deliverable state, the ownership interest in the goods, unless a different intention appears, presumably is not intended to pass until the seller has completed his duties with respect to the goods.

(C) When the agreement is not for the sale of specific goods but involves merely the supply of a certain amount of goods answering a particular description, no ownership interest passes at the time of the bargain.

(D) Delivery of goods under a contract to sell,

thereby giving control and present use and enjoyment of the goods, is generally a clear indication of the intention of the parties that the ownership interest in the property was to pass to the buyer immediately.

(E) When goods are delivered to the buyer with an arrangement that indicates a present sale but gives the buyer an option to return the goods instead of paying the price, the ownership of the goods, unless a different intention appears, passes to the buyer when the goods are delivered.

DIRECTIONS: The law case described below is followed by several legal principles. These principles may be either real or imaginary, but for purposes of this test you are to assume them to be valid. Following each legal principle are four statements regarding the possible applicability or inapplicability of the principle to the law case. You are to select the *one* statement which most appropriately describes the applicability or inapplicability of the principle to the law case and blacken the space beneath the letter of the statement you select.

These questions do not presuppose any specific legal knowledge on your part; you are to arrive at your answers entirely by the ordinary processes of logical reasoning.

After having bought a ticket to Far City, Mrs. P was waiting on the platform for her train. A train going to Near City stopped and Mr. X, carrying a package, almost fell as he hurriedly jumped aboard the train. A guard of the railroad pushed X so roughly and negligently into the car that X dropped his package. The package contained fireworks, though neither the railroad company nor the guard knew this. The fireworks exploded, throwing down some scales many feet away at the other end of the platform. The scales struck Mrs. P and injured her severely. Mrs. P sues the railroad for the injuries which she claims were caused by the negligent act of the guard.

11. By statute it is a criminal offense, punishable by a prison term and a fine, for a person to carry a package of fireworks upon a bus, trolley car, or train without first notifying the operators of the intention to do so and securing their permission for the trip.

The above principle is

(A) *applicable* since the operators of the railroad would have given Mr. X permission to carry his fireworks on the railroad had he requested it

(B) *applicable* since the statute demonstrates

an attempt by the legislature to regulate and make safe the transportation of fireworks on public carriers

(C) *not applicable* since Mrs. P is interested in securing money damages from the railroad, not in pressing a criminal prosecution against X

(D) *not applicable* since the operators of the railroad would never have given Mr. X permission to carry his fireworks on the railroad had he requested it.

12. When one acts negligently and the negligent act causes injury to a person in a manner not reasonably foreseeable, the person so acting is in no way liable to the person injured by the negligent act.

The above principle is

(A) *applicable* since Mr. X had no way of knowing that Mrs. P was standing near scales which were not securely fastened and which, therefore, might injure her.

(B) *applicable* since the guard could not have been expected to foresee that an explosion of such force would result from the dropping of the package

(C) *not applicable* since Mr. X must have known that any blow to the fireworks might result in injury to anyone standing on the platform

(D) *not applicable* since the guard and other railroad employees knew that the scales were not securely fastened to the wall and might easily be jarred by an explosion.

13. Railroads are absolutely liable for damage done to personal property of any passenger while he is on railroad property; there is no burden on the owner of such property to show that either the railroad or its employee acted negligently.

The above principle is

(A) *applicable* since each railroad must exercise a high degree of care in its operation and must compensate those who suffer through its negligence

(B) *applicable* since the only injury suffered by Mr. X was to his property, the package of fireworks.

(C) *not applicable* since the guard acted negligently when he pushed Mr. X

(D) *not applicable* since Mrs. P has made no claims for damages other than those for the injury to her person.

Nonverbal Reasoning

DIRECTIONS: Each of these problems consists of two groups of figures, labeled 1 and 2. These are followed by five lettered answer figures. For each problem you are to decide what characteristic *each* of the figures in group 1 has that *none* of the figures in group 2 has. Then select the lettered answer figure that has this characteristic.

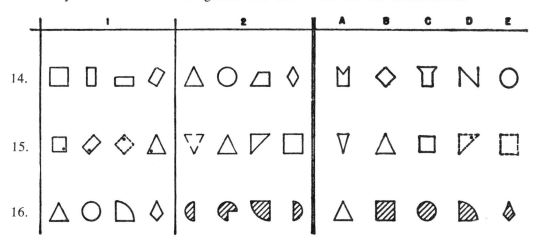

(In sample problem 14 you will note that all the figures in group 1 are rectangles but none of the figures in group 2 is a rectangle. In sample problem 15, all the figures in group 1 include a dot but none of the figures in group 2 includes a dot. The figures in group 1 sample problem 16 are all white figures, but none of the group 2 figures is white.)

Graphs, Charts, and Tables

DIRECTIONS: This section of the test consists of questions based on charts, tables, and graphs. Each question is followed by five choices, only *one* of which is correct. Whenever the option "Not answerable" appears, it is to be understood to mean "Not answerable on the basis of the data given."

Select the correct answer to each question and mark the corresponding space on the answer sheet.

DISTRIBUTION OF EMPLOYMENT IN NEW JERSEY BY INDUSTRY AND SEX—1940

1. Manufacturing
2. Trade—wholesale and retail
3. Personal services
4. Transportation, communication, utilities
5. Professional and related
6. Finance, insurance, real estate
7. Construction
8. Government
9. Agriculture
10. All other, including those not reported

Questions 17-19 are based on the graph above.

17. Which of the industries listed employed the greatest proportion of women?
(A) 1   (B) 2
(C) 3   (D) 7
(E) 8

18. Approximately how many thousand men were employed in the construction industry?
(A) 4   (B) 6
(C) 8   (D) 10
(E) Not answerable

19. Out of every 100 persons employed in the manufacturing industry, approximately how many were women?
(A) 10   (B) 20
(C) 30   (D) 40
(E) Not answerable

AFTERNOON SESSION

I. TEST OF WRITING ABILITY

Recognizing Errors

DIRECTIONS: Among the sentences in this group are some which cannot be accepted in formal, written English for one or another of the following reasons:

Poor Diction: The use of a word which is improper either because its meaning does not fit the sentence or because it is not acceptable in formal writing.

Example: The audience was strongly <u>effected</u> by the senator's speech.

Verbosity: Repetitious elements adding nothing to the meaning of the sentence and not justified by any need for special emphasis.

Example: At that time there was <u>then</u> no right of petition.

Faulty Grammar: Word forms and expressions which do not conform to the grammatical and structural usages required by formal written English (errors in case, number, parallelism, and the like).

Example: Everyone in the delegation had <u>their</u> reasons for opposing the measure.

No sentence has more than one of these errors. Some sentences have no errors. Read each sentence carefully; then on your answer sheet blacken the space under:

D if the sentence contains an error in <u>diction</u>,
V if the sentence is <u>verbose</u>,
G if the sentence contains <u>faulty grammar</u>,
O if the sentence contains <u>none</u> of these errors.

20. In the last decade movie production has advanced forward with great strides.

21. In spite of their remarkable display of fortitude, the gallant defenders were plenty discouraged.

22. Neither of the men was seriously hurt in the accident.

23. The commission decided to reimburse the property owners, to readjust the rates, and that they would extend the services in the near future.

24. Who it was that invented the wheel has never been determined and is not known.

25. Holding the heavy log made his right hand ache so that he threw it into the fire.

26. The dean made an illusion to the Boer War in his talk.

Organization of Ideas

DIRECTIONS: Each set of questions in this test consists of several statements. Most of the statements refer to the same subject or idea. The statements can be classified as follows:

(A) the *central idea* to which most of the statements are related

(B) *main supporting ideas,* which are general points directly related to the central idea;

(C) *illustrative facts* or detailed statements, which document the main supporting ideas;

(D) statements *irrelevant* to the central idea.

The statements may be regarded as headings in an outline: they are *not* sentences taken from one complete paragraph. The outline might, for example, have the following form:

A. The Central Idea
 B. Main Supporting Idea
  C. Illustrative Fact
 B. Main Supporting Idea
  C. Illustrative Fact
  C. Illustrative Fact

Classify the following sentences according to the scheme set forth above:

27. The Roman roads connected all parts of the Empire with Rome.

28. The Roman roads were so well built that some of them remain today.

29. One of the greatest achievements of the Romans was their extensive and durable system of roads.

30. Wealthy travelers in Roman times used horse-drawn coaches.

31. Along Roman roads caravans would bring to Rome luxuries from Alexandria and the East.

32. In present-day Italy some of the roads used are original Roman roads.

EDITING ABILITY

Directions: A sentence is given in which one part is underlined. Following the sentence are five choices. The first (A) choice simply repeats the underlined part. The subsequent four choices suggest other ways to express the underlined part of the original sentence. If you think that the underlined part is correct as it stands, write the answer A. If you believe that the underlined part is incorrect, select from among the other choices (B or C or D or E) the one you think is correct. Grammar, sentence structure, word usage, and punctuation are to be considered in your decision, and the original meaning of the sentence must be retained.

33. My younger brother insists <u>that he is as tall as me.</u>
    (A) that he is as tall as me.
    (B) that he is so tall as me.
    (C) that he is tall as me.
    (D) that he is as tall as I.
    (E) he is as tall as me.

34. It is so dark that <u>I can't hardly see.</u>
    (A) I can't hardly see.
    (B) I can hardly see.
    (C) I cannot hardly see.
    (D) I cannot see hardly.
    (E) I can see hardly.

35. <u>After it had laid in the rain all night,</u> it was not fit for use again.
    (A) After it had laid in the rain all night,
    (B) After it lay in the rain all night,
    (C) After it laid in the rain all night,
    (D) After it lied in the rain all night,
    (E) After it had lain in the rain all night,

II. TEST OF GENERAL BACKGROUND

Humanities

36. All the following pairs of people were contemporaries *except*
    (A) Johann Sebastian Bach and Voltaire
    (B) Joseph Haydn and Alexander Hamilton
    (C) Robert Schumann and Edgar Allan Poe
    (D) Richard Wagner and Adolph Hitler
    (E) Giuseppe Verdi and Queen Victoria.

37. What would be the probable type of a musical program devoted solely to the compositions of Mahler, Beethoven, Shostakovitch, and Hindemith?
    (A) Piano recital
    (B) Symphony orchestra concert
    (C) String quartet recital
    (D) Organ recital
    (E) Song recital.

Science

38. Which of the following explained the retrograde motion of the planets by the use of epicycles?
    I. Ptolemy
    II. Galileo
    III. Kepler
    (A) I only   (B) II only
    (C) III only   (D) I and II only
    (E) I, II, and III

39. The reason for the red appearance of the setting sun is also the reason why
    (A) a red barn looks redder at sunset than at noon
    (B) red is a better color than blue for the navigation lights on top of radio transmission towers
    (C) a blue object looks black in red light
    (D) the flame from burning calcium is red
    (E) blood looks red under white light

Social Science

40. A truly laissez-faire economic system **came** closest to existing in
    (A) Europe in the Middle Ages
    (B) Great Britain in the eighteenth century
    (C) Great Britain and the United States in the nineteenth century
    (D) The United States in the twentieth century
    (E) France and Germany in the nineteenth century

41. By which of the following has the Middle East been seriously handicapped in its economic development?
    I. Lack of adequate water resources
    II. Lack of a substantial middle class
    III. Low rate of investment of native capital
    (A) I only   (B) I and II only
    (C) I and III only   (D) II and III only
    (E) I, II, and III

ANSWER KEY TO SAMPLE QUESTIONS

1. D	9. C	17. C	25. G	33. D
2. B	10. A	18. E	26. D	34. B
3. E	11. C	19. C	27. B	35. E
4. A	12. B	20. V	28. B	36. D
5. E	13. D	21. D	29. A	37. B
6. B	14. B	22. O	30. D	38. A
7. D	15. D	23. G	31. C	39. B
8. B	16. A	24. V	32. C	40. C
				41. E

WHEN SHOULD YOU TAKE THE LSAT?

The Law School Admission Test is given several times a year. In certain sections of the country there may be a more frequent administering of the test than in other sections. The question is: "When should the LSAT be taken?"

If you are taking the test because it is required by a law school to which you plan to have your scores sent, you will take the LSAT when that particular school specifies that you are to take the examination.

On the other hand, if you are taking the test to determine your fitness for a law career, it would be advisable for you to register for the LSAT as soon as possible. In this way, you will discover without delay the "exploratory" results of the examination.

APPLYING FOR THE EXAMINATION

1. Find out from the law school(s) of your choice whether or not you are to take the Law School Admission Test. If it is required or recommended, find out on what date you should take it. Plan to take the test on the earliest date your law school specifies.

2. Registration for the LSAT does not constitute application for admission to law school. Such application must be made by filing appropriate papers with the institution concerned.

3. Choose a convenient examination center.

4. Detach the application from the LSAT bulletin and fill it out completely, indicating the date on which you want to take the LSAT and send it with a check or money order to Educational Testing Service.

5. After your application has been received and found in order, ETS will send you a ticket of admission giving the exact address of the examination center and the test date.

TRANSMITTING THE RESULTS

One copy of your score report will be sent directly to you. In addition, ETS will send a score report to each of the law schools you list on your application. No one law school will know the number or the names of other law schools to which you may be applying for admission. The scoring range is 200 to 800; that is, 200 is the lowest score a candidate may get—800 is the highest. 500 is the average score and about two-thirds of those tested receive scores between 400 and 600.

With your score, you will receive a memorandum describing the score system and giving a distribution of scores for a large group of applicants. The distribution of scores, which gives the percentages of candidates whose scores fall below each of several selected scores, will enable you to determine your standing among all applicants who have taken the test over a number of years. If your score is very high in this group your chances of being accepted are quite good, whereas if your score is very low you are less likely to be accepted although the exact degree of likelihood will vary depending on the schools to which you apply.

Suggestions Before You Take The Sample Test

The first thing we want you to do, in solid preparation for the Law School Admission Test, is to administer to yourself the Sample (A).

This test follows the general pattern of a recent Law School Admission Test. The Sample Test is designed to give you familiarity with the types of questions which you will face on the actual test.

Put yourself under strict examination conditions. Allow yourself exactly three hours and thirty minutes of working time for the Morning Session and two hours of working time for the Afternoon Session.

LSAT TIMETABLE*

Morning Session

SECTION I: Nonverbal Reasoning—35 minutes

SECTION II: Reading Comprehension—40 minutes

SECTION III: Graphs, Charts, and Tables—45 minutes

NOW TAKE A TEN-MINUTE BREAK

After the break, proceed immediately to Section IV

SECTION IV: Law Interpretation—35 minutes

SECTION V: Nonverbal Reasoning—35 minutes

SECTION VI: Remembering Main Ideas—20 minutes

Afternoon Session*

SECTION I: Recognizing Errors—20 minutes

SECTION II: Organization of Ideas—20 minutes

SECTION III: Editing Ability—20 minutes

SECTION IV: Humanities (Literature, Art, Music)—30 minutes

SECTION V: Science—15 minutes

SECTION VI: Social Science—15 minutes

---

* The allocation of questions for the MORNING TEST and for the AFTERNOON TEST is not to be taken strictly. For example, Recognizing Errors may be given in the Morning Test and/or the Afternoon Test.

$$\boxed{\begin{matrix} L^s \\ a_t \end{matrix}}$$

PART TWO

Law School Admission Test

(SAMPLE A)

This test closely resembles the actual test. Take this Sample Test now for guidance to determine how best to pinpoint your practice and study effort.

The actual test which you are going to take may, in some areas, have more difficult questions than you will encounter in this Sample Test. On the other hand, the questions may be less difficult, but don't bank on this. We trust that in your use of this book, you will gain confidence — not overconfidence.

Use the special Answer Sheet (next page) to record your answers.

ANSWER SHEET FOR SAMPLE TEST A
Morning Session

	A	B	C	D	E			A	B	C	D	E			A	B	C	D	E			A	B	C	D	E			A	B	C	D	E
1							30							59							88							117					
2							31							60							89							118					
3							32							61							90							119					
4							33							62							91							120					
5							34							63							92							121					
6							35							64							93							122					
7							36							65							94							123					
8							37							66							95							124					
9							38							67							96							125					
10							39							68							97							126					
11							40							69							98							127					
12							41							70							99							128					
13							42							71							100							129					
14							43							72							101							130					
15							44							73							102							131					
16							45							74							103							132					
17							46							75							104							133					
18							47							76							105							134					
19							48							77							106							135					
20							49							78							107							136					
21							50							79							108							137					
22							51							80							109							138					
23							52							81							110							139					
24							53							82							111							140					
25							54							83							112							141					
26							55							84							113							142					
27							56							85							114							143					
28							57							86							115							144					
29							58							87							116							145					

	A	B	C	D	E			A	B	C	D	E			A	B	C	D	E			A	B	C	D	E			A	B	C	D	E
146							149							152							155							158					
147							150							153							156							159					
148							151							154							157							160					

Afternoon Session

	A	B	C	D	E			A	B	C	D	E			A	B	C	D	E			A	B	C	D	E			A	B	C	D	E
1							27							53							79							105					
2							28							54							80							106					
3							29							55							81							107					
4							30							56							82							108					
5							31							57							83							109					
6							32							58							84							110					
7							33							59							85							111					
8							34							60							86							112					
9							35							61							87							113					
10							36							62							88							114					
11							37							63							89							115					
12							38							64							90							116					
13							39							65							91							117					
14							40							66							92							118					
15							41							67							93							119					
16							42							68							94							120					
17							43							69							95							121					
18							44							70							96							122					
19							45							71							97							123					
20							46							72							98							124					
21							47							73							99							125					
22							48							74							100							126					
23							49							75							101							127					
24							50							76							102							128					
25							51							77							103							129					
26							52							78							104							130					

Morning Session

SECTION I — NONVERBAL REASONING
(35 minutes)

DIRECTIONS: In each of these questions, look at the symbols in the first two boxes. Something about the three symbols in the first box makes them alike; something about the two symbols in the other box with the question mark makes them alike. Look for some characteristic that is common to all symbols in the same box, yet makes them different from the symbols in the other box. Among the five answer choices, find the symbol that can best be substituted for the question mark, because it is *like* the symbols in the second box, and, *for the same reason*, different from those in the first box.

1.

A   B   C   D   E

2.

A   B   C   D   E

3.

A   B   C   D   E

4.

A   B   C   D   E

5.

A   B   C   D   E

6.

A   B   C   D   E

7.

A   B   C   D   E

8.

A   B   C   D   E

9.

A   B   C   D   E

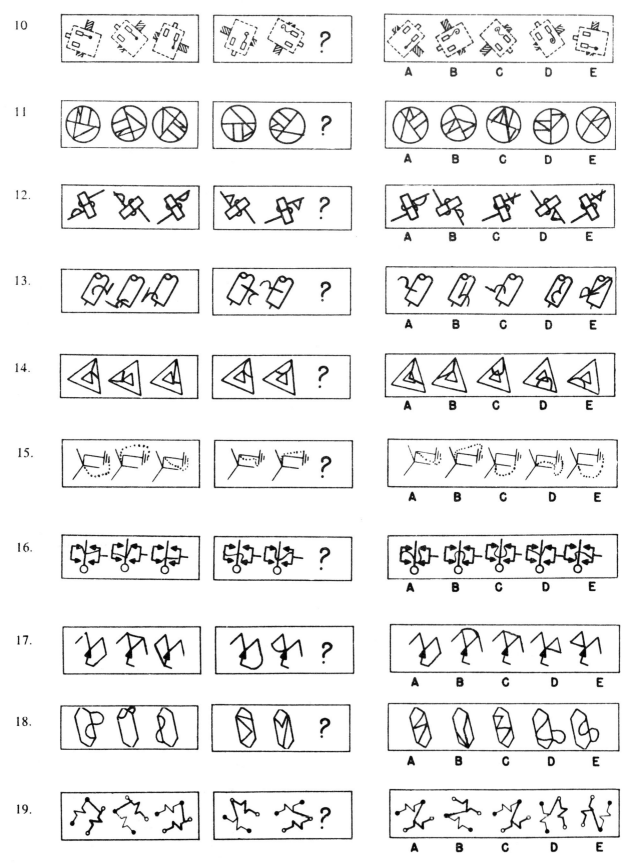

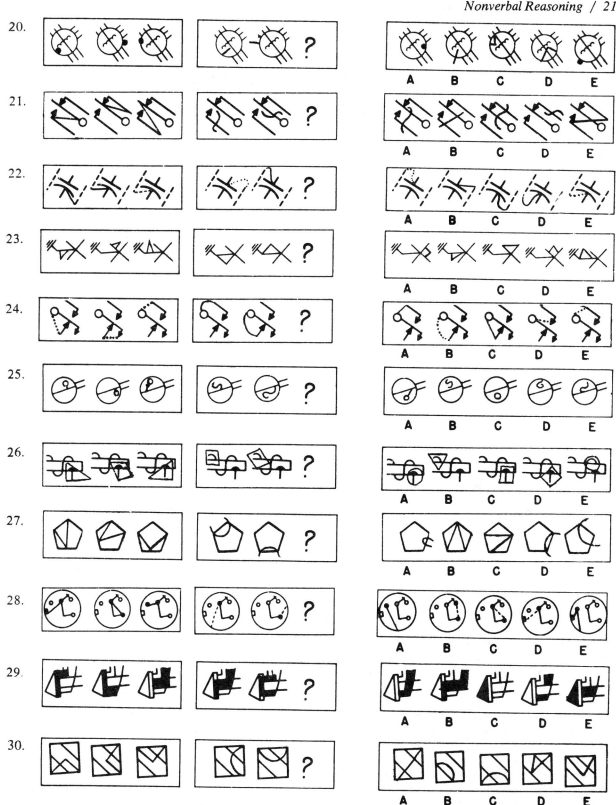

End Of Section I

If you finish before time is called, check your work on this section only.

When time is called, proceed directly to the next section and do not return to this section.

SECTION II — READING COMPREHENSION
(40 Minutes)

Directions: Below each of the following passages, you will find questions or incomplete statements about the passage. Each statement or question is followed by lettered words or expressions. Select the word or expression that most satisfactorily completes each statement or answers each question in accordance with the meaning of the passage. Write the letter of that word or expression on your answer paper.

If a man were called to fix the period in the history of the world, during which the condition of the human race was most happy and prosperous, he would, without hesitation, name that which elapsed from the death of Domitian to the accession of Commodus [96–180 A.D.]. The vast extent of the Roman empire was governed by absolute power, under the guidance of virtue and wisdom. The armies were restrained by the firm but gentle hand of four successive emperors, whose characters and authority commanded involuntary respect. The forms of the civil administration were carefully preserved by Nerva, Trajan, Hadrian, and the Antonines, who delighted in the image of liberty, and were pleased with considering themselves as the accountable ministers of the laws. Such princes deserved the honour of restoring the republic, had the Romans of their days been capable of enjoying a rational freedom.

The labours of these monarchs were overpaid by the immense reward that inseparably waited on their success; by the honest pride of virtue, and by the exquisite delight of beholding the general happiness of which they were the authors. A just, but melancholy reflection embittered, however, the noblest of human enjoyments. They must often have recollected the instability of a happiness which depended on the character of a single man. The fatal moment was perhaps approaching, when some licentious youth, or some jealous tyrant, would abuse, to the destruction, that absolute power, which they had exerted for the benefit of their people. The ideal restraints of the senate and the laws might serve to display the virtues, but could never correct the vices, of the emperor. The military force was a blind and irresistible instrument of oppression; and the corruption of Roman manners would always supply flatterers eager to applaud, and ministers prepared to serve, the fear or the avarice, the lust or the cruelty, of their masters.

These gloomy apprehensions had been already justified by the experience of the Romans. The annals of the emperors exhibit a strong and various picture of human nature, which we should vainly seek among the mixed and doubtful characters of modern history. In the conduct of those monarchs we may trace the utmost lines of vice and virtue; the most exalted perfection, and the meanest degeneracy of our own species. The golden age of Trajan and the Antonines had been preceded by an age of iron. It is almost superfluous to enumerate the unworthy successors of Augustus. Their unparalled vices, and the splendid theater on which they were acted, have saved them from oblivion. The dark unrelenting Tiberius, the furious Caligula, the feeble Claudius, the profligate and cruel Nero, the beastly Vitellius, and the timid inhuman Domitian, are condemned to everlasting infamy. During fourscore years (excepting only the short and doubtful respite of Vespasian's reign) Rome groaned beneath an unremitting tyranny, which exterminated the ancient families of the republic, and was fatal to almost every virtue and every talent that arose in that unhappy period.

31. The emperor group which is spoken of favorably consists of
    (A) Trajan, Caligula, Hadrian
    (B) the Antonines, Vespasian, Domitian
    (C) Nerva, Claudius, Vitellius
    (D) Claudius, Caligula, the Antonines
    (E) Vespasian, Trajan, Hadrian.

32. The period during which the Roman Empire showed greatest stability was the
    (A) second century B.C.
    (B) first century B.C.
    (C) second century A.D.
    (D) first century A.D.
    (E) none of the above.

33. The passage implies that
    (A) the military element in a government has a worthwhile function
    (B) a benevolent despot may have doubts about one-man rule
    (C) there is something good in every wicked ruler
    (D) most of the Roman emperors were degenerates
    (E) the later Roman emperors were superior rulers.

34. The Roman emperors are unique in history in that
    (A) they represent greater variety of moral conduct than any other group of leaders
    (B) they are unmatched for their cruelty
    (C) their life spans were shorter than those of any other group of rulers
    (D) they were the most capable leaders in all history
    (E) they encouraged the building of roads and temples.

35. The writer impresses you as being
    (A) in favor of the dictatorial type of govment
    (B) of the opinion that the Roman citiens, under the later emperors, were in a wretched state
    (C) doubtful of the capability of the people of Rome to appreciate freedom
    (D) tolerant and hopeful of the motives of the military
    (E) in favor of the checks and balances feature of government.

36. The author of this article is
    (A) Pushkin
    (B) Dewey
    (C) Symington
    (D) Stowe
    (E) Gibbon.

Do students learn from programed instruction? The research leaves us in no doubt of this. They do, indeed, learn. They learn from linear programs, from branching programs built on the Skinnerian model, from scrambled books of the Crowder type, from Pressey review tests with immediate knowledge of results, from programs on machines or programs in texts. Many kinds of students learn—college, high school, secondary, primary, preschool, adult, professional, skilled labor, clerical employees, military, deaf, retarded, imprisoned—every kind of student that programs have been tried on. Using programs, these students are able to learn mathematics and science at different levels, foreign languages, English language correctness, the details of the U.S. Constitution, spelling, electronics, computer science, psychology, statistics, business skills, reading skills, instrument flying rules, and many other subjects. The limits of the topics which can be studied efficiently by means of programs are not yet known.

For each of the kinds of subject matter and the kinds of student mentioned above, experiments have demonstrated that a considerable amount of learning can be derived from programs; this learning has been measured either by comparing pre- and post-tests or the time and trials needed to reach a set criterion of performance. But the question, how well do students learn from programs as compared to how well they learn from other kinds of instruction, we cannot answer quite so confidently.

Experimental psychologists typically do not take very seriously the evaluative experiments in which learning from programs is compared with learning from conventional teaching. Such experiments are doubtless useful, they say, for school administrators or teachers to prove to themselves (or their boards of education) that programs work. But whereas one can describe fairly well the characteristics of a program, can one describe the characteristics of a classroom teaching situation so that the result of the comparison will have any generality? What kind of teacher is being compared to what kind of program? Furthermore, these early evaluative experiments with programs are likely to suffer from the Hawthorne effect: that is to say, students are in the spotlight when testing something new, and are challenged to do well. It is very hard to make allowance for this effect. Therefore, the evaluative tests may be useful administratively, say many of the experimenters, but do not contribute much to science, and should properly be kept for private use.

These objections are well taken. And yet, do they justify us in ignoring the evaluative studies? The great strength of a program is that it permits the student to learn efficiently by himself. Is it not therefore important to know how much and what kind of skills, concepts, insights, or attitudes he can learn by himself from a program as compared to what he can learn from a teacher? Admittedly, this is a very difficult and complex research problem, but that should not keep us from trying to solve it.

37. The word Skinnerian refers to
    (A) a plastic model
    (B) a nineteenth century textbook
    (C) a psychologist
    (D) a pedagogical principle
    (E) a culinary device.

38. The article implies that programed instruction
    (A) is inferior to other instruction
    (B) is superior to other instruction
    (C) is beneficial regardless of the type of programing used
    (D) is best for certain educational levels
    (E) is probably of temporary duration.

39. Psychologists view the results of program experiments
    (A) lightly
    (B) enthusiastically
    (C) with distaste
    (D) with complete acceptance
    (E) with risibility.

40. The article indicates that, with programed instruction, the teacher
    (A) may be dispensed with
    (B) may prove of negative value
    (C) and principal must work together
    (D) must be superior to get results
    (E) remains an important factor.

41. Programed learning
    (A) is a recent educational innovation
    (B) has been used in our schools for many years
    (C) is confined to teaching machines
    (D) refers to a student's school program
    (E) is always in linear form.

42. The expression "scrambled books" refers to a program type in which the student
    (A) eats while he learns
    (B) learns in a disorganized manner
    (C) learns by referring to various reference materials
    (D) is directed to different pages not in consecutive order
    (E) must be self-directed in his selection of research materials.

"I have considered the structure of all volant animals, and find the folding continuity of the bat's wings most easily accommodated to the human form. Upon this model I shall begin my task tomorrow, and in a year expect to tower into the air beyond the malice or pursuit of man. But I will work only on this condition, that the art shall not be divulged, and that you shall not require me to make wings for any but ourselves."

"Why," said Rasselas, "should you envy others so great an advantage? All skill ought to be exerted for universal good; every man has owed much to others, and ought to repay the kindness that he has received."

"If men were all virtuous," returned the artist, "I should with great alacrity teach them all to fly. But what would be the security of the good, if the bad could at pleasure invade them from the sky? Against an army sailing through the clouds neither wall, nor mountains, nor seas, could afford any security. A flight of northern savages might hover in the wind, and light at once with irresistible vio-

lence upon the capital of a fruitful region that was rolling under them. Even this valley, the retreat of princes, the abode of happiness, might be violated by the sudden descent of some of the naked nations that swarm on the coast of the southern sea."

43. The word "volant," according to the context, means
    (A) crawling
    (B) violent
    (C) carnivorous
    (D) ferocious
    (E) flying.

44. The author of the passage expresses a philosophy which
    (A) is currently applicable
    (B) expresses optimism
    (C) was valid only in his day
    (D) reminds one of a military strategist
    (E) is similar to existentialism.

45. The person whom Rasselas is speaking to is
    (A) a tailor
    (B) a gambler
    (C) a bat
    (D) an artist
    (E) a biologist.

46. The attitude of the person giving his point of view is one of
    (A) optimism
    (B) sprightliness
    (C) distrust
    (D) innocence
    (E) sarcasm.

47. In this selection, the author is employing the literary device of
    (A) onomatopoeia   (B) flashback
    (C) symbolism   (D) alliteration
    (E) irony.

48. Worldwide peace, according to the passage, could come about by
    (A) arming for defense
    (B) eliminating evil tendencies
    (C) resorting to stratagem
    (D) establishing firm controls
    (E) letting the intellectuals govern.

Shams and delusions are esteemed for soundest truths, while reality is fabulous. If men would steadily observe realities only, and not allow themselves to be deluded, life, to compare it with such things as we know, would be like a fairy tale and the Arabian Nights' Entertainments. If we respected only what is inevitable and has a right to be, music and poetry would resound along the streets. When we are unhurried and wise, we perceive that only great and worthy things have any permanent and absolute existence, — that petty fears and petty pleasures are but the shadow of the reality. This is always exhilarating and sublime. By closing the eyes and slumbering, and consenting to be deceived by shows, men establish and confirm their daily life of routine and habit everywhere, which still is built on purely illusory foundations. Children, who play life, discern its true law and relations more clearly than men, who fail to live it worthily, but who think that they are wiser by experience, that is, by failure. I have read in a Hindoo book, that "there was a king's son, who, being expelled in infancy from his native city, was brought up by a forester, and, growing up to maturity in that state, imagined himself to belong to the barbarous race with which he lived. One of his father's ministers having discovered him, revealed to him what he was, and the misconception of his character was removed, and he knew himself to be a prince. So soul," continues the Hindoo philosopher, "from the circumstances in which it is placed, mistakes its own character, until the truth is revealed to it by some holy teacher, and then it knows itself to be *Brahme*." We think that that *is* which *appears* to be. If a man should give us an account of the realities he beheld, we should not recognize the place in his description. Look at a meeting-house, or a court-house, or a jail, or a shop, or a dwelling-house, and say what that thing really is before a true gaze, and they would all go to pieces in your account of them. Men esteem truth remote, in the outskirts of the system, behind the farthest star, before Adam and after the last man. In eternity there is indeed something true and sublime. But all these times and places and occasions are now and here. God himself culminates in the present moment, and will never be more divine in the lapse of all ages. And we are enabled to apprehend at all what is sublime and noble only by the perpetual instilling and drenching of the reality that surrounds us. The universe constantly and obediently answers to our conceptions; whether we travel fast or slow, the track is laid for us. Let us spend our lives in conceiving then. The poet or the artist never yet had so fair and noble a design but some of his posterity at least could accomplish it.

49. **The writer's attitude toward the arts is one of**
    (A) indifference   (B) suspicion
    (C) admiration   (D) repulsion
    (E) flippancy.

50. The author believes that a child
    (A) should practice what the Hindoos preach
    (B) frequently faces vital problems better than grownups do
    (C) prefers to be a barbarian than to be a prince
    (D) hardly ever knows his true origin
    (E) is incapable of appreciating the arts.

51. The passage implies that human beings
    (A) cannot distinguish the true from the untrue
    (B) are immoral if they are lazy
    (C) should be bold and fearless
    (D) believe in fairy tales
    (E) have progressed culturally throughout history.

52. The word "fabulous" in the second line means
    (A) wonderful
    (B) delicious
    (C) birdlike
    (D) incomprehensible
    (E) nonexistent.

53. The passage urges the reader
    (A) to view the stars in their true light
    (B) to travel slowly or rapidly, as the occasion demands
    (C) to appraise the present for its true value
    (D) to be observant in regard to his environment
    (E) to be deeply religious.

54. You would suspect that the author
    (A) was noted for his books predominantly on historical, military, and naval subjects
    (B) was one of the world's great satirists
    (C) was a first-rate scientist
    (D) was a rebel against the restraints imposed by society
    (E) was a devotee of a cult.

Suppose you go into a fruiterer's shop, wanting an apple—you take up one, and, on biting it, you find it is sour; you look at it, and see that it is hard and green. You take up another one, and that too is hard, green, and sour. The shopman offers you a third; but, before biting it, you examine it, and find that it is hard and green, and you immediately say that you will not have it, as it must be sour, like those that you have already tried.

Nothing can be more simple than that, you think; but if you will take the trouble to analyse and trace out into its logical elements what has been done by the mind, you will be greatly surprised. In the first place you have performed the operation of induction. You found that, in two experiences, hardness and greenness in apples went together with sourness. It was so in the first case, and it was confirmed by the second. True, it is a very small basis, but still it is enough to make an induction from; you generalise the facts, and you expect to find sourness in apples where you get hardness and greenness. You found upon that a general law, that all hard and green apples are sour; and that, so far as it goes, is a perfect induction. Well, having got your natural law in this way, when you are offered another apple which you find is hard and green, you say, "All hard and green apples are sour; this apple is hard and green, therefore this apple is sour." That train of reasoning is what logicians call a syllogism, and has all its various parts and terms—its major premiss, its minor premiss, and its conclusion. And, by the help of further reasoning, which, if drawn out, would have to be exhibited in two or three other syllogisms, you arrive at your final determination, "I will not have that apple." So that, you see, you have, in the first place, established a law by induction, and upon that you have founded a deduction, and reasoned out the special particular case. Well now, suppose, having got your conclusion of the law, that at some times afterwards, you are discussing the qualities of apple with a friend; you will say to him, "It is a very curious thing, but I find that all hard and green apples are sour!" Your friend says to you, "But how do you know that?" You at once reply, "Oh, because I have tried them over and over again, and have always found them to be so." Well, if we were talking science instead of common sense, we should call that an experimental verification. And, if still opposed, you go further, and say, "I have heard from the people in Somersetshire and Devonshire, where a large number of apples are grown, that they have observed the same thing. It is also found to be the case in Normandy, and in North America. In short, I find it to be the universal experience of mankind wherever attention has been directed to the subject." Whereupon, your friend, unless he is a very unreasonable man, agrees with you, and is convinced that you are quite right in the conclusion you have drawn. He believes, although perhaps he does not know he believes it, that the more extensive verifications have been made, and

results of the same kind arrived at—that the more varied the conditions under which the same results are attained, the more cerain is the ultimate conclusion, and he disputes the question no further. He sees that the experiment has been tried under all sorts of conditions, as to time, place, and people, with the same result; and he says with you, therefore, that the law you have laid down must be a good one, and he must believe it.

55. The writer is probably
    (A) French
    (B) English
    (C) American
    (D) Italian
    (E) none of the above.

56. "All men are mortal;
    Socrates was a man;
    Socrates was mortal."
    The foregoing represents reasoning that is
    (A) verification
    (B) inductive
    (C) syllogistic
    (D) experimental
    (E) developmental.

57. Apples are used
    (A) in order to convince the reader that fruit has no intellect
    (B) as an analogy
    (C) to give color to the story
    (D) for sarcasm
    (E) to compare various types of persons.

58. The word "premiss" as it appears is more commonly spelled
    (A) promise   (B) permit
    (C) premit   (D) premise
    (E) in none of the above ways.

59. The author has the approach of
    (A) a scientist   (B) an artist
    (C) a novelist   (D) an economist
    (E) a businessman.

60. You would expect the following to be the writer of this article:
    (A) William Babington Macaulay
    (B) Henry Steele Commager
    (C) Sir Francis Bacon
    (D) Thomas Henry Huxley
    (E) John Steinbeck.

END OF SECTION II

If you finish before time is called, check your work on this section only. When time is called, proceed directly to the next section and do not return to this section.

SECTION III—GRAPHS, CHARTS, AND TABLES
(45 Minutes)

DIRECTIONS: This section of the test consists of questions based on charts, tables, and graphs. Each question is followed by five choices, only *one* of which is correct. Select the correct answer to each question and mark the corresponding space on the answer sheet.

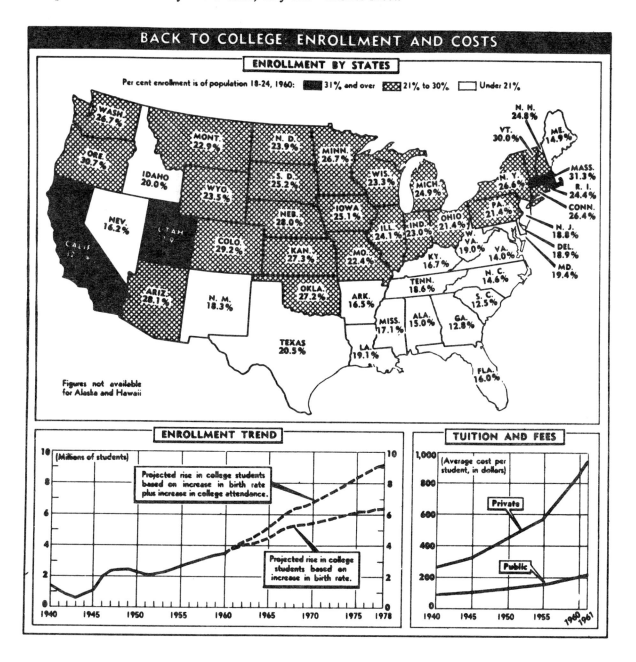

Questions 61-66 are to be answered with reference to the above chart-graph.

61. The states that have the highest and lowest per cent enrollment are
    (A) South Carolina and Utah

(B) California and Georgia
(C) Massachusetts and Idaho
(D) Delaware and Texas
(E) Florida and Washington

62. In 1961, the average tuition and fees cost per

private student was approximately how many times what it was for the public student?
(A) twice   (B) three times
(C) five times   (D) seven times
(E) eight times

63. A steady and uninterrupted rise in the enrollment of college students began in
(A) 1943   (B) 1945
(C) 1950   (D) 1952
(E) 1955

64. There is over a 20% college enrollment of the 18-24 group in all the states of this section of the country:
(A) south-central   (B) western
(C) eastern   (D) north-eastern
(E) north-central

65. The projected rise in college student enrollment by 1975 based on increase in birth rate, in relationship with the 1960 figures, will be approximately
(A) 40%   (B) 50%
(C) 60%   (D) 70%
(E) 100%

66. It is true that
(A) for the period 1945-1950, there was a direct relationship between the tuition rise (public and private) and the enrollment trend
(B) in every case, the larger the state the greater the per cent of college enrollment
(C) since the end of the great depression of the 30's, there has been an uninterrupted rise in the college enrollment trend
(D) college enrollment in 1950 doubled since 1945
(E) California has about one-half the number of college students enrolled that Nevada has

Questions 67-71 are to be answered with reference to the graph in the next column.

67. The increase in passenger-miles during the following two-year periods was greatest in
(A) 1950-1952
(C) 1953-1955
(E) 1958-1960

68. It is not true that
(A) Excluding 1960, there were more deaths in the aggregate, per 100 million passen-

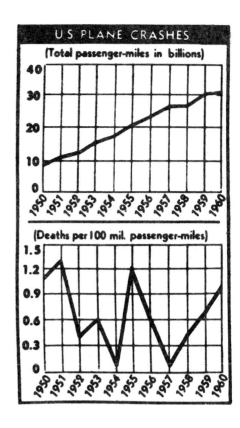

ger-miles, during the odd years than during the even years
(B) There was an increase in passenger miles flown from 1950 to 1957
(C) There has been an increase in deaths every year since 1950
(D) There were more deaths in 1960 than in 1950
(E) 30 billion passenger-miles were flown in 1959

69. The greatest and the least number of deaths occurred during
(A) 1950 and 1957   (B) 1951 and 1957
(C) 1952 and 1955   (D) 1953 and 1956
(E) 1954 and 1957

70. In 1955, there were approximately
(A) 24 deaths   (B) 240 deaths
(C) 2400 deaths   (D) 24,000 deaths
(E) 240,000 deaths

71. The sharpest drop in deaths was during the period of
(A) 1951-1952   (B) 1953-1954
(C) 1954-1955   (D) 1955-1956
(E) 1957-1958

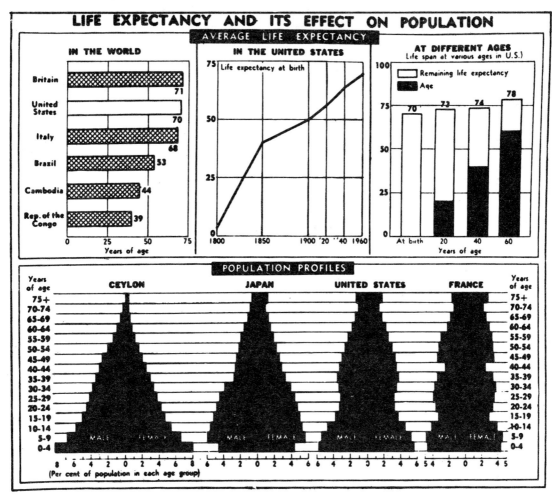

LIFE EXPECTANCY AND ITS EFFECT ON POPULATION

Questions 72-77 are to be answered with reference to the above chart-graph.

72. The country which has the highest per cent in the "75 and over" group among the countries listed is
    (A) Ceylon   (B) Japan
    (C) United States   (D) France
    (E) not determinable from chart

73. Among the countries of Ceylon, Japan, the United States, and France, there are as many females as males, or more females than males, in all of these countries in this age group:
    (A) 0-4   (B) 30-34
    (C) 45-49   (D) 55-59
    (E) 75+

74. The life expectancy in this country as of 1960 has, since 1825,
    (A) remained about the same
    (B) doubled
    (C) tripled
    (D) quadrupled
    (E) not been determined

75. A person of 20 in this country, according to life expectancy findings, has lived about what per cent of his life?
    (A) 15%   (B) 25%
    (C) 35%   (D) 40%
    (E) 45%

76. The life expectancy of people in the Republic of the Congo is how many years under the average life expectancy of people in the United States, Britain, and Italy?
    (A) 25   (B) 27
    (C) 29   (D) 31
    (E) 33

77. In Japan, there are more people in which age group than in any other age group?
    (A) 0-4   (B) 5-9
    (C) 10-14   (D) 15-19
    (E) 20-24

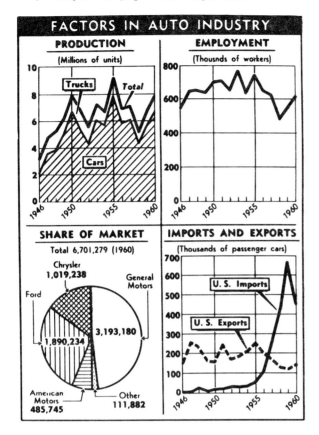

FACTORS IN AUTO INDUSTRY

Questions 78-83 are to be answered with reference to the graph-chart above.

78. The number of auto workers in 1960 was about what per cent of the peak year of employment?
(A) 55%   (B) 70%
(C) 80%   (D) 88%
(E) 95%

79. These auto industry graphs and charts will not be able to tell you the following for the 1946-1960 period:
(A) how employment in one year compared with employment in another year
(B) the per cent of production that trucks have constituted
(C) the breakdown of the Chrysler Company types of cars which have been sold
(D) the number of U. S.-made passenger cars marketed abroad
(E) how many passenger cars were produced

80. In 1960, the exports of cars made up approximately what part of the import-export total?
(A) one-eighth   (B) one-seventh
(C) one-fourth   (D) one-third
(E) one-half

81. General Motors and Ford combined have about what per cent of the entire market?
(A) 50%   (B) 60%
(C) 75%   (D) 85%
(E) 90%

82. The years in which the number of passenger car imports and exports were a) about the same and b) farthest apart were
(A) 1955 and 1950   (B) 1957 and 1959
(C) 1946 and 1957   (D) 1960 and 1959
(E) 1960 and 1957

83. The number of trucks produced in 1960 was closest to
(A) 650,000   (B) 100,000
(C) 8,000,000   (D) 1,000,000
(E) 4,000,000

Questions 84-90 are to be answered with reference to the above graph.

84. The decade during which there were the two greatest extremes in the price of silver is
    (A) 1920-1930   (B) 1930-1940
    (C) 1940-1950   (D) 1950-1960
    (E) not the kind of information given

85. The years when the price of silver was highest (2 separate years) and lowest (2 separate years) were
    (A) 1920, 1931, 1933, 1959
    (B) 1917, 1920, 1935, 1959
    (C) 1920, 1925, 1935, 1945
    (D) 1932, 1935, 1955, 1956
    (E) 1915, 1930, 1945, 1960

86. The average price of silver for the years 1931 through 1934 was approximately
    (A) 25¢   (B) 35¢
    (C) 45¢   (D) 50¢
    (E) 55¢

87. The price was most steady during the period
    (A) 1915-1917   (B) 1929-1931
    (C) 1935-1937   (D) 1943-1945
    (E) 1954-1956

88. The graph indicates that the price of silver, since 1940, has
    (A) risen slightly   (B) risen sharply
    (C) fallen slightly   (D) fallen sharply
    (E) remained about the same

89. A year during which the price was approximately the same as the year immediately preceding was
    (A) 1919   (B) 1929
    (C) 1935   (D) 1944
    (E) 1951

90. A 10 year period during which silver was under 85¢ a pound was
    (A) 1920-1930   (B) 1930-1940
    (C) 1940-1950   (D) 1950-1960
    (E) none of the above

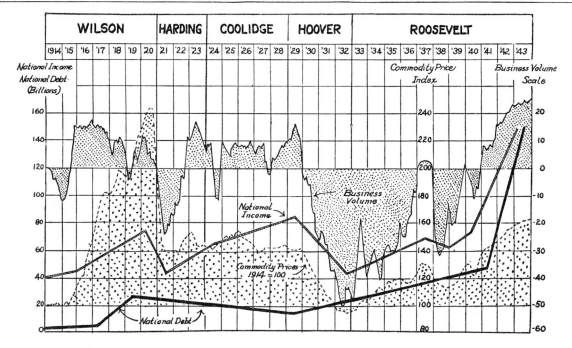

Questions 91-95 are to be answered with reference to the preceding graph.

Note these dates:
    WORLD WAR I – 1914-1918
    WORLD WAR II – 1939-1945
    STOCK MARKET CRASH – 1929
    GREAT DEPRESSION – 1929-1933

91. Which of the following statements about the national debt of the United States are true?
    a. It increased sharply during both World Wars.

    b. It increased throughout the great depression.

    c. It decreased a third between World War I and the stock market crash.

    d. In 1943 it had reached the highest point up to that time.

    (A) a, b   (B) a, c
    (C) a, d   (D) c, d
    (E) all of them

92. Which of the following statements about the national income of the United States are true?
   a. It reached its highest point in the period between the declaration of World War I and the declaration of World War II.
   b. It increased constantly after Franklin D. Roosevelt became President.
   c. It increased more in Republican than in Democratic administrations.
   (A) none of them   (B) a only
   (C) a, b   (D) a, c
   (E) b, c

93. As shown by the chart, the index of the cost of living in the United States
   a. is based upon commodity prices in 1914
   b. rose at approximately the same rate in both wars
   c. remained fairly constant throughout the administrations of Harding and Coolidge
   d. reached a maximum of 165 during World War I
   (A) a, b   (B) a, c
   (C) a, d   (D) b, c
   (E) b, d

94. Which of the following statements about the volume of business in the United States are true?
   a. It has fluctuated widely in the period covered by the chart.
   b. It has shown the same general trends as the national income.
   c. In the period shown, it has been both highest and lowest under Republican Presidents.
   d. It tends to increase in wartime.
   (A) a, b, c   (B) a, b, d
   (C) a, c, d   (D) b, c, d
   (E) all of them

95. In the period shown, which of the following statements about the value of money in the United States are true?
   a. It was greatest at the end of 1932.
   b. It showed an upward trend during the New Deal.
   c. It rose sharply at the close of the Harding administration.
   d. It remained higher in World War II than in World War I.
   (A) a, b   (B) a, d
   (C) b, c   (D) b, d
   (E) c, e

End Of Section III

If you finish before time is called, check your work on this section only.

Take a ten minute break . . . . then proceed to Section IV.

SECTION IV — LAW INTERPRETATION
(35 minutes)

Part A. Cases and Principles

DIRECTIONS: This group of questions consists of the list of law cases followed by a list of legal principles. These principles may be either real or imaginary, but for purposes of this test you are to assume them to be valid. For each case you are to select the legal principle which is *most applicable* to the case. To indicate your answer blacken the space beneath the letter on the answer sheet which corresponds to the letter of the legal principle you select.

These questions do not presuppose any specific legal knowledge on your part; you are to base your answers entirely on the ordinary processes of logical reasoning.

CASES

96. X sets on fire his own building which is not insured. His purpose was to defraud the insurance company in connection with his contents and not to destroy the building. X claims, therefore, that he is not guilty of arson.

97. X is charged with setting on fire a building which is owned by Y. In pleading his case, X proves that Y's building, being run down, was of very little value.

98. X wilfully sets on fire in the night time, a house which is ordinarily occupied at night, although no person was in it at the time the fire started. The fire was put out with very little damage having occurred. X claims he is not guilty under the circumstances.

99. X deliberately sets fire to a building. The fire spreads and destroys three other buildings. X says that he can be tried for only one arson.

100. X, with the intention of causing a fire in a warehouse at some future time, placed cans of gasoline among the bales of cotton stored in the building. His plan was to return in one week and set fire to the gasoline. His plan is detected before he can do the job. He claims, therefore, that there is no guilt on his part.

PRINCIPLES

(A) The attempt to burn constitutes the intention of causing a fire by placing inflammables in or about a building.

(B) The value of property involved is never an essential element in determining the degree of arson committed.

(C) Where an appurtenance to a building is so situated with reference to such a building, or where any building is so situated with reference to any other building, that the burning of one will manifestly endanger the other, a burning of one is deemed a burning of the other.

(D) Arson, 2nd degree, is constituted by the wilful burning at night of a structure ordinarily occupied at night, although it may not be occupied at the time of burning.

(E) In order to constitute arson, it must be shown that the building was insured at the time of burning, and not merely that the contents were insured.

CASES

101. A carelessly jostles B causing him to fall and sustain injuries. A is charged with assault.

102. While operating an automobile, A purposely strikes B causing the latter slight injury. A is charged with assault.

103. While operating his automobile in an unjustifiably careless manner, A runs down a pedestrian injuring him severely. A is charged with assault.

104. A, intending to rob B, points a loaded revolver at him. A is charged with assault.

105. A detective, Jones, arrives at the home of Smith in order to execute a search warrant which has lawfully been issued by the court. Smith refuses to admit Jones into the house. When Jones insists, Smith strikes him with his fist causing Jones' nose to bleed. Smith is charged with assault.

PRINCIPLES

(A) Assault 2nd degree occurs when the offender wilfully and wrongfully assaults another by the use of a weapon, instrument, or thing likely to produce bodily harm.

(B) Assault 1st degree occurs when there is intent to kill a human being or to commit a felony upon the person or property of another or the person assaulted.

(C) Assault 3rd degree occurs when one operates a vehicle of any kind in a culpably negligent manner, whereby another suffers bodily harm.

(D) Suppressing evidence occurs when one practices deceit or uses threats or violence with intent to prevent witness from attending or to prevent production of evidence.

(E) When there is an intentional attempt to do injury to another or if the deliberate act induces reasonable fear of bodily injury, an assault occurs. Carelessness and negligence do not ordinarily amount to an assault.

Part B. Law Comprehension

DIRECTIONS: Several paragraphs pertaining to law are included in Part B. After each paragraph are questions that are to be answered in the light of the contents of that paragraph. Legal background is not required.

Questions 106 and 107 pertain to the following section of the Penal Code:

"Section 1942. A person who, after having been three times convicted within this state, of felonies or attempts to commit felonies, or under the law of any other state, government or country, of crimes which if committed within this state would be felonious, commits a felony, other than murder, first or second degree, or treason, within this state, shall be sentenced upon conviction of such fourth, or subsequent, offense to imprisonment in a state prison for an indeterminate term the minimum of which shall be not less than the maximum term provided for first offenders for the crime for which the individual has been convicted, but, in any event, the minimum term upon conviction for a felony as the fourth or subsequent, offense, shall be not less than fifteen years, and the maximum thereof shall be his natural life."

106. Under the terms of the above quoted portion of Section 1942 of the Penal Law, a person must receive the increased punishment therein provided, if

(A) He is convicted of a felony and has been three times previously convicted of felonies

(B) He has been three times previously convicted of felonies, regardless of the nature of his present conviction

(C) His fourth conviction is for murder, first or second degree, or treason

(D) He has previously been convicted three times of murder, first or second degree, or treason.

107. Under the terms of the above quoted portion of Section 1942 of the Penal Law, a person convicted of a felony for which the penalty is imprisonment for a term not to exceed ten years, and who has been three times previously convicted of felonies in this state, shall be sentenced to a term the minimum of which shall be
(A) ten years   (B) fifteen years
(C) indeterminate   (D) his natural life.

Answer questions 108 to 111 on the basis of the following statement:

"Disorderly conduct, in the abstract, does not constitute any crime known to law; it is only when it tends to a breach of the peace under the circumstances detailed in section 1458 of the Consolidation Act, that it constitutes a minor offense cognizable by the police magistrate of the City of Metropolis, and when it in fact threatens to disturb the peace it is a misdemeanor as well under section 675 of the Penal Code as at common law, and not within the jurisdiction of the police magistrate, but of the Court of Special Sessions."

108. Of the following, the most accurate statement on the basis of the above paragraph is that
(A) an act which merely threatens to disturb the peace is not a crime
(B) disorderly conduct, by itself, is not a crime
(C) some types of disorderly conduct are indictable
(D) a minor offense may or may not be cognizable by the police
(E) some facts threaten to disturb the peace.

109. Of the following, the least accurate statement on the basis of the above paragraph is that
(A) disorderly conduct which threatens to disturb the peace is within the jurisdiction of a police magistrate.
(B) disorderly conduct which "tends to a breach of the peace" may constitute a minor offense
(C) section 1458 of the Consolidated Act discusses a "breach of the peace"
(D) disorderly conduct which "tends to a breach of the peace" is not the same as that which threatens to disturb the peace
(E) the Court of Special Sessions considers some cases resulting from disorderly conduct.

110. The above quotation distinguishes least sharply between
(A) jurisdiction of a police magistrate and jurisdiction of the Court of Special Sessions
(B) disorderly conduct as a crime and disorderly conduct as no crime
(C) what "tends to a breach of the peace" and what threatens to disturb the peace
(D) a minor offense and a misdemeanor
(E) the Penal Code and the Common Law.

111. Of the following generalizations, the one which is best illustrated by the above paragraph is that
(A) acts which in themselves are not criminal may become criminal as a result of their effect
(B) abstract conduct may, in and of itself, be criminal
(C) criminal acts are determined by results rather than by intent
(D) an act which is criminal to begin with may not be criminal if it fails to have the desired effect
(E) all law consists of a detailing of circumstances under which a crime is committed.

Answer questions 112 and 113 solely on the basis of the following paragraph:

"If a motor vehicle fails to pass inspection, the owner will be given a rejection notice by the inspection station. Repairs must be made within ten days after this notice is issued. It is not necessary to have the required adjustment or repairs made at the station where the inspection occurred. The vehicle may be taken to any other garage. Re-inspection after repairs may be made at any official inspection station, not necessarily the same station which made the initial inspection. The registration of any motor vehicle for which an inspection sticker has not been obtained as required, or which is not repaired and inspected within ten days after inspection indicates defects, is subject to suspension. A vehicle cannot be used on public highways while its registration is under suspension."

112. According to the above paragraph, the owner of a car which does not pass inspection must
(A) have repairs made at the same station which rejected his car
(B) take the car to another station and have it re-inspected
(C) have repairs made anywhere and then have the car re-inspected
(D) not use the car on a public highway until the necessary repairs have been made.

113. According to the above paragraph, the one of the following which may be cause for suspension of the registration of a vehicle is that
    (A) an inspection sticker was issued before the rejection notice had been in force for ten days
    (B) it was not re-inspected by the station that rejected it originally
    (C) it was not re-inspected either by the station that rejected it originally or by the garage which made the repairs
    (D) it has not had defective parts repaired within ten days after inspection.

114. A statute states: "A person who steals an article worth less than $100 where no aggravating circumstances accompany the act, is guilty of petit larceny. If the article is worth $100 or more it may be larceny second degree." If all you know is that Edward Smith stole an article worth $100, it may reasonably be said that
    (A) Smith is guilty of petit larceny
    (B) Smith is guilty of larceny second degree
    (C) Smith is guilty of neither petit larceny nor larceny second degree
    (D) precisely what charge will be placed against Smith is uncertain.

115. An ordinance reads: "All vehicles, such as motorcycles, passenger automobiles, automobile trucks, horsedriven wagons, or any other type of conveyance, are prohibited from using any street designated as a play street, except as the requirements of the residents of the property abutting such play street may call for." John White, who had only recently arrived in the city from Montreal, Canada, where he had lived all his life, was given a summons by Patrolman Kelly for violating this ordinance. At the time he received the summons he was delivering groceries to a resident on the play street for the Smith Grocery Company, for whom he had started to work the day before. There were no children playing on the street at the time and he did not know that it was a play street. Patrolman Kelly should be told that the summons should not have been issued because
    (A) there were no children on the street at the time
    (B) he was delivering groceries to a resident on the street
    (C) not being a citizen of the United States, he is not completely subject to our jurisdiction
    (D) he did not know that it was a play street
    (E) he did not know that traffic was prohibited on play streets.

Answer Questions 116-118 on the basis of the following paragraph:

"The City Police Department will accept for investigation no report of a person missing from his residence, if such residence is located outside of the city. The person reporting same will be advised to report such fact to the police department of the locality where the missing person lives, which will, if necessary, communicate officially with the City Police Department. However, a report will be accepted of a person who is missing from a temporary residence in the city, but the person making the report will be instructed to make a report also to the police department of the locality where the missing person lives."

116. According to the above paragraph, a report to the City Police Department of a missing person whose permanent residence is outside of the city will
    (A) always be investigated provided that a report is also made to his local police authorities
    (B) never be investigated unless requested officially by his local police authorities
    (C) be investigated in cases of temporary residence in the city, but a report should always be made to his local police authorities
    (D) be investigated if the person making the report is a city resident
    (E) always be investigated and a report will be made to the local police authorities by the City Police Department.

117. Of the following, the most likely reason for the procedure described in the above paragraph is that
    (A) non-residents are not entitled to free police service from the city
    (B) local police authorities would resent interference in their jurisdiction
    (C) local police authorities sometimes try to unload their problems on the City Police
    (D) local police authorities may be better able to conduct an investigation
    (E) few persons are erroneously reported as missing.

118. Mr. Smith of Oldtown and Mr. Jones of Newtown had an appointment in the city, but Mr. Jones doesn't appear. Mr. Smith, after trying repeatedly to phone Mr. Jones the next day, believes that something has happened to him. According to the above paragraph, Mr. Smith should apply to the police of
    (A) Oldtown

(B) Newtown
(C) Newtown and the city
(D) Oldtown and the city
(E) Newtown, Oldtown and the city.

119. Police Department Rule 5 reads as follows: "A Deputy Commissioner acting as Police Commissioner shall carry out the orders of the Police Commissioner, previously given, and such orders shall not, except in cases of extreme emergency, be countermanded." This means most nearly that, except in case of extreme emergency,
   (A) the orders given by a Deputy Commissioner acting as Police Commissioner may not be revoked
   (B) a Deputy Commissioner acting as Police Commissioner should not revoke orders previously given by the Police Commissioner

(C) a Deputy Commissioner acting as Police Commissioner is vested with the same authority to issue orders as the Police Commissioner himself
(D) only a Deputy Commissioner acting as Police Commissioner may issue orders in the absence of the Police Commissioner himself.

120. "A 'crime' is an act committed or omitted in violation of a public law either forbidding or commanding it." This statement implies most nearly that
   (A) crimes can be omitted
   (B) a forbidding act if omitted is a crime
   (C) an act of omission may be criminal
   (D) to commit an act not commanded is criminal
   (E) some acts are acts of commission.

End Of Section IV

If you finish before time is called, check your work on Section IV only.

When time is called, proceed directly to the next section and do not return to this section.

SECTION V — NONVERBAL REASONING
(35 minutes)

DIRECTIONS: The following questions consist of a series of five symbols at the left and five other symbols labeled (A), (B), (C), (D), and (E) at the right. In each question, first study the series of symbols at the left; then from the symbols at the right, labeled (A), (B), (C), (D), and (E) select the one which continues the series most completely.

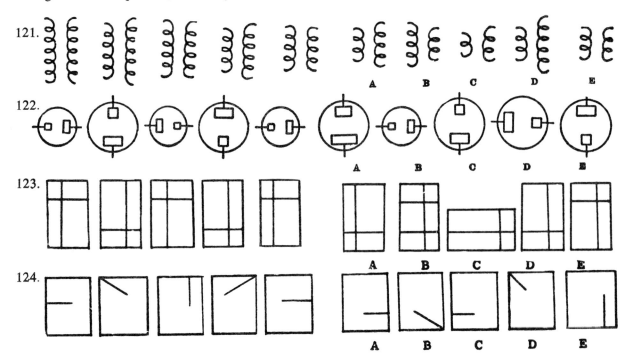

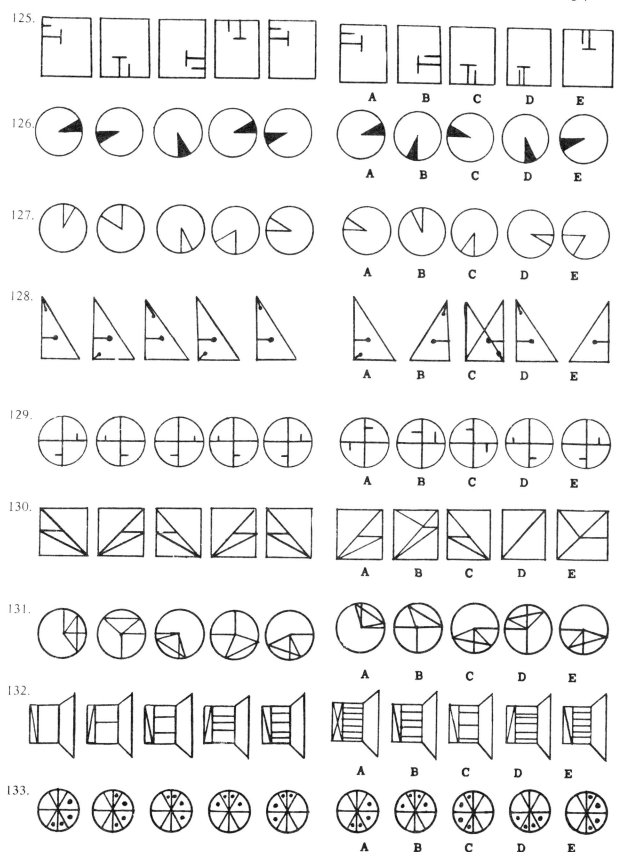

DIRECTIONS: In the following questions, the symbols in columns 1 and 2 ·have a relationship to each other. Select from the symbols in columns A, B, C, D and E the symbol which has the same relationship to the symbol in column 3, as the symbol in column 2 has to the symbol in column 1.

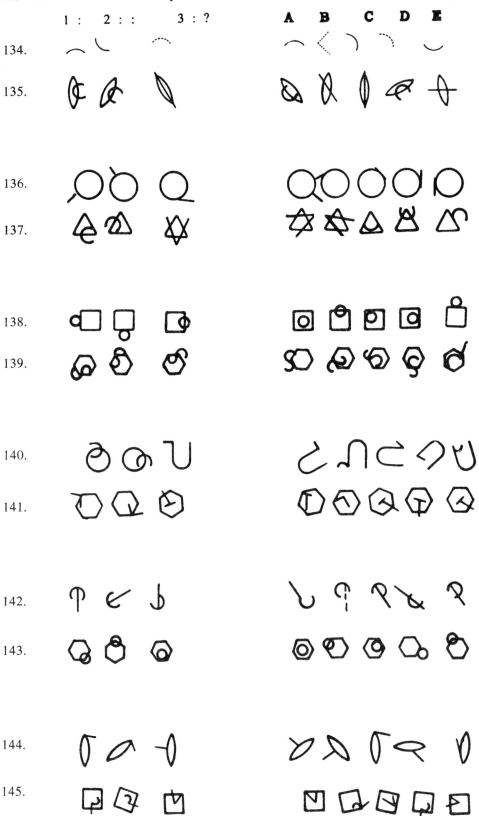

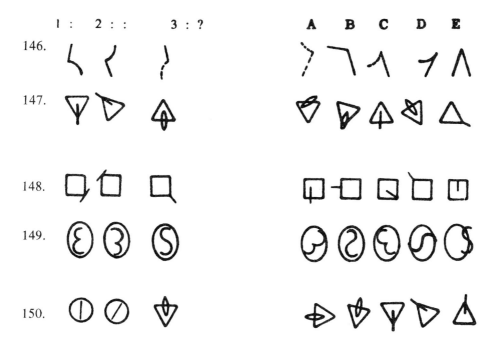

End Of Section V

If you finish before time is called, check your work on this section only.   **When time is called, proceed directly to the next section and do not return to this section.**

SECTION VI — REMEMBERING MAIN IDEAS AND DETAILS
(20 minutes)

PART A. (10 minutes)

DIRECTIONS: This is a test to determine your ability to remember main ideas and significant details. You are to read the four passages that follow in a period of ten minutes altogether. It is suggested that you divide your time equally among the four passages. When the time is up, you will be asked to recall certain ideas and facts about the four passages. You will not be able to refer back to the passages after 10 minutes.

PASSAGE 1

If one is tempted to reflect on the type of language which is used in polite society, and, more particularly, if one is inclined to interpret it literally, one must conclude that social intercourse involves a collection of inanities and a tissue of lies. We say "Good morning" to the boss although the weather is foul and our temper is no better. We say "Pleased to meet you" when we really mean, "I hope I'll never see you again in my life." We chatter aimlessly at a tea about matters that are not fit to exercise the mind of a child of two.

To say "Pleased to meet you" or "Good morning" or to chatter at tea are examples of the ceremonial function of language. Language used in this way is not informational. It simply celebrates whatever feelings are responsible for bringing men together in social groups. It is said that the custom of shaking hands originated when primitive men held out empty hands to indicate that they had no concealed weapons and were thus amicably disposed. In the same way, when we say "How do you do," or "Good morning," we perform a sort of ceremony to indicate community of feeling with the person so addressed.

PASSAGE 2

Too often we retire people who are willing and able to continue working, according to Federal Security Agency Administrator Oscar R. Ewing in addressing the first National Conference on Aging, to point up the fact that chronological age is no longer an effective criterion in determining whether or not an individual is capable of working. The second World War proved this point when it became necessary to hire older experienced people to handle positions in business and industry vacated by personnel called to serve their country. As shown by production records set during the war period, the employment of older people helped us continue, and even better, our high level of production.

It was also pointed out at the conference that our

SECTION VI — REMEMBERING MAIN IDEAS AND DETAILS
(20 minutes)

PART A. (10 minutes)

Directions: This is a test to determine your ability to remember main ideas and significant details. You are to read the four passages that follow in a period of ten minutes altogether. It is suggested that you divide your time equally among the four passages. When the time is up, you will be asked to recall certain ideas and facts about the four passages. You will not be able to refer back to the passages after 10 minutes.

PASSAGE 1

As befits a nation made up of immigrants from all over the Christian world, Americans have no distinctive Christmas symbols; but we have taken the symbols of all the nations and made them our own. The Christmas tree, the holly and the ivy, the mistle-toe, the exchange of gifts, the myth of Santa Claus, the carols of all nations, the plum pudding and the wassail bowl are all elements in the American Christmas of the mid-twentieth century. Though we have no Christmas symbols of our own, the American Christmas still has a distinctive aura by virtue of two characteristic elements.

The first of these is that, as might be expected in a nation as dedicated to the carrying on of business as the American nation, the dominant role of the Christmas festivities has become to serve as a stimulus to retail business. The themes of Christmas advertising begin to appear as early as September, and the open season on Christmas shopping begins in November. Fifty years ago, Thanksgiving Day was regarded as the opening day of the season for Christmas shopping; today, the season opens immediately after Halloween. Thus virtually a whole month has been added to the Christmas season—for shopping purposes.

Second, the Christmas season of festivities has insensibly combined with the New Year's celebration into one lengthened period of Saturnalia. This starts with the "office parties" a few days before Christmas, continues on Christmas Eve, now the occasion in America of one of two large-scale revels that mark the season—save that the Christmas Eve revels are often punctuated by a visit to one of the larger churches for midnight Mass, which has increasingly tended to become blended into a part of the entertainment aspect of the season—and continues in spirited euphoria until New Year's Eve, the second of the large-scale revels. New Year's Day is spent resting, possibly regretting one's excesses, watching a football "bowl" game, and indulging in the lenitive of one's choice. January 2 marks, for most, the return to temperance and decorum and business as usual.

PASSAGE 2

Those early principles discovered in 1775 are the same as those upon which blueprinting is based today. Light, be it sun or electric, has a decided effect on a chemical compound known as ferro-prussiate; it turns the color from a pale green to a deep blue. Thus, if a sheet of white paper is coated with a solution of ferro-prussiate and is so covered that only a portion of it is exposed to light, that exposed part will turn blue while the unexposed section remains its original color. Then, if the paper is washed in water which both removes the unexposed coating, revealing the white paper, and fixes (makes permanent) the exposed blue coating, a print is obtained in blue and white. This, then, is a blueprint.

The principles of all copying processes which depend on sensitized paper to obtain a print are similar. In photography, photostating, blueprinting, and so on, light, to make a print, must reach and react upon a chemically sensitized surface only in the places permitted by an original copy.

There are several of these processes divided into two general groups: (1) direct, and (2) indirect. Of these two, direct copying is the more widely used because it is less expensive and requires less equipment.

Blueprinting, probably the best known and most widely used direct copying method, prints from a tracing of the original or from the original itself, according to the process involved. Because of possible shrinkage or stretch of the tracings as well as inaccuracies accrued in the tracing process the direct copying method does not ordinarily produce copies as true as those obtained by the indirect.

Chief process of the indirect method is photostating. Known as "Indirect" because it takes the print through a lens, it can always work from the original without a tracing and can enlarge or reduce the copy as desired. This flexibility and photographic accuracy have made indirect copying popular.

End Of Section VI — Part A

When time is called, proceed directly to Part B and do not return to Part A.

SECTION VI — Part B.

PART B. (10 minutes)

Directions: Answer the following questions in accordance with the contents of the preceding passages. You are not to turn back to the passages.

PASSAGE ON CHRISTMAS

151. The author's attitude toward the manner in which Christmas is celebrated in the United States is
    (A) sarcastic   (D) critical
    (B) laudatory   (E) jocose.
    (C) mildly approving

152. A statement which is most closely associated with the philosophy expressed in this passage is the following:
    (A) In Puritan Massachusetts Bay Colony, it was a crime, punishable by the stocks, to observe Christmas.
    (B) Christmas customs that have prevailed in the European and American practices with the Feast of the Nativity were not originally Christian at all.
    (C) Many American clergymen produce annual diatribes calling on their flocks to "return" to the traditional religious celebration of Christmas.
    (D) The custom of wassailing trees continued well into the nineteenth century.
    (E) In widely separated areas of the world, religious observances tend to cluster around striking natural phenomena.

153. The passage implies that, during the Christmas season,
    (A) few celebrants drink and are merry
    (B) hard-hearted persons love their fellowmen more than during the rest of the year
    (C) church-going is more sincere now than it was in previous years
    (D) Europeans have just as much merriment
    (E) business interests take advantage of the seasonal opportunity, caring little for religious aspects.

154. According to the passage,
    (A) Americans should be credited with originality in regard to Christmas representations
    (B) there is a variety of entertainment associated with the Christmas season
    (C) the period of celebration seems to be growing shorter

(D) the belief in Santa Claus should be encouraged
(E) parties and football games have little justification in our social structure.

PASSAGE ON COPYING METHODS

155. According to the paragraph, the most accurate statement is that
    (A) blueprinting was discovered in 1775
    (B) the principles behind blueprinting were discovered in 1775
    (C) since 1775, no new information has been discovered regarding blueprinting
    (D) the effect of electricity on a chemical compound was discovered in 1775
    (E) blueprinting was discovered because of the start of the American Revolution.

156. In making a blueprint, a sheet is covered with a chemical compound and light is permitted to fall on those parts which later on are seen as
    (A) white   (D) deep blue
    (B) black   (E) yellow.
    (C) pale green

157. Photostating, compared with blueprinting,
    (A) is cheaper
    (B) is a more direct method
    (C) requires a tracing
    (D) makes possible enlargement of copy
    (E) is more expensive.

158. Of the following, the most accurate statement is that blueprinting, compared with photostating,
    (A) is called the indirect method
    (B) is as true as photostating
    (C) does not require a lens
    (D) is not widely used
    (E) is inferior in quality.

159. Where the lowest cost and least equipment are desired, the copying would be done by the
    (A) direct method with a lens
    (B) direct method without a lens
    (C) indirect method with a lens
    (D) indirect method without a lens
    (E) indirect-direct method combination.

160. Generally, a more accurate copy of the original can be obtained by the
    (A) direct method without a lens
    (B) indirect method with or without a lens
    (C) indirect method without a lens
    (D) indirect method with a lens
    (E) direct method with a lens.

End Of Section VI
When time is called, stop work on this section.
The Morning Session part of the test is now concluded.

ANSWER KEY TO LAW SCHOOL ADMISSION TEST （A）

Morning Session

1. B	17. B	33. B	49. C	65. D	81. C	97. B	113. D	129. D	145. E
2. C	18. B	34. A	50. B	66. D	82. B	98. D	114. D	130. A	146. A
3. E	19. D	35. B	51. A	67. D	83. D	99. C	115. B	131. B	147. A
4. D	20. B	36. E	52. E	68. C	84. A	100. A	116. C	132. D	148. D
5. B	21. D	37. C	53. C	69. B	85. A	101. E	117. D	133. C	149. B
6. A	22. A	38. C	54. D	70. B	86. B	102. A	118. B	134. D	150. B
7. D	23. C	39. A	55. B	71. A	87. D	103. C	119. B	135. C	151. D
8. D	24. B	40. E	56. C	72. D	88. B	104. B	120. C	136. D	152. C
9. A	25. E	41. A	57. B	73. E	89. D	105. A	121. A	137. B	153. E
10. C	26. B	42. D	58. D	74. C	90. B	106. A	122. C	138. B	154. B
11. A	27. D	43. E	59. A	75. B	91. E	107. B	123. D	139. C	155. B
12. D	28. A	44. A	60. D	76. D	92. A	108. B	124. B	140. A	156. D
13. A	29. B	45. D	61. A	77. B	93. B	109. A	125. C	141. E	157. D
14. E	30. C	46. C	62. C	78. C	94. B	110. E	126. D	142. C	158. C
15. C	31. E	47. C	63. D	79. C	95. B	111. A	127. E	143. C	159. B
16. E	32. C	48. B	64. E	80. C	96. E	112. C	128. A	144. A	160. D

Afternoon Session

SECTION I — RECOGNIZING ERRORS
(20 minutes)

DIRECTIONS: Among the sentences in this group are some which cannot be accepted in formal, written English for one or another of the following reasons:

Poor Diction: The use of a word which is improper either because its meaning does not fit the sentence or because it is not acceptable in formal writing.
Example: The audience was strongly <u>effected</u> by the senator's speech.

Verbosity: Repetitious elements adding nothing to the meaning of the sentence and not justified by any need for special emphasis.
Example: At that time there was <u>then</u> no right of petition.

Faulty Grammar: Word forms and expressions which do not conform to the grammatical and structural usages required by formal written English (errors in case, number, parallelism, and the like).
Example: Everyone in the delegation had <u>their</u> reasons for opposing the measure.

No sentence has more than one of these errors. Some sentences have no errors. Read each sentence carefully; then on your answer sheet blacken the space under:

    D if the sentence contains an error in <u>diction</u>,
    V if the sentence is <u>verbose</u>,
    G if the sentence contains <u>faulty grammar</u>,
    O if the sentence contains <u>none of these errors</u>.

1. The two companies were hopeful of eventually affecting a merger, if the government didn't object.

2. The ore, pitchblende, is an important source of radium, which is found in many parts of the world.

3. The jury are still arguing over the credibility of one of the witnesses.

4. He is different, in many respects, than his predecessor in the office of dean.

5. Due to the mechanic's carelessness or a fault in the construction of the plans, forty lives were lost.

6. The umpire said that the penalty would be meted out to whomever had been at fault.

7. The language in Faulkner is somewhat like Proust, although Faulkner is much more inclined to sesquipedalianism.

8. He said he thought he would buy two pairs of shoes and save one pair for rare special occasions.

9. Four former past presidents of the United States have been graduated from Harvard University.

10. Asia is as valuable and more fully developed than Africa.

11. One or the other of those books have presented a much better interpretation of the event than the text you are now studying.

12. Neither the diplomats nor our president were to blame for the international fiasco.

13. You or your friend seems to have broken the regulations.

14. Only one of the rooms which is vacant is on the fourth floor.

15. "Don Quixote," which is a fantasy to a child, is a work of sober philology to the serious thinker.

16. Rather than ignore civil service, it would be advisable for you to consider its bearing on modern democracy.

17. I don't doubt but what the party of my choice will win the election.

18. The secret of happiness lies not in doing what you like, but to like what you do.
19. It takes all kinds of readers to make a classic survive to live on and on.
20. The train having been delayed, he drove to work.

End Of Section I

If you finish before time is called, check your work on this section only.

When time is called, proceed directly to the next section and do not return to this section.

SECTION II — ORGANIZATION OF IDEAS (20 minutes)

Directions: Each set of questions in this test consists of several statements. Most of the statements refer to the same subject or idea. The statements can be classified as follows:

(A) the *central idea* to which most of the statements are related;

(B) *main supporting ideas,* which are general points directly related to the central idea;

(C) *illustrative facts* of detailed statements, which document the main supporting ideas;

(D) statements *irrelevant* to the central idea.

The statements may be regarded as headings in an outline: they are *not* sentences taken from one complete paragraph. The outline might, for example, have the following form:

  A. The Central Idea
    B. Main Supporting Idea
      C. Illustrative Fact
    B. Main Supporting Idea
      C. Illustrative Fact
      C. Illustrative Fact.

Classify the following sentences according to the scheme set forth above:

USE THIS SPACE FOR YOUR SCRATCHWORK

SET A

21. What things there are to write, if one could only write them.
22. It matters not whether we are in business, in the professions, or working in the shop.
23. The foundation of industrial democracy is a self-discipline.
24. Such a standard of living can be preserved only by work by all of us and respect and regard for the other fellow.
25. This fundamental truth applies to all of us.
26. The only way to preserve the American standard of equality in goods and low cost is through cooperation of all the forces of production and distribution.
27. Our standard of living is the highest in the world.

SET B

28. These consisted of the following: to exploit himself, to exploit his fellows, or to reduce the problem to its lowest common denominator.
29. The single business of Henry Thoreau was to discover an economy calculated to provide a satisfying life.
30. The problem of economics offered, in his way of thinking, three possible solutions.
31. Reading is the art of getting the meaning from the printed page.
32. His one concern, that gave to his ramblings in Concord fields a value of high adventure, was to explore the true meaning of wealth.
33. Common prefixes, stems, and suffixes form the innumerable words in our language.

**USE THIS SPACE
FOR YOUR SCRATCHWORK**

SET C

34. She had been raised among the hills of Media.
35. These terraces were provided with earth deep enough to accommodate trees of great size.
36. Ancient writers tell us that the lavish king Nebuchadnezzar built this skyscraper of foliage to gratify his wife Amytis.
37. The Hanging Gardens rose from a river in the north of Babylon.
38. She soon wearied of the flat plains of Babylon.
39. They rose in a series of terraces.
40. Virtue and talent are not enough to procure a man a welcome wherever he goes.

End Of Section II

If you finish before time is called, check your work on this section only.

When time is called, proceed directly to the next section and do not return to this section.

SECTION III — EDITING ABILITY (20 minutes)

Directions: A sentence is given, of which one part is underlined. Following the sentence are five choices. The first (A) choice simply repeats the underlined part. Then you have four additional choices which suggest other ways to express the underlined part of the original sentence. If you think that the underlined part is correct as it stands, write the answer A. If you believe that the underlined part is incorrect, select from the other choices (B or C or D or E) whichever you think is correct. Grammar, sentence structure, word usage, and punctuation are to be considered in your decision. The original meaning of the sentence must be retained.

41. She insisted on me going.
    - (A) on me going.
    - (B) on I going.
    - (C) for me to go.
    - (D) upon me going.
    - (E) on my going.

42. I was really very much excited at the news, that's why I dropped the vase.
    - (A) at the news, that's why
    - (B) by the news, that's why
    - (C) at the news; that's why
    - (D) at the news, that is why
    - (E) at the news that's why

43. We can't do their job since its difficult to do even ours.
    - (A) its difficult to do even ours.
    - (B) its difficult to do even our's.
    - (C) its' difficult to do even ours'.
    - (D) it's difficult to do even ours.
    - (E) its difficult to do ours even.

44. Do you think that Alice has shown more progress than any girl in the class?
    - (A) more progress than any girl in the class?
    - (B) greater progress than any girl in the class?
    - (C) more progress than any girl in the class has shown?
    - (D) more progress than any other girl in the class?
    - (E) more progress from that shown by any girl in the class?

45. He supposed me to be him.
    - (A) He supposed me to be him.
    - (B) He supposed me to be he.
    - (C) He supposed I to be him.
    - (D) He supposed I to be he.
    - (E) He thought me to be he.

46. With a sigh of contentment, she set her doll in the carriage; then she herself laid down and fell asleep.
    - (A) she set her doll in the carriage; then she herself laid down
    - (B) she sat her doll in the carriage; then she herself laid down
    - (C) she sat her doll in the carriage; then she herself lay down
    - (D) she set her doll in the carriage; then she herself lay down
    - (E) she set her doll in the carriage; then herself she laid down

47. Is the climate of Italy somewhat like Florida?
    - (A) somewhat like Florida?
    - (B) somewhat similar to Florida?
    - (C) somewhat like that of Florida?
    - (D) something like Florida?
    - (E) similar to Florida?

48. Everyone except Ruth and I knows her.
    (A) Everyone except Ruth and I knows her.
    (B) Everyone except Ruth and I know her.
    (C) Everyone besides Ruth and me knows her.
    (D) Everyone except I and Ruth knows her.
    (E) Everyone except Ruth and me knows her.

49. The reason I plan to go is because she will be disappointed if I don't.
    (A) because she will be disappointed
    (B) that she will be disappointed
    (C) because she will have a disappointment
    (D) on account of she will be disappointed
    (E) because she shall be disappointed

50. Our teacher won't leave us come into the room after the gong sounds.
    (A) Our teacher won't leave us come
    (B) Our teacher won't let us come
    (C) Our teacher refuses to leave us come
    (D) Our teacher won't leave us enter
    (E) Our teacher won't allow that we come

51. Everyone, including Anne and Helen, was there.
    (A) Everyone, including Anne and Helen, was there.
    (B) Everyone including Anne and Helen, was there.
    (C) Everyone, including Anne and Helen, were there.
    (D) Everyone including Anne, and Helen, was there.
    (E) Everyone including Anne and Helen was there.

52. Being an intelligent person, the slur was disregarded by him.
    (A) Being an intelligent person, the slur was disregarded by him.
    (B) Being that he was an intelligent person, the slur was disregarded by him.
    (C) Being an intelligent person, he disregarded the slur.
    (D) Being that he was an intelligent person, he disregarded the slur.
    (E) As an intelligent person, the slur was disregarded by him.

53. Instead of him going home, he went to a movie.
    (A) Instead of him going home
    (B) Instead that he went home
    (C) Instead of him going on home
    (D) Instead of his going home
    (E) Instead that he was going home

54. If the parent would have shown more interest, her daughter would have been in college today.
    (A) If the parent would have shown more interest
    (B) If the parent had shown more interest
    (C) If the parent would have showed more interest
    (D) If the parent would have been showing more interest
    (E) Should the parent have shown more interest

55. Having eaten a hearty luncheon, the judge was ready to seriously consider the circumstances.
    (A) to seriously consider the circumstances.
    (B) seriously to consider the circumstances.
    (C) to consider seriously the circumstances.
    (D) to consider the circumstances seriously.
    (E) with seriousness to consider the circumstances.

56. Such of his stories as was original were accepted.
    (A) Such of his stories as was original were accepted.
    (B) Such of his stories as were original was accepted.
    (C) Such of his stories as were original were accepted.
    (D) Such of his stories as were original were excepted.
    (E) His stories such as were original were excepted.

57. She never has and she never will do any work.
    (A) She never has and she never will do any work.
    (B) She never has and she never will do no work.
    (C) She never has, and she never will do any work.
    (D) Never has she and never will she do any work.
    (E) She never has done and she never will do any work.

58. I could not but help feel that her reasons for coming here were not honest.
    (A) I could not but help feel
    (B) I could not but feel
    (C) I couldn't help only to feel
    (D) I could not help feel
    (E) I could but not feel

59. He is not as talented as his wife.
    (A) He is not as talented as his wife.
    (B) He is not so talented as his wife.
    (C) He is not talented like his wife is.
    (D) As his wife, he is not as talented.
    (E) He doesn't have the talent as his wife.

60. Did you see James's hat?
    (A) Did you see James's hat?
    (B) Did you see James hat?
    (C) Have you seen Jame's hat?
    (D) Have you seen James hat?
    (E) Have you saw James hat?

End Of Section III

SECTION IV — HUMANITIES
(30 minutes)

DIRECTIONS: In each of the following, select the one of the choices which will make the sentence most nearly correct. On the answer sheet blacken the space corrsponding to your choice.

61. "Boot, saddle, to horse, and away"
    "God's in His Heaven—
    All's right with the World."
    "Just for a handful of silver he left us"
    All of these were written by
    (A) Tennyson   (B) Longfellow
    (C) Kipling   (D) Browning.

62. The pen name of Theodore Geisel is
    (A) Lewis Carroll   (B) Dr. Seuss
    (C) Leslie Brooks   (D) Munro Leaf.

63. A small Italian village provides the background for most of the action of
    (A) West's "The Devil's Advocate"
    (B) Huxley's "Point Counter Point"
    (C) Hersey's "The Wall"
    (D) Dreiser's "Sister Carrie."

64. The author of "Tales of the South Pacific" also wrote
    (A) The Good Earth
    (B) Of Human Bondage
    (C) The Moon and Sixpence
    (D) Sayonara.

65. Of the four titles listed, the two that are the titles of books written by Jules Verne are
    a. Around the World in Eighty Days
    b. Twenty Thousand Leagues Under the Sea
    c. The War of the Worlds
    d. The Time Machine.
    (A) a, b   (B) a, d
    (C) b, c   (D) b, d

66. The author of "How do I love thee? Let me count the ways" is
    (A) Elizabeth Barrett Browning
    (B) John Keats
    (C) Lord Byron
    (D) Percy Bysshe Shelley.

67. Byam, Christian, and Bligh are characters in the work of
    (A) Beaumont and Fletcher
    (B) Nordhoff and Hall
    (C) Joseph Conrad
    (D) C. S. Forrester.

68. Of the following, the one Shaw did *not* write is
    (A) Lady Windermere's Fan
    (B) Man and Superman
    (C) Candida
    (D) Arms and the Man.

69. Robert Louis Stevenson wrote all of the following *except*
    (A) Kidnapped
    (B) Markheim
    (C) Treasure Island
    (D-) The Outcast of the Islands.

70. The main theme of "Arrowsmith" by Sinclair Lewis deals with
    (A) the medical profession
    (B) business and industry
    (C) politics in America
    (D) religion in America.

71. Of the following names, the one which is the surname of the celebrated Renaissance painter Michelangelo is
    (A) Buonarroti   (B) Theotokopulos
    (C) Van Rijn   (D) Le Douanier.

72. Of the following cities, the one that is of *least* importance in the history of Italian painting is
    (A) Rome   (B) Palermo
    (C) Venice   (D) Florence.

73. Of the following, a modern painter with religious overtones is
    (A) Grant Wood   (B) Orozco
    (C) Duchamp   (D) Rouault.

74. The flying buttress is
    (A) an ornamental gargoyle
    (B) an element in modern sculpture
    (C) a structural unit in Gothic architecture
    (D) a device introduced by Frank Lloyd Wright.

75. Colonial Williamsburg has been reconstructed through the money and interest of the
    (A) Morgans   (B) Fords
    (C) Rockefellers   (D) Mellons.

76. Fired clay
    (A) can always be made plastic and fluid again

(B) can never again be made plastic and fluid
(C) is called green ware
(D) is discarded ceramic material.

77. A nineteenth century artist noted for his life among and paintings of natives of the South Sea Islands is
(A) Vincent Van Gogh   (B) Paul Gauguin
(C) Paulo Uccello   (D) Henri Matisse.

78. Gouge, knife, roller, veiner, relief printing are all terms associated with
(A) etching
(B) linoleum block printing
(C) wood carving
(D) leather work.

79. A portrait of George Washington that has frequently been reproduced was painted by
(A) George Innes   (B) Gilbert Stuart
(C) John Singer Sargent (D) Cass Gilbert.

80. Marin, eminent American water colorist, took for his locale the
(A) Deep South
(B) Middle West
(C) streets of San Francisco
(D) Maine coast and New England.

81. Of the following, the partners who first popularized the operetta in England were
(A) George and Ira Gershwin
(B) Gilbert and Sullivan
(C) Rodgers and Hammerstein
(D) Elgar and Williams.

82. The key signature for E major is
(A) 2 sharps   (B) 3 sharps
(C) 4 sharps   (D) no sharps.

83. A "concerto" is a
(A) musical instrument
(B) composition for solo instrument with orchestral accompaniment
(C) type of vocal solo with organ accompaniment
(D) composition for chorus.

84. The words, "I looked over Jordan, and what did I see" are found in the spiritual
(A) Steal Away
(B) Deep River
(C) Were You There
(D) Swing Low Sweet Chariot.

85. The "Golliwog's Cakewalk" is taken from a larger composition known as
(A) The Children's Corner—Debussy
(B) The Peer Gynt Suite—Grieg
(C) The Sorcerer's Apprentice—Dukas
(D) The Nutcracker Suite—Tschaikowsky.

86. The opera by Verdi first performed at the opening of an opera house in Cairo is
(A) Il Trovatore   (B) Aida
(C) Rigoletto   (D) Rienzi.

87. Of the following, the song which was not composed by Stephen Foster is
(A) Nelly Bly
(B) Jeanie with the Light Brown Hair
(C) Beautiful Dreamer
(D) Carry Me Back to Old Virginny.

88. The foreign artist, Emil Gilels, who won acclaim in this country, is a
(A) singer   (B) pianist
(C) violinist   (D) conductor.

89. Of the following, the one in which Figaro is a character is
(A) Pagliacci
(B) The Barber of Seville
(C) Madame Butterfly
(D) La Tosca.

90. Of the following, the composer best known for his large number of song compositions is
(A) Johann Strauss   (B) Franz Schubert
(C) Richard Wagner (D) Anton Rubinstein.

End Of Section IV

If you finish before time is called, check your work on this section only.

When time is called, proceed directly to the next section and do not return to this section.

SECTION V — SCIENCE
(15 minutes)

91. Each of the following bodily functions is correctly paired with a physiological part *except*
    (A) circulation—clavicle
    (B) elimination—pore
    (C) digestion—saliva
    (D) respiration—trachea.

92. Of the following, the one most likely to speed soil erosion is
    (A) planting trees   (B) removing trees
    (C) contour plowing   (D) terracing.

93. Of the following, Vitamin B_{12} is most useful in combatting
    (A) anemia   (B) night blindness
    (C) rickets   (D) goiter.

94. Both malaria and yellow fever are
    (A) caused by protozoans
    (B) cured with antibiotics
    (C) prevented by vaccination
    (D) controlled by swamp drainage.

95. The tassel of a corn plant
    (A) produces pollen (B) provides protection
    (C) forms the pistil (D) produces ovules.

96. The heliocentric theory of the solar system is associated with the name of
    (A) Tycho   (B) Copernicus
    (C) Harvey   (D) Archimedes.

97. A cold-blooded animal is one that
    (A) lacks red corpuscles
    (B) lacks white corpuscles
    (C) has a variable temperature
    (D) lives in arctic regions.

98. Of the following, the one which represents the conversion of a liquid to a gas is
    (A) evaporation   (B) condensation
    (C) oxidation   (D) sublimation.

99. The time that it takes for the earth to complete a 60 degree rotation is
    (A) 1 hour   (B) 4 hours
    (C) 6 hours   (D) 24 hours.

100. Of the following, the most common metal found in the earth's crust is
    (A) iron   (B) copper
    (C) aluminum   (D) tin.

101. Of the following, the gas which is needed for burning is
    (A) carbon dioxide   (B) oxygen
    (C) nitrogen   (D) argon.

102. Of the following, the process which will result in water that is the most nearly chemically pure is
    (A) aeration   (B) chlorination
    (C) distillation   (D) filtration.

103. The number of degrees on the Fahrenheit thermometer between the freezing point and the boiling point of water is
    (A) 100 degrees   (B) 180 degrees
    (C) 212 degrees   (D) 273 degrees.

104. Of the following planets, the one which has the largest number of satellites is
    (A) Jupiter   (B) Mercury
    (C) Neptune   (D) Pluto.

105. The Beaufort Scale indicates
    (A) temperature   (B) air pressure
    (C) wind force   (D) wind direction.

106. Of the following, the string with the lowest pitch would be a
    (A) tight, thick string (B) loose, thick string
    (C) tight, thin string (D) loose, thin string.

107. Washing soda is composed of the chemical elements sodium, oxygen and
    (A) nitrogen   (B) chlorine
    (C) sulfur   (D) carbon.

108. One is most likely to feel the effects of static electricity on a
    (A) cold, damp day   (B) cold, dry day
    (C) warm, humid day   (D) warm, dry day.

109. Of the following, the part of a ship which gives it stability by lowering the center of gravity is the
    (A) bulkhead   (B) anchor
    (C) keel   (D) prow.

110. A wax begonia often turns reddish in a classroom because
    (A) it is not receiving enough sunlight
    (B) the soil is too rich
    (C) the soil is too dry
    (D) it is receiving too much sunlight.

End Of Section V

If you finish before time is called, check your work on this section only.

When time is called, proceed directly to the next section and do not return to this section.

SECTION VI — SOCIAL SCIENCE
(15 minutes)

111. If the cost of living index rises from 120 to 130, the purchasing power of the dollar
    (A) rises
    (B) falls
    (C) remains the same
    (D) is automatically adjusted.

112. Of the following, the one which *incorrectly* pairs a person with a field of achievement is
    (A) Phidias—sculpture
    (B) Plato—philosophy
    (C) Aeschylus—drama
    (D) Pericles—poetry.

113. Of the following, the width in longitude of each standard time zone is closest to
    (A) 5 degrees
    (B) 10 degrees
    (C) 15 degrees
    (D) 20 degrees.

114. The Elastic Clause gives Congress
    (A) reserved powers
    (B) delegated powers
    (C) enumerated powers
    (D) implied powers.

115. The opening of the Erie Canal in 1825
    (A) held back the growth of Syracuse and Rochester
    (B) decreased the business of the New York Central railroad
    (C) brought western trade to the port of New York
    (D) discouraged pioneers from settling in the land west of the Mohawk Valley.

116. In reference to the following Southern cities, the description that appears next to each is approximate *except* in the case of
    (A) Birmingham—Pittsburgh of the South
    (B) New Orleans—Gateway to the Mississippi Valley
    (C) Atlanta—Business Capital of the South
    (D) Louisville—Sugar Bowl of the South.

117. " . . . and secure the blessings of liberty to ourselves and our posterity . . . " is quoted from the
    (A) Atlantic Charter
    (B) Preamble, United States Constitution
    (C) Preamble, United Nations Charter
    (D) Declaration of Independence.

118. Of the following, the one which provides for an eighty-day "cooling off" period in labor disputes is the
    (A) Taft-Hartley Act
    (B) Wagner Labor Relations Act
    (C) Norris-LaGuardia Anti-Injunction Act
    (D) Clayton Anti-Trust Act.

119. Of the following, the most stable government in Latin America during the past twenty-five years has been
    (A) Argentina
    (B) Cuba
    (C) Venezuela
    (D) Mexico.

120. Japan defied the League of Nations in 1931 when she invaded
    (A) Korea
    (B) Formosa
    (C) Manchuria
    (D) Indochina.

121. "The American High School Today" by James Bryant Conant, published in 1959, advocated
    (A) no radical change in high schools
    (B) abolition of junior high schools
    (C) no high schools with a graduating class of over one hundred
    (D) all mathematics and science to be electives.

122. The policy and position of England with respect to Continental Europe through most of the nineteenth century was once aptly described by a British statesman as a policy of
    (A) dollar diplomacy
    (B) inextricable entanglement
    (C) splendid isolation
    (D) collective security.

123. The cartoonist who drew the first Tammany tiger and who created the Republican elephant was
    (A) Thomas Nast
    (B) Horace Greeley
    (C) Edmund Duffy
    (D) Nelson Harding.

124. During the 1930's, immigration into the United States declined chiefly because of
    (A) depressed economic conditions
    (B) the easing of religious intolerance in Europe
    (C) more attractive opportunities in other lands
    (D) restrictive United States legislation.

125. All of the following usually tend to encourage inflation *except*
    (A) advances in production technology
    (B) lowering of rediscount rate
    (C) decrease in Federal income tax rates
    (D) increase in military spending.

126. Time is usually reckoned by using as a starting point
    (A) Greenwich—England
    (B) the International Date Line
    (C) the Equator
    (D) the Tropic of Capricorn.

127. Sinn Fein is a political party that was active in attempts to gain independence for
    (A) Ireland   (B) China
    (C) Malaya   (D) French Cameroons.

128. All of the following states border New York State *except*
    (A) Massachusetts   (B) New Hampshire
    (C) New Jersey   (D) Vermont.

129. During the entire period from 1800 to 1850, the greatest number of immigrants to the United States came from
    (A) Germany   (B) England
    (C) Scandinavia   (D) Ireland.

130. Voting qualifications in the United States are
    (A) determined by the states, subject to constitutional restrictions
    (B) established by Congress, subject to constitutional restrictions
    (C) enumerated in the Bill of Rights
    (D) specifically defined in the Federal Constitution.

End Of Section VI

When time is called, stop work on this section
The Afternoon Session part of the test is now concluded

ANSWER KEY TO LAW SCHOOL ADMISSION TEST [A]
Afternoon Session

1. D	16. G	31. D	46. D	61. D	76. B	91. A	106. B	121. A
2. O	17. O	32. B	47. C	62. B	77. B	92. B	107. D	122. C
3. O	18. G	33. D	48. E	63. A	78. B	93. A	108. B	123. A
4. D	19. V	34. C	49. B	64. D	79. B	94. D	109. C	124. D
5. D	20. O	35. C	50. B	65. A	80. D	95. A	110. D	125. A
6. G	21. D	36. B	51. A	66. A	81. B	96. B	111. B	126. A
7. D	22. C	37. A	52. C	67. B	82. C	97. C	112. D	127. A
8. V	23. A	38. C	53. D	68. A	83. B	98. A	113. C	129. A
9. V	24. C	39. B	54. B	69. D	84. D	99. B	114. D	128. B
10. G	25. B	40. D	55. C	70. A	85. A	100. C	115. C	130. A
11. G	26. B	41. E	56. C	71. A	86. B	101. B	116. D	
12. G	27. C	42. C	57. E	72. B	87. D	102. C	117. B	
13. O	28. C	43. D	58. B	73. D	88. B	103. B	118. A	
14. G	29. A	44. D	59. B	74. C	89. B	104. A	119. D	
15. D	30. B	45. A	60. A	75. C	90. B	105. C	120. C	

Suggestions After You Take The Sample LSAT

*Now that you have finished the Sample Test,
proceed as follows:*

STEP ONE — Check your answers with the Answer Key that follows the Sample Test. Then compare your total score with the Unofficial Percentile Ranking Table below. Although this table is not official, it will give you a reasonably good idea of how you would stand with others taking the same test. For example, if your percentile ranking, according to your score, is 61, this means that you are superior to 60% of those who have taken the test and inferior to 39%. As stated previously, the percentile ranking on the Law School Admission Test is a major factor among many law schools in determining fitness for a career in law.

Percentile Ranking Table
(unofficial)

Approximate Percentile Ranking	Score On Morning Test	Score On Afternoon Test	Approximate Percentile Ranking	Score On Morning Test	Score On Afternoon Test
99	158–160	129–130	68	105	83
98	155–157	127–128	67	104	82
97	152–154	125–126	66	103	81
96	149–151	123–124	65	102	80
95	146–148	121–122	64	101	79
94	143–145	119–120	63	100	78
93	140–142	117–118	62	99	77
92	137–139	115–116	61	98	76
91	135–137	113–114	60	97	75
90	133–134	111–112	59	96	74
89	131–132	109–110	58	95	73
88	129–130	107–108	57	94	72
87	127–128	105–106	56	93	71
86	125–126	103–104	55	92	70
85	123–124	101–102	54	91	69
84	121–122	99–100	53	90	68
83	120	98	52	89	67
82	119	97	51	88	66
81	118	96	50	87	65
80	117	95	49	86	64
79	116	94	48	85	63
78	115	93	47	84	62
77	114	92	46	83	61
76	113	91	45	82	60
75	112	90	44	81	59
74	111	89	43	80	58
73	110	88	42	79	57
72	109	87	41	78	56
71	108	86	40	77	55
70	107	85	0–39	0–76	0–54
69	106	84			

STEP TWO—Use the results of the test in a diagnostic manner. Pinpoint the areas in which you show the greatest weakness. The following Diagnostic Table will help you to spotlight the places where you need the most practice.

Diagnostic Table

Area	Strong	Average	Weak
	Number Correct on Trial Examination		
NONVERBAL REASONING 60 questions	56–60	45–55	0–44
READING COMPREHENSION 30 questions	28–30	20–27	0–19
GRAPHS, CHARTS, AND TABLES 35 questions	32–35	23–31	0–22
LAW INTERPRETATION 25 questions	23–25	16–22	0–15
REMEMBERING MAIN IDEAS 10 questions	9–10	6–8	0–5
RECOGNIZING ERRORS 20 questions	17–20	12–16	0–11
ORGANIZATION OF IDEAS 20 questions	17–20	12–16	0–11
EDITING ABILITY 20 questions	17–20	12–16	0–11
LITERATURE 10 questions	9–10	6–8	0–5
ART 10 questions	9–10	6–8	0–5
MUSIC 10 questions	9–10	6–8	0–5
SCIENCE 20 questions	18–20	13–17	0–12
SOCIAL SCIENCE 20 questions	18–20	13–17	0–12

STEP THREE—Use the following CHECK LIST to establish areas that require the greatest application on your part. One check (√) after the item means *moderately weak;* two checks (√√) means *seriously weak.*

Area of Weakness	Check Below
NONVERBAL REASONING	
READING COMPREHENSION	
GRAPHS, CHARTS, AND TABLES	
LAW INTERPRETATION	
REMEMBERING MAIN IDEAS	
RECOGNIZING ERRORS	
ORGANIZATION OF IDEAS	
EDITING ABILITY	
LITERATURE	
ART	
MUSIC	
SCIENCE	
SOCIAL SCIENCE	

STEP FOUR—The Pinpoint Practice section, which is the next part of this book, has considerable drill material to cover every phase of the Law School Admission Test. Be systematic in your plan of attack. Concentrate on the areas of weakness first. Answer the practice questions in these areas. As you will discover, the material is presented so that the areas tested in the actual exam are individually treated in this book.

L
s
a
t

3

PART THREE

Pinpoint Practice To Raise Your Mark

PINPOINT PRACTICE FOR THE MORNING AND AFTERNOON SESSIONS

We are now ready to eliminate our weaknesses in preparation for each part of the LSAT. The questions which you encountered in the Trial Examination (starting on page 17) should have spotlighted your strong and weak points.

At this stage it is important for you to concentrate on the "soft spots" (your weaknesses). This Pinpoint section is so-called because you will, in the following pages, be able to locate accurately and quickly the areas that offer practice where you need it most. You are strongly advised to deal first with the phases of the examination in which you need the greatest work. You will find in the pages to come plenty of practice tests in each of the areas of the LSAT. The coverage in this section consists of questions in

LAW INTERPRETATION
NONVERBAL REASONING

RECOGNIZING ERRORS
ORGANIZATION OF IDEAS
EDITING ABILITY
LITERATURE
ART
MUSIC
SCIENCE
SOCIAL SCIENCE

The Supplement of this book contains additional practice material in

GRAPHS, CHARTS, AND TABLES
MATCHING PARTS AND FIGURES
(Nonverbal Reasoning)

Law Interpretation Tests

DIRECTIONS: This group of questions consists of law cases followed by a list of legal principles. These principles may be either real or imaginary, but for purposes of this test you are to assume them to be valid. For each case you are to select the legal principle which is *most applicable* to the case. To identify your answer blacken the space beneath the letter on the answer sheet which corresponds to the letter of the legal principle you select.

These questions do not presuppose any specific legal knowledge on your part; you are to base your answers entirely on the ordinary processes of logical reasoning.

LAW INTERPRETATION: TEST 1

CASES

1. Brown offers to give the sum of $1000 to Jones, who is about to be called as a witness in a criminal trial, with the understanding that Jones perjure himself at the trial. Jones refuses the money and reports the incident to the district attorney.

2. Smith, a basketball coach, approaches Greene, a known gambler, and offers to limit the margin of his team's victory to a low score in a game scheduled for the same evening, if Greene agrees to buy him a new automobile. Greene accepts the offer. Greene's attorney claims that his client was innocently taken by Smith.

3. Black, returning from work late at night, discovered that he did not have the keys to his house. Raising a window of a house which he believed to be his home, he entered a room only to realize that he was not in his home. As he was about to leave the house, he picked up a watch from the table and pocketed it. He opened the front door of the dwelling and left. He is charged with burglary. His attorney presses for the lesser charge of unintentional trespass.

4. Black left the outer door of his home open and White slipped in unnoticed by Black and hid in the closet. When he and his family were about to retire, Black closed and locked the outer door. Later White came out of the closet, took some valuable jewelry, unlocked the outer door, opened it and made good his escape. White is charged with burglary. His attorney presses for the lesser charge of larceny.

5. Smith and Jones, both armed, break into and enter the home of Walters in mid-afternoon, while Walters is asleep in another part of the dwelling. After taking some valuable jewelry, Smith and Jones depart through the back door. The criminals are charged with burglary. Their attorney presses for the lesser charge of larceny.

PRINCIPLES

(A) Anyone who breaks into and enters a dwelling at night with a person therein, with intent to commit a crime therein, and who is armed with a dangerous weapon, or is assisted by a confederate actually present, or assaults a person while entering or escaping from such building, is guilty of burglary, 1st degree.

(B) Guilt in bribery extends to all participants contributing to the fulfilment of the bribe.

(C) A person, who, being in a building, commits a crime, whether or not there is original intent to do so, and then breaks out of the building, is guilty of burglary, 3rd degree.

(D) A person who gives or offers a bribe for false testimony is guilty of the charge of bribing a witness.

(E) Anyone who breaks into and enters a dwelling during the day with a person therein, with intent to commit a crime therein, is guilty of burglary, 2nd degree.

Answers: Test 1

1. D   2. B   3. C   4. C   5. E

LAW INTERPRETATION: TEST 2

CASES

1. Jones, aware that there are human beings in a house, fires several shots into it, knowing that someone could be killed. One of the occupants is killed. A charge of murder is asked for Jones by the district attorney.

2. An eleven-year old child kills a human being with intent to kill and with deliberation and premeditation. On the basis of these facts, a relative of the slain person insists that the child be charged with murder.

3. A assaults B with a loaded revolver. The gun accidentally discharges and the bullet kills B.

A's attorney contends that A is not guilty of felony murder.

4. D entered his father's room and held him at bay with a loaded rifle, warning him that he would be shot if he stepped forward. D's wife tried to stop D from threatening his father. D pushed his wife aside. She fell and was killed when her head struck the brick wall of the fireplace. The district attorney claims that D is guilty of murder.

5. When Jones was being questioned by two police officers as a criminal suspect, he drew his gun and shot and killed one of the policemen. In order to avoid being arrested, Jones shot and killed the second officer. The district attorney claims that Jones is guilty of two murders.

PRINCIPLES

(A) A person who kills another to prevent the latter from carrying out a legal function is guilty of deliberate and premeditated murder.

(B) A child between the ages of 7 and 12 years is presumed incapable of committing crime. This presumption of incapacity is rebuttable by evidence of ability to understand the difference between right and wrong.

(C) When a person, guilty of assault with intent to murder, kills someone else instead by accident, the assaulter is guilty of murder.

(D) A killing resulting from an act imminently dangerous to others, evincing a depraved mind, is considered murder although there may be no premeditated design to effect the death of any individual.

(E) When a person, guilty of assault, kills the assaulted without intent to do so, the felony is merged in the homicide on the person killed and does not constitute felony murder.

Answers: Test 2

1. D   2. B   3. E   4. C   5. A

LAW INTERPRETATION: TEST 3

CASES

1. X was asleep on a park bench. Y attempted to waken him by shaking him. When X failed to respond, he shook him more violently. Finally X opened his eyes, began to grapple

with Y, drew a revolver from his pocket and shot him. X had never seen Y before and had no apparent motive for the shooting. X proved that he was of good character but had been a sleep-walker since infancy, and was not conscious of what he was doing at the time of the shooting. The district attorney asks for a manslaughter charge.

2. X, while driving a stolen car far beyond the speed limit, hit and killed a pedestrian. The district attorney asks for a manslaughter charge.

3. X, a guard at a mental institution, wilfully encouraged and assisted Y, an inmate, in attempting suicide by supplying him with a poisonous drug. The district attorney asks for a manslaughter charge.

4. Brown steals $100 from the cash register of Sim's store. Keefe, having knowledge of the theft, aids Brown to escape apprehension. Keefe's attorney claims that his client was simply trying to help out a friend and that Keefe, therefore, should be given no sentence.

5. A, without B's knowledge, placed his hand in B's pocket, seized B's wallet containing a large amount of money, and had partly lifted it out of the pocket when he was apprehended by a detective behind him. A's attorney claims A is not guilty of larceny because the attempt to steal was foiled.

PRINCIPLES

(A) When, in an attempt to take and carry away property, the property is moved from its original position but the carrying away is not completed, there is an act of larceny by trespass.

(B) One who knowingly aids a person before, during, or after the commission of a crime, is a principal to the crime and punishable in the same manner as if he had committed the crime.

(C) Criminal negligence occurs when a person operates a vehicle in a culpably negligent manner causing death of a human being.

(D) Manslaughter occurs when there is no design to effect death, but death has occurred as a result of the person's heat of passion.

(E) If an attempt at suicide is successful, the abettor is guilty of manslaughter.

Answers: Test 3

1. D   2. C   3. E   4. B   5. A

LAW INTERPRETATION: TEST 4
CASES

1. Jones was arrested for stealing clothing from his employer. In order to trap Brown as the receiver of stolen goods, the police, with the employer's consent, gave Jones the clothing with orders to sell them to Brown as stolen merchandise. Brown, believing that the goods were stolen, purchased them from Jones. Brown's attorney claims that his client has committed no crime.

2. X placed his hand in Y's pocket intending to steal Y's wallet. Y felt the hand in his pocket and grabbed X. Y's pocket, at the same time, contained nothing. X's attorney claims that his client has committed no crime.

3. Smith paid his hotel bill by means of a check and received $25 in change. The check was returned for insufficient funds. The hotel claims that Smith, in receiving money for a bad check, has committed larceny.

4. Jones and Black were partners in a business venture. According to their agreement, each was allowed to draw checks on the funds of the partnership. Jones drew a check to himself for $200 against the funds of the partnership and cashed the check, using the money for his personal pleasure. Black says Jones should be charged with larceny.

5. Smith agreed to buy a dozen lottery tickets from Jones. Jones told Smith that he would send a messenger to his office the next day at noon to deliver the tickets and receive payment. Brown overheard the conversation and the next day called at Smith's office. He pretended to be the messenger from Jones and delivered to Smith a sealed envelope, receiving $150 therefor. The envelope was found to contain blank papers. Brown's attorney claims that it is illegal to buy and sell lottery tickets. Therefore, Brown is without guilt.

PRINCIPLES

(A) If an agreement is specific as to the use and application of partnership funds, any deviation of such use constitutes larceny.

(B) Jostling, a disorderly conduct offense, occurs if the evidence shows that the pickpocket's hand is in the proximity of another person's pocket. If the hand is actually in the pocket, attempted larceny results.

(C) If the owner of goods consents to a transaction, another person purchasing same goods cannot be charged with purchasing stolen goods.

(D) Criminal intent to deprive and defraud an owner constitutes larceny. The fact that the consideration involved is illegal does not initigate the circumstances of a commission of larceny.

(E) If the evidence establishes criminal intent on the part of a person to defraud, he may be convicted of larceny for obtaining property by fraudulent order.

Answers: Test 4

1. C   2. B   3. E   4. A   5. D

LAW INTERPRETATION: TEST 5

CASES

1. X found a diamond bracelet with a tag attached showing the name and address of the owner. Without making any effort to locate the owner, X gave the bracelet to his wife. X claims he has committed no wrong since the bracelet has been recovered and returned by the police to its owner.

2. Jones, over a period of 3 months, stole 144 articles from a department store. The aggregate value of all the articles exceeded $500 although none of the separate articles stolen involved that amount. The district attorney claims that Jones has hereby committed several larcenies.

3. Jones breaks into and enters Smith's apartment at night. He enters Smith's bedroom, takes an envelope from Smith's coat in the closet, while Smith is sound asleep. The envelope contains a certified copy of Smith's marriage certificate. Jones' attorney claims that his client, having

taken nothing of value to himself, is guilty of unlawful entry only.

4. A stock broker appropriated money belonging to one of his customers. He restores the money at a later date before a complaint is filed. The customer involved insists that larceny has nevertheless been committed.

5. X, a chauffeur for the Y family, takes Y's car valued at $4000, without obtaining Y's permission, and drives his (X's) family to the seashore. At the end of the day, X returns the car to the garage after replacing the gasoline which had been consumed. X's employer claims that X is guilty of larceny.

PRINCIPLES

(A) Breaking into a dwelling with intent to commit a crime constitutes larceny.

(B) Where a number of individual stealings spell out the fact that each stealing was one step in the completion of a common scheme, then each of the individual thefts can be joined together to constitute a single larceny.

(C) Taking of property without the owner's consent constitutes larceny.

(D) The intent to return property alleged to have been stolen, particularly if returned before complaint, is always relevant as evidence of lack of felonious intent.

(E) A person who finds property under circumstances which give means of inquiry as to the true owner, and who appropriates such property without having first made every reasonable effort to locate the owner for restoration, is guilty of larceny.

Answers: Test 5

1. E   2. B   3. A   4. D   5. C

Nonverbal Reasoning Tests

DIRECTIONS: Each question consists of 3 drawings followed by 5 alternative drawings, lettered A, B, C, D, and E. The first two drawings in each question are related in some way. Choose the alternative that is related to the third drawing in the same way that the second drawing is related to the first.

Examples:

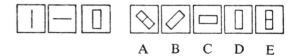

A   B   C   D   E

The correct answer is **C.** A vertical line has the same relationship to a horizontal line that rectangle standing on its end has to a rectangle lying on its side.

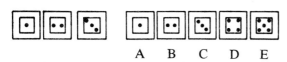

The second square has one more dot than the first square. Therefore the correct answer is alternative D, which has one more dot than the third square.

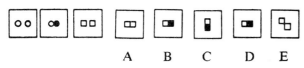

In the second drawing the circles are moved together and the circle on the right darkened. Therefore the correct answer is B, in which the squares are moved together and the right-hand square darkened.

Now answer the questions below in the same way.

NONVERBAL REASONING: TEST 1

1.

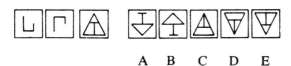

2.

3.

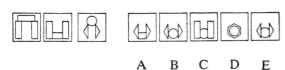

4.

5.

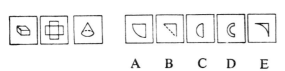

Answers: Test 1

1. E   2. D   3. E   4. E   5. A

NONVERBAL REASONING: TEST 2

1.

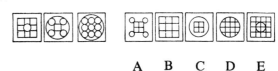

2.

3.

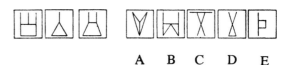

4.

5.

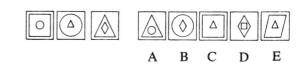

Answers: Test 2

1. B   2. B   3. D   4. A   5. D

EXPLANATION OF ANSWERS

1. In the second figure, the squares are changed to circles and the circles to squares.

2. In the second figure, the upper darkened area has moved two squares to left; the lower, two squares to right.

3. The second figure has a flat base, like the first.

4. The sum of sides and dots in the second figure equals that of the first.

5. The outside part of the second figure is the inside part of the first.

NONVERBAL REASONING: TEST 3

1.

A B C D E

2.

A B C D E

3.

A B C D E

4.

A B C D E

5.

A B C D E

Answers: Test 3

1. C 2. C 3. B 4. C 5. E

EXPLANATION OF ANSWERS

1. The second figure is constructed from the lines given in the first.

2. The second figure is obtained rfom the first by rotating it 135 degrees.

3. The second figure is the bisector of the area of the first.

4. The second figure is obtained from the first by deleting all the vertical lines.

5. The second figure contains two blocks more than the first.

The Need for the Writing Ability and Cultural Background Tests

"The Law School Admission Test Policy Committee, which is composed of representatives of the law schools making major use of the test and which determines the general policies governing the test, has for some time been exploring ways of using the test to obtain additional data about law school applicants. In particular law schools are interested in learning more about the writing ability of their applicants and about the extent to which they have acquired a broad background in the liberal arts. The first of these concerns is prompted by the fact that the student of law and the lawyer must be able to communicate effectively in writing as well as by the spoken word. There is no time in law school for formal training in the techniques of correct and effective writing and the law schools wish to ensure, so far as possible, that their entering students are reasonably competent in writing skills. The interest of law schools in breadth of background results from their belief that a lawyer should be more than a mere technician ignorant of the cultural and historical context within which the law functions. To take his proper place in the community the lawyer should have an informal awareness of the world around him and of its relation to the past."

—*excerpt from Educational Testing Service Memorandum for Deans and Advisers of Pre-Law Students*

Accordingly, an additional testing session was introduced into the LSAT program in November 1961. This session is made up of two parts:

A. WRITING ABILITY—a test of about an hour and twenty minutes, designed to measure the candidate's ability to

1. recognize common errors
2. organize a connected piece of prose
3. edit a sentence.

B. CULTURAL BACKGROUND—a test of approximately an hour, designed to measure the candidate's general knowledge in

1. Humanities (Literature, Art, Music)
2. Science
3. Social Science.

The importance of basic writing skills for lawyers is clearly brought out by the dean of the Columbia University Law School, Professor William C. Warren, in his statement that incoming law students write papers that are "for the most part graceless and too often distressingly ungrammatical."

Law students, he noted, have almost without exception completed four years of college for bachelor's degrees. "Yet what can we do? We are teachers of law and not of rhetoric."

Dean Warren expresses the opinion that no student should be admitted to law school without minimal writing skills. "I have proposed that all law applicants be tested in this single area of achievement," he adds

This deficiency in writing ability among law school students is further brought out by Professor Thomas M. Cooley II, dean of the School of Law, University of Pittsburgh. Writing in the *Saturday Review,* he cogently states:

"We have students in our law schools who, we are sure, have mastered substantial amounts of legal information. They have, in effect, *learned* enough. But they cannot put this learning into words on their examinations or in their term papers so that we who have supervised the very learning which they seek to express can understand what they are talking about. They cannot organize and express what it is that they know. How much less, then, can these unfortunates advise a client, or someone else who knows little or nothing of the substance of the legal issues, of what it is that needs to be communicated? The faculty of doing so is simply not being developed in the current system of American education."

Error Recognition Tests

DIRECTIONS: Among the sentences in this group are some which cannot be accepted in formal, written English for one or another of the following reasons:

Poor Diction:
The use of a word which is improper either because its meaning does not fit the sentence or because it is not acceptable in formal writing.
Example: The audience was strongly effected by the senator's speech.

Verbosity:
Repetitious elements adding nothing to the meaning of the sentence and not justified by any need for special emphasis.
Example: At that time there was then no right of petition.

Faulty Grammar:
Word forms and expressions which do not conform to the grammatical and structural usages required by formal written English (errors in case, number, parallelism, and the like).
Example: Everyone in the delegation had their reasons for opposing the measure.

No sentence has more than one of these errors. Some sentences have no errors. Read each sentence carefully; then on your answer sheet blacken the space under:

D if the sentence contains an error in diction,
V if the sentence is verbose,
G if the sentence contains faulty grammar,
O if the sentence contains none of these errors.

ERROR RECOGNITION: TEST 1

1. Beside us, he can count upon few of his constituents.

2. He had a chance to invest wisely, establish his position, and displaying his ability as an executive.

3. Picknicking in these woods is one way to effectively avoid the noise and crowds of the metropolitan areas.

4. The pretensions of the old charlatan were so absurd that they amused his host, a man who had had a lot of experience dealing with similar frauds.

5. The snow fell during the night so that it was laying in big drifts on the highway the next morning.

6. Why don't you try to please the customers, Ted, so they're satisfied?

7. The coach with his entire team are traveling by plane.

8. Credible as she usually is, even Mrs. Brown refused to believe such an implausible story.

9. Having finished his homework, his new records were played.

10. He replied, when she asked him about the project, that he hoped to have finished it soon.

Answers: Test 1

| 1. D | 3. G | 5. D | 7. G | 9. G |
| 2. G | 4. D | 6. V | 8. D | 10. G |

ERROR RECOGNITION: TEST 2

1. "We were never formerly introduced," she answered gaily.

2. This is one of those tricky questions which has two answers.

3. The director gave little assistance to the applicants; all he did was criticize their grammar and make irrevelant remarks about their clothes.

4. Before I met him, I heard stories about his skill in argument.

5. The work had been done long before the date specified in the original agreement.

6. In some books printed years ago, the s's look like f's.

7. To make sure your speech is audible, practice in an auditorium is helpful.

8. His ambiguous remarks were inconsistent with his reputation for intelligence.

9. The dialogue was so irreverent and sacrilegious, I refused to listen to it.

10. A fool and his gold is soon parted.

Answers: Test 2

| 1. D | 3. D | 5. O | 7. G | 9. V |
| 2. G | 4. G | 6. O | 8. O | 10. G |

ERROR RECOGNITION: TEST 3

1. We found no precedence for his outrageous rulings.

2. The results of the poll had little or no affect on the actions of the legislature.

3. These platitudinous observations did little to embellish his speech.

4. She did the work very well, however, she showed no interest in anything beyond her assignment.

5. Such fallacious reasoning can be detected by an inexperienced debater easily.

6. Roberts, a man who we trusted with the most difficult task of all, proved loyal to his country.

7. The consensus of those present favors the suggestion.

8. He felt badly when he heard the news.

9. "They will soon be here," John replied. "Please wait for them."

10. It was hard to even believe that conscientious pupils could misspell so many words in their quizzes.

Answers: Test 3

| 1. D | 3. O | 5. G | 7. O | 9. O |
| 2. D | 4. G | 6. G | 8. D | 10. G |

ERROR RECOGNITION: TEST 4

1. He had a large amount of friends until he lost all his money.

2. Neither John nor I are going to join such an organization.

3. I'd like to present my colleague, Tom Rover, who helped me in all my investigative research.

4. Seldom have so many gathered to honor so few.

5. Spending the money, it made him feel like a wealthy man.

6. He prefers us to believe he is an ancestor of a distinguished Colonial official.

7. Although the table was supposed to be stationery, it was readily moved.

8. The attorney cited a ruling of the Supreme Court as an instance of the application of this principal.

9. We took Jean, Mary, and she to the dance.

10. Would you agree to Parson's having full control of the operation?

Answers: Test 4

| 1. D | 3. V | 5. G | 7. D | 9. G |
| 2. G | 4. O | 6. D | 8. D | 10. O |

ERROR RECOGNITION: TEST 5

1. If they were in a position to speedily accomplish it, they would certainly do so.

2. He had no sooner entered the room than the group came to attention.

3. What makes this beverage taste so peculiarly?

4. When studying the animals, it is important to keep alert to those you believe to be of a venomous disposition.

5. Had you explained how colossal the task would become, you would not be in this predicament at present.

6. In the melee, he thought the disputant to be me.

7. Award the cup to whomever receives the majority of the judges' votes.

8. She was promoted because she had made less errors than the other secretary.

9. Treat me as if I was your brother.

10. These kinds of excuses are hard to accept.

Answers: Test 5

1. G	3. G	5. O	7. G	9. G
2. O	4. G	6. O	8. D	10. O

ERROR RECOGNITION: TEST 6

1. Having lain on the beach all afternoon, he suffered a severe sunburn.

2. She is a person who we know people can trust.

3. I have learned many lessons when I worked for you.

4. The jury are divided in their opinions.

5. The lecture finished, the audience began asking questions.

6. George did like his mother told him, despite the importunities of his playmates.

7. At the conference, it transpired that the president had absconded with the stolen funds six months before.

8. Do you believe that Ted is more brilliant than she?

9. There isn't but one grocery store in the neighborhood.

10. The data which he collected are not relevant to the matter.

Answers: Test 6

1. O	3. G	5. O	7. V	9. V
2. G	4. O	6. G	8. O	10. O

ERROR RECOGNITION: TEST 7

1. The reason why I flunked was that I had not studied my lesson.

2. At the fringe of the crowd, peering through all those bodies, stood Henry and I.

3. The man who I thought was my friend deceived me.

4. The possession of certain skills and abilities are necessary for that type of work.

5. The beautiful elm trees are in danger of being killed by a disease which was taken here from Europe.

6. These criteria help to prove that his statements are well-founded.

7. He lay the book down on the table and angrily stalked out of the room.

8. He read inserts from his new novel to John and me.

9. Maugham has the ability to hold his readers' attention to keep reading.

10. Coming in on the train, the high school building is seen on the left.

Answers: Test 7

1. D	3. O	5. D	7. D	9. V
2. O	4. G	6. O	8. D	10. G

ERROR RECOGNITION: TEST 8

1. When the toy baloon burst the child screamed piercingly with fright.

2. I shall relay the message to my secretary upon her arrival, when she comes.

3. He is very different than his brother in temperament.

4. Does neither of them expect to attend the reception?

5. He had scarcely finished his lines when the audience began to applaud wildly with enthusiasm.

6. He told Marjorie and me that he would not come.

7. Each of the wheels on these trucks have twelve spokes.

8. It looked like it was going to be a pleasant day, so we left our umbrella at home.

9. The judge said that punishment would be dished out to whoever deserved it.

10. It is I who am mistaken.

Answers: Test 8

1. V	3. D	5. V	7. G	9. D
2. V	4. O	6. O	8. G	10. O

ERROR RECOGNITION: TEST 9

1. Is it John or Mary who stand at the head of the class?

2. At first glance, the old man believed him to be me.

3. The scenery in Banff is somewhat like Switzerland, although Banff is much farther north.

4. There must be some faraway place where one can spend a quiet and placid holiday.

5. The boy looked like he had gone through a trying period.

6. A series of biographical sketches is to be released soon.

7. Beside Mr. Truman there is one other former president living.

8. The flower smells sweet after a chemical spraying.

9. There is an increasing number of retarding readers in the ninth year.

10. Many pupils seem to enjoy playing games alone but not to lose in these games.

Answers: Test 9

1. G	3. G	5. G	7. D	9. D
2. O	4. V	6. O	8. O	10. G

ERROR RECOGNITION: TEST 10

1. The prize should be given to whomever the committee chooses.

2. The further you walk, the more lovely the road becomes.

3. Give the answer to whoever opens the door first.

4. Born in India and educated in England, Kipling's stories have the flavor of both countries.

5. The teacher, together with his pupils, was late for the bus.

6. Irregardless of consequences, he flew his plane toward the sound barrier.

7. Bring this book to the librarian.

8. Although he is playing golf only two years, he has already won three tournaments.

9. None of the boys is better able to cope with the problem than he.

10. His first answer, not his other answers, is open to question.

Answers: Test 10

1. O	3. O	5. O	7. D	9. O
2. D	4. G	6. D	8. G	10. O

Organization of Ideas Tests

Directions: Each set of questions in this test consists of several statements. Most of the statements refer to the same subject or idea. The statements can be classified as follows:

- (A) the *central idea* to which most of the statements are related;
- (B) *main supporting ideas,* which are general points directly related to the central idea;
- (C) *illustrative facts* of detailed statements, which document the main supporting ideas;
- (D) statements *irrelevant* to the central idea.

The statements may be regarded as headings in an outline: they are *not* sentences taken from one complete paragraph. The outline might, for example, have the following form:

A. The Central Idea
  B. Main Supporting Idea
    C. Illustrative Fact
  B. Main Supporting Idea
    C. Illustrative Fact
    C. Illustrative Fact.

Classify the following sentences according to the scheme set forth above:

USE THIS SPACE FOR YOUR SCRATCH WORK

Answers Test 1	
1.	C
2.	A
3.	B
4.	B
5.	C

Answers Test 2	
1.	C
2.	A
3.	C
4.	B
5.	C
6.	D

ORGANIZATION TEST 1

1. I learned this in my forty years in China from many friends, who, though illiterate, were wise and sophisticated.

2. I contend that this is a myth: that since most Chinese are illiterate they are, therefore, ignorant.

3. It all adds up to this—knowing how to read does not mean that one reads or thinks.

4. Actually there is surprisingly little connection between illiteracy and ignorance.

5. I learned it again in my own country, where I have found literacy and ignorance in frequent combination.

ORGANIZATION TEST 2

1. The actors are the only unashamed artists in the theatre.

2. A surprising number of *great* plays—and I fear this means *old* plays–has been seen on Broadway.

3. Not that they are sheer idealists—it so happens that the great roles are in the great plays.

4. Since neither the public nor the critics nor the producers can be said to have demanded them, one must give credit to the handful of star actors who insisted on playing in them.

5. The obstacles in the path of, say, a Shakespeare production would never be overcome but for the zeal of an Olivier, a Gielgud, a Katherine Cornell, or a Maurice Evans.

6. Shakespeare was born in 1564 and died in 1616.

USE THIS SPACE FOR YOUR SCRATCHWORK

ORGANIZATION TEST 3

1. Death is caused by another importation, Dutch elm disease, a fungus infection which the beetles carry from tree to tree.

2. During the past fourteen years, thousands of top-lofty United States elms have been marked for death by the activities of the tiny European elm bark beetle.

3. Every household and village that prizes an elm-shaded lawn or commons must now watch for this disease.

4. The beetles, however, do not do fatal damage.

5. Since there is yet no cure for it, the infected trees must be pruned or felled, and the wood must be burned in order to protect other healthy trees.

ORGANIZATION TEST 4

1. The fleurs-de-lis were the blazon of the delta country until 1762.

2. Iberville appropriated it to France when he colonized Louisiana in 1700.

3. Control of the Mississippi had always been the goal of nations having ambitions in the New World.

4. Then Spain claimed all of Louisiana and, with it, control of the great river.

5. La Salle claimed it for France in 1682.

6. The Mississippi is one of the world's longest rivers.

Answers Test 3

1. B
2. A
3. C
4. B
5. C

Answers Test 4

1. C
2. B
3. A
4. C
5. B
6. D

Directions: Each set of questions in this test consists of several statements. Most of the statements refer to the same subject or idea. The statements can be classified as follows:

(A) the *central idea* to which most of the statements are related

(B) *main supporting ideas,* which are general points directly related to the central idea;

(C) *illustrative facts* of detailed statements, which document the main supporting ideas;

(D) statements *irrelevant* to the central idea.

The statements may be regarded as headings in an outline: they are *not* sentences taken from one complete paragraph. The outline might, for example, have the following form:

A. The Central Idea
  B. Main Supporting Idea
    C. Illustrative Fact
  B. Main Supporting Idea
    C. Illustrative Fact
    C. Illustrative Fact.

Classify the following sentences according to the scheme set forth above:

USE THIS SPACE FOR YOUR SCRATCHWORK

ORGANIZATION TEST 5

1. When he lived in a cave with stone implements, his mind no less than his actions was grooved into simple channels.

2. And, as he moved along the road, he questioned each step, as indeed he should, for he trod upon the beliefs of his ancestors.

3. It is elemental that the greater the development of man, the greater the problems he has to concern him.

4. Each step upon this later road posed more questions than the earlier ones.

5. Every new invention, every new way of doing things, posed fresh problems for him.

6. Some of the greatest inventors emerged from circumstances of poverty.

ORGANIZATION TEST 6

1. On the other hand, if he faces his problems squarely he dwells in a real world with real people.

2. If his responses to thwartings are emotional explosions and irrational excuses, he is tending to live in an unreal world.

3. Just why some individuals choose one way of adjusting to their difficulties and others choose another way is not known.

4. Yet what an individual does when he is thwarted remains a reasonably good key to the understanding of his personality.

5. In any case, it is the part of wisdom to learn the nature of the world and of oneself in relation to it, and to meet each situation as intelligently and as adequately as one can.

Answers Test 5
1. B
2. C
3. A
4. C
5. C
6. D

Answers Test 6
1. C
2. C
3. A
4. B
5. B

**USE THIS SPACE
FOR YOUR SCRATCHWORK**

ORGANIZATION TEST 7

1. We can understand, then, why the literary history of the late nineteenth and early twentieth centuries is full of theories and "isms"—Symbolism, Futurism, Imagism, Vorticism, Expressionism, Dadaism, Surrealism—which provided artistic creeds for artist groups, and set the individual artist apart from the community in the popular opinion.

2. There were many reasons why the whole character of the twentieth century should be very different from that of the nineteenth.

3. But literature, which had been nourished by the general vigor of the time, and not at all by the practical interests of the period, declined as the spirit itself dispersed.

4. Before the end of the century that positive, homogeneous, energetic social culture which collaborated with the great Victorian writers had disintegrated.

5. The great wave of vitality and national expansions, which, during the Victorian period, swept both England and America to a high water

ORGANIZATION TEST 8

1. What the Greeks discovered, or rather how they made their discoveries and how they brought a new world to birth out of the dark confusion of an old world that had crumbled away, is full of meaning for us today.

2. Greece has a claim upon our attention not only because we are by our spiritual and mental inheritance partly Greek.

3. It is full of meaning for us who have seen an old world vanish in the space of two or three decades.

4. Greek and Latin are, as languages, related in some respects.

5. She has a direct contribution for us as well.

6. The actual Greek remains are so few and so far away, so separated from us by space and strange, difficult language, they are felt to be matters for the travelers and the scholars and no more.

Answers Test 7

1. C
2. A
3. C
4. C
5. B

Answers Test 8

1. A
2. C
3. B
4. D
5. C
6. B

Directions: Each set of questions in this test consists of several statements. Most of the statements refer to the same subject or idea. The statements can be classified as follows:

(A) the *central idea* to which most of the statements are related;

(B) *main supporting ideas,* which are general points directly related to the central idea;

(C) *illustrative facts* or detailed statements, which document the main supporting idea;

(D) statements *irrelevant* to the central idea.

The statements may be regarded as headings in an outline: they are *not* sentences taken from one complete paragraph. The outline might, for example, have the following form:

A. The Central Idea
  B. Main Supporting Idea
    C. Illustrative Fact
  B. Main Supporting Idea
    C. Illustrative Fact
    C. Illustrative Fact

**USE THIS SPACE
FOR YOUR SCRATCH WORK**

Answers Test 9
1. B
2. D
3. C
4. C
5. C

Answers Test 10
1. B
2. C
3. C
4. A
5. C

ORGANIZATION TEST 9

1. The full import of the war we cannot even now comprehend, but one of the effects stands out in sharp relief—the coming of the air age.

2. Some authorities quote statistics to prove that jets are safer than propeller planes.

3. This new master of time and space, fruit of man's inventive genius, has come to stay, smalling the earth and smoothing its surface.

4. To all of us, then, to youth and to adult alike, comes the winged challenge to get ourselves ready—to orient ourselves for living in an age which the airplane seems destined to mold.

5. The airplane, which played a relatively minor part in World War I, has already soared to heights undreamed of save by the few with mighty vision.

ORGANIZATION TEST 10

1. Dr. Bernard Vonnegut, his disciple, has added that unless there is police regulation, unrestrained cloud seeding will hamper earnest scientists who are trying to develop a new meteorological art.

2. In California one public utility company seeded clouds over a watershed a hundred miles square.

3. As a result of this action, in three successive years enough rain was brought down to supply a city of 50,000 with water enough for three months.

4. Last June Dr. Irving Langmuir warned that enthusiastic but unscientific rain-making might actually prevent rain from falling.

5. On the other hand, the Arizona Date Institute has threatened rain-makers with suits if the date crop is damaged by too much man-made rain.

**USE THIS SPACE
FOR YOUR SCRATCHWORK**

ORGANIZATION TEST 11

1. We recommend a pair of these.

2. Hearts, like doors, will ope' with ease.

3. They're "Thank you, sir" and "Will you please."

4. A childhood ditty about courtesy that I shall never forget is the following:

5. You simply need some little keys.

6. Not every key will open a door.

ORGANIZATION TEST 12

1. One can understand, then, that to Camus life is without purpose and without meaning.

2. Man, animals, plants live and die.

3. Camus' ideas belong in the broad stream of contemporary thought called Existentialism.

4. There is no God and therefore no supernatural intelligence directs their process of life.

5. He rejects the traditional view that there is a divine purpose in the universe and in human life.

Answers Test 11

1. C
2. B
3. C
4. A
5. C
6. D

Answers Test 12

1. B
2. C
3. A
4. C
5. B

Directions: Each set of questions in this test consists of several statements. Most of the statements refer to the same subject or idea. The statements can be classified as follows:

(A) the *central idea* to which most of the statements are related.

(B) *main supporting ideas,* which are general points directly related to the central idea;

(C) *illustrative facts* or detailed statements, which document the main supporting idea.

(D) statements *irrelevant* to the central idea.

The statements may be regarded as headings in an outline: they are *not* sentences taken from one complete paragraph. The outline might, for example, have the following form:

A. The Central Idea
  B. Main Supporting Idea
    C. Illustrative Fact
  B. Main Supporting Idea
    C. Illustrative Fact
    C. Illustrative Fact

ORGANIZATION TEST 13

1. The process may save some papers as much as 50% in capital investment.

2. Newsmen have long been looking for a way to cut towering newspaper costs.

3. Moreover, operating costs may well be reduced by 25%.

4. Lately they have eyed offset printing, a lithographic process used mostly for reproducing pictures.

5. Offset is cheap because it does away with such standard processes as engraving, form makeup, and stereotyping.

ORGANIZATION TEST 14

1. On the other hand, punctuation does not form an ornament of style; it forms a part of style.

2. We conclude, then, that punctuation has grace —as practiced by a master.

3. Good punctuation is more than a craft; it is an art, for it demands variety and subtlety.

4. At the outset we must recognize that punctuation does not create; it assists.

5. So far from being haphazard and perfunctory, punctuation is—or should be—consistent and thorough and is, therefore, a skilled craft.

Answers Test 13
5. B
1. C
2. A
3. C
4. B
5. C

Answers Test 14
1. B
2. C
3. C
4. A
5. C

Editing Ability Tests

Editing Test 1

Directions: A passage is given in which words or phrases are underlined. Following the passage are four choices for each word or phrase underlined. The first (A) choice simply repeats the underlined part. Then you have four additional choices which suggest to you other ways to express the underlined part of the original sentence. If you think that the underlined part is correct as it stands, write the answer A. If you believe that the underlined part is incorrect, select from the other choices (B or C or D) whichever you think is correct. Grammar, sentence structure, word usage, and punctuation are to be considered in your decision. Regardless which choice you make, the original meaning of the sentence must be retained.

The six year <u>old child</u> is about the best <u>kind of</u> example that can be found of that type of inquisitive-ness that <u>cause</u> some <u>aggravated</u> adults to <u>exclaim,</u> "curiosity killed the cat." To him, the world is a fascinating place to be explored and investigated <u>with great thoroughness,</u> but such a world is bounded by the environment in which he or the people <u>who</u> he knows live. It is constantly expanding through new <u>experiences. Which</u> bring many eager questions from members of any group of first-graders, as each one tries to figure out new relationships—to know and accept <u>their</u> place within the family, the school, and the community—to understand all around him. There are adults who find it quite annoying to be presented with such rank inquisitiveness. But this is no purposeless prying, no idle curiosity! It is that quality characteristic of the successful adult, inherent <u>in</u> the good citizen—intellectual curiosity.

1. (A) old child (C) old
   (B) oldster (D) old-child

2. (A) kind of example
   (B) kinds of example
   (C) sort of example
   (D) example

3. (A) cause (C) exhort
   (B) causes (D) exhorts

4. (A) aggravated (C) irritated
   (B) mad (D) gravitated

5. (A) exclaim, "curiosity
   (B) exclaim, "Curiosity
   (C) exclaim; "curiosity
   (D) exclaim! "Curiosity

6. (A) with great thoroughness
   (B) with a great thoroughness
   (C) quite thoroughly
   (D) in a manner that is very thorough

7. (A) who (C) which
   (B) whom (D) what

8. (A) experiences. Which
   (B) experiences: Which
   (C) experiences; which
   (D) experiences, which

9. (A) their (C) his
   (B) there (D) each

10. (A) of (C) on
    (B) to (D) in

Answers to Test 1

1. C	3. B	5. B	7. B	9. C
2. D	4. C	6. C	8. D	10. A

EDITING TEST 2

Hail is at once the <u>cruelest</u> weapon in Nature's
armory. And the most incalculable. It can destroy
one <u>farmers</u> prospects of a harvest in a matter of
seconds; it can leave his neighbor's unimpaired. It
can <u>slay</u> a flock of sheep (it has killed children
before now) in one field, while the sun continues
to <u>brightly shine</u> in the next. To the harassed mete-
orologist, <u>it's</u> behavior is even more Machiavellian
than <u>an ice storm</u>. Difficult as it undoubtedly is for
him to forecast the onset of an ice storm, <u>he sort of</u>
knows what the course and duration will be once
it has started; just about all he can do with a hail-
storm is <u>measuring</u> the size of the stones—and they
have a habit of <u>melting</u> as soon as he gets his hands
on them.

1. (A) cruelest
   (B) most cruelest
   (C) crueler
   (D) cruel

2. (A) armory. And
   (B) armory: And
   (C) armory; and
   (D) armory, and

3. (A) farmers
   (B) farmer's
   (C) farmers'
   (D) farmers's

4. (A) slay
   (B) sleigh
   (C) sly
   (D) slew

5. (A) to brightly shine
   (B) to shine brightly
   (C) brightly to shine
   (D) brightly shining

6. (A) it's
   (B) its
   (C) its'
   (D) it is

7. (A) an ice storm
   (B) an ice storm is
   (C) a storm of ice
   (D) that of an ice storm

8. (A) he sort of knows
   (B) he kind of knows
   (C) he gets to know
   (D) he in a way knows

9. (A) measuring
   (B) the measuring
   (C) to measure
   (D) a measure of

10. (A) melting
    (B) to melt
    (C) as if to melt
    (D) going into a melt

Answers to Test 2

1. A	3. B	5. B	7. D	9. C
2. D	4. A	6. B	8. C	10. A

EDITING TEST 3

Disregard for odds and complete confidence in
<u>ones self</u> have produced many of our great successes.
But every young man who wants to go <u>into business</u>
for <u>themselves</u> should raise certain questions and
answer them in a straightforward manner. What has
he to offer that is new or better? Has he special
talents, special know-how, a new invention or
service, or more <u>capital than the average competi-</u>
tor? Has he the most important <u>thing</u> of all, a will-
ingness to work harder than <u>any one else</u>? A man
who is working for himself without <u>limitation</u> of
hours can run circles around any operation that
relies on paid help. But he must forget the eight-
hour day, the forty-hour week, and the <u>vacation
once a year</u>. The successful self-employed man in-
variably works harder and <u>has more worries</u> than
the man <u>on</u> a salary.

1. (A) ones   (C) one's
   (B) one   (D) ones'

2. (A) into   (C) to
   (B) in   (D) at

3. (A) themselves   (C) hisself
   (B) theirselves   (D) himself

4. (A) service, or   (C) service: or
   (B) service. Or   (D) service; or

5. (A) thing   (C) qualification
   (B) talent   (D) possession

6. (A) any one else   (C) any one
   (B) anyone else   (D) anyone

7. (A) limitation   (C) a limiting
   (B) a limit   (D) limitment

8. (A) vacation once a year
   (B) once-a-year vacation
   (C) annual vacation
   (D) vacation one time a year

9. (A) has more worries
   (B) has greater worries
   (C) is worried more
   (D) worries more

10. (A) on   (C) by
    (B) in   (D) from

Answers to Test 3

1. C   3. D   5. C   7. A   9. D

2. A   4. A   6. B   8. C   10. A

EDITING TEST 4

The most magnificent display of color in all the Kingdom of plants is the Fall foliage of the trees of ¹North America. Even an acid English visitor broke down her British reservation in praise of our au-²tumns. The granite soils of New England especially turn up a display of gloriousness. It is interesting to
³   ⁴

note that our dry uplands flame more brilliant than ⁵the trees in low ground, on account of a reduced ⁶ground-water supply is a contribution to color. Chief of all reasons for our splendors of the autumn season ⁷is in view of the fact that there are a greater variety ⁸   ⁹ of deciduous trees, shrubs, and vines in our country than any other part of the temperate zone.
¹⁰

1. (A) Fall foliage   (C) fall foliage
   (B) Fall Foliage   (D) fall's foliage

2. (A) reservation   (C) reserve manner
   (B) reserve   (D) reservationism

3. (A) turn up   (C) give up
   (B) carry in   (D) bring forth

4. (A) gloriousness   (C) glory
   (B) glorification   (D) glow

5. (A) more brilliant
   (B) brillianter
   (C) with a brilliance that is greater
   (D) more brilliantly

6. (A) on account of
   (B) since
   (C) in consideration that
   (D) in that

7. (A) splendors of the autumn season
   (B) autumn seasonal splendor
   (C) autumn splendors
   (D) splendidness of autumn

8. (A) in view of the fact
   (B) the fact
   (C) explained by the fact
   (D) on the basis

9. (A) are   (C) have been
   (B) will be   (D) is

10. (A) any other part
    (B) any part
    (C) any other parts
    (D) in any other part

Answers to Test 4

1. C	3. D	5. D	7. C	9. D
2. B	4. C	6. B	8. B	10. D

EDITING TEST 5

Lamarck's theory of evolution, although at one time generally in discredit, has now been made to revive by a great amount of prominent biologists. According to Lamarck, changes in an animal occur through use and a lacking in use. Organs which are specially exercised becomes specially developed. The need for this special exercise is aroused from the conditions in which the animal live; thus a changing environment, by making different demands on an animal, changes the animal. The giraffe, for an instance, has developed its long neck in periods of relative scarcity by endeavoring to browse on higher and higher branches of trees. On the other hand, organs that are never exercised tend to disappear altogether. The eyes of animals that have taken to live in the dark grow smaller and smaller, generation after generation. Until the late descendants are born eyeless.

1. (A) in discredit
   (B) in a discredited position
   (C) discreditable
   (D) discredited

2. (A) made to revive   (C) in revival
   (B) revived   (D) reviving

3. (A) amount   (C) portion
   (B) number   (D) bunch

4. (A) lacking in use   (C) no use
   (B) disuse   (D) lack of use

5. (A) is aroused   (C) arises
   (B) rises up   (D) is raised

6. (A) live   (C) exist
   (B) lives   (D) are existing

7. (A) for an instance   (C) for instance
   (B) for one instance   (D) by an instance

8. (A) altogether   (C) all-together
   (B) all together   (D) al-together

9. (A) to live   (C) to the living
   (B) to living   (D) to a living

10. (A) generation. Until
    (B) generation; until
    (C) generation until
    (D) generation, until

Answers to Test 5

1. D	3. B	5. C	7. C	9. B
2. B	4. B	6. B	8. A	10. D

Reading Comprehension Practice

HELPFUL HINTS FOR THE READING COMPREHENSION PART OF THE EXAM

1. Do all of the reading comprehension questions in this book. You will find these questions in Sample Test A (pp. 22-26, 32-36, 40-41); Pinpoint Practice Section (pp. 57-60, 79-92); and Sample Test B (pp. 119-124, 132-135, 139-141).

2. Get additional practice by reading the following:

   (a) Editorial pages of various newspapers.

   (b) Book reviews (also drama and movies reviews).

   (c) Magazine articles.

For each selection that you read, do the following:

   (a) Jot down the main idea of the article.

   (b) Look up the meanings of words that you don't know or that you aren't sure of.

Four Steps To Reading Comprehension Success

1. Read the entire selection to get the general sense. Look for the topic sentence in each paragraph.

2. Underline the important ideas.

3. Read each choice. Eliminate the "impossible" choices.

4. With the "possible" choices in mind, go back to the selection (if you are permitted to). Look for specific information in the selection which will give you the only correct choice.

Avoid The Traps

Trap #1 — Sometimes the question cannot be answered on the basis of the stated facts. You may be required to make a deduction from the facts given.

Trap #2 — Eliminate your personal opinions.

Trap #3 — Search out significant details that are nestled in the selection. Reread the selection or parts of the selection as many times as necessary.

COMPREHENSION TEST 1 *

Directions: Below each of the following passages, you will find questions or incomplete statements about the passage. Each statement or question is followed by lettered words or expressions. Select the word or expression that most satisfactorily completes each statement or answers each question in accordance with the meaning of the passage. Write the letter of that word or expression on your answer paper.

The standardized educational or psychological tests, that are widely used to aid in selecting, classifying, assigning, or promoting students, employees, and military personnel have been the target of recent attacks in books, magazines, the daily press, and even in Congress. The target is wrong, for in attacking the tests, critics divert attention from the fault that lies with ill-informed or incompetent users. The tests themselves are merely tools, with characteristics that can be measured with reasonable precision under specified conditions. Whether the results will be valuable, meaningless, or even misleading depends partly upon the tool itself but largely upon the user.

All informed predictions of future performance are based upon some knowledge of relevant past performance: school grades, research productivity, sales records, batting averages, or whatever is appropriate. How well the predictions will be validated by later performance depends upon the amount, reliability, and appropriateness of the information used and on the skill and wisdom with which it is interpreted. Anyone who keeps careful score knows that the information available is always incomplete and that the predictions are always subject to error.

Standardized tests should be considered in this context. They provide a quick, objective method of getting some kinds of information about what a person has learned, the skills he has developed, or the kind of person he is. The information so obtained has, qualitatively, the same advantages and shortcomings as other kinds of information. Whether to use tests, other kinds of information, or both in a particular situation depends, therefore, upon the empirical evidence concerning comparative validity, and upon such factors as cost and availability.

In general, the tests work most effectively when the traits or qualities to be measured can be most precisely defined (for example, ability to do well in a particular course or training program) and

least effectively when what is to be measured or predicted cannot be well defined (for example, personality or creativity). Properly used, they provide a rapid means of getting comparable information about many people. Sometimes they identify students whose high potential has not been previously recognized. But there are many things they do not do. For example, they do not compensate for gross social inequality, and thus do not tell how able an underprivileged youngster might have been had he grown up under more favorable circumstances.

Professionals in the business and the conscientious publishers know the limitations as well as the values. They write these things into test manuals and in critiques of available tests. But they have no jurisdiction over users; an educational test can be administered by almost anyone, whether he knows how to interpret it or not. Nor can the difficulty be controlled by limiting sales to qualified users; some attempts to do so have been countered by restraint-of-trade suits.

In the long run it may be possible to establish better controls or to require higher qualifications. But in the meantime, unhappily, the demonstrated value of these tests under many circumstances has given them a popularity that has led to considerable misuse. Also unhappily, justifiable criticism of the misuse now threatens to hamper proper use. Business and government can probably look after themselves. But school guidance and selection programs are being attacked for using a valuable tool, because some of the users are unskilled.

—by Watson Davis, Sc.D., Director of Science Service (reprinted with permission)

1. The essence of this article on educational tests is:
   (A) These tests do not test adequately what they set out to test.
   (B) Don't blame the test—blame the user.
   (C) When a student is nervous or ill, the test results are inaccurate.
   (D) Publishers of tests are without conscience.
   (E) Educators are gradually losing confidence in the value of the tests.

2. Tests like the College Entrance Scholastic Aptitude Test are, it would seem to the author,
   (A) generally unreliable
   (B) generally reliable
   (C) meaningless
   (D) misleading
   (E) neither good nor bad.

3. The selection implies that, more often, the value of an educational test rests with
   (A) the interpretation of results
   (B) the test itself
   (C) the testee
   (D) emotional considerations
   (E) the directions.

4. Which statement is not true, according to the passage, about educational tests?
   (A) Some students "shine" unexpectedly
   (B) Predictions do not always hold true
   (C) Personality tests often fail to measure the true personality
   (D) The supervisor of the test must be very well trained
   (E) Publishers cannot confine sales to highly skilled administrators.

5. The worthwhileness of a test requires, most of all,
   (A) cooperation on the part of the person tested
   (B) sufficient preparation on the part of the applicant
   (C) clearcut directions
   (D) one answer—and ony one—for each question
   (E) specificity regarding what is to be tested.

COMPREHENSION TEST 2

When television is good, nothing—not the theatre, not the magazines, or newspapers—nothing is better. But when television is bad, nothing is worse. I invite you to sit down in front of your television set when your station goes on the air and stay there without a book, magazine, newspaper, or anything else to distract you and keep your eyes glued to that set until the station signs off. I can assure you that you will observe a vast wasteland. You will see a procession of game shows, violence, audience participation shows, formula comedies about totally unbelievable families, blood and thunder, mayhem, more violence, sadism, murder, Western badmen, Western goodmen, private eyes, gangsters, still more violence, and cartoons. And, endlessly, commercials that scream and cajole and offend. And most of all, boredom. True, you will see a few things you will enjoy. But they will be very, very few. And if you think I exaggerate, try it.

Is there no room on television to teach, to inform, to uplift, to stretch, to enlarge the capacities of our children? Is there no room for programs to deepen the children's understanding of children in other lands? Is there no room for a children's news show explaining something about the world for them at their level of understanding? Is there no room for reading the great literature of the past, teaching them the great traditions of freedom? There are some fine children's shows, but they are drowned out in the massive doses of cartoons, violence, and more violence. Must these be your trademarks? Search your conscience and see whether you cannot offer more to your young beneficiaries whose future you guard so many hours each and every day.

There are many people in this great country, and you must serve all of us. You will get no argument from me if you say that, given a choice between a Western and a symphony, more people will watch the Western. I like Westerns and private eyes, too—but a steady diet for the whole country is obviously not in the public interest. We all know that people would more often prefer to be entertained than stimulated or informed. But your obligations are not satisfied if you look only to popularity as a test of what to broadcast. You are not only in show business; you are free to communicate ideas as well as to give relaxation. You must provide a wider range of choices, more diversity, more alternatives. It is not enough to cater to the nation's whims—you must also serve the nation's needs. The people own the air. They own it as much in prime evening time as they do at 6 o'clock in the morning. For every hour that the people give you—you owe them something. I intend to see that your debt is paid with service.

—excerpt from speech by Newton N. Minow, chairman of the Federal Communications Commission, before the National Association of Broadcasters.

1. The wasteland referred to describes
   (A) Western badmen and Western goodmen
   (B) average television programs
   (C) the morning shows
   (D) television shows with desert locales
   (E) children's programs.

2. Minow's attitude is one of
   (A) sullenness
   (B) reconciliation
   (C) determination
   (D) rage
   (E) hopelessness.

3. The National Association of Broadcasters probably accepted Minow's remarks with
   (A) considerable enthusiasm
   (B) shocked wonderment
   (C) complete agreement
   (D) some disagreement
   (E) absolute rejection.

4. The Federal Communications Commission chairman is, in effect, telling the broadcasters that
   (A) the listener, not the broadcaster, should make decisions about programs
   (B) chilldren's shows are worthless
   (C) mystery programs should be banned
   (D) television instruction should be a substitute for classroom lessons
   (E) they had better mend their ways.

5. Concerning programs for children, Minow believes that programs should
   (A) eliminate cartoons
   (B) provide culture
   (C) be presented at certain periods during the day
   (D) eliminate commercials
   (E) not deal with the West.

6. The statement that "the people own the air" implies that
   (A) citizens have the right to insist on worthwhile television programs
   (B) television should be socialized
   (C) the government may build above present structures
   (D) since air is worthless, the people own nothing
   (E) the broadcasters have no right to commercialize on television.

7. Minow indicates that
   (A) the broadcasters are trying to do the right thing but are failing
   (B) foreign countries are going to pattern their programs after ours
   (C) there is a great deal that is worthwhile in present programs
   (D) the listeners do not necessarily know what is good for them
   (E) 6 A.M. is too early for a television show.

COMPREHENSION TEST 3

If Johnny can't write, one of the reasons may be a conditioning based on speed rather than respect for the creative process. Speed is neither a valid test of nor a proper preparation for competence in writing. It makes for murkiness, glibness, disorganization. It takes the beauty out of the language. It rules out respect for the reflective thought that should precede expression. It runs counter to the word-by-word and line-by-line reworking that enables a piece to be finely knit.

This is not to minimize the value of genuine facility. With years of practice, a man may be able to put down words swiftly and expertly. But it is the same kind of swiftness that enables a cellist, after having invested years of efforts, to negotiate an intricate passage from Haydn. Speed writing is for stenographers and court reporters, not for anyone who wants to use language with precision and distinction.

Thomas Mann was not ashamed to admit that he would often take a full day to write 500 words, and another day to edit them, out of respect for the most difficult art in the world. Flaubert would ponder a paragraph for hours. Did it say what he wanted it to say—not approximately but exactly? Did the words turn into one another with proper rhythm and grace? Were they artistically and securely fitted together? Were they briskly alive, or were they full of fuzz and ragged edges? Were they likely to make things happen inside the mind of the reader, igniting the imagination and touching off all sorts of new anticipations? These questions are relevant not only for the established novelist but for anyone who attaches value to words as a medium of expression and communication.

E. B. White, whose respect for the environment of good writing is exceeded by no word-artist of our time, would rather have his fingers cut off than to be guilty of handling words lightly. No sculptor chipping away at a granite block in order to produce a delicate curve or feature has labored more painstakingly than White in fashioning a short paragraph. Obviously, we can't expect our schools to make every Johnny into a White or a Flaubert or a Mann, but it is not unreasonable to expect more of them to provide the conditions that promote clear, careful, competent expression. Certainly the cumulative effort of the school experience should not have to be undone in later years.

—by Norman Cousins, Editor of *Saturday Review* (reprinted with permission)

1. Johnny
   (A) represents the average American elementary or high school student
   (B) is probably the name of the writer's son
   (C) stands for the male student—not the female
   (D) is probably related to Thomas Mann
   (E) is a musician.

2. Mr. Cousins is saying, in effect, that
   (A) writing should never be done rapidly
   (B) E. B. White was a writer as well as a sculptor
   (C) Thomas Mann averaged 500 words a day
   (D) Flaubert would study and restudy his writing
   (E) all authors write slowly.

3. Our schools, according to the passage,
   (A) are providing proper conditions for good writing
   (B) should not stress writing speed on a test
   (C) should give essay tests rather than multiple-choice tests
   (D) teach good writing primarily through reading
   (E) correlate art and music with writing instruction.

4. In describing White as a "word-artist," the author means that White
   (A) was also a cartoonist
   (B) illustrated his stories
   (C) was colorful in his descriptions
   (D) had artistic background
   (E) was a great writer.

5. It is obvious that Cousins himself is outstanding as a(n)
   (A) artist
   (B) publisher
   (C) teacher
   (D) journalist
   (E) musician.

COMPREHENSION TEST 4

Recent scientific discoveries are throwing new light on the basic nature of viruses and on the possible nature of cancer, genes and even life itself. These discoveries are providing evidence for relationships among these four subjects which indicate that one may be dependent upon another to an extent not fully appreciated heretofore. Too often one works and thinks within too narrow a range and hence fails to recognize the significance of certain facts for other areas. Sometimes the important new ideas and subsequent fundamental discoveries come from the borderline areas between two well-established fields of investigation. This will result in the synthesis of new ideas regarding viruses, cancer, genes and life. These ideas in turn will result in the doing of new experiments which may provide the basis for fundamental discoveries in these fields.

There is no doubt that of the four topics, life is the one most people would consider to be of the greatest importance. However, life means different things to different people and it is in reality difficult to define just what we mean by life. There is no difficulty in recognizing an agent as living so long as we contemplate structures like a man, a dog or even a bacterium, and at the other extreme a piece of iron or glass or an atom of hydrogen or a molecule of water. The ability to grow or reproduce and to change or mutate has long been regarded as a special property characteristic of living agents along with the ability to respond to external stimuli. These are properties not shared by bits of iron or glass or even by a molecule of hemoglobin. Now if viruses had not been discovered, all would have been well. The organisms of the biologist would have ranged from the largest of animals all the way down to the smallest of the bacteria which are about 200 millimicra. There would have been a definite break with respect to size; the largest molecules known to the chemist were less than 20 millimicra in size. Thus life and living agents would have been represented by those structures which possessed the ability to reproduce themselves and to mutate and were about ten times larger than the largest known molecule. This would have provided a comfortable area of separation between living and non-living things.

Then came the discovery of the viruses. These infectious, disease-producing agents are characterized by their small size, by their ability to grow or reproduce within specific living cells, and by their ability to change or mutate during reproduction. This was enough to convince most people that viruses were merely still smaller living organisms. When the sizes of different viruses were determined, it was found that some were actually smaller than certain protein molecules. When the first virus was isolated in the form of a crystallizable material it was found to be a nucleoprotein. It was found to possess all the usual properties associated with protein molecules yet was larger than any molecule previously described. Here was a molecule that possessed the ability to reproduce itself and to mutate. The distinction between living and non-living things seemed to be tottering. The gap in size between 20 and 200 millimicra has been filled in completely by the viruses, with some actual overlapping at both ends. Some large viruses are larger than some living organisms, and some small viruses are actuallly smaller than certain protein molecules.

Let us consider the relationship between genes and viruses since both are related to life. Both genes and viruses seem to be nucleoproteins and both reproduce only within specific living cells. Both possess the ability to mutate. Although viruses generally reproduce many times within a given cell, some situations are known in which they appear to reproduce only once with each cell division. Genes usually reproduce once with each cell division, but here also the rate can be changed. Actually the similarities between genes and viruses are so remarkable that viruses were referred to as "naked genes" or "genes on the loose."

Despite the fact that today viruses are known to cause cancer in animals and in certain plants, there exists a great reluctance to accept viruses as being of importance in human cancer. Basic biological phenomena generally do not differ strikingly as one goes from one species to another. It should be recognized that cancer is a biological problem and not a problem that is unique for man. Cancer originates when a normal cell suddenly becomes a cancer cell which multiplies widely and without apparent restraint. Cancer may originate in many differrent kinds of cells, but the cancer cell usually continues to carry certain traits of the cell of origin. The transformation of a normal cell into a cancer cell may have more than one kind of cause, but there is good reason to consider the relationships that exist between viruses and cancer.

Since there is no evidence that human cancer, as generally experienced, is infectious, many persons believe that because viruses are infectious agents they cannot possibly be of importance in human cancer. However, viruses can mutate and examples are known in which a virus that never kills its host can mutate to form a new strain of virus that always kills its host. It does not seem unreasonable to assume that an innocuous latent virus might mutate to form a strain that causes cancer. Certainly the experimental evidence now available is consistent with the idea that viruses as

we know them today, could be the causative agents of most, if not all cancer, including cancer in man.

1. People were convinced that viruses were small living organism, because viruses
   (A) are disease-producing
   (B) reproduce within living cells
   (C) could be grown on artificial media
   (D) consist of nucleoproteins.

2. Scientists very often do not apply the facts learned in one subject area to a related field of investigation because
   (A) the borderline areas are too close to both to give separate facts
   (B) scientists work in a very narrow range of experimentation
   (C) new ideas are synthesized only as a result of new experimentation
   (D) fundamental discoveries are based upon finding close relationships in related sciences.

3. Before the discovery of viruses, it might have been possible to distinguish living things from non-living things by the fact that
   (A) animate objects can mutate
   (B) non-living substances cannot reproduce themselves
   (C) responses to external stimuli are characteristic of living things
   (D) living things were greater than 20 millimicra in size.

4. The size of viruses is presently known to be
   (A) between 20 and 200 millimicra
   (B) smaller than any bacterium
   (C) larger than any protein molecule
   (D) larger than most nucleoproteins.

5. That genes and viruses seem to be related might be shown by the fact that
   (A) both are ultra-microscopic
   (B) each can mutate but once in a cell
   (C) each reproduces but once in a cell
   (D) both appear to have the same chemical structure.

6. Viruses were called "genes on the loose" because they
   (A) seem to wander at will within cells
   (B) like genes, seem to be able to mutate
   (C) seemed to be genes without cells
   (D) could loosen genes from cells.

7. Cancer should be considered to be a biological problem rather than a medical one because
    (A) viruses are known to cause cancers in animals
    (B) at present, human cancer is not believed to be contagious
    (C) there are many known causes for the transformation of a normal cell to a cancer cell
    (D) results of experiments on plants and animals do not vary greatly from species to species.

8. The possibility that a virus causes human cancer is indicated by
    (A) the fact that viruses have been known to mutate
    (B) the fact that a cancer-immune individual may lose his immunity
    (C) the fact that reproduction of human cancer cells might be due to a genetic factor
    (D) the fact that man is host to many viruses.

9. The best title for this passage is
    (A) New Light on the Cause of Cancer
    (B) The Newest Theory on the Nature of Viruses
    (C) Viruses, Genes, Cancer and Life
    (D) On the Nature of Life.

10. It is quite possible that viruses unknown today, may be discovered by scientists in the future, since
    (A) viruses have been known to mutate
    (B) the crystalline structure of viruses can be changed
    (C) viruses have been known that cause cancer in animals
    (D) viruses must reproduce only within a specific cell.

COMPREHENSION TEST 5

An action of apparent social significance among animals is that of migration. But several different factors are at work causing such migrations. These may be concerned with food–getting, with temperature, salinity, pressure and light changes; with the action of sex hormones and probably other combinations of these factors.

The great aggregations of small crustaceans, such as copepods found at the surface of the ocean, swarms of insects about a light, or the masses of unicellular organisms making up a part of the plankton in the lakes and oceans, are all examples of nonsocial aggregations of organisms brought together because of the presence or absence of certain factors in their environment, such as air currents, water currents, food or the lack of it, oxygen or carbon dioxide, or some other contributing causes.

Insects make long migrations, most of which seem due to the urge for food. The migrations of the locust, both in this country and elsewhere, are well known. While fish, such as salmon, return to the same stream where they grew up, such return migrations are rare in insects, the only known instance being in the monarch butterfly. This is apparently due to the fact that it is long-lived and has the power of strong flight. The mass migrations of the Rocky Mountain and the African species of locust seem attributable to the need for food. Locusts live, eat, sun themselves and migrate in groups. It has been suggested that their social life is in response to the two fundamental instincts, aggregation and imitation.

Migrations of fish have been studied carefully by many investigators. Typically the migrations are from deep to shallow waters, as in the herring, mackerel and many other marine fish. Fresh-water fish in general exhibit this type of migration in the spawning season. Spawning habits of many fish show a change in habitat from salt to fresh water. Among these are the shad, salmon, alewife and others. In the North American and European eels, long migrations take place at the breeding season. All these migrations are obviously not brought about by a quest for food, for the salmon and many other fish feed only sparingly during the spawning season, but are undoubtedly brought about by metabolic changes in the animal initiated by the interaction of sex hormones. If this thesis holds, then here is the beginning of social life.

Bird migrations have long been a matter of study. The reasons for the migration of the golden plover from the Arctic regions to the tip of South America and return in a single year are not fully explainable. Several theories have been advanced, although none have been fully proved. The reproductive "instinct," food scarcity, temperature and light changes, the metabolic changes brought about by the activity of the sex hormones and the length of the day, all have been suggested, and ultimately several may prove to be factors. Aside from other findings, it is interesting to note that bird migrations take place year after year on about the same dates. Recent studies in the biochemistry of metabolism, showing that there is a seasonal cycle in the blood sugar that has a definite relation to activity and food, seem to be among the most promising leads.

In mammals the seasonal migrations that take place, such as those of the deer, which travel from the high mountains in summer to the valleys in winter, or the migration of the caribou in the northern areas of Canada, are based on the factor of temperature which regulates the food supply. Another mystery is the migration of the lemming, a small ratlike animal found in Scandinavia and Canada. The lemming population varies greatly from year to year, and, at times when it greatly increases, a migration occurs in which hordes of lemmings march across the country, swimming rivers and even plunging into the ocean if it bars their way. This again cannot be purely social association of animals. The horde is usually made up entirely of males, as the females seldom migrate.

1. The migration of the lemmings cannot be considered one of social association since
   (A) only males migrate
   (B) migrations occur only with population increases
   (C) it is probably due to the absence of some factor in the environment
   (D) the migrants do not return.

2. Animals which apparently migrate in quest of food are the
   (A) fish
   (B) birds
   (C) mammals
   (D) **insects.**

3. A characteristic of migration is the return of the migrants to their former home areas. This is, however, not true of the
   (A) birds
   (B) **insects**
   (C) mammals
   (D) fish.

4. The reproductive instinct is probably not a factor in the actual migration of
   (A) shad
   (B) lemming
   (C) golden plover
   (D) monarch butterfly.

5. In paragraph 1, several probable factors causing migrations are given. None of these seem to explain the migrations of
   (A) lemming
   (B) caribou
   (C) salmon
   (D) locusts.

6. The reasons for the migrations of birds may ultimately be determined by scientists working in the field of
   (A) population studies
   (B) ecology
   (C) metabolism chemistry
   (D) reproduction.

7. The group in which "egg laying" seems to be a known factor in migration is
   (A) fish
   (B) insects
   (C) mammals
   (D) birds.

8. Animals which migrate back and forth between the same general areas are
   (A) locusts and salmon
   (B) salmon and golden plover
   (C) golden plover and lemming
   (D) monarch butterfly and caribou.

9. The shortest distance covered by any migrating group is taken by
   (A) insects
   (B) fish
   (C) birds
   (D) mammals.

10. The author indicates that careful investigation has shown that fish migration is probably concerned with
    (A) spawning habits
    (B) feeding habits
    (C) neither spawning nor feeding
    (D) both spawning and feeding.

11. Return migrations are usually associated with animals that
    (A) make long migrations
    (B) are long-lived
    (C) migrate to spawn
    (D) make short migrations.

COMPREHENSION TEST 6

As the world's population grows, the part played by man in influencing plant life becomes more and more important. In old and densely populated countries, as in central Europe, man determines almost wholly what shall grow and what shall not grow. In such regions, the influence of man on plant life is in large measure a beneficial one. Laws, often centuries old, protect plants of economic value and preserve soil fertility. In newly settled countries the situation is unfortunately quite the reverse. The pioneer's life is too strenuous a one for him to think of posterity.

Some years ago Mt. Mitchell, the highest summit east of the Mississippi, was covered with a magnificent forest. A lumber company was given full rights to fell the trees. Those not cut down were crushed. The mountain was left a wasted area where fire would rage and erosion would complete the destruction. There was no stopping the devastating foresting of the company, for the contract had been given. Under a more enlightened civilization this could not have happened. The denuding of Mt. Mitchell is a minor chapter in the destruction of lands in the United States; and this country is by no means the only or chief sufferer. China, India, Egypt, and East Africa all have their thousands of square miles of waste land, the result of man's indifference to the future.

Deforestation, grazing, and poor farming are the chief causes of the destruction of land fertility. Wasteful cutting of timber is the first step. Grazing then follows lumbering in bringing about ruin. The Caribbean slopes of northern Venezuela are barren wastes owing first to ruthless cutting of forests and then to destructive grazing. Hordes of goats have roamed these slopes until only a few thorny acacias and cacti remain. Erosion completed the desvastation. What is there illustrated on a small scale is the story of vast areas in China and India, countries where famines are of regular occurrence.

Man is not wholly to blame, for Nature is often merciless. In parts of India and China, plant life, when left undisturbed by man, cannot cope with either the disastrous floods of wet seasons or the destructive winds of the dry season. Man has learned much; prudent land management has been the policy of the Chinese people since 2700 B. C., but even they have not learned enough.

When the American forestry service was in its infancy, it met with much opposition from legislators who loudly claimed that the protected land would in one season yield a crop of cabbages of more value than all the timber on it. Herein lay the fallacy, that one season's crop is all that need be thought of. Nature, through the years, adjusts crops to the soil and to the climate. Forests usually occur where precipitation exceeds evaporation. If the reverse is true, grasslands are found; and where evaporation is still greater, desert or scrub vegetation alone survives. The phytogeographic map of a country is very similar to the climatic map based on rainfall, evaporation, and temperature. Man ignores this natural adjustment of crops and strives for one "bumper" crop in a single season; he may produce it, but "year in and year out the yield of the grassland is certain, that of the planted fields, never."

Man is learning; he sprays his trees with insecticides and fungicides; he imports ladybugs to destroy aphids; he irrigates, fertilizes, and rotates his crops; but he is still indifferent to many of the consequences of his short-sighted policies. The great dust storms of the western United States are proof of this indifference.

In spite of the evidence to be had from this country, the people of other countries, still in the pioneer stage, farm as wastefully as did our own pioneers. In the interiors of Central and South American Republics, natives fell superb forest trees and leave them to rot in order to obtain virgin soil for cultivation. Where the land is hillside, it readily washes and after one or two seasons is unfit for crops. So the frontier farmer pushes back into the primeval forest, moving his hut as he goes, and fells more monarchs to lay bare another patch of ground for his plantings to support his family. Valuable timber which will require a century to replace is destroyed and the land laid waste to produce what could be supplied for a pittance.

How badly man can err in his handling of land is shown by the draining of extensive swamp areas, which to the uninformed would seem to be a very good thing to do. One of the first effects of the drainage is the lowering of the water-table, which may bring about the death of the dominant species and leave to another species the possession of the soil, even when the difference in water level is little more than an inch. Frequently, bog country will yield marketable crops of cranberries and blueberries but, if drained, neither these nor any other economic plant will grow on the fallow soil. Swamps and marshes have their drawbacks but also their virtues. When drained they may leave waste land, the surface of which rapidly erodes to be then blown away in dust blizzards disastrous to both man and wild beasts.

1. The best title for this passage is
    (A) How to Increase Soil Productivity
    (B) Conservation of Natural Resources
    (C) Man's Effect on Soil
    (D) Soil Conditions and Plant Growth.

2. A policy of good management is sometimes upset by
   (A) the indifference of man
   (B) centuries-old laws
   (C) floods and winds
   (D) grazing animals.

3. Areas in which the total amounts of rain and snow falling on the ground are greater than that which is evaporated will support
   (A) forests
   (B) grasslands
   (C) scrub vegetation
   (D) no plants.

4. Pioneers do not have a long range view on soil problems since they
   (A) are not protected by laws
   (B) live under adverse conditions
   (C) use poor methods of farming
   (D) must protect themselves from famine.

5. Phytogeographic maps are those that show
   (A) areas of grassland
   (B) areas of bumper crops
   (C) areas of similar climate
   (D) areas of similar plants.

6. The basic cause of frequent famines in China and India is probably due to
   (A) allowing animals to roam wild
   (B) drainage of swamps
   (C) over-grazing of the land
   (D) destruction of forests.

7. With a growing world population, the increased need for soil for food production may be met by
   (A) draining unproductive swamp areas
   (B) legislating against excess lumbering
   (C) trying to raise bumper crops each year
   (D) irrigating desert areas.

8. What is meant by "the yield of the grassland is certain; that of the planted field, never" is that
   (A) it is impossible to get more than one bumper crop from any one cultivated area
   (B) crops, planted in former grassland, will not give good yields
   (C) through the indifference of man, dust blizzards have occurred in former grasslands
   (D) if man does not interfere, plants will grow in the most suitable environment.

9. The first act of prudent land management might be to
   (A) prohibit drainage of swamps
   (B) use irrigation and crop rotation in planted areas
   (C) increase use of fertilizers
   (D) prohibit excessive forest lumbering.

10. The results of good land management may usually be found in
    (A) heavily populated areas
    (B) areas not given over to grazing
    (C) underdeveloped areas
    (D) ancient civilizations.

COMPREHENSION TEST 7

Regarding physical changes that have been and are now taking place on the surface of the earth, the sea and its shores have been the scene of the greatest stability. The dry land has seen the rise, the decline, and even the disappearance, of vast hordes of various types and forms within times comparatively recent, geologically speaking; but life in the sea is today virtually what it was when many of the forms now extinct on land had not yet been evolved. Also, it may be parenthetically stated here, the marine habitat has been biologically the most important in the evolution and development of life on this planet. Its rhythmic influence can still be traced in those animals whose ancestors have long since left that realm to abide far from their primary haunts. For it is now generally held as an accepted fact that the shore area of an ancient sea was the birthplace of life.

Still, despite the primitive conditions still maintained in the sea, its shore inhabitants show an amazing diversity, while their adaptive characters are perhaps not exceeded in refinement by those that distinguish the dwellers of dry land. Why is this diversity manifest? We must look for an answer into the physical factors obtaining in that extremely slender zone surrounding the continents, marked by the rise and fall of the tides.

It will be noticed by the most casual observer that on any given seashore the area exposed between the tide marks may be roughly divided into a number of levels each characterized by a certain assemblage of animals. Thus in proceeding from high- to low-water mark, new forms constantly become predominant while other forms gradually drop out. Now, provided that the character of the substratum does not change, these differences in the types of animals are determined almost exclusively by the duration of time that the individual forms may remain exposed to the air without harm. Indeed, so regularly does the tidal rhythm act on certain animals (the barnacles, for instance), that certain species have come to require a definite period of exposure in order to maintain themselves, and will die out if kept continuously submerged. Although there are some forms that actually require periodic exposure, the number of species inhabiting the shore that are able to endure exposure every twelve hours, when the tide falls, is comparatively few.

With the alternate rise and fall of the tides, the successive areas of the tidal zone are subjected to force of wave-impact. In certain regions the waves often break with considerable force. Consequently, wave-shock has had a profound influence on the structure and habits of shore animals. It is characteristic of most shore animals that they shun definitely exposed places, and seek shelter in nooks and crannies and such refuges as are offered under stones and seaweed; particularly is this true of those forms living on rock and other firm foundations. Many of these have a marked capacity to cling closely to the substratum; some, such as anemones and certain snails, although without the grasping organs of higher animals, have special powers of adhesion; others, such as sponges and sea squirts, remain permanently fixed, and if torn loose from their base are incapable of forming a new attachment. But perhaps the most significant method of solving the problem presented by the surf has been in the adaptation of body-form to minimize friction. This is strikingly displayed in the fact that seashore animals are essentially flattened forms. Thus, in the typically shore forms the sponges are of the encrusting type, the non-burrowing worms are leaflike, the snails and other mollusks are squat forms and are without the spines and other ornate extensions such as are often produced on the shells of many mollusks in deeper and quieter waters. The same influence is no less marked in the case of the crustaceans; the flattening is either lateral, as in the amphipods, or dorso-ventral, as in the isopods and crabs.

In sandy regions, because of the unstable nature of substratum, no such means of attachment as indicated in the foregoing paragraph will suffice to maintain the animals in their almost ceaseless battle with the billows. Most of them must perforce depend on their ability quickly to penetrate into the sand for safety. Some forms endowed with less celerity, such as the sand dollars, are so constructed that their bodies offer no more resistance to wave impact than does a flat pebble.

Temperature, also, is a not inconsiderable factor among those physical forces constantly operating to produce a diversity of forms among seashore animals. At a comparatively shallow depth in the sea, there is small fluctuation of temperatures; and life there exists in surroundings of serene stability; but as the shore is approached, the influence of the sun becomes more and more manifest and the variation is greater. This variation becomes greatest between the tide marks where, because of the very shallow depths and the fresh water from the land, this area is subjected to wide changes in both temperature and salinity.

Nor is a highly competitive mode of life without its bearing on structure as well as habits. In this phase of their struggle for existence, the animals of both the sea and the shore have become possessed of weapons for offense and defense that are correspondingly varied.

Although the life in the sea has been generally considered and treated as separate and distinct from the more familiar life on land, that supposition has no real basis in fact. Life on this planet is one vast unit, depending for its existence chiefly on the same sources of supply. That portion of animal life living in the sea, notwithstanding its strangeness and unfamiliarity, may be considered as but the aquatic fringe of the life on land. It is supported largely by materials washed into the sea, which are no longer available for the support of land animals. Perhaps we have been misled in these considerations of sea life because of the fact that approximately three times as many major *types* of animals inhabit salt water as live on the land: of the major types of animals no fewer than ten are exclusively marine, that is to say, nearly half again as many as land-dwelling types together. A further interesting fact is that despite the greater variety in the form and structure of sea animals about three-fourths of all known *kinds* of animals live on the land, while only one-fourth lives in the sea. In this connection it is noteworthy that sea life becomes scarcer with increasing distance from land; toward the middle of the oceans it disappears almost completely. For example, the central south Pacific is a region more barren than is any desert area on land. Indeed, no life of any kind has been found in the surface water, and there seems to be none on the bottom.

Sea animals are largest and most abundant on those shores receiving the most copious rainfall. Particularly is this true on the most rugged and colder coasts where it may be assumed that the material from the land finds its way to the sea unaltered and in greater quantities.

1. The best title for this passage is
   (A) Between the Tides
   (B) Seashore Life
   (C) The Tides
   (D) The Seashore.

2. Of the following adaptations, the one that would enable an organism to live on a sandy beach is
   (A) the ability to move rapidly
   (B) the ability to burrow deeply
   (C) a flattened shape
   (D) spiny extensions of the shell.

3. The absence of living things in mid-ocean might be due to
   (A) lack of rainfall in mid-ocean
   (B) the distance from material washed into the sea
   (C) larger animals feeding on smaller ones which must live near the land
   (D) insufficient dissolved oxygen.

4. A greater variety of living things exist on a rocky shore than on a sandy beach because
   (A) rocks offer a better foothold than sand
   (B) sandy areas are continually being washed by the surf
   (C) temperature changes are less drastic in rocky areas
   (D) the water in rock pools is less salty.

5. Organisms found living at the high-tide mark are adapted to
   (A) maintain themselves in the air for a long time
   (B) offer no resistance to wave impact
   (C) remain permanently fixed to the substratum
   (D) burrow in the ground.

6. The author holds that living things in the sea represent the aquatic fringe of life on land. This is so because
   (A) there are relatively fewer marine forms of animals than there are land-living forms
   (B) there is greater variety among land-living forms

(C) marine animals ultimately depend upon material from the land
(D) there are three times as many kinds of animals on land than there are in the sea.

7. A biologist walking along the shore at the low-tide line would not easily find many live animals since
   (A) their flattened shapes make them indistinguishable
   (B) they are washed back and forth by the waves
   (C) they burrow deeply
   (D) they move rapidly.

8. The intent of the author in the next to the last paragraph is to show that
   (A) the temperature and salinity of the sea determine the variety among shore animals
   (B) marine animals are vastly different from terrestrial organisms
   (C) colder areas can support more living things than warm areas
   (D) marine forms have the same problems as terrestrial animals.

9. A scientist wishing to study a great variety of living things would do well to hunt for them
   (A) in shallow waters
   (B) on a rocky seashore
   (C) on a sandy seashore
   (D) on any shore between the tide lines.

10. The most primitive forms of living things in the evolutionary scale are to be found in the sea because
    (A) the influence of the sea is found in land animals
    (B) the sea is relatively stable
    (C) many forms have become extinct on land
    (D) land animals are supposed to have evolved from sea organisms.

COMPREHENSION TEST 8

A vast health checkup is now being conducted in the western Swedish province of Varmland with the use of an automated apparatus for high-speed multiple-blood analyses. Developed by two physician brothers, the apparatus can process more than 4,000 blood samples a day, subjecting each to 10 or more tests. Automation has cut the cost of the analyses by about 90 per cent.

The results so far have been astonishing, for hundreds of Swedes have learned that they have silent symptoms of disorders that neither they nor their physicians were aware of. Among them were iron-deficiency anemia, hypercholesterolemia hypertension and even diabetes.

The automated blood analysis apparatus was developed by Dr. Gunnar Jungner, 49-year-old associate professor of clinical chemistry at Goteborg University, and his brother, Ingmar, 39, the physician in charge of the chemical central laboratory of Stockholm's Hospital for Infectious Diseases.

The idea was conceived 15 years ago when Dr. Gunnar Jungner was working as clinical chemist in northern Sweden and was asked by local physicians to devise a way of performing multiple analyses on a single blood sample. The design was ready in 1961.

Consisting of calorimeters, pumps and other components, many of them American-made, the Jungner apparatus was set up here in Stockholm. Samples from Varmland Province are drawn into the automated system at 90-second intervals.

The findings clatter forth in the form of numbers printed by an automatic typewriter.

The Jungners predict that advance knowledge about a person's potential ailments made possible by the chemical screening process will result in considerable savings in hospital and other medical costs. Thus, they point out, the blood analyses will actually turn out to cost nothing.

In the beginning, the automated blood analyses ran into considerable opposition from some physicians who had no faith in machines and saw no need for so many tests. Some laboratory technicians who saw their jobs threatened also protested. But the opposition is said to be waning.

1. Automation is viewed by the writer with
   (A) animosity
   (B) indecision
   (C) remorse
   (D) indifference
   (E) favor.

2. The results of the use of the Jungner apparatus indicate that
   (A) person may become aware of an ailment not previously detected
   (B) blood diseases can be cured very easily
   (C) diabetes does not respond to the apparatus
   (D) practically all Swedish physicians have welcomed the invention
   (E) only one analysis may be made at a time.

3. Which statement is *not* true?
   (A) Eventually it will cost nothing to analyze blood
   (B) The Jungners are physicians
   (C) The blood analysis results are recorded numerically
   (D) One of the Jungner brothers first thought up the apparatus when he was a young physician
   (E) Lab technicians don't care much for the Jungner apparatus.

4. According to the passage
   (A) the original idea for the apparatus was conceived in Stockholm
   (B) American engineering is, in part, responsible for the development of the apparatus
   (C) people throughout the world have already benefited from the invention
   (D) test results are fed into the mechanism every hour
   (E) the device reveals symptoms that a physician coult not find.

5. The prediction process that the Jungners use is essentially
   (A) biological
   (B) physiological
   (C) chemical
   (D) anatomical
   (E) biophysical.

COMPREHENSION TEST 9

In discussing human competence in a world of change, I want to make it crystal-clear that I am not ready to accept all the changes that are being pressed on us. I am not at all prepared to suggest that we must blindly find new competences in order to adjust to all the changes or in order to make ourselves inconspicuous in the modern habitat. Let me be specific. I see no reason in the world why modern man should develop any competence whatsoever to pay high rents in order to be permitted to live in buildings with walls that act as soundtracks rather than sound-absorbers. Nor do I believe that this problem can or should be overcome by developing such novel engineering competences as "acoustical perfume"—artificial noise to drown out next-door noises. When I don't wish to be a silent partner to the bedroom conversation of the neighbors, I am not at all satisfied by having the sound effects of a waterfall, the chirping of crickets, or incidental music superimposed on the disturbance, just to cover up the incompetence or greed of modern builders.

The other day I found myself wandering through the desolate destruction of Pennsylvania Station in New York, thoroughly incompetent in my efforts to find a ticket office. Instead I found a large poster which said that "your new station" was being built and that this was the reason for my temporary inconvenience. Nonsense! my station was not being built at all. My station is being destroyed, and I do not need the new competence of an advertising copy writer or a public relations consultant to obscure the facts. The competence that was needed—and which I and great numbers of like-minded contemporaries lacked—was the competence to prevent an undesirable change. In plain language—the competence to stop the organized vandalism which, in the name of progress and change, is tearing down good buildings to put up flimsy ones; is dynamting fine landmarks to replace then with structures that can be ripped down again twenty years later without a tear.

When the packaging industry finds it increasingly easy to design containers that make reduced contents appear to be an enlarged value at a steeper price, the change does not call for the competence of a consumer psychologist to make the defrauded customer feel happy. The change calls simply for a tough public prosecutor.

Lest I be mistaken for a political or even a sentimental reactionary who wants to halt progress and change, let me add another example of modern life the improvement of which may call for radical public action rather than for any new competence. Commuter rail transportation has fallen into decline in many parts of the country. Persons dependent on it find themselves frustrated and inconvenienced. In reply to their plight, they are given explanations such as the economic difficulties facing the railroad. Explanations, however, are no substitute for remedies. The competence required here is not technological or mechanical. After all, it would be difficult to persuade any sane citizen that a technology able to dispatch men into space and return them on schedule is mechanically incapable of transporting commuters from the suburbs to the cities in comfort, in safety, and on time.

The competence lacking here is one of general intelligence of the kind that is willing to shed doctrinaire myths when they stand in the way of the facts of modern life. To make millions of commuters suffer (and I use this example only because it is readily familiar, not because it is unique today) merely because the doctrine of free, competitive enterprise must be upheld, even after competition has disappeared as a vital ingredient, is an example of ludicrous mental incompetence. So is the tendency to worry whether a public takeover of a public necessity that is no longer being adequately maintained by private enterprise constitutes socialism or merely the protection of citizens' interests.

We ought to place the stress of competence in such a fashion that we can use it to mold, control, and—in extreme instances—even to block change rather than merely to adjust or submit to it.

—by Fred M. Hechinger (reprinted with permission)

1. The attitude of the writer is
   (A) sardonic and uncompromising
   (B) critical and constructive
   (C) petulant and forbidding
   (D) maudlin and merciful
   (E) reflective and questioning.

2. A "doctrinaire myth" (next to last paragraph) may be defined as a belief based on the false premises of
   (A) a deluded lexicographer
   (B) a public relations man
   (C) an insincere politician
   (D) a quack
   (E) an impractical theorist.

3. In the article, the author urges us
   (A) to fight against unethical political deals
   (B) to disregard the claims of the advertiser
   (C) to be opposed to many of the changes going on in our society today
   (D) not to rent a luxury apartment
   (E) to avoid becoming a commuter.

4. An appropriate title for this article would be
   (A) Antidotes for Incompetence
   (B) The Suffering Commuter
   (C) Unwarranted Destruction
   (D) Structured Vandalism
   (E) Progress and Change.

5. The passage, in no way, states or implies that
   (A) much construction today is inferior to what it was in other years
   (B) the razing of the Pennsylvania Station was justifiable
   (C) consumers are often deceived
   (D) some engineering devices are not worth the trouble spent in contriving them
   (E) space scientists have made great progress.

6. You would expect the author to say that
   (A) there is no reason for the United States to send nuclear-powered submarines to Japanese ports
   (B) a great deal of confusion reigns in credit card circles
   (C) a truly fundamental need in our society is honesty of thought and attitude
   (D) the damage done to our language by the structural linguists is not altogether irreparable
   (E) the world's population seems now to be increasing out of all proportion to the world's ability to provide food and education.

COMPREHENSION TEST 10

There is a time in every man's education when he arrives at the conviction that envy is ignorance; that imitation is suicide; that he must take himself for better for worse as his portion; that though the wide universe is full of good, no kernel of nourishing corn can come to him but through his toil bestowed on that plot of ground which is given him to till. The power which resides in him is new in nature, and none but him knows what he can do, nor does he know until he has tried.

Society everywhere is in conspiracy against the manhood of every one of its members. Society is a joint-stock company, in which the members agree for the better securing of his bread to each shareholder, to surrender the liberty and culture of the eater. The virtue in most request is conformity. Self-reliance is its aversion. It loves not realities and creators, but names and customs.

Whoso would be a man, must be a nonconformist. He who would gather immortal palms must not be hindered by the name of goodness, but must explore if it be goodness. Nothing is at last sacred but the integrity of your own mind. Absolve you to yourself, and you shall have the suffrage of the world.

A foolish consistency is the hobgoblin of little minds, adored by little statemen and philosophers and divines. With consistency a great soul has simply nothing to do. He may as well concern himself with his shadow on the wall. Speak what you think now in hard words, and tomorrow speak what tomorrow thinks in hard words again, though

it contradict everything you said today. "Ah, so you shall be sure to be misunderstood." Is it so bad, then, to be misunderstood? Pythagoras was misunderstood, and Socrates, and Jesus, and Luther, and Copernicus, and Galileo, and Newton, and every pure and wise spirit that ever took flesh. To be great is to be misunderstood. . . .

1. According to the passage, the practice of adhering, at all times, to the regulations is
   (A) praiseworthy
   (B) characteristic of inadequate people
   (C) a matter of democratic choice
   (D) reserved only for the intelligent
   (E) not workable

2. The writer, in effect, is saying that one
   (A) must always change his opinions
   (B) who agrees with the findings of Newton may also agree with those of Copernicus, Pythagoras, Socrates, Jesus, Luther, and Galileo
   (C) must join a group to survive in our society
   (D) should continue to appraise the facts at the cost of changing a previous conclusion
   (E) can find solace only in a belief in the hereafter

3. You may infer that the author
   (A) was a philosopher-humorist
   (B) once remarked that Toil, Want, Truth, and Mutual Faith were the four angels of his home
   (C) was a leader of oyster pirates, a deck hand on a North Pacific sealer, a mill worker hobo, and college student for a time
   (D) achieved a reputation as a clever business entrepreneur
   (E) was a vivid personality who led a strenuous life and became president of the United States

4. Society, so the selection implies,
   (A) does not encourage an individual to be creative
   (B) wants its members to be self-starters
   (C) can thrive only under democratic rule
   (D) encourages investments in stocks and bonds
   (E) will not improve unless the quality of its leaders improve

ANSWER KEY TO READING COMPREHENSION PRACTICE TESTS

Test 1	*Test 4*	*Test 6*	*Test 8*
1. B	1. B	1. C	1. E
2. B	2. B	2. C	2. A
3. A	3. D	3. A	3. B
4. D	4. A	4. B	4. B
5. E	5. D	5. D	5. C
	6. A	6. D	
Test 2	7. D	7. B	*Test 9*
1. B	8. A	8. D	1. B
2. C	9. C	9. D	2. E
3. D	10. A	10. A	3. C
4. E			4. A
5. B	*Test 5*	*Test 7*	5. B
6. A	1. A	1. B	6. C
7. D	2. D	2. A	
	3. B	3. B	*Test 10*
Test 3	4. B	4. B	1. B
1. A	5. A	5. A	2. D
2. D	6. C	6. C	3. B
3. B	7. A	7. D	4. A
4. E	8. B	8. D	
5. D	9. D	9. D	
	10. D	10. B	
	11. B		

Literature Tests

DIRECTIONS: Select from the choices offered in each of the following, the one which is correct or most nearly correct.

LITERATURE: TEST 1

1. Which one of the following is a biting satire for adults, rather than a book for children?
   (A) Homer Price — Robert McCloskey
   (B) The Matchlock Gun — Walter D. Edmonds
   (C) The Peterkin Papers — Lucretia Hale
   (D) Animal Farm — George Orwell.

2. All of the following poems are in rhyme except
   (A) Little Boy Blue — Eugene Field
   (B) Paul Revere's Ride — Henry Wadsworth Longfellow
   (C) The Fog — Carl Sandburg
   (D) Stopping by Woods on a Snowy Evening — Robert Frost.

3. The story of the Forsyte family is told in a series of novels and short stories by
   (A) John Galsworthy   (B) H. G. Wells
   (C) Arnold Bennett   (D) J. B. Priestley.

4. Roger Chillingworth seeks revenge in Hawthorne's
   (A) The Marble Faun
   (B) The House of the Seven Gables
   (C) The Scarlet Letter
   (D) The Blithedale Romance.

5. In Drury's "Advise and Consent," when Leffingwell's nomination to a cabinet post has not been confirmed, he
   (A) is jailed for perjury
   (B) is offered another post in the government
   (C) blames the President
   (D) commits suicide.

6. All of the following literary characters are correctly identified except
   (A) Thunderhead — lighthouse
   (B) Little Toot — tugboat
   (C) Flag — fawn
   (D) Bambi — deer.

7. The poem in which Father William stands on his head was written by
   (A) Lewis Carroll   (B) Hilaire Belloc
   (C) A. A. Milne   (D) Carl Sandburg.

8. Each of the following book titles is correctly paired with a drama or a musical based on the book except
   (A) Washington Square — The Heiress
   (B) The Autobiography of Helen Keller — The Miracle Worker
   (C) The Once and Future King — Camelot
   (D) All the King's Men — Wildcat.

9. Of the following, the work not generally regarded as a historical novel is
   (A) Maugham's "Of Human Bondage"
   (B) Roberts' "Northwest Passage"
   (C) Churchill's "The Crisis"
   (D) Reade's "The Cloister and the Hearth."

10. All of the following are the first lines of sonnets by Shakespeare except
    (A) Shall I compare thee to a summer's day
    (B) When to the sessions of sweet silent thought
    (C) Let me not to the marriage of true minds
    (D) Death be not proud, though some have called thee.

Answers: Test 1

1. D	3. A	5. B	7. A	9. A
2. C	4. C	6. A	8. D	10. D

LITERATURE: TEST 2

1. The Snopes family appears in many of the books of
   (A) Ernest Hemingway (B) William Faulkner
   (C) Thomas Mann   (D) Thomas Wolfe.

2. A famous Phi Beta Kappa address entitled "The American Scholar" was delivered at Harvard in 1837 by
   (A) Ralph Waldo Emerson
   (B) Henry David Thoreau
   (C) Henry Wadsworth Longfellow
   (D) Louisa May Alcott.

3. Of the following, the author who has not written an important work dealing with Thomas Becket is
   (A) Jean Anouilh   (B) Alfred Duggan
   (C) Evelyn Waugh   (D) T. S. Eliot.

4. "Thou shalt see me at Philippi" is the warning of
   (A) Hamlet's father to Hamlet
   (B) Caesar's ghost to Brutus
   (C) Antony to Cleopatra
   (D) Tybalt to Romeo.

5. In "The Highwayman," Bess was betrayed to the soldiers by
   (A) the tavern keeper
   (B) Jim, the peddler
   (C) Tim, the ostler
   (D) Tom, the farmhand.

6. Mrs. Bennet and her five daughters appear in Jane Austen's
   (A) Northanger Abbey
   (B) Pride and Prejudice
   (C) Mansfield Park
   (D) Sense and Sensibility.

7. In Nobel prize winner Juan Jimenez's book, "Platero and I," Platero is the name of a (an)
(A) orphan boy   (B) affectionate pup
(C) itinerant peddler   (D) small donkey.

8. "Exodus" by Leon Uris is
(A) a retelling of the Biblical account of the Jews' departure from Egypt
(B) the story of the struggle to build the modern state of Israel
(C) the story of the world's refugees
(D) the story of a defector from a Soviet camp.

9. Of the following, the one who is *not* famous as a writer of humorous stories and essays is
(A) Robert Benchley   (B) Mark Twain
(C) James Thurber   (D) Thomas Merton.

10. In revenge for the slaying of Patroclus, Achilles killed
(A) Paris   (B) Priam
(C) Nestor   (D) Hector.

Answers: Test 2

1. B	3. C	5. C	7. D	9. D
2. A	4. B	6. B	8. B	10. D

LITERATURE: TEST 3

1. Life in a Middle West town is depicted by means of epitaphs in which former inhabitants tell their life stories in the work entitled:
(A) Spoon River Anthology
(B) Winesburg, Ohio
(C) Main Street
(D) The Story of a Country Town.

2. "They shall beat their swords into plowshares, and their spears into pruning hooks" is a quotation from:
(A) War and Peace
(B) The Bible
(C) The Charter of the United Nations
(D) Lee's Farewell to His Officers.

3. The creator of Diedrich Knickerbocker also created the character of:
(A) Ichabod Crane   (D) Poor Richard.
(C) Hiawatha   (B) Uncle Remus

4. "Adonais" is an elegy written by Shelley on the death of:
(A) Keats   (B) Wordsworth
(C) Byron   (D) Milton.

5. "With malice toward none; with charity for all" is a quotation from a speech by:
(A) George Washington
(B) Franklin D. Roosevelt

(C) Abraham Lincoln
(D) Theodore Roosevelt.

6. The Argonauts were the sailors under the direction of:
(A) Ulysses   (B) Jason
(C) Aeneas   (D) Perseus.

7. Descriptive phrases like "wine-dark" and "rosy-fingered" are characteristic of:
(A) Paradise Lost
(B) morality plays
(C) The Comedy of Errors
(D) The Odyssey.

8. "I believe a leaf of grass is no less than the journey-work of the stars" was written by:
(A) Thoreau   (B) Dickinson
(C) Whitman   (D) Freneau.

9. In the quotation:
"As idle as a painted ship
Upon a painted ocean,"
The figure of speech is a:
(A) metaphor   (B) hyperbole
(C) apostrophe   (D) simile.

10. Of the following, the poet whose work is most closely identified with New England is:
(A) Vachel Lindsay   (B) Amy Lowell
(C) Carl Sandburg   (D) Robert Frost.

Answers: Test 3

1. A	3. A	5. C	7. D	9. D
2. B	4. A	6. B	8. C	10. D

LITERATURE: TEST 4

1. The author of "A Farewell to Arms" also wrote:
(A) Look Homeward, Angel
(B) Giant
(C) The Old Man and the Sea
(D) East of Eden.

2. "Old Marley was as dead as a doornail" is a quotation from:
(A) Oliver Twist
(B) David Copperfield
(C) A Christmas Carol
(D) Nicholas Nickleby.

3. "Profiles in Courage," the Pulitzer Prize winning biography was written by a:
(A) senator of the United States
(B) justice of the Supreme Court
(C) mountain climber
(D) pioneer in aviation.

4. He was known as the Household Poet. He was professor of languages at Harvard. He is the

author of a great epic of the American Indian. These statements describe:

(A) Whittier   (B) Lowell
(C) Longfellow   (D) Holmes.

5. In a poem by Poe, "Nevermore" is the oft-repeated word spoken by:

(A) Annabel Lee   (B) the Raven
(C) Israfel   (D) Ulalume.

6. An English poet and novelist also known for his animal stories for children is:

(A) Robert Louis Stevenson
(B) Carl Sandburg
(C) Rudyard Kipling
(D) John Masefield.

7. A Shakespearean critic who collaborated with his sister to write synopses of the plots of Shakespeare's plays is:

(A) William Wordsworth
(B) Charles Lamb
(C) William Hazlitt
(D) Dante Gabriel Rossetti.

8. Of the following poets, the one who is associated most closely with World War I is:

(A) Dylan Thomas
(B) Stephen Spender
(C) T. S. Eliot
(D) Wilfred Owen.

9.
    "I never saw a moor
    I never saw the sea
    Yet I know how the heather looks
    And what a wave must be."

This is a quotation from:

(A) Chartless   (B) Marshes of Glynn
(C) Indian Summer   (D) Renascence.

10. A poet who frequently used inexact rhymes, like "Heaven" and "given," is:

(A) Edwin Markham
(B) Joyce Kilmer
(C) Emily Dickinson
(D) Thomas Bailey Aldrich.

Answers: Test 4

1. C	3. A	5. B	7. B	9. A
2. C	4. C	6. C	8. D	10. C

LITERATURE: TEST 5

1. "Whereat with blade, with bloody, shameful blade
He bravely broached his boiling bloody breast"
is an example of

(A) personification   (B) apostrophe
(C) hyperbole   (D) alliteration.

2. King Arthur's treacherous sister was

(A) Morgan Le Fay   (B) Lynette
(C) Enid   (D) Elaine of Astolat.

3. All of the following characters are matched correctly with the authors who created them *except*

(A) Lennie Small — John Steinbeck
(B) Jim Smiley — Mark Twain
(C) Uncle Remus — Joel Chandler Harris
(D) Hawkeye — Washington Irving.

4. All of the following poems are by Robert Frost *except*

(A) The Death of the Hired Man
(B) The Mountain Whippoorwill
(C) Mending Wall
(D) Birches.

5. "The Status Seekers" by Vance Packard is a recent work dealing mainly with

(A) social classes in the United States
(B) teenagers and their problems
(C) the struggle of underprivileged nations for recognition
(D) the changing role of the teacher in American society.

6. The Greek hero who killed Hector was

(A) Paris   (B) Ulysses
(C) Achilles   (D) Aeneas.

7. Of the following authors, the one whose literary pseudonym is *incorrectly* given is

(A) Joel Chandler Harris — Uncle Remus
(B) William Sidney Porter — O. Henry
(C) Washington Irving — Diedrich Knickerbocker
(D) William Makepeace Thackeray — Boz.

8. "Make me thy lyre, even as the forest is" was Shelley's request of

(A) the west wind   (B) a skylark
(C) a cloud   (D) autumn.

9. Of the following, the one in which a Greek deity is *not* correctly paired with the Roman counterpart is

(A) Ares — Mars
(B) Demeter — Proserpina
(C) Poseidon — Neptune
(D) Eros — Cupid.

10. All of the following are daughters of King Lear *except*

(A) Goneril   (B) Regan
(C) Cordelia   (D) Calpurnia.

Answers: Test 5

1. D	3. D	5. A	7. D	9. B
2. A	4. B	6. C	8. A	10. D

Art Tests

DIRECTIONS: Select from the choices offered in each of the following, the one which is correct or most nearly correct.

ART: TEST 1

1. One of the finest painters of marine pictures is
   (A) George Bellows (B) John Steuart Curry
   (C) El Greco   (D) Winslow Homer
   (E) James McNeill Whistler.

2. A contemporary illustrator whose magazine cover designs have become known for their interpretation of American types and scenes is
   (A) Elmore J. Brown   (B) Walt Disney
   (C) R. John Holmgren (D) Rockwell Kent
   (E) Norman Rockwell.

3. What American woman painter is known for her use of exquisite colors and abstract representations of flower forms?
   (A) Lillian Westcott Hale
   (B) Violet Oakley
   (C) Georgia O'Keeffe
   (D) Marie Danforth Page
   (E) Jessie Willcox Smith.

4. A painter of decorative, barbaric Tahitian landscapes was
   (A) Edgar Degas   (B) Paul Gauguin
   (C) George Inness   (D) Pierre Renoir
   (E) Vincent Van Gogh.

5. In painting or drawing a scene, the most important thing to do is to
   (A) represent the scene exactly as it appears to the eye
   (B) have all the perspective exact
   (C) use a wide variety of colors
   (D) plan a good design
   (E) lay in the color smoothly.

6. Rhythm in a drawing or painting is achieved by
   (A) repetition of lines
   (B) using contrasting colors adjacent to one another
   (C) using a variety of straight and curved lines
   (D) using the strongest colors for the centers of interest
   (E) careful attention to balance.

7. Transitional lines are those which
   (A) are horizontal
   (B) tie shapes together to give them unity
   (C) are vertical

(D) throw a pattern off balance
(E) repeat a shape.

8. Of the six faces of a cube, the greatest number that can be shown in a perspective drawing is
   (A) one   (B) two
   (C) three   (D) four
   (E) five.

9. Which of these landscapes shows best design?

   (A)   (B)   (C)   (D)   (E)

10. Which candle-and-candlestick combination is most artistic?

   (A)   (B)   (C)   (D)   (E)

Answers: Test 1

| 1. D | 3. C | 5. D | 7. B | 9. E |
| 2. E | 4. B | 6. A | 8. C | 10. D |

ART: TEST 2

1. Floor coverings, such as rugs, paint and linoleum, should be darker in color than the walls because
   (A) they are less likely to show soil
   (B) they make a better background for furniture
   (C) they are warmer
   (D) dark dyes do not weaken the fabrics so much as light dyes
   (E) dark colors are heavy and belong at the bottom.

2. The table pictured here is in the style made popular by
   (A) The Adam brothers
   (B) Chippendale
   (C) Duncan Phyfe
   (D) Paul Revere
   (E) Sheraton.

3. Painting with the airbrush was perfected by the
   (A) Dutch School   (B) French School
   (C) Florentine School   (D) English School
   (E) Commercial art school.

4. *The Victory of Samothrace* is a famous
   (A) bas-relief   (B) cathedral
   (C) mural   (D) statue
   (E) tapestry.

5. The raised design on a cameo is an example of
   (A) bas-relief   (B) intaglio
   (C) modeling   (D) sculpture
   (E) sgraffito.

6. The word PRECISION is printed in type known as
   (A) sans-serif   (B) modern
   (C) roman   (D) Gothic
   (E) old English.

7. As a designer of the fine type, one of America's foremost contributors to the art of printing has has been
   (A) Boris Artzybasheff
   (B) Frederick W. Goudy
   (C) Johann Gutenberg
   (D) Alfred Stieglitz
   (E) N. C. Wyeth.

8. Which of the following arts best expresses the social background of a period.
   (A) architecture   (B) minor arts
   (C) painting   (D) sculpture.
   (E) graphic arts.

9. A Florentine sculptor and goldsmith who lived in the 16th century was
   (A) Giovanni Bellini
   (B) Benvenuto Cellini
   (C) Giovanni Cimabue
   (D) Leonardo DaVinci
   (E) Michelangelo.

10. In which period of art were stained glass windows introduced for church decoration?
    (A) Roman   (B) Gothic
    (C) Renaissance   (D) Classical
    (E) Futuristic.

Answers: Test 2

1. E	3. E	5. A	7. B	9. B
2. C	4. D	6. C	8. A	10. B

ART: TEST 3

1. The city of Washington was planned by
   (A) Ralph Adams Cram
   (B) Cass Gilbert
   (C) Thomas Jefferson
   (D) Pierre L'Enfant
   (E) Frank Lloyd Wright.

2. The most important American contribution to the development of architecture has been
   (A) glass brick
   (B) revolving doors
   (C) elevators
   (D) reinforced concrete
   (E) steel-frame construction.

3. Which of the following would be designed by an industrial designer?
   (A) a mural   (B) a frieze
   (C) an electric flatiron   (D) a poster
   (E) the facade of a building.

4. Which of the following is a contemporary American industrial designer?
   (A) Norman Bel Geddes
   (B) Thomas Hart Benton
   (C) Margaret Bourke-White
   (D) Charles E. Burchfield
   (E) Edward Steichen.

5. A pioneer in the production of animated cartoons is
   (A) Malvina Hoffman   (B) Diego Rivera
   (C) Lee Simonson   (D) Paul Terry
   (E) Walter Dorwin Teague.

6. Thomas Jefferson practiced with considerable skill the art of
   (A) blacksmithing   (B) architecture
   (C) ceramics   (D) painting.

7. The style of the Lincoln Memorial in Washington is derived from
   (A) Greek architecture
   (B) Gothic architecture
   (C) Romanesque architecture
   (D) Modern architecture.

8. The picture writing of the ancient Egyptians is known as
   (A) cuneiform   (B) cursive
   (C) hieroglyphics   (O) sans-serif.

9. Of the following, the painter whose work is well known for its rich and exciting color is
   (A) Courbet   (B) Chardin
   (C) Matisse   (D) Daumier.

10. Goya, a Spanish artist, achieved fame chiefly as a
    (A) court painter
    (B) painter of madonnas
    (C) painter of the sea
    (D) satirist.

Answers: Test 3

1. D	3. C	5. D	7. A	9. D
2. E	4. A	6. B	8. C	10. D

ART: TEST 4

1. Of the following movements in art, the one with which Picasso has been most closely identified is
   - (A) Futurism
   - (B) Fauvism
   - (C) Cubism
   - (D) Surrealism.

2. All of the following works are by Michelangelo *except* the
   - (A) painting, "The Last Judgment"
   - (B) portal of the baptistery in Florence, "The Gates of Paradise"
   - (C) statue of Moses
   - (D) fresco on the ceiling of the Sistine Chapel.

3. The Seven Wonders of the World included all of the following *except* the
   - (A) Great Pyramid of Khufu
   - (B) Colossus of Rhodes
   - (C) Hanging Gardens of Babylon
   - (D) Taj Mahal at Agra.

4. Of the following, the artist who is best known for his peasant scenes, painted with robustness, realism, and humor, is
   - (A) Rubens
   - (B) Van Dyck
   - (C) Bruegel
   - (D) Van Eyck.

5. The term "Expressionism" in relation to art refers to
   - (A) content with little or no resemblance to objects in nature
   - (B) distortion of forms and colors to achieve an emotional or esthetic effect
   - (C) the use of subject matter with political, social, or economic content
   - (D) exact, realistic technique applied to improbable or dream-like subject matter.

6. The statement "The objective of the Impressionist (painter) was to create an illusion of light and atmosphere" best describes the work of
   - (A) Pissarro
   - (B) Courbet
   - (C) Daumier
   - (D) Millet.

7. All of the following artists are known primarily as sculptors *except*
   - (A) Wilhelm Lehmbruck
   - (B) Aristide Maillol
   - (C) Constantin Brancusi
   - (D) Amadeo Modigliani.

8. The *incorrectly* matched pair is
   - (A) Bosch—"Temptation of St. Anthony'
   - (B) Leonardo da Vinci—"The Birth of Venus"
   - (C) Hogarth—"The Shrimp Girl"
   - (D) Rembrandt—"The Anatomy Lesson."

9. All of the following are well known designers of modern furniture *except*
   - (A) Willem de Kooning
   - (B) Ludwig Mies van der Rohe
   - (C) Le Corbusier
   - (D) Marcel Breuer.

10. All of the following famous churches are Gothic in style *except*
    - (A) Chartres
    - (B) Amiens
    - (C) St. Peter's
    - (D) Notre Dame.

Answers: Test 4

1. C	3. D	5. B	7. D	9. A
2. B	4. C	6. A	8. B	10. C

ART: TEST 5

1. The eighteenth century English artist who won prominence primarily for his landscapes was
   - (A) Reynolds
   - (B) Lely
   - (C) Lawrence
   - (D) Constable.

2. Of the following artists, the one who is famous for his paintings of sporting events is
   - (A) John LaFarge
   - (B) George Bellows
   - (C) Winslow Homer
   - (D) Albert Ryder.

3. Some of the most incisive portrayals of the horrors and brutality of war are the work of
   - (A) Titian
   - (B) Stuart
   - (C) Valasquez
   - (D) Goya.

4. The correct association of the artist and the subject matter of his cartoons is
   - (A) Hirschfeld—social criticism
   - (B) Kirby—domestic life
   - (C) Low—international politics
   - (D) "Herblock"—affairs of the theatre.

5. The term "value," when used of a color, refers to
   - (A) the degree of its darkness or lightness
   - (B) its intensity
   - (C) its hue
   - (D) its texture.

6. In painting, emphasis on inner emotions, sensations, or ideas rather than actual appearances is called
   - (A) impressionism
   - (B) futurism
   - (C) expressionism
   - (D) cubism.

7. The statue of Abraham Lincoln in the Lincoln Memorial in Washington, D.C., was created by
   (A) Augustus St. Gaudens
   (B) Frederick William MacMonnies
   (C) Paul Manship
   (D) Daniel Chester French.

8. "Toledo in a Storm" is the work of
   (A) Diego Velasquez
   (B) Francisco Goya
   (C) El Greco
   (D) Bartolome Murillo.

9. The rounded arch was a dominant form of architectural construction in
   (A) Gothic cathedrals (B) Egyptian temples
   (C) Assyrian temples (D) Roman basilicas.

10. The ceiling of the Sistine Chapel depicts
    (A) The Temptation of St. Anthony
    (B) The Last Judgment
    (C) The Creation of Man
    (D) The Resurrection.

Answers: Test 5

1. D	3. D	5. A	7. D	9. D
2. B	4. C	6. C	8. C	10. C

Music Tests

DIRECTIONS: Select from the choices offered in each of the following, the one which is correct or most nearly correct.

MUSIC: TEST 1

1. Which of these composers did *not* earn his reputation as a leading composer by writing operas?
   (A) Bizet   (B) Brahms
   (C) Puccini   (D) Verdi
   (E) Wagner.

2. All of the following have composed famous church music *except*
   (A) Chopin   (B) Franck
   (C) Gounod   (D) Mendelssohn
   (E) Palestrina.

3. Which of these musical compositions is not in the classical style?
   (A) "Surprise Symphony" by Haydn
   (B) "Gavotte" by Mozart
   (C) "Passacaglia In C Minor" by Bach
   (D) "Tales of The Vienna Woods" by Strauss
   (E) "Largo" by Handel.

4. The "Carnival of Animals," a suite of short compositions each of which depicts an animal in a Mardi gras, was written by
   (A) Cherubini   (B) DeBussy
   (C) Dvorak   (D) Grieg
   (E) Saint-Saens.

5. Which of the following would you *not* be likely to hear in a musical program?
   (A) "Caprice Viennois" played by Fritz Kreisler
   (B) "William Tell Overture" played by the New York Philharmonic-Symphony Orchestra
   (C) "The Flight of The Bumblebee" sung by Lily Pons
   (D) "Water Boy" sung by Lawrence Tibbett
   (E) "Minute Waltz" played by Jose Iturbi.

6. Humperdinck composed the music for
   (A) Rigoletto
   (B) Madame Butterfly
   (C) The Magic Flute
   (D) Orpheus and Eurydice
   (E) Hansel and Gretel

7. The Russian composer of "Scheherazade Suite" is
   (A) Borodin   (B) Prokofieff
   (C) Shostakovitch   (D) Tschaikowsky
   (E) Rimsky-Korsakoff.

8. Which of these musical performers does *not* belong to the same category as the others?
   (A) Marian Anderson   (B) Patrice Munsel
   (C) Fritz Reiner   (D) Paul Robeson
   (E) John Charles Thomas.

9. Which of the following instruments belong to the reed family?
   (A) cornet   (B) oboe
   (C) trombone   (D) trumpet
   (E) French horn.

10. Which of these instruments is sometimes considered a percussion instrument?
    (A) oboe   (B) piano
    (C) trumpet   (D) viola
    (E) violin.

Answers: Test 1

1. B	3. D	5. C	7. E	9. B
2. A	4. E	6. E	8. C	10. B

MUSIC: TEST 2

1. Which of these is *not* found in $\frac{2}{4}$ time?

   (A) ♩   (B) ♪

   (C) ♩.   (D) ♪

   (E) 𝅝

2. Which of the following terms is *not* related to the others?
   (A) allegro   (B) sforzando
   (C) andante   (D) presto
   (E) largo.

3. Which of the following musical terms is *incorrectly* interpreted?
   (A) adagio—slow
   (B) allegretto—moderately quick
   (C) diminuendo—gradually softer
   (D) cadenza—quick and spirited
   (E) poco a poco—little by little.

4. A song about the syllable tones of the musical scale comes from the musical comedy
   (A) My Fair Lady
   (B) Most Happy Fella
   (C) The Sound of Music
   (D) The Music Man.

5. Which of these operas is based upon the legend of the Holy Grail?
   (A) "Don Giovanni"   (B) "Falstaff"
   (C) "Pagliacci"   (D) "Parsifal"
   (E) "La Traviata."

6. Which of the following does *not* refer to a degree of loudness?
   (A) piano   (B) forte
   (C) pianoforte   (D) mezzo forte
   (E) pianissimo.

7. A symphony is made up of several parts containing different themes and played at different tempos. Thes parts are called
   (A) arias   (B) cantatas
   (C) leitmotifs   (D) movements
   (E) sonatas.

8. The ninth symphony by Beethoven is referred to as the
   (A) Choral   (B) Pastoral
   (C) Eroica   (D) C-Minor.

9. Of the following, the one in which the music is expected to evoke scenes of Christmas fantasy is
   (A) Tales from the Vienna Woods
   (B) The Man in the Drum
   (C) Children's Corner
   (D) The Nutcracker Suite.

10. The lines:
   "When at night I go to sleep
   Fourteen angels watch do keep"
   occur in a musical selection sung in
   (A) H.M.S. Pinafore
   (B) The Music Man
   (C) The Pastoral Symphony
   (D) Hansel and Gretel.

Answers: Test 2

1. E	3. D	5. D	7. D	9. D
2. B	4. C	6. C	8. A	10. D

MUSIC: TEST 3

1. A vocal arrangement in which the same melody is sung by several voices starting one after the other at regular intervals to produce pleasant harmony and rhythm is called a(n)
   (A) art song   (B) round
   (C) descant   (D) a cappella.

2. Of the following musical terms, the one which is out of place in the following group is
   (A) forte   (B) piano
   (C) crescendo   (D) presto.

3. In the ascending scale of C major, the note after G is
   (A) H   (B) A
   (C) F   (D) G sharp.

4. Of the following, the one in which the musical story theme concerns the adventures of a boy who has run away from his mountain home is
   (A) Grand Canyon Suite
   (B) The Gondoliers
   (C) An American in Paris
   (D) The Peer Gynt Suite.

5. The flute's airy theme evokes the image of a faun in a descriptive orchestral piece by
   (A) Saint-Saens   (B) Ravel
   (C) Debussy   (D) Chopin.

6. In a musical composition, a coda is a(n)
   (A) introduction
   (B) solo for one instrument
   (C) concluding passage
   (D) motive.

7. The section of a concerto played by the soloist without the accompaniment of the orchestra is known as the
   (A) cadenza   (B) canzone
   (C) scherzo   (D) leitmotiv.

8. The symphonic poem "Fountains of Rome" was composed by
   (A) Pietro Mascagni   (B) Ottorio Respighi
   (C) Giacomo Puccini   (D) Niccolo Paganini.

9. Of the following operas, the one that was *not* composed by Puccini is
   (A) La Boheme
   (B) Madama Butterfly
   (C) The Girl of the Golden West
   (D) Falstaff.

10. All of the following composed symphonies *except*
   (A) Gustav Mahler
   (B) Frederic Chopin
   (C) Jakob Mendelssohn
   (D) Cesar Franck.

Answers: Test 3

1. B	3. B	5. C	7. A	9. D
2. D	4. D	6. C	8. B	10. B

MUSIC: TEST 4

1. Of the following descriptive terms, the one that best describes the fugue is
   (A) homophonic   (B) antiphonal
   (C) polyphonic   (D) lyric.

2. Of the following, the composer who best exemplifies the Baroque era in music is
   (A) Johann Sebastian Bach
   (B) Ernest Bloch
   (C) Franz Joseph Haydn
   (D) Giovanni Pierluigi da Palestrina.

3. Of the following ballets, the one that was *not* composed by Stravinsky is
   (A) Fire Bird
   (B) Afternoon of a Faun
   (C) Rite of Spring
   (D) Petrushka.

4. All of the following operas are correctly paired with their composers *except*
   (A) Billy Budd — Benjamin Britten
   (B) The Rake's Progress — Igor Stravinsky
   (C) Wozzeck — Francis Poulenc
   (D) War and Peace — Serge Prokofiev.

5. In the classical symphony, the third movement was usually a
   (A) caprice   (B) gavotte
   (C) rondo   (D) minuet.

6. Gilbert and Sullivan composed all of the following *except*
   (A) Princess Ida   (B) Ruddigore
   (C) The Red Mill   (D) Patience.

7. All of the following operas are included in the famous Ring Cycle *except*
   (A) Siegfried
   (B) Die Gotterdammerung
   (C) Die Walkure
   (D) Die Meistersinger.

8. Of the following, the opera which was *not* composed by Mennotti is
   (A) The Saint of Bleecker Street
   (B) Amahl and the Night Visitors
   (C) The King's Henchman
   (D) The Medium.

9. Impressionism in the field of music is best exemplified by
   (A) Strauss   (B) Debussy
   (C) Berlioz   (D) Franck.

10. In musical terminology the word "dynamics" refers to
   (A) harmony   (B) rhythm
   (C) theory   (D) volume.

Answers: Test 4

1. C	3. B	5. D	7. D	9. B
2. A	4. C	6. C	8. C	10. D

MUSIC: TEST 5

1. A concerto is music for
   (A) a prelude to an opera
   (B) the organ
   (C) two players
   (D) solo and orchestra.

2. Schiller's "Ode to Joy" is the setting for the chorale in a symphony by
   (A) Beethoven   (B) Tschaikovsky
   (C) Hanson   (D) Menotti.

3. The "Revolutionary Etude" for piano was composed by
   (A) Shostakovitch   (B) Chopin
   (C) Von Bulow   (D) MacDowell.

4. The "Grand Canyon Suite" was written by
   (A) Carpenter   (B) Grofe
   (C) Gershwin   (D) Blitztein.

5. Of the following the one that was *not* written by George Gershwin is
   (A) The Rhumba Symphony
   (B) Porgy and Bess
   (C) Concerto in F
   (D) An American in Paris.

6. The name of Pablo Casals is associated with the
   (A) piano   (B) cello
   (C) organ   (D) violin.

7. Brilliant music written to display the range of a voice or the skill of a performer is designated by the term
(A) animato   (B) virtuoso
(C) bravura   (D) allegro affettuoso.

8. Guido Cantelli was a(n)
(A) singer   (B) orchestra conductor
(C) music critic   (D) organist.

9. An opera not composed by Richard Wagner is
(A) Das Rheingold   (B) Tristan und Isolde
(C) Otello   (D) Rienzi.

10. Of the following, the one which is not part of the "Nutcracker Suite" is (the)
(A) Dance of the Sugarplum Fairy
(B) Golliwog's Cakewalk
(C) Chinese Dance
(D) Waltz of the Flowers.

Answers: Test 5

1. D	3. B	5. A	7. B	9. C
2. A	4. B	6. B	8. B	10. B

Science Tests

DIRECTIONS: Select from the choices offered in each of the following, the one which is correct or most nearly correct.

SCIENCE: TEST 1

1. The normal height of a mercury barometer at sea level is
(A) 15 inches   (B) 30 inches
(C) 32 feet   (D) 34 feet.

2. Of the following phases of the moon, the invisible one is called
(A) crescent   (B) full moon
(C) new moon   (D) waxing and waning.

3. Of the following, the statement that best describes a "high" on a weather map is
(A) the air extends farther up than normal
(B) the air pressure is greater than normal
(C) the air temperature is higher than normal
(D) the air moves faster than normal.

4. The nerve endings for the sense of sight are located in the part of the eye called the
(A) cornea   (B) sclera
(C) iris   (D) retina.

5. Of the following, the one which causes malaria is
(A) a bacterium   (B) a mosquito
(C) a protozoan   (D) bad air.

6. A 1000-ton ship must displace a weight of water equal to
(A) 500 tons   (B) 1000 tons
(C) 1500 tons   (D) 2000 tons.

7. Of the following instruments, the one that can convert light into an electric current is the
(A) radiometer
(B) dry cell
(C) electroylsis apparatus
(D) photo-electric cell.

8. On the film in a camera, the lens forms an image which, by comparison with the original subject, is
(A) right side up and reversed from left to right
(B) upside down and reversed from left to right
(C) right side up and not reversed from left to right
(D) upside down and not reversed from left to right.

9. Of the following, the plant whose seeds are *not* spread by wind is the
(A) cocklebur   (B) maple
(C) dandelion   (D) milkweed.

10. Of the following, the insect which is harmful to man's food supply is the
(A) dragonfly   (B) grasshopper
(C) ladybug   (D) praying mantis.

Answers: Test 1

1. B	3. B	5. C	7. D	9. A
2. C	4. D	6. B	8. B	10. B

SCIENCE: TEST 2

1. One-celled animals belong to the group of living things known as
(A) protozoa   (B) porifera
(C) annelida   (D) arthropoda.

2. Spiders can be distinguished from insects by the fact that spiders have
(A hard outer coverings
(B) large abdomens
(C) four pairs of legs
(D) biting mouth parts.

3. An important ore of uranium is called
   (A) hematite   (B) bauxite
   (C) chalcopyrite   (D) pitchblende.

4. Of the following, the lightest element known on earth is
   (A) hydrogen   (B) helium
   (C) oxygen   (D) air.

5. Of the following gases in the air, the most plentiful is
   (A) argon   (B) nitrogen
   (C) oxygen   (D) carbon dioxide.

6. The time it takes for light from the sun to reach the earth is approximately
   (A) four years   (B) four months
   (C) eight minutes   (D) sixteen years.

7. Of the following types of clouds, the ones which occur at the greatest height are called
   (A) cirrus   (B) cumulus
   (C) nimbus   (D) stratus.

8. The time that it takes for the earth to rotate 45° is
   (A) one hour   (B) three hours
   (C) four hours   (D) ten hours.

9. Of the following glands, the one which regulates the metabolic rate is the
   (A) adrenal   (B) salivary
   (C) thyroid   (D) thymus.

10. All of the following are Amphibia *except* the
   (A) salamander   (B) lizard
   (C) frog   (D) toad.

Answers: Test 2

1. A	3. D	5. B	7. A	9. C
2. C	4. A	6. C	8. B	10. B

SCIENCE: TEST 3

1. Of the following planets, the one which has the shortest revolutionary period around the sun is
   (A) Earth   (B) Mercury
   (C) Jupiter   (D) Venus.

2. A popular shrub that produces bell-shaped, yellow flowers in early spring is the
   (A) tulip   (B) azalea
   (C) forsythia   (D) flowering dogwood.

3. A circuit breaker is used in many homes instead of a
   (A) switch   (B) fuse
   (C) fire extinguisher (D) meter box.

4. Of the following, which is closest to the speed of sound in air at sea level?
   (A) 1/5th of a mile per second
   (B) 1/2 mile per second
   (C) 1 mile per second
   (D) 5 miles per second.

5. In the production of sounds, the greater the number of vibrations per second
   (A) the greater the volume
   (B) the higher the tone
   (C) the lower the volume
   (D) the lower the tone.

6. Of the following media, the one in which the speed of sound is greatest is
   (A) cold air   (B) warm air
   (C) steel   (D) water.

7. What is the name of the negative particle which circles the nucleus of the atom?
   (A) neutron   (B) proton
   (C) meson   (D) electron.

8. Which of the following rocks can be dissolved with a weak acid?
   (A) sandstone   (B) granite
   (C) gneiss   (D) limestone.

9. Of the following methods, the one which is correct to use in converting a steel knitting needle into a permanent magnet is
   (A) heating
   (B) jarring
   (C) stroking with a magnet
   (D) passing electricity through it.

10. Which of the following minerals is restored to the soil by plants of the pea and bean family?
   (A) sulfates   (B) nitrates
   (C) carbonates   (D) phosphates.

Answers: Test 3

1. B	3. B	5. B	7. D	9. C
2. C	4. A	6. C	8. D	10. B

SCIENCE: TEST 4

1. Of the following, the scientist who originated and developed the system of classifying the plants and animals of the earth was
   (A) Linnaeus   (B) Darwin
   (C) Mendel   (D) Agassiz.

2. Of the following substances, the one which is non-magnetic is
   (A) iron   (B) nickel
   (C) aluminum   (D) cobalt.

3. A scientist noted for his work in the field of antibiotics is:

(A) Salk   (B) Koch
(C) Banting   (D) Waksman.

4. The vascular system of the body is concerned with:

(A) respiration   (B) circulation of blood
(C) sense of touch   (D) enzymes.

5. The "bite," that is, the meeting of the teeth of the upper and lower jaws is described as:

(A) junction   (B) fixation
(C) occlusion   (D) mastication.

6. The transparent, slightly bulging tissue which covers the front sixth of the eyeball and is frequently referred to as the "window of the eyes" is the:

(A) iris   (B) cornea
(C) sciera   (D) retina.

7. The technical term for "cross-eyes" is

(A) myopia   (B) hyperopia
(C) strabismus   (D) trachoma.

8. A boy caught Japanese beetles, large and small, in an insect trap. One would be correct in assuming that the small ones:

(A) had been in the trap for a long time
(B) had recently hatched from eggs
(C) were adults
(D) were younger than the large ones.

9. To reduce soil acidity a farmer should use:

(A) lime   (B) manure
(C) phosphate   (D) peat moss.

10. Proteins are used by the body chiefly to:

(A) build cells
(B) develop antibodies
(C) maintain body heat
(D) produce nutrients.

Answers: Test 4

| 1. A | 3. D | 5. C | 7. C | 9. A |
| 2. C | 4. B | 6. B | 8. C | 10. A |

SCIENCE: TEST 5

1. In four hours the earth rotates:

(A) 20 degrees   (B) 40
(C) 60   (D) 120.

2. The cyclotron is used to:

(A) measure radioactivity
(B) measure the speed of the earth's rotation
(C) split atoms
(D) store radioactive energy.

3. Fossils are least often found in:

(A) igneous rock   (B) limestone
(C) metamorphic rock   (D) uranium.

4. The most efficient absorber of rays given off by radioactive substances is:

(A) carbon 14   (B) the Geiger counter
(C) lead   (D) uranium.

5. A person is more buoyant when swimming in salt water than in fresh water because:

(A) he keeps his head out of salt water
(B) salt coats his body with a floating membrane
(C) salt water has greater tensile strength
(D) salt water weighs more than an equal volume of fresh water.

6. The air around us is composed mostly of:

(A) carbon   (B) hydrogen
(C) nitrogen   (D) oxygen.

7. Of the following, the one which expands when it freezes is:

(A) carbon dioxide   (B) glass
(C) iron   (D) water.

8. Of the following statements about the auroras, the one which is correct is:

(A) they were studied during the IGY
(B) they are present most often at dawn
(C) they are seen only in the northern hemisphere
(D) they are solar flares.

9. Egg yolks cause silver to tarnish chiefly because they contain:

(A) carbon   (B) hydrogen
(C) nitrogen   (D) sulphur.

10. Of the following, the food which contains the largest amount of Vitamin C is:

(A) carrots   (B) lima beans
(C) sweet potatoes   (D) tomatoes.

Answers: Test 5

| 1. C | 3. A | 5. D | 7. D | 9. D |
| 2. C | 4. C | 6. C | 8. A | 10. D |

Social Science Tests

DIRECTIONS: Select from the choices offered in each of the following, the one which is correct or most nearly correct.

SOCIAL SCIENCE: TEST 1

1. The most important factor in England's rise to power in the 16th Century was the
   (A) riches brought home through expeditions to the New World
   (B) destruction of the Spanish naval power
   (C) world trip of Sir Francis Drake
   (D) conquest of New Amsterdam.

2. The Foreign Ministers Conference of Geneva, held in early 1959, dealt mainly with the problem of
   (A) West Berlin and the unification of Germany
   (B) the limitation of armaments
   (C) the withdrawal of Allied troops from Europe
   (D) international trade.

3. Of the following, the body of water that is completely land-locked is the
   (A) Black Sea   (B) Tyrrhenian Sea
   (C) Ionian Sea   (D) Caspian Sea.

4. The term "savanna" best describes large
   (A) forest areas of central Africa
   (B) swamp areas in the southern part of the United States
   (C) grassland regions of Brazil
   (D) constellations in the Milky Way.

5. The practical effect on persons traveling westward across the International Date Line would be to place them in time
   (A) back 24 hours   (B) ahead 12 hours
   (C) back 12 hours   (D) ahead 24 hours.

6. An excerpt from a biographical dictionary which reads as follows: "A great compromiser, author of the 'American System', member of the War-Hawk group during the War of 1812" would best fit
   (A) Henry Clay   (B) Daniel Webster
   (C) John C. Calhoun   (D) Stephen Douglas.

7. The ruling of the Supreme Court of the United States of America that racial segregation in public schools is unconstitutional is based on the
   (A) 5th Amendment
   (B) 13th Amendment
   (C) 14th Amendment
   (D) 15th Amendment

8. The Eisenhower Doctrine empowered the President of the United States to
   (A) construe an attack upon any member nation of NATO as an attack upon the United States
   (B) grant military aid to any SEATO nation according to the terms set forth in the agreement
   (C) use armed force to assist any nation in the Middle East that requests it to put down acts of Communist aggression upon that nation
   (D) withdraw financial aid granted an underdeveloped nation if that nation should fall within the Communist orbit.

9. In the United States of America, the most important factor among the following for the development of economic life since the Civil War has been the
   (A) acquisition of new territory
   (B) development of mass production
   (C) growth of the merchant marine
   (D) reforms in state banking.

10. The right of the United States Supreme Court to pass upon the constitutionality of laws is
    (A) expressly stated in the Federal Constitution
    (B) the result of Congressional action
    (C) assumed by the Supreme Court as a necessary function
    (D) the result of an amendment to the Federal Constitution.

Answers: Test 1

1. B	3. D	5. D	7. C	9. B
2. A	4. C	6. A	8. C	10. C

SOCIAL SCIENCE: TEST 2

1. The seating of an elected United States Senator or Representative follows his election except when
   (A) two-thirds of the membership of the House to which he was elected disallows it
   (B) a majority of both Houses sitting in joint session disallows it
   (C) disapproval by the legislature of his home state is sustained by the Judiciary Committee of the House to which he was elected
   (D) the governor of his state finds good cause for invalidating the election.

2. Which of the following features of our federal government can be traced most directly to our heritage of government in the English fashion?
    (A) our written constitution
    (B) our bicameral legislature
    (C) the supremacy of our federal judiciary
    (D) our system of checks and balances.

3. When a condition exists in which there is a decline in employment and an increase in government spending for relief, one would probably also find
    (A) an increase in bank loans
    (B) a decline in imports
    (C) an increase in installment buying
    (D) a reduction in bond purchases as compared with purchases of stocks.

4. In which of the following ways did the frontier influence American foreign policy?
    (A) it led to foreign alliances
    (B) it led to the development of a policy of isolation
    (C) it encouraged trade agreements with European nations
    (D) it stimulated interest in hemispheric co-operation.

5. The Conservation Movement in the United States of America got its major impetus from Theodore Roosevelt and
    (A) James G. Blaine
    (B) Gifford Pinchot
    (C) Elihu Root
    (D) William Jennings Bryan.

6. Which one of the following has changed from being a part of our "unwritten constitution" to being a part of our written Constitution?
    (A) limiting the number of terms of the presidency
    (B) formation of political parties
    (C) senatorial courtesy
    (D) provision for a President's cabinet.

7. In which one of the following paired events did the first event lead directly to the second?
    (A) bombing of Pearl Harbor — annexing of Hawaii by the United States of America
    (B) purchase of Alaska — cold war with Russia
    (C) failure of the League of Nations — World War I
    (D) assassination of President Garfield — passage of the Pendleton Civil Service Act.

8. Which item below pairs an outstanding American with a noteworthy contribution made by him?

    (A) Benjamin Franklin — leader of the Minutemen
    (B) Samuel Adams — Writs of Assistance
    (C) Haym Solomon — raising of funds to help Washington
    (D) James Otis — Boston Tea Party.

9. The defeat of the Persians by the Greek states may be likened in its effect on future history to the
    (A) defeat of the Moors at Tours
    (B) defeat of the Britons by Roman Legions
    (C) capture of the Philippines by the Japanese
    (D) rout of the Russians at Tannenberg Forest.

10. Which of the following events is the result of the three others mentioned?
    (A) the formation of the Holy Alliance
    (B) pronouncement of the Monroe Doctrine
    (C) revolts in Spanish territories in the Americas
    (D) Russian claims on the Pacific Coast of North America.

Answers: Test 2

1. A	3. B	5. B	7. D	9. A
2. B	4. B	6. A	8. C	10. B

SOCIAL SCIENCE: TEST 3

1. The stated purposes of UNESCO include all of the following *except*
    (A) to promote collaboration among nations to further human rights
    (B) to achieve freedom for all peoples without distinction of race, sex, language, or religion
    (C) to aid in the attainment by all peoples of the highest possible level of health
    (D) to use education, science, and culture to further justice throughout the world.

2. "Dependent on outside sources for iron ore, recent development of hydroelectric power, large consumption of wheat products, rainfall scarce in southern portion" — this description applies chiefly to
    (A) West Germany   (B) Italy
    (C) Sweden   (D) Soviet Union.

3. The difference between the rigorous climate of Labrador and the relatively salubrious climate of Norway is due chiefly to
    (A) prevailing winds and latitude
    (B) latitude and altitude
    (C) altitude and atmospheric pressure
    (D) water currents and prevailing winds.

4. Of the following geographic factors, the one that has most influenced the history of Russia is
   (A) its limited number of ice-free ports
   (B) its separation from Central Europe by high mountains
   (C) the lack of navigable rivers
   (D) the scarcity of rain.

5. In spite of a very short growing season, crops can be grown in the valley regions of Alaska because of the
   (A) heavy rainfall
   (B) long summer days
   (C) heavy winter snowfall
   (D) northeast trade winds.

6. All of the following reasons are given for the dwindling United States gold reserves *except*
   (A) United States imports exceed exports
   (B) American tourists spend millions of dollars abroad each year
   (C) United States industrial firms have invested heavily in foreign businesses
   (D) Foreign-made goods are purchased for United States military installations overseas.

7. Of the following, the chief cargo carried by ships going from the United States to South America is
   (A) cotton   (B) wheat
   (C) manufactured goods (D) fertilizer.

8. The term *parity price* is most directly associated with
   (A) a wholesaler's price
   (B) a middleman's profit
   (C) the rate fixed by the Federal Power Commission
   (D) the federal government's price support for farm produce.

9. In the event of the death or resignation of a United States Senator before his term expires, it is general practice to determine his successor for the remainder of that term by
   (A) appointment by the state legislature
   (B) an appointment by the President of the Senate
   (C) a temporary appointment by the governor of the state
   (D) the election of a Senator-at-large.

10. All of the following countries achieved national unity during the 19th Century *except*
    (A) Greece   (B) Czechoslovakia
    (C) Germany   (D) Italy.

Answers: Test 3

1. C	3. D	5. B	7. C	9. C
2. B	4. A	6. A	8. D	10. B

SOCIAL SCIENCE: TEST 4

1. Abraham Lincoln, Theodore Roosevelt, and Franklin Roosevelt had all of the following policies in common *except*
   (A) expansion of executive powers
   (B) economic betterment of the common man
   (C) land reforms
   (D) regulation of giant industries.

2. All of the following generally tend to retard inflation *except*
   (A) the purchase of Government bonds
   (B) the limitation of purchases on the installment plan
   (C) a high rate of taxation
   (D) the devaluation of the currency.

3. The Emancipation Proclamation was a (an)
   (A) law passed by Congress
   (B) amendment to the Federal Constitution
   (C) presidential order
   (D) joint resolution of Congress.

4. Of the following educational institutions, the one that was founded in colonial times is
   (A) Cornell University
   (B) College of William and Mary
   (C) Pennsylvania State University
   (D) University of New Hampshire.

5. Each of the following names is correctly matched with a historical movement *except*
   (A) Martin Luther — The Reformation
   (B) Jean Jacques Rousseau — The French Revolution
   (C) Edmund Cartwright — The Agricultural Revolution
   (D) Rudyard Kipling — Imperialism.

6. Of the following, the World War I ally that suffered the fewest military casualties was
   (A) Russia   (B) France
   (C) Italy   (D) United States.

7. A former New York State Governor who resigned his office to become a Justice of the United States Supreme Court was
   (A) Samuel J. Tilden
   (B) Herbert H. Lehman
   (C) Charles Evans Hughes
   (D) Grover Cleveland.

8. "The Politics of Upheaval" is one volume of a four-volume study of the Age of Roosevelt by
   (A) Allan Nevins

(B) A. M. Schlesinger, Jr.
(C) Eleanor Roosevelt
(D) Charles A. Beard.

9. The equity in a corporation that each share of capital stock represents is called its
(A) par value   (B) face value
(C) book value   (D) market value.

10. The Grand Coulee Dam harnesses the waters of the
(A) Colorado River   (D) Columbia River.
(C) Tennessee River   (B) Missouri River

Answers: Test 4

1. D	3. C	5. C	7. C	9. C
2. D	4. B	6. D	8. B	10. D

SOCIAL SCIENCE: TEST 5

1. Of the following statements, the one that best explains why Africa's interior remained undeveloped until recent times is:
(A) it has no large rivers
(B) it is entirely made up of jungle
(C) it has a very regular coastline
(D) it was completely unknown to the ancient and medieval worlds.

2. Of the following, the one that best describes a great circle on the globe is
(A) any parallel of latitude
(B) any meridian of longitude
(C) the air route taken over the Arctic
(D) a globe-circling line connecting places of equal temperature.

3. In the event that a presidential candidate does not receive a majority of the electoral votes, the president is elected by a
(A) majority of the members of both Houses of Congress
(B) majority vote in the House of Representatives, each state having one vote
(C) majority of the members of the Senate
(D) majority vote in the Senate, each state having one vote.

4. All of the following statements are taken from the Bill of Rights of the United States Constitution *except*
(A) the accused shall enjoy the right to have the assistance of counsel for his defense
(B) no religious test should ever be required as a qualification to any office or public trust in the United States

(C) no soldier shall, in time of peace, be quartered in any house, without the consent of the owner
(D) nor shall private property be taken for public use without just compensation.

5. Basic to the idea of a federal system of government is the
(A) existence of a strong executive
(B) division of power between national and state governments
(C) distribution of powers between two branches of the legislature
(D) existence of a Supreme Court.

6. Of the following, the European nation that dominated trade in Asia and the East Indies during the sixteenth century was
(A) Portugal   (B) Spain
(C) Holland   (D) England.

7. Of the following statements, the one which best describes the term "gerrymandering" is:
(A) organized pressure on legislators to pass certain legislation
(B) the rearrangement of election districts in the states so that the party in power gains control of as many as possible
(C) a practice whereby legislators secure support for enactment of laws by trading votes with their colleagues
(D) a clamoring for war or aggressive policy in foreign affairs.

8. Of the following, the event directly associated with the early history of New York State was
(A) Shays' Rebellion
(B) the publication of The Liberator
(C) the Whiskey Rebellion
(D) the trial of John Peter Zenger.

9. The United States has declared war at some time or other against all of the following countries *except*
(A) England   (B) Russia
(C) Spain   (D) Italy.

10. "In the field of world policy, I would dedicate this nation to the policy of the good neighbor" is a quotation from the speeches of
(A) Franklin D. Roosevelt
(B) Theodore Roosevelt
(C) Abraham Lincoln
(D) Calvin Coolidge.

Answers: Test 5

1. C	3. B	5. B	7. B	9. B
2. B	4. B	6. A	8. D	10. A

LSAT

PART FOUR

Law School Admission Test

(SAMPLE B)

You have studied the preceding material in this book faithfully — we trust. At this point, let us determine how much your study has done for you since you took the Sample LSAT on page 19.

The Sample Test you are about to take is patterned after the actual Law School Admission Test which you are going to take. Review the suggestions for taking the Sample Test (see page 13).

After you have taken this test, determine your unofficial percentile ranking by using the table on page 52. Compare this ranking with the ranking you achieved after taking the first Sample Test. The difference indicates the extent to which you have improved yourself by the study plan presented in this book.

Use the special Answer Sheet (next page) to record your answers.

ANSWER SHEET FOR SAMPLE TEST B

Morning Session

1 A B C D E	30 A B C D E	59 A B C D E	88 A B C D E	117 A B C D E
2 A B C D E	31 A B C D E	60 A B C D E	89 A B C D E	118 A B C D E
3 A B C D E	32 A B C D E	61 A B C D E	90 A B C D E	119 A B C D E
4 A B C D E	33 A B C D E	62 A B C D E	91 A B C D E	120 A B C D E
5 A B C D E	34 A B C D E	63 A B C D E	92 A B C D E	121 A B C D E
6 A B C D E	35 A B C D E	64 A B C D E	93 A B C D E	122 A B C D E
7 A B C D E	36 A B C D E	65 A B C D E	94 A B C D E	123 A B C D E
8 A B C D E	37 A B C D E	66 A B C D E	95 A B C D E	124 A B C D E
9 A B C D E	38 A B C D E	67 A B C D E	96 A B C D E	125 A B C D E
10 A B C D E	39 A B C D E	68 A B C D E	97 A B C D E	126 A B C D E
11 A B C D E	40 A B C D E	69 A B C D E	98 A B C D E	127 A B C D E
12 A B C D E	41 A B C D E	70 A B C D E	99 A B C D E	128 A B C D E
13 A B C D E	42 A B C D E	71 A B C D E	100 A B C D E	129 A B C D E
14 A B C D E	43 A B C D E	72 A B C D E	101 A B C D E	130 A B C D E
15 A B C D E	44 A B C D E	73 A B C D E	102 A B C D E	131 A B C D E
16 A B C D E	45 A B C D E	74 A B C D E	103 A B C D E	132 A B C D E
17 A B C D E	46 A B C D E	75 A B C D E	104 A B C D E	133 A B C D E
18 A B C D E	47 A B C D E	76 A B C D E	105 A B C D E	134 A B C D E
19 A B C D E	48 A B C D E	77 A B C D E	106 A B C D E	135 A B C D E
20 A B C D E	49 A B C D E	78 A B C D E	107 A B C D E	136 A B C D E
21 A B C D E	50 A B C D E	79 A B C D E	108 A B C D E	137 A B C D E
22 A B C D E	51 A B C D E	80 A B C D E	109 A B C D E	138 A B C D E
23 A B C D E	52 A B C D E	81 A B C D E	110 A B C D E	139 A B C D E
24 A B C D E	53 A B C D E	82 A B C D E	111 A B C D E	140 A B C D E
25 A B C D E	54 A B C D E	83 A B C D E	112 A B C D E	141 A B C D E
26 A B C D E	55 A B C D E	84 A B C D E	113 A B C D E	142 A B C D E
27 A B C D E	56 A B C D E	85 A B C D E	114 A B C D E	143 A B C D E
28 A B C D E	57 A B C D E	86 A B C D E	115 A B C D E	144 A B C D E
29 A B C D E	58 A B C D E	87 A B C D E	116 A B C D E	145 A B C D E

A B C D E   A B C D E   A B C D E   A B C D E   A B C D E

146   149   152   155   158

147   150   153   156   159

148   151   154   157   160

Afternoon Session

1   27   53   79   105
2   28   54   80   106
3   29   55   81   107
4   30   56   82   108
5   31   57   83   109
6   32   58   84   110
7   33   59   85   111
8   34   60   86   112
9   35   61   87   113
10   36   62   88   114
11   37   63   89   115
12   38   64   90   116
13   39   65   91   117
14   40   66   92   118
15   41   67   93   119
16   42   68   94   120
17   43   69   95   121
18   44   70   96   122
19   45   71   97   123
20   46   72   98   124
21   47   73   99   125
22   48   74   100   126
23   49   75   101   127
24   50   76   102   128
25   51   77   103   129
26   52   78   104   130

Morning Session

SECTION I — NONVERBAL REASONING
(35 minutes)

DIRECTIONS: In each of these questions, look at the symbols in the first two boxes. Something about the three symbols in the first box makes them alike; something about the two symbols in the other box with the question mark makes them alike. Look for some characteristic that is common to all symbols in the same box, yet makes them different from the symbols in the other box. Among the five answer choices, find the symbol that can best be substituted for the question mark, because it is *like* the symbols in the second box, and, *for the same reason,* different from those in the first box.

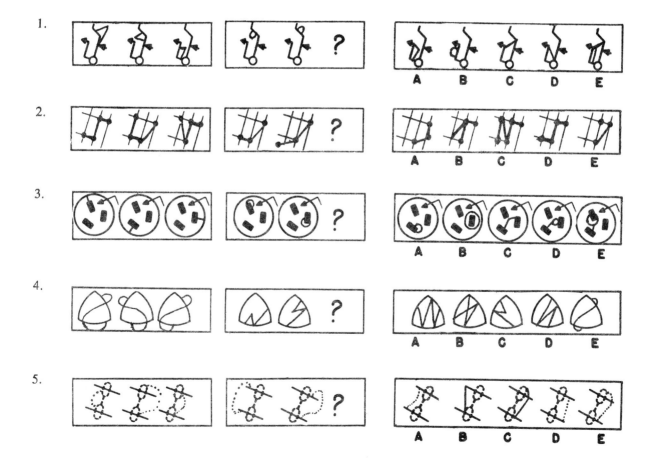

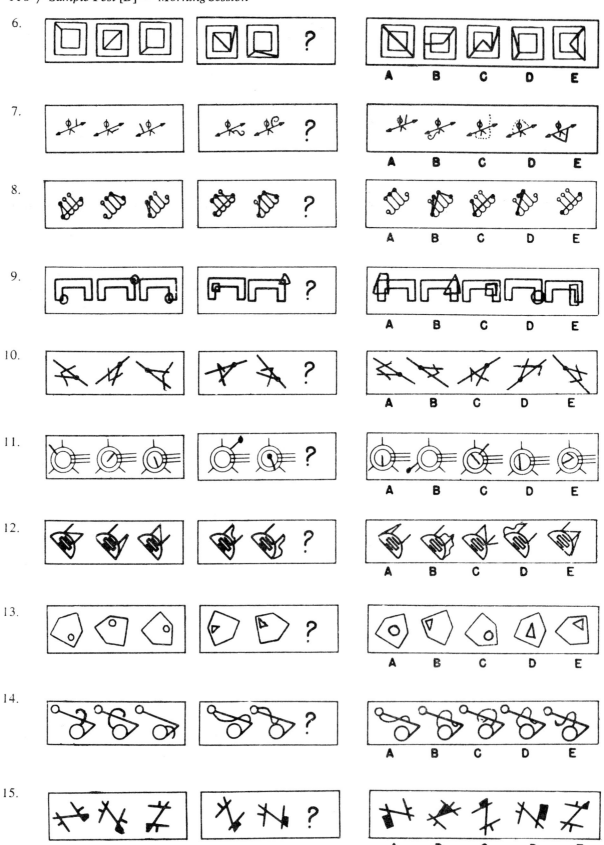

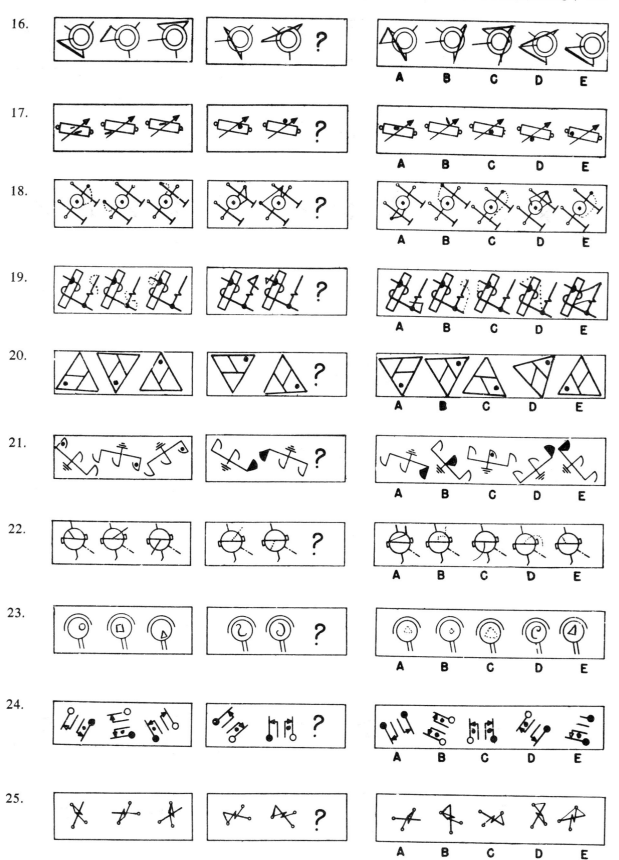

26.

27.

28.

29.

30.

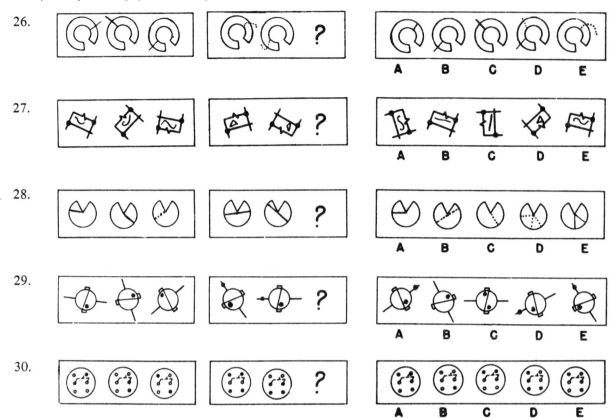

End Of Section I

If you finish before time is called, check your work on this section only.

When time is called, proceed directly to the next section and do not return to this section.

SECTION II — READING COMPREHENSION
(40 Minutes)

Directions: Below each of the following passages, you will find questions or incomplete statements about the passage. Each statement or question is followed by lettered words or expressions. Select the word or expression that most satisfactorily completes each statement or answers each question in accordance with the meaning of the passage. Write the letter of that word or expression on your answer paper.

Every profession or trade, every art, and every science has its technical vocabulary, the function of which is partly to designate things or processes which have no names in ordinary English, and partly to secure greater exactness in nomenclature. Such special dialects, or jargons, are necessary in technical discussion of any kind. Being universally undestood by the devotees of the particular science or art, they have the precision of a mathematical formula. Besides, they save time, for it is much more economical to name a process than to describe it. Thousands of these technical terms are very properly included in every large dictionary, yet, as a whole, they are rather on the outskirts of the English language than actually within its borders.

Different occupations, however, differ widely in the character of their special vocabularies. In trades and handicrafts, and other vocations, like farming and fishery, that have occupied great numbers of men from remote times, the technical vocabulary, is very old. It consists largely of native words, or of borrowed words that have worked themselves into the very fibre of our language. Hence, though highly technical in many particulars, these vocabularies are more familiar in sound, and more generally understood, than most other technicalities. The special dialects of law, medicine, divinity, and philosophy have also, in their older strata, become pretty familiar to cultivated persons, and have contributed much to the popular vocabulary. Yet every vocation still possesses a large body of technical terms that remain essentially foreign, even to educated speech. And the proportion has been much increased in the last fifty years, particularly in the various departments of natural and political science and in the mechanic arts. Here new terms are coined with the greatest freedom, and abandoned with indifference when they have served their turn. Most of the new coinages are confined to special discussions, and seldom get into general literature or conversation. Yet no profession is nowadays, as all professions once were, a close guild. The lawyer, the physician, the man of science, the divine, associates freely with his fellow-creatures, and does not meet them in a merely professional way. Furthermore, what is called "popular science" makes everybody acquainted with modern views and recent discoveries. Any important experiment, though made in a remote or provincial laboratory, is at once reported in the newspapers, and everybody is soon talking about it—as in the case of the Roentgen rays and wireless telegraphy. Thus our common speech is always taking up new technical terms and making them commonplace.

31. This passage is primarily concerned with
   (A) a new language
   (B) technical terminology
   (C) various occupations and professions
   (D) scientific undertakings
   (E) popular science.

32. Special words used in technical discussion
   (A) never last long
   (B) should be confined to scientific fields
   (C) should resemble mathematical formulae
   (D) are considered artificial speech
   (E) may become part of common speech.

33. It is true that
   (A) the average man often uses in his own vocabulary what was once technical language not meant for him
   (B) various professions and occupations often interchange their dialects and jargons
   (C) there is always a clearcut non-technical word that may be substituted for the technical word
   (D) an educated person would be expected to know most technical terms
   (E) everyone is interested in scientific findings.

34. In recent years, there has been a marked increase in the number of technical terms in the nomenclature of
   (A) farming   (B) government
   (C) botany   (D) fishing
   (E) sports.

35. The writer of this article was, no doubt,
    (A) a linguist   (B) an attorney
    (C) a scientist   (D) an essayist
    (E) a physician.

36. If we were to add a sentence to the end of this passage, it could very well be: The process began with
    (A) the conversion of the Anglo-Saxons, soon after their settlement of Britain.
    (B) the crossing of the Indus by Alexander the Great.
    (C) the birth of Italian fascism in 1914.
    (D) the advent of John Ruskin, a leader of the protest movement commonly called the "Esthetic Revolt."
    (E) embellishments of manuscripts by means of colored decorations.

It is almost a definition of a gentleman to say he is one who never inflicts pain. This description is both refined and, as far as it goes, accurate. He is mainly occupied in merely removing the obstacles which hinder the free and unembarrassed action of those about him; and he concurs with their movements rather than takes the initiative himself. His benefits may be considered as parallel to what are called comforts or conveniences in arrangements of a personal nature: like an easy chair or a good fire, which do their part in dispelling cold and fatigue, though nature provides both means of rest and animal heat without them. The true gentleman, in like manner, carefully avoids whatever may cause a jar or a jolt in the minds of those with whom he is cast;—all clashing of opinion, or collision of feeling, all restraint, or suspicion, or gloom, or resentment; his great concern being to make everyone at their ease and at home. He has his eyes on all his company; he is tender towards the bashful, gentle towards the distant, and merciful towards the absurd; he can recollect to whom he is speaking; he guards against unseasonable allusions, or topics which may irritate; he is seldom prominent in conversation, and never wearisome. He makes light of favors while he does them, and seems to be receiving when he is conferring. He never speaks of himself except when compelled, never defends himself by a mere retort, he has no ears for slander or gossip, is scrupulous in imputing motives to those who interfere with him, and interprets everything for the best. He is never mean or little in his disputes, never takes unfair advantage, never mistakes personalities or sharp sayings for arguments, or insinuates evil which he dare not say out. From a longsighted prudence, he observes the maxim of the ancient sage, that we should ever conduct ourselves towards our enemy as if he were one day to be our friend. He has too much good sense to be affronted at insults, he is too well employed to remember injuries, and too indolent to bear malice. He is patient, forbearing, and resigned, on philosophical principles; he submits to pain, because it is inevitable, to bereavement, because it is irreparable, and to death, because it is his destiny. If he engages in controversy of any kind, his disciplined intellect preserves him from the blundering discourtesy of better, perhaps, but less educated minds; who, like blunt weapons, tear and hack instead of cutting clean, who mistake the point in argument, waste their strength on trifles, misconceive their adversary, to leave the question more involved than they find it. He may be right or wrong in his opinion, but he is too clear-headed to be unjust; he is as simple as he is forcible, and as brief as he is decisive. Nowhere shall we find greater candor, consideration, indulgence: he throws himself into the minds of his opponents, he accounts for their mistakes. He knows the weakness of human reason as well as its strength, its province, and its limits. If he be an unbeliever, he will be too profound and large-minded to ridicule religion or to act against it; he is too wise to be a dogmatist or fanatic in his infidelity. He respects piety and devotion; he even supports institutions as venerable, beautiful, or useful, to which he does not assent; he honors the ministers of religion, and it contents him to decline its mysteries without assailing or denouncing them. He is a friend of religious toleration, and that, not only because his philosophy has taught him to look on all forms of faith with an impartial eye, but also from the gentleness and effeminacy of feeling, which is the attendant on civilization.

Not that he may not hold a religion too, in his own way, even when he is not a Christian. In that case his religion is one of imagination and sentiment; it is the embodiment of those ideas of the sublime, majestic, and beautiful, without which there can be no large philosophy. Sometimes he acknowledges the being of God, sometimes he invests an unknown principle or quality with the attributes of perfection. And this deduction of his reason, or creation of his fancy, he makes the occasion of such excellent thoughts, and the starting-point of so varied and systematic a teaching, that he even seems like a disciple of Christianity itself. From the very accuracy and steadiness of his logical powers, he is able to see what sentiments are consistent in those who hold any religious doctrine at all, and he appears to others to feel and to hold a whole circle of theological truths, which exist in his mind no otherwise than as a number of deductions.

37. According to the concept of a gentlemen expressed here, who would best fit the requirements of a gentleman?
    (A) Gen. George S. Patton
    (B) Richard Wagner
    (C) Friedrich Wilhelm Nietzsche
    (D) Robert Frost
    (E) Andrew Jackson.

38. A gentleman, here, is equated with
    (A) a jar or jolt
    (B) an easy chair or a good fire
    (C) a blunt weapon
    (D) a sharp saying
    (E) collisions and restraints.

39. A person who is "scrupulous in imputing motives" is
    (A) careful about accusing others
    (B) eager to prove another guilty
    (C) willing to falsify
    (D) unable to make decisions
    (E) suspicious concerning the actions of others.

40. This passage does not take into account a commonly held concept of a gentleman—namely,
    (A) consideration for others
    (B) refusal to slander
    (C) leniency toward the stupid
    (D) neatness in attire
    (E) willingness to forgive.

41. The most appropriate title for this passage would be
    (A) A Gentleman Now and Before
    (B) Definition of a Gentleman
    (C) Intellectualism and the Gentleman
    (D) Can a Gentleman Be Religious?
    (E) Gentlemen Prefer Easy Chairs.

42. The word "effeminacy" as used in this selection really means
    (A) femininity
    (B) childishness
    (C) cowardice
    (D) indecision
    (E) delicacy.

Monseigneur, one of the great lords in power at the Court, held his fortnightly reception in his grand hotel in Paris. Monseigneur was in his inner room, his sanctuary of sanctuaries, the Holiest of Holiests to the crowd of worshippers in the suite of rooms without. Monseigneur was about to take his chocolate. Monseigneur could swallow a great many things with ease, and was by some few sullen minds supposed to be rather rapidly swallowing France; but, his morning's chocolate could not so much as get into the throat of Monseigneur, witthout the aid of four strong men besides the Cook.

Yes. It took four men, all four a-blaze with georgeous decoration, and the Chief of them unable to exist with fewer than two gold watches in his pocket, emulative of the noble and chaste fashion set by Monseigneur, to conduct the happy chocolate to Monseigneur's lips. One lacquey carried the chocolate-pot into the sacred presence; a second milled and frothed the chocolate with the little instrument he bore for that function; a third presented the favoured napkin; a fourth (he of the two gold watches) poured the chocolate out. It was impossible for Monseigneur to dispense with one of these attendants on the chocolate and hold his high place under the admiring Heavens. Deep would have been the blot upon his escutcheon if his chocolate had been ignobly waited on by only three men; he must have died of two.

Monseigneur had been out at a little supper last night, where the Comedy and the Grand Opera were charmingly represented. Monseigneur was out at a little supper most nights, with fascinating company. So polite and so impressible was Monseigneur, that the Comedy and the Grand Opera had far more influence with him in the tiresome articles of state affairs and state secrets, than the needs of all France. A happy circumstance for France, as the like always is for all countries similarly favoured!—always was for England (by way of example), in the regretted days of the merry Stuart who sold it.

Monseigneur had one truly noble idea of general public business, which was, to let everything go on in its own way; of particular public business, Monseigneur had the other truly noble idea that it must all go his way—tend to his own power and pocket. Of his pleasures, general and particular, Monseigneur had the other truly noble idea, that the world was made for them. The text of his order (altered from the original by only a pronoun, which is not much) ran: "The earth and the fulness thereof are mine, saith Monseigneur."

43. The locale of this passage is
    (A) the opera
    (B) a sweet shop
    (C) the field of battle
    (D) an apartment
    (E) a church.

44. The tone of the selection is
    (A) serious
    (B) sarcastic
    (C) inquiring
    (D) objective
    (E) informative.

45. The chronological placement is the
    (A) twentieth century
    (B) eighteenth century
    (C) sixteenth century
    (D) fourteenth century
    (E) indefinite past or future.

46. Monseigneur represents
    (A) a person who elicits sympathy
    (B) a simpleton who cannot provide for himself
    (C) a profligate who cares little about others
    (D) an intellectual who dabbles in business matters
    (E) a miser who has moments of extravagance.

47. This passage was written by
    (A) John Steinbeck
    (B) Anatole France
    (C) Thomas Carlyle
    (D) Edna St. Vincent Millay
    (E) Charles Dickens.

48. The author is, with his reference to Monseigneur, using a literary device called
    (A) onomatopoeia
    (B) denouement
    (C) symbolism
    (D) psychogenesis
    (E) euphemism.

It is not easy to write a familiar style. Many people mistake a familiar for a vulgar style, and suppose that to write without affectation is to write at random. On the contrary, there is nothing that requires more precision, and, if I may so say, purity of expression, than the style I am speaking of. It utterly rejects not only all unmeaning pomp, but all low, cant phrases, and loose, unconnected slipshod allusions. It is not to take the first word that offers, but the best word in common use; it is not to throw words together in any combinations we please, but to follow and avail ourselves of the true idiom of the language. To write a genuine familiar or truly English style is to write as anyone would speak in common conversation who had a thorough command and choice of words, or who could discourse with ease, force, and perspicuity, setting aside all pedantic and oratorical flourishes. Or, to give another illustration, to write naturally is the same thing in regard to common conversation as to read naturally is in regard to common speech. It does not follow that it is an easy thing to give the true accent and inflection to the words you utter, because you do not attempt to rise above the level of ordinary life and colloquial speaking. You do not, assume, indeed, the solemnity of the pulpit, or the tone of stage declamation; neither are you at liberty to gabble on at a venture, without emphasis or discretion, or to resort to vulgar dialect or clownish pronunciation. You must steer a middle course. You are tied down to a given appropriate articulation, which is determined by the habitual associations between sense and sound, and which you can only hit by entering into the author's meaning, as you must find the proper words and style to express yourself by fixing your thoughts on the subject you have to write about. Anyone may mouth out a passage with a theatrical cadence, or get upon stilts to tell his thoughts; but to write or speak with propriety and simplicity is a more difficult task. Thus it is easy to affect a pompous style, to use a word twice as big as the thing you want to express: it is not so easy to pitch upon the very word that exactly fits it. Out of eight or ten words equally common, equally intelligible, with nearly equal pretensions, it is a matter of some nicety and discrimination to pick out the very one the preferableness of which is scarcely perceptible, but decisive.

49. According to the passage,
    (A) one should be permitted to speak in any way he wishes to
    (B) getting on stilts should aid one in speaking more effectively
    (C) it is easier to write pompously than simply
    (D) the preacher is a model of good speech speech
    (E) a grammatical background is not necessary for good writing.

50. If we were to break this selection up into two paragraphs, the second paragraph would best start with
    (A) "It is not to take the first word..."
    (B) "To write a genuine familiar..."
    (C) "It does not follow that..."
    (D) "You do not assume..."
    (E) "Or, to give another illustration..."

51. When the writer says, "You must steer a middle course," he means that
    (A) you should speak neither too loudly or too softly
    (B) you should speak neither too guardedly or too loosely
    (C) you should write as well as speak
    (D) you should not come to any definite conclusion about what is proper or not proper in speech
    (E) you should write neither too fast or too slowly.

52. By "cant phrases" is meant
    (A) a type of language which is peculiar to a particular class
    (B) a sing-song type of speech
    (C) expressions which consistently indicate refusal to do another's bidding
    (D) obscene language
    (E) obsolete expressions.

53. The passage implies
    (A) a large vocabulary is quite a worthwhile thing to have
    (B) actors are very good speakers
    (C) one's writing style may very well be one's speaking style
    (D) people should act familiar even with strangers
    (E) it doesn't make much difference whether you use one word or another.

54. The author
    (A) is critical of the person who converses in a manner which is easy to understand
    (B) implies that foreigners do not speak well
    (C) feels that there is no relationship between the sound of a word and its meaning
    (D) criticizes pomposity of style more so than vulgarity of style
    (E) urges us to speak like the actor or the preacher.

Studies serve for delight, for ornament, and for ability. Their chief use for delight, is in privateness and retiring; for ornament, is in discourse; and for ability, is in the judgment and disposition of business. For expert men can execute, and perhaps judge of particulars, one by one; but the general counsels, and the plots and marshalling of affairs, come best from those that are learned. To spend too much time in studies is sloth; to use them too much for ornament is affectation; to make judgment wholly by their rules, is the humour of a scholar. They perfect nature, and are perfected by experience: for natural abilities are like natural plants, that need pruning by study; and studies themselves do give forth directions too much at large, except they be bounded in by experience. Crafty men contemn studies, simple men admire them, and wise men use them; for they teach not their own use; but that is a wisdom without them, and above them, won by observation. Read not to contradict and confute; nor to believe and take for granted; nor to find talk and discourse; but to weigh and consider. Some books are to be tasted, others to be swallowed, and some few to be chewed, and digested; that is, some books are to read only in parts; others to be read, but not curiously; and some few to be read wholly, and with diligence and attention. Some books also may be read by deputy, and extracts made of them by others; but that would be only in the less important arguments, and the meaner sort of books; else distilled books are like common distilled waters, flashy things. Reading maketh a full man; conference a ready man; and writing an exact man. And therefore, if a man write little, he had need have a great memory; if he confer little, he had need have a present wit; and if he read little, he had need have much cunning, to seem to know that he doth not. Histories make men wise; poets witty; the mathematics subtle; natural philosophy deep; moral grave; logic and rhetoric able to contend. *Abeunt studia in mores.* Nay, there is no stond or impediment in the wit, but may be wrought out by fit studies: like as diseases of the body may have appropriate exercises. Bowling is good for the stone and reins; shooting for the lungs and breast; gentle walking for the stomach; riding for the head, and the like. So if a man's wit be wandering, let him study the mathematics; for in demonstrations, if his wit be called away ever so little, he must begin again. If his wit be not apt to distinguish and find differences, let him study the schoolmen, for they are *cymini sectores.* If he be not apt to beat over matters, and to call up one thing to prove and illustrate another, let him study the lawyers' cases. So every defect of the mind may have a special receipt.

55. The author believes that
    (A) every book should be read "from cover to cover"
    (B) in reading a book, one should skip a page or two if he feels tired
    (C) the technique of reading one book may, for the same person, be different from that of reading another book
    (D) some books ought to be destroyed
    (E) an interest in sports will result in more effective reading.

56. "Reading maketh a full man" means that
    (A) if one reads widely, he will be knowledgeable about many things
    (B) a man who reads much will grow tired of reading
    (C) a man is not really a man unless he reads
    (D) reading may allay a man's physical hunger
    (E) if you look at a person, you can tell what he reads.

57. It is obvious that the writer is a
    (A) modern writer
    (B) romanticist
    (C) playwright
    (D) classical scholar
    (E) sports reporter.

58. The passage indicates agreement with
    (A) the faculty psychologists
    (B) the existentialists
    (C) the dadaists
    (D) structural linguists
    (E) phoneticians.

59. The attitude expressed toward reading outlines rather than the books themselves is one of
    (A) modified approval
    (B) utter disdain
    (C) enthusiastic acceptance
    (D) complete indifference
    (E) pretended acclaim.

60. The word "stond" is obsolete for
    (A) astonishment
    (B) resistance
    (C) star
    (D) slander
    (E) understanding.

End Of Section II

If you finish before time is called, check your work on this section only.

When time is called, proceed directly to the next section and do not return to this section.

SECTION III — GRAPHS, CHARTS, AND TABLES
(45 minutes)

DIRECTIONS: This section of the test consists of questions based on charts, tables, and graphs. Each question is followed by five choices, only *one* of which is correct. Select the correct answer to each question and mark the corresponding space on the answer sheet.

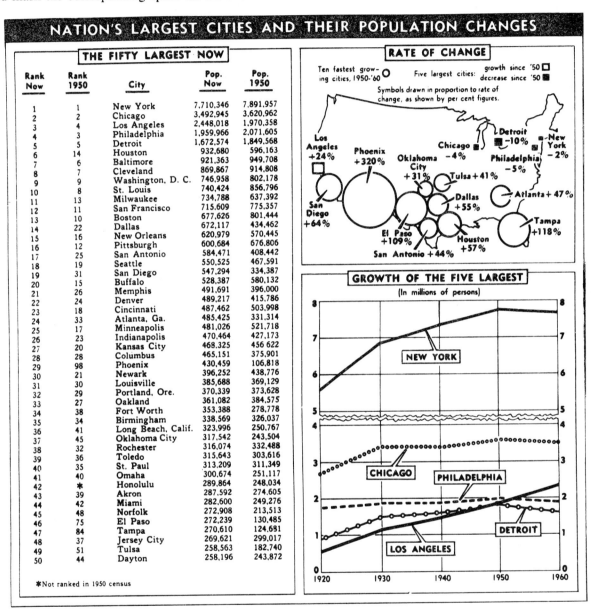

NATION'S LARGEST CITIES AND THEIR POPULATION CHANGES

THE FIFTY LARGEST NOW

Rank Now	Rank 1950	City	Pop. Now	Pop. 1950
1	1	New York	7,710,346	7,891,957
2	2	Chicago	3,492,945	3,620,962
3	4	Los Angeles	2,448,018	1,970,358
4	3	Philadelphia	1,959,966	2,071,605
5	5	Detroit	1,672,574	1,849,568
6	14	Houston	932,680	596,163
7	6	Baltimore	921,363	949,708
8	7	Cleveland	869,867	914,808
9	9	Washington, D. C.	746,958	802,178
10	8	St. Louis	740,424	856,796
11	13	Milwaukee	734,788	637,392
12	11	San Francisco	715,609	775,357
13	10	Boston	677,626	801,444
14	22	Dallas	672,117	434,462
15	16	New Orleans	620,979	570,445
16	12	Pittsburgh	600,684	676,806
17	25	San Antonio	584,471	408,442
18	19	Seattle	550,525	467,591
19	31	San Diego	547,294	334,387
20	15	Buffalo	528,387	580,132
21	26	Memphis	491,691	396,000
22	24	Denver	489,217	415,786
23	18	Cincinnati	487,462	503,998
24	33	Atlanta, Ga.	485,425	331,314
25	17	Minneapolis	481,026	521,718
26	23	Indianapolis	470,464	427,173
27	20	Kansas City	468,325	456,622
28	28	Columbus	465,151	375,901
29	98	Phoenix	430,459	106,818
30	21	Newark	396,252	438,776
31	30	Louisville	385,688	369,129
32	29	Portland, Ore.	370,339	373,628
33	27	Oakland	361,082	384,575
34	38	Fort Worth	353,388	278,778
35	34	Birmingham	338,569	326,037
36	41	Long Beach, Calif.	323,996	250,767
37	45	Oklahoma City	317,542	243,504
38	32	Rochester	316,074	332,488
39	36	Toledo	315,643	303,616
40	35	St. Paul	313,209	311,349
41	40	Omaha	300,674	251,117
42	*	Honolulu	289,864	248,034
43	39	Akron	287,592	274,605
44	42	Miami	282,600	249,276
45	48	Norfolk	272,908	213,513
46	75	El Paso	272,239	130,485
47	84	Tampa	270,610	124,681
48	37	Jersey City	269,621	299,017
49	51	Tulsa	258,563	182,740
50	44	Dayton	258,196	243,872

*Not ranked in 1950 census

RATE OF CHANGE

Ten fastest growing cities, 1950-'60 ○   Five largest cities: growth since '50 □ decrease since '50 ■

Symbols drawn in proportion to rate of change, as shown by per cent figures.

Detroit −10%   ■New York −2%
Chicago ■ −4%   Philadelphia −5%
Los Angeles +24%   Phoenix +320%   Oklahoma City +31%   Tulsa +41%   Atlanta +47%
San Diego +64%   Dallas +55%   Tampa +118%
El Paso +109%   Houston +57%
San Antonio +44%

GROWTH OF THE FIVE LARGEST
(In millions of persons)

NEW YORK
CHICAGO   PHILADELPHIA
DETROIT
LOS ANGELES

1920   1930   1940   1950   1960

Questions 61-67 are to be answered with reference to the above table-chart.

61. Next to the fastest and next to the slowest cities in growth among the following since 1950 are:
   (A) Chicago and El Paso
   (B) San Diego and New York
   (C) Tampa and Philadelphia
   (D) Detroit and Phoenix
   (E) Tulsa and Dallas.

62. Cities that did not decrease in population rank since 1950 are:
   (A) Los Angeles, Houston, St. Paul, Detroit
   (B) New York, Fort Worth, New Orleans, Seattle
   (C) Milwaukee, Dallas, Cincinnati, Denver
   (D) Omaha, Memphis, San Diego, San Antonio

(E) El Paso, Phoenix, Indianapolis, Washington.

63. Among the five largest cities, a significant population decline occurred:
(A) 1920-1930　　(B) 1930-1940
(C) 1940-1950　　(D) 1950-1960
(E) at no time.

64. The smallest per cent of decrease since 1950 has taken place in:
(A) Jersey City　　(B) Los Angeles
(C) Boston　　(D) Minneapolis
(E) New York.

65. The greatest per cent of increase since 1950 has occurred in:
(A) Omaha　　(B) Miami
(C) Houston　　(D) Louisville
(E) San Antonio.

66. The city that will probably show a population increase in 1970, according to the general pattern is:
(A) Philadelphia　　(B) New York
(C) Detroit　　(D) Los Angeles
(E) Chicago.

67. Three cities west of Chicago that make up about a million people in the aggregate are:
(A) Tulsa, Phoenix, and Oklahoma City
(B) Phoenix, Los Angeles, and El Paso

(C) San Diego, Oklahoma City, and Dallas
(D) Omaha, Tampa, and Phoenix
(E) San Antonio, Houston, and San Diego.

68. From 1920 to 1960, petroleum increased in use:
(A) 2 times　　(B) 6 times
(C) 12 times　　(D) 20 times
(E) 25 times

69. Nuclear use will have approximately how many consumption units in 1980?
(A) 9　　(B) 5
(C) 3　　(D) 1
(E) none of the above.

70. By 1980, coal-lignite is expected to have how many more consumption units than nuclear material will have?
(A) 2　　(B) 10
(C) 20　　(D) 30
(E) 40

71. The graph shows that there has been—or there is expected to be—an interruption in the increase in the use of coal-lignite and
(A) natural gas　　(B) shale
(C) petroleum　　(D) nuclear material
(E) "other" material.

72. The estimated use of nuclear materials in 1980 is what part of all other combined sources of world energy estimated for 1980?
(A) a little over one-half
(B) a little over one-quarter
(C) a little over three-quarters
(D) a little over one-seventh
(E) about equal.

Questions 73-79 are to be answered with reference to the graph on the next page.

73. The graph shows that there has been a steady increase in total degrees awarded from:
(A) 1900 to 1959　　(B) 1950 to 1959
(C) 1920 to 1959　　(D) 1890 to 1950
(E) 1900 to 1950

74. There have been more Bachelor's degrees granted in Education than in these fields combined:
(A) Business and Engineering
(B) Social Sciences and Business
(C) Engineering and Social Sciences
(D) Social Sciences, English, and Biological Sciences
(E) Business, English, Biological Sciences, and Physical Sciences.

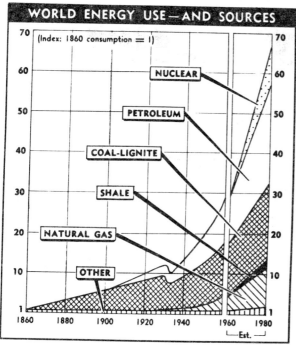

Questions 68-72 are to be answered with reference to the graph above.

AT GRADUATION TIME: DEGREES AND FIELDS OF STUDY

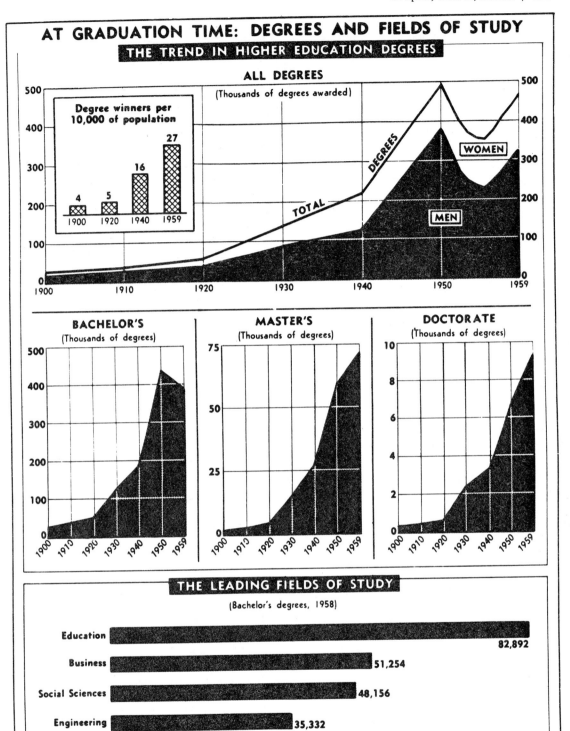

THE TREND IN HIGHER EDUCATION DEGREES

ALL DEGREES
(Thousands of degrees awarded)

Degree winners per 10,000 of population

1900	1920	1940	1959
4	5	16	27

DEGREES

TOTAL

WOMEN

MEN

BACHELOR'S
(Thousands of degrees)

MASTER'S
(Thousands of degrees)

DOCTORATE
(Thousands of degrees)

THE LEADING FIELDS OF STUDY
(Bachelor's degrees, 1958)

Field	Degrees
Education	82,892
Business	51,254
Social Sciences	48,156
Engineering	35,332
English	16,669
Biological Sciences	14,408
Physical Sciences	14,352
Fine and Applied Arts	12,252

75. In 1959, men earned about ? times the number of degrees that women earned?
    (A) 1½   (B) 2
    (C) 3   (D) 4
    (E) 5.

76. In 1950, the ratio of degrees earned in this order: Bachelor's — Master's — Doctorate . . . was approximately:
    (A) 5:2:1   (B) 50:10:1
    (C) 10:5:2   (D) 100:10:1
    (E) 70:10:1.

77. The sharpest rise in the acquisition of Doctorate degrees occurred between:
    (A) 1940-1950   (B) 1930-1940
    (C) 1920-1930   (D) 1910-1920
    (E) 1900-1910.

78. In 1950, Bachelor degrees constituted about what per cent of all degrees?
    (A) 65%   (B) 70%
    (C) 78%   (D) 86%
    (E) 92%.

79. A general trend upward in the number of degrees granted began in:
    (A) 1950   (B) 1951
    (C) 1953   (D) 1955
    (E) 1957.

ONE NEW YORK SCHOOL PROBLEM

Origins of newly admitted pupils who have lived in city for less than a year at time of registration.

Questions 80-84 are to be answered with reference to the graph above.

80. Puerto Rican children comprised approximately what part of newly admitted pupils in 1960?
    (A) one-twentieth   (B) one-tenth
    (C) one-fourth   (D) one-half
    (E) three-fourths.

81. The average number of newly admitted children from European and other countries for the period 1955-1960 is:
    (A) 6,600   (B) 36,000
    (C) 660   (D) 360
    (E) 10,000.

82. The total of newly admitted children from Europe and other countries and from Puerto Rico in 1957-1958 was about:
    (A) 10,000   (B) 15,000
    (C) 20,000   (D) 30,000
    (E) 40,000.

83. Newly admitted Puerto Rican pupils in 1960 increased over the same type of pupil admitted in 1950 by about:
    (A) 15%   (B) 25%
    (C) 40%   (D) 55%
    (E) 70%.

84. The graph cannot be used to give us the following information:
    (A) the combined total of the newly admitted pupils from Puerto Rico, Continental United States, and European and other countries
    (B) the per cent of Continental United States newly admitted pupils in relation to the total of the three groups of newly admitted pupils
    (C) the difference in number of newly admitted pupils from one period to another
    (D) the combined total of newly admitted Puerto Rican pupils and other Puerto Rican pupils
    (E) the increases and decreases of newly admitted pupils.

Questions 85-90 are to be answered with reference to the chart on the next page.

85. The population of Brazil in 2000 is expected to be about:
    (A) 100 million   (B) 150 million
    (C) 200 million   (D) 250 million
    (E) 300 million.

86. The growth rate of India, Japan, and Britain

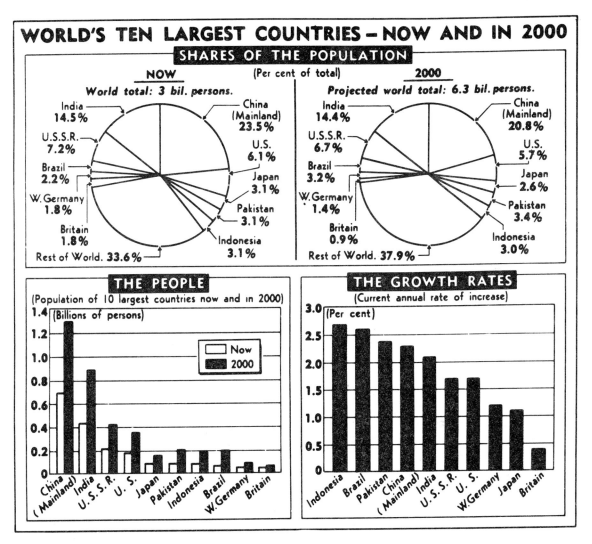

expressed as a combined average per cent of increase is approximately:

(A) 1%   (B) 2%
(C) 3%   (D) 4%
(E) 5%.

87. The per cent change in the population of the U. S. S. R. from now to 2000 is expected to be about:

(A) 50%   (B) 70%
(C) 80%   (D) 90%
(E) 100%.

88. The present population ratio for Britain, W. Germany, and the U. S. S. R. is:

(A) 1:1:4   (B) 1:1:2
(C) 1:2:3   (D) 1:3:5
(E) 1:3:3.

89. In 2000 the U. S. S. R. population is expected to exceed that of the United States by about:

(A) 40 million   (B) 60 million
(C) 80 million   (D) 100 million
(E) 120 million.

90. The combined population of the U. S. S. R. and China (Mainland) is expected to be approximately what part of the world population in 2000?

(A) one-tenth   (B) three-quarters
(C) one-fifth   (D) one-quarter
(E) one-half.

YEARLY INCIDENCE OF MAJOR CRIMES FOR COMMUNITY Z 1957-1959

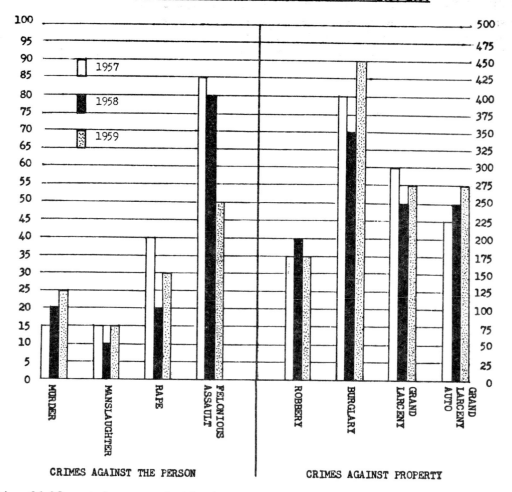

CRIMES AGAINST THE PERSON   CRIMES AGAINST PROPERTY

Questions 91-95 are to be answered with reference to the above chart.

91. Of the following crimes, the one for which the 1959 figure was greater than the average of the previous two years was:
    (A) grand larceny   (B) manslaughter
    (C) rape   (D) robbery
    (E) none of these.

92. If the incidence of burglary in 1960 were to increase over 1959 by the same number as it increased in 1959 over 1958, then the average for this crime for the four-year period from 1957 through 1960 would be, most nearly:
    (A) 100   (B) 400
    (C) 415   (D) 440
    (E) 480.

93. The above graph indicates that the *percentage* increase in grand larceny auto from 1958 to 1959 was:
    (A) 5%   (B) 10%
    (C) 15%   (D) 20%
    (E) 25%

94. The one of the following which cannot be determined because there is *not* enough information in the above graph to do so is
    (A) In regard to "Crimes Against Property," for the three-year period what percentage was committed in 1957?
    (B) In regard to all "Crimes Against the Person," for the three-year period what percentage were murders committed in 1958?
    (C) In regard to "Major Crimes," for the three-year period what percentage was committed in the first six months of 1958?
    (D) Which major crimes followed a pattern of continuing yearly increases for the three-year period?
    (E) For 1959, what was the ratio of robbery, burglary, and grand larceny crimes?

95. According to this graph, the combined number of all "Crimes Against Property" and all

"Crimes Against The Person" for 1959, as compared with the total for 1958,

(A) was twice as large
(B) was half as large
(C) was the same
(D) cannot be determined
(E) a little larger.

End Of Section III

If you finish before time is called, check your work on this section only.

When time is called, stop work.

Take a ten minute break . . . then proceed to Section IV.

SECTION IV — LAW INTERPRETATION
(35 minutes)

Part A. Cases and Principles

DIRECTIONS: This group of questions consists of the list of law cases followed by a list of legal principles. These principles may be either real or imaginary, but for purposes of this test you are to assume them to be valid. For each case you are to select the legal principle which is *most applicable* to the case. To indicate your answer blacken the space beneath the letter on the answer sheet which corresponds to the letter of the legal principle you select. These questions do not presuppose any specific legal knowledge on your part; you are to base your answers entirely on the ordinary processes of logical reasoning.

CASES

96. Black approaches a Ford convertible, breaks the glass in the side window, inserts his arm into the car and removes a lady's handbag. Black's attorney claims that his client's action does not constitute the crime of burglary.

97. Black breaks into an office building with the intention of stealing some furs stored therein. One of the floors of this building contains an apartment for the building superintendent and his family. Black is charged with 2nd degree burglary.

98. Black, intending to steal from the store of White, bored a hole through the floor with a centerbit but before he could proceed any further he was discovered and arrested. Part of the woodchips were found on the inside of the store, indicating that the end of the center-bit had penetrated into the building. Black's attorney claims that his client has not committed burglary since the instrument was used for effecting an entry only.

99. Black breaks into White's apartment with the intention of entering Brown's apartment next door for the purpose of committing larceny therein. Before he can effect an entry into

Brown's apartment, he is apprehended. Black's attorney claims that the extent of his client's offense is disorderly conduct.

100. Black, finding the door of the White Warehouse unlocked, pushed it open and entered the building. When apprehended by Patrolman Smith, he was examining the contents of the safe which he had apparently opened. Black's attorney claims that there is no basis for a charge of robbery.

PRINCIPLES

(A) If a building is so constructed as to consist of two or more parts occupied by different tenants separately for any purpose, each part or apartment is considered a separate building. The distinction is important for the purpose of establishing the degree of burglary committed since first or second degree burglary is committed only when a dwelling house is involved.

(B) Attempted burglary occurs when there is a breaking into of any degree.

(C) A passenger automobile is not a building within the meaning of the burglary statute.

(D) Malicious mischief requires some degree of destructiveness on the part of the offender.

(E) Robbery consists of the unlawful taking of personal property from the person against his will by force, violence, or fear of injury.

CASES

101. Jones deliberately poisons Smith with intent to kill him. Smith does not die from the effects of the poison until two years later. The prosecutor contends that Jones is guilty of murder.

102. X, intending to kill Y, discharges a revolver at him but the bullet misses Y and accidentally kills Z. The prosecutor contends that X is guilty of murder.

103. Tom Brown, aged 14 years, in company with 22 year old Frank Roe, held up a drug store. During the course of the hold-up, the proprietor in an attempt to resist the robbery, was shot and killed by Brown. The prosecutor contends that Roe is guilty of murder.

104. Jones encourages Smith to commit suicide by supplying him with a deadly drug. The prosecutor contends that Jones is guilty of murder.

105. A police officer is arresting a person for a misdemeanor. The latter attempts to slash the officer with a razor. The officer shoots and kills the attacker. The prosecutor contends that the officer is guilty of a crime.

PRINCIPLES

(A) A person who wilfully, in any manner, advises, encourages, abets or assists another person in taking the latter's life, is guilty of manslaughter.

(B) An adult may be charged with murder as a principal even though the killing was committed by his accomplice.

(C) Lawful defense of oneself, family or other person, upon reasonable grounds of belief that the slain person had intended to do great personal injury to the slayer or others, constitutes justifiable homicide.

(D) When there is deliberation and premeditation coupled with intent to kill, murder in the first degree is the appropriate charge. It is immaterial when the victim dies.

(E) Where the perpetrator has a specific intent to commit a crime, the law presumes that such intent applies to the natural and probable results of the act specifically intended. The specific intent which he had for the first crime is transferred as the constructive intent for the second crime.

Part B. Law Comprehension

DIRECTIONS: Several paragraphs pertaining to law are included in Part B. After each paragraph are questions that are to be answered in the light of the contents of that paragraph. Legal background is not required.

106. "He who by command, counsel or assistance procures another to commit a crime is, in morals and in law, as culpable as the visible actor himself, for the reason that the criminal act, whichever it may be, is imputable to the person who conceived it and set the forces in motion for its actual accomplishment." Of the following, the most accurate inference from the above sentence is that

(A) a criminal act does not have to be committed for a crime to be committed

(B) acting as counsellor for a criminal is a crime

(C) the mere counseling of a criminal act can never be a crime if no criminal act is committed

(D) only the visible actor himself can be criminal

(E) a person acting only as an adviser may be guilty of committing a criminal act.

107. "A 'felony' is a crime punishable by death or imprisonment in a state prison, and any other crime is a 'misdemeanor.'" According to this quotation the decisive distinction between "felony" and "misdemeanor" is the

(A) degree of criminality

(B) type of crime

(C) place of incarceration

(D) length of imprisonment

(E) judicial jurisdiction.

Answer questions 108 to 111 on the basis of the following statement:

"The question, whether an act, repugnant to the Constitution, can become the law of the land, is a question deeply interesting to the United States; but, happily, not of an intricacy proportioned to its interest. It seems only necessary to recognize certain principles, supposed to have been long and well established, to decide it. That the people have an original right to establish, for their future government, such principles as, in their opinion, shall most conduce to their own happiness, is the basis on which the whole American fabric has been erected. The exercise of this original right is a very great exertion; nor can it, nor ought it, to be frequently repeated. The principles, therefore, so established, are deemed fundamental: and as the authority from which they proceed is supreme, and can seldom act, they are designed to be permanent."

108. The best title for the above paragraph would be

(A) Principles of the Constitution

(B) The Root of Constitutional Change

(C) Only People Can Change the Constitution

(D) Methods of Constitutional Change.

109. According to the above paragraph, original right is

(A) fundamental to the principle that the people may choose their own form of government

(B) established by the Constitution

(C) the result of a very great exertion and should not often be repeated

(D) supreme, can seldom act, and is designed to be permanent.

110. Whether an act not in keeping with Constitutional principles can become law is, according to the above paragraph

(A) an intricate problem requiring great thought and concentration

(B) determined by the proportionate interests of legislators

(C) an intricate problem but not too complicated to be solved

(D) determined by certain long established principles, fundamental to Constitutional law

(E) an intricate problem, but less intricate than it would seem from the interest shown in it.

111. According to the above paragraph, the phrase, "and can seldom act," refers to

(A) the principles early enacted into law by Americans when they chose their future form of government

(B) the original rights of the people as vested in the Constitution

(C) the original framers of the Constitution

(D) the established, fundamental principles of government

(E) the body of laws by which the life and actions of all people are governed.

Answer Questions 112 to 115 solely on the basis of the following paragraph:

A foundling is an abandoned child whose identity is unknown. Desk officers shall direct the delivery, by a policewoman if available, of foundlings actually or apparently under two years of age to the New York Foundling Hospital, or if actually or apparently two years of age or over, to the Children's Center. In all other cases of dependent or neglected children, other than foundlings, requiring shelter, desk officers shall provide for obtaining such shelter as follows: between 9 a.m. and 5 p.m., Monday through Friday, by telephone direct to the Bureau of Child Welfare, in order to ascertain the shelter to which the child shall be sent; at all other times, direct the delivery of a child actually or apparently under two years of age to the New York Foundling Hospital, or if the child is actually or apparently two years of age or over to the Children's Center.

112. According to this paragraph, it would be most correct to state that

(A) a foundling as well as a neglected child may be delivered to the New York Foundling Hospital

(B) a foundling but not a neglected child may be delivered to the Children's Center

(C) a neglected child requiring shelter, regardless of age, may be delivered to the Bureau of Child Welfare

(D) the Bureau of Child Welfare may determine the shelter to which a foundling may be delivered.

113. According to this paragraph, the desk officer shall provide for obtaining shelter for a neglected child, apparently under two years of age, by

(A) directing its delivery to Children's Center if occurrence is on a Monday between 9 a.m. and 5 p.m.

(B) telephoning the Bureau of Child Welfare if occurrence is on a Sunday

(C) directing its delivery to the New York Foundling Hospital if occurrence is on a Wednesday at 4 p.m.

(D) telephoning the Bureau of Child Welfare if occurrence is at 10 a.m. on a Friday.

114. According to this paragraph, the desk officer should direct delivery to the New York Foundling Hospital of any child who is

(A) actually under 2 years of age and requires shelter

(B) apparently under two years of age and is neglected or dependent

(C) actually 2 years of age and is a foundling

(D) apparently under 2 years of age and has been abandoned.

115. A 12-year-old neglected child requiring shelter is brought to a police station on Thursday at 2 p.m. Such a child should be sent to

(A) a shelter selected by the Bureau of Child Welfare

(B) a shelter selected by the desk officer

(C) the Children's Center

(D) the New York Foundling Hospital when a brother or sister, under 2 years of age, also requires shelter.

Answer Questions 116 to 118 solely on the basis of the following paragraph:

"All applicants for an original license to operate a catering establishment shall be fingerprinted. This shall include the officers, employees and stockholders of the company and the members of a partnership. In case of a change, by addition or substitution, occurring during the existence of a license, the person added or substituted shall be fingerprinted. However, in the case of a hotel containing more than 200 rooms, only the officer or manager filing the application is required to be fingerprinted. The police commissioner may also at his discretion exempt the employees and stockholders of any company. The fingerprints shall be taken on one copy of form C.E. 20 and on two copies of C.E. 21. One copy of form C.E. 21 shall accompany the application. Fingerprints are not required with a renewal application."

116. According to this paragraph, an employee added to the payroll of a licensed catering establishment which is not in a hotel
    (A) must always be fingerprinted
    (B) must be fingerprinted unless he has been previously fingerprinted for another license
    (C) must be fingerprinted unless exempted by the police commissioner
    (D) must be fingerprinted only if he is the manager or an officer of the company.

117. According to this paragraph, it would be most accurate to state that
    (A) form C.E. 20 must accompany a renewal application
    (B) form C.E. 21 must accompany all applications
    (C) form C.E. 21 must accompany an original application
    (D) both forms C.E. 20 and C.E. 21 must accompany all applications.

118. A hotel of 270 rooms has applied for a license to operate a catering establishment on the premises. According to the instructions for fingerprinting given in this paragraph
    (A) the officers, employees and stockholders shall be fingerprinted
    (B) the officers and the manager shall be fingerprinted
    (C) the employees shall be fingerprinted
    (D) the officer filing the application shall be fingerprinted.

Questions 119 and 120 are to be answered solely on the basis of the following paragraph:

"If the second or third felony is such that, upon a first conviction, the offender would be punishable by imprisonment for any term less than his natural life, then such person must be sentenced to imprisonment for an indeterminate term, the minimum of which shall be not less than one-half of the longest term prescribed upon a first conviction, and the maximum of which shall be not longer than twice such longest term; provided, however, that the minimum sentence imposed hereunder upon such second or third felony offender shall in no case be less than five years; except that where the maximum punishment for a second or third felony offender hereunder is five years or less, the minimum sentence must be not less than two years."

119. According to this paragraph, a person who has a second felony conviction, shall receive as a sentence for that second felony an indeterminate term
    (A) not less than twice the minimum term prescribed upon a first conviction as a maximum
    (B) not less than one-half the maximum term of his first conviction as a minimum
    (C) not more than twice the minimum term prescribed upon a first conviction as a minimum
    (D) with a maximum of not more than one-half the longest term prescribed upon conviction for his first crime
    (E) with a maximum of not more than twice the longest term prescribed for a first conviction for this crime.

120. According to this paragraph, if the term for this crime for a first offender is up to three years, the possible indeterminate term for this crime as a second or third felony shall have a
    (A) minimum of not less than five years
    (B) maximum of not more than five years
    (C) minimum of not less than one and one-half years
    (D) maximum of not less than six years
    (E) minimum of not more than two years.

End Of Section IV

SECTION V — NONVERBAL REASONING
(30 minutes)

DIRECTIONS: The following questions consist of five symbols at the left and five other symbols labeled (A), (B), (C), (D), and (E) at the right. In each question, first study the series of symbols at the left; then from the symbols at the right, labeled (A), (B), (C), (D), and (E) select the one which continues the series most completely.

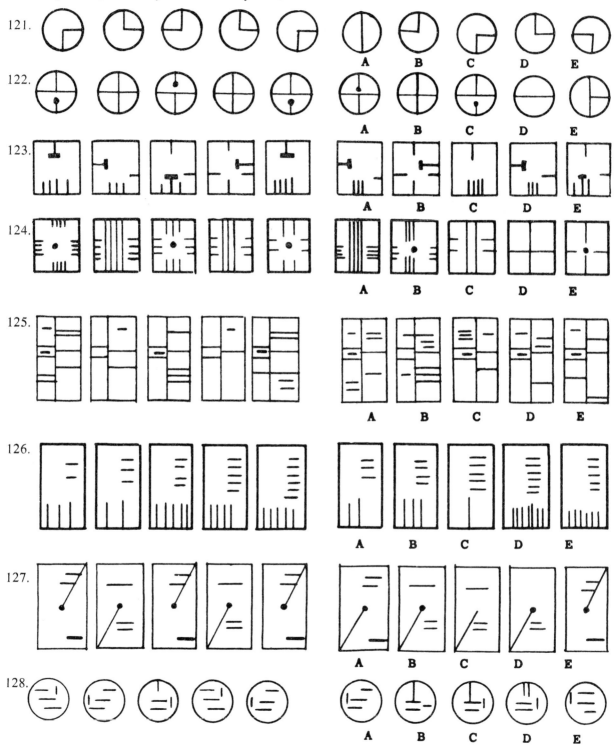

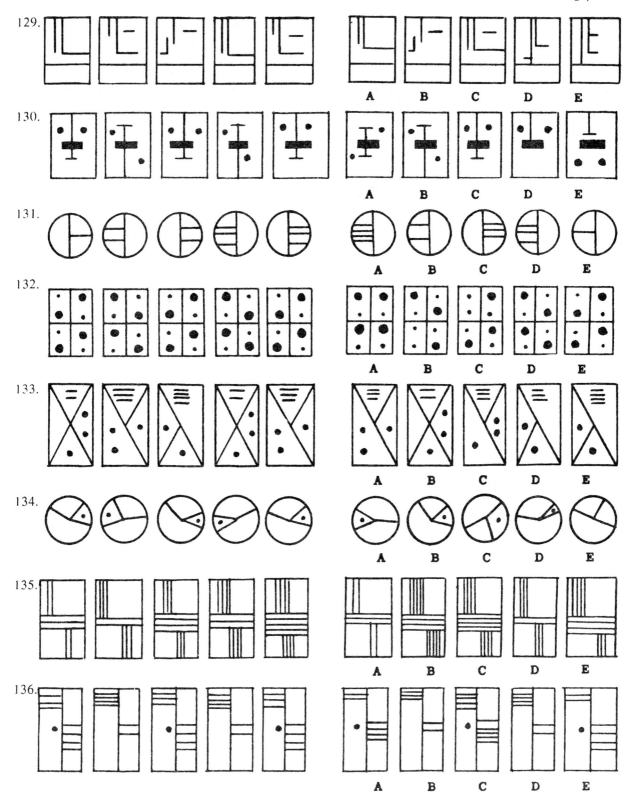

129.

130.

131.

132.

133.

134.

135.

136.

A   B   C   D   E

DIRECTIONS: In the following questions, the symbols in columns 1 and 2 have a relationship to each other. Select from the symbols in columns (A), (B), (C), (D) and (E) the symbol which has the same relationship to the symbol in column 3, as the symbol in column 2 has to the symbol in column 1.

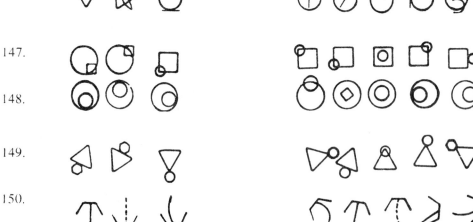

1 : 2 : : 3 : ?

A B C D

137.

138.

139.

140.

A B C D E

141.

142.

143.

144.

145.

146.

147.

148.

149.

150.

End Of Section V

If you finish before time is called, check your work on this section only.

When time is called, proceed directly to the next section and do not return to this section.

SECTION VI — REMEMBERING MAIN IDEAS AND DETAILS (20 minutes)

PART A. (10 minutes)

Directions: This is a test to determine your ability to remember main ideas and significant details. You are to read the four passages that follow in a period of 10 minutes altogether. It is suggested that you divide your time equally among the four passages. When the time is up, you will be asked to recall certain ideas and facts about the four passages. You will not be able to refer back to the passages after 10 minutes.

PASSAGE 1

Of all the areas of learning the most important is the development of attitudes. Emotional reactions as well as logical thought processes affect the behavior of most people.

"The burnt child fears the fire" is one instance; another is the rise of despots like Hitler. Both these examples also point up the fact that attitudes stem from experience. In the one case the experience was direct and impressive; in the other it was indirect and cumulative. The Nazis were indoctrinated largely by the speeches they heard and the books they read.

The classroom teacher in the elementary school is in a strategic position to influence attitudes. This is true partly because children acquire attitudes from those adults whose word they respect.

Another reason it is true is that pupils often delve somewhat deeply into a subject in school that has only been touched upon at home or has possibly never occurred to them before. To a child who had previously acquired little knowledge of Mexico, his teacher's method of handling such a unit would greatly affect his attitude toward Mexicans.

The media through which the teacher can develop wholesome attitudes are innumerable. Social studies (with special reference to races, creeds and nationalities), science, matters of health and safety, the very atmosphere of the classroom . . . these are a few of the fertile fields for the inculcation of proper emotional reactions.

However, when children come to school with undesirable attitudes, it is unwise for the teacher to attempt to change their feelings by cajoling or scolding them. She can achieve the proper effect by helping them obtain constructive experiences.

To illustrate, first-grade pupils afraid of policemen will probably alter their attitudes after a classroom chat with the neighborhood officer in which he explains how he protects them. In the same way, a class of older children can develop attitudes through discussion, research, outside reading and all-day trips.

Finally, a teacher must constantly evaluate her own attitudes, because her influence can be deleterious if she has personal prejudices. This is especially true in respect to controversial issues and questions on which children should be encouraged to reach their own decisions as a result of objective analysis of all the facts.

PASSAGE 2

The operation of the gelatin process is undoubtedly the simplest of all modern duplicating methods. In order to reproduce copies of typewritten matter, for example, the copy is typed on an ordinary sheet of paper by any typist in the customary way. The only difference between this first operation and regular everyday typing is that a special typewriter ribbon impregnated with hectograph ink is necessary. The typed copy is then transferred to the gelatin by pressing the typed matter tightly against the gelatin surface, leaving it for a few minutes, and then removing the paper that bore the original copy. The gelatin is simply a spongy, jelly-like material in sheet form that absorbs and holds in reverse any copy done in hectograph ink. Thus, when blank impression paper is pressed against the inked portion of the gelatin it picks up a print of the image. This can be repeated as many as 100 times, with the gelatin releasing just a little of the ink each time. This factor of single inking is the reason for the gradual lightening of copies on a run of more than fifty copies.

After the desired copies have been made the gelatin may be used again but not at a future time or for different copy without additional preparation. Aniline inks sink gradually down into the gelatin; after an hour of either use or non-use, they no longer reproduce satisfactory copies. The gelatin's preparation for further use consists simply of allowing it to remain untouched for about eight hours. At the end of this time the ink will have sunk far enough below the gelatin surface so that it will no longer print. New copy can then be transferred from a new master to the newly cleared surface. This gelatin sheet may thus be used over and over again for a considerable length of time. It is time and exposure to natural elements rather than usage that determine the life of this gelatin duplicating medium.

End Of Section VI — Part A

When time is called, proceed directly to Part B and do not return to Part A.

SECTION VI — Part B.

PART B. (10 minutes)

Directions: Answer the following questions in accordance with the contents of the preceding passages. You are not to turn back to the passages.

PASSAGE ON EDUCATION

151. The central idea conveyed in the above passage is that
    (A) attitudes affect our actions
    (B) teachers play a significant role in developing or changing pupils' attitudes
    (C) attitudes can be changed by some classroom experiences
    (D) by their attitudes, teachers inadvertently affect pupils' attitudes
    (E) attitudes have nothing to do with our actions.

152. The author implies that
    (A) the teacher should guide all discussions by revealing her own attitude
    (B) in some aspects of social studies a greater variety of methods can be used in the upper grades than in the lower grades
    (C) people usually act on the basis of reasoning rather than on emotion
    (D) children's attitudes often come from those of other children
    (E) parents are not responsible for pupil attitudes.

153. A statement *not* made or implied in the passage is that
    (A) attitudes can be based on the learning of falsehoods
    (B) a child can develop in the classroom an attitude about the importance of brushing his teeth
    (C) attitudes cannot easily be changed by rewards and lectures
    (D) the attitudes of children are influenced by all the adults in their environment
    (E) attitudes may be measured scientifically.

154. The passage specifically states that
    (A) direct experiences are more valuable than indirect ones
    (B) whatever attitudes a child learns in school have already been introduced at home

(C) teachers should always conceal their own attitudes
(D) teachers can sometimes have an unwholesome influence on children
(E) policemen must not regard all children alike.

155. The writer does *not* bring out
    (A) the importance of experience in building attitudes
    (B) how fear sometimes governs attitudes
    (C) how attitudes can be changed in the home environment
    (D) how reading affects attitudes
    (E) the place of attitudes in education.

PASSAGE ON GELATIN

156. When preparing typed material for transfer to the gelatin, the typing is done
    (A) with a regular typewriter ribbon
    (B) with a special typewriter ribbon impregnated with hectograph ink
    (C) with a special carbon paper ribbon
    (D) without any ribbon so that the type can cut into the gelatin
    (E) with gelatin ribbon.

157. When preparing typed material for transfer to the gelatin, the material should first be typed on
    (A) regular paper
    (B) carbon paper
    (C) gelatin paper
    (D) waxed paper
    (E) tissue paper.

158. The typed material is transferred to the gelatin by pressing the typed side of the paper against the
    (A) gelatin surface
    (B) reverse of the gelatin surface
    (C) blank impression paper
    (D) reverse of the blank impression paper
    (E) typewriter carriage.

159. Copy done in hectograph ink is absorbed and held by the gelatin
    (A) from the blank impression paper
    (B) from the carbon copy
    (C) upside down
    (D) in reverse
    (E) by osmosis.

160. Blank impression paper picks up its material directly from
    (A) the uninked portion of the gelatin
    (B) the uninked portion of the original copy
    (C) the inked portion of the gelatin
    (D) the inked portion of the original copy
    (E) the inked portion of the carbon copy.

End Of Section VI

When time is called, stop work on this section.

The Morning Session part of the test is now concluded.

ANSWER KEY TO LAW SCHOOL ADMISSION TEST (B)

Morning Session

1. B	17. D	33. A	49. C	65. C	81. A	97. A	113. D	129. B	145. E
2. A	18. A	34. B	50. C	66. D	82. C	98. B	114. D	130. B	146. D
3. A	19. A	35. A	51. B	67. A	83. D	99. B	115. A	131. A	147. A
4. C	20. A	36. A	52. A	68. B	84. D	100. E	116. C	132. D	148. D
5. A	21. D	37. D	53. C	69. A	85. C	101. D	117. C	133. E	149. D
6. D	22. E	38. B	54. D	70. A	86. A	102. E	118. D	134. A	150. C
7. B	23. D	39. A	55. C	71. C	87. E	103. B	119. E	135. B	151. B
8. B	24. D	40. D	56. A	72. D	88. A	104. A	120. C	136. D	152. B
9. C	25. C	41. B	57. D	73. E	89. B	105. C	121. E	137. A	153. D
10. C	26. E	42. E	58. A	74. D	90. D	106. E	122. B	138. A	154. D
11. B	27. D	43. D	59. A	75. B	91. B	107. C	123. A	139. B	155. C
12. D	28. B	44. B	60. B	76. E	92. D	108. B	124. C	140. C	156. B
13. B	29. E	45. B	61. C	77. A	93. B	109. A	125. B	141. A	157. A
14. A	30. C	46. C	62. B	78. D	94. C	110. E	126. E	142. B	158. A
15. C	31. B	47. E	63. D	79. D	95. E	111. A	127. B	143. D	159. D
16. B	32. E	48. C	64. E	80. C	96. C	112. A	128. C	144. E	160. C

Afternoon Session

SECTION I — RECOGNIZING ERRORS
(20 minutes)

DIRECTIONS: Among the sentences in this group are some which cannot be accepted in formal, written English for one or another of the following reasons:

Poor Diction: The use of a word which is improper either because its meaning does not fit the sentence or because it is not acceptable in formal writing.
Example: The audience was strongly effected by the senator's speech.

Verbosity: Repetitious elements adding nothing to the meaning of the sentence and not justified by any need for special emphasis.
Example: At that time there was then no right of petition.

Faulty Grammar: Word forms and expressions which do not conform to the grammatical and structural usages required by formal written English (errors in case, number, parallelism and the like).
Example: Everyone in the delegation had their reasons for opposing the measure.

No sentence has more than one of these errors. Some sentences have no errors. Read each sentence carefully; then on your answer sheet blacken the space under:

D if the sentence contains an error in diction,

V if the sentence is verbose,

G if the sentence contains faulty grammar,

O if the sentence contains none of these errors.

1. It was he, not I, who became nauseous because of the boat's motion.
2. If he would have heeded my warning, he would have remained alive.
3. Making friends is more rewarding than to be antisocial.
4. Although Richard graduated high school with honors, he failed three subjects as a college freshman.
5. Sitting on that bench are a student who is majoring in English and one who is majoring in French.
6. The chief attraction of the garden is the azaleas.
7. She wrung her hands in her distress.
8. Jerry Cruncher was very aggravated by his wife's praying.
9. Two qualities of a true gentleman are respect and trust in his fellow men.
10. He found the climate of Arizona very healthful.
11. He is one of those people who do their best work solely alone.
12. They invited my whole family to the cookout— my father, my mother, my sister and I.
13. Having raked the beach for hours, the search for the lost ring was abandoned.
14. According to the last census, there are less men than women in big cities.
15. The cake turned out heavy because she used too much excess flour.
16. Such a large amount of pupils in a room is bound to cause confusion.
17. Her brother never has and never will be dependable.
18. Have you ever swum out to the breakwater?
19. My mother is making chicken for dinner tonight, and I don't want to miss it.
20. Paul asked, "Do you believe in the proverbial maxim, "Misery loves company?"

End Of Section I
If you finish before time is called, check your work on this section only.
When time is called, proceed directly to the next section and do not return to this section.

SECTION II—ORGANIZATION OF IDEAS (20 minutes)

Directions: Each set of questions in this test consists of several statements. Most of the statements refer to the same subject or idea. The statements can be classified as follows:

(A) the *central idea* to which most of the statements are related;

(B) *main supporting ideas,* which are general points directly related to the central idea;

(C) *illustrative facts* or detailed statements, which document the main supporting idea;

(D) statements *irrelevant* to the central idea.

The statements may be regarded as headings in an outline: they are *not* sentences taken from one complete paragraph. The outline might, for example, have the following form:

> A. The Central Idea
>   B. Main Supporting Idea
>   C. Illustrative Fact
>   B. Main Supporting Idea
>   C. Illustrative Fact
>   C. Illustrative Fact

USE THIS SPACE FOR YOUR SCRATCHWORK

SET A

21. In the great later tragedies, the internal conflict is more emphasized.
22. In as excellent an early tragedy as *Romeo and Juliet,* the hero fights more with outside obstacles than with himself.
23. Ben Jonson was a contemporary of Shakespeare's.
24. In his earlier plays, his men and women are more engaged with external forces than with internal struggles.
25. Consider later plays such as *Hamlet* and *Macbeth.*
26. The change in the treatment of his characters is a significant index to Shakespeare's growth as a dramatist.

SET B

27. It contains an enormous variety of regions and cultures.
28. Another region consists of pioneer Russian farm settlements.
29. All of these tribes are subjected to the powerful impact of the Soviet Revolution.
30. Still another region is made up of old colorful oases.
31. Soviet Asia is a vividly interesting area.
32. One such region is the frozen tundra toward the Arctic.
33. There is a mosaic of peoples and tribes in this Asiatic part of the Soviet Union.
34. They are further influenced by tendencies toward modernization and industrialization.

SET C

35. He is the only poet since the 18th century who has been a public man in his own country.
36. He saw his dreams of liberty blotted out in horror by "innumerable clanging wings that have put out the moon."
37. Yeats wrote a number of plays.
38. In width of scope, Yeats far exceeds any of his contemporaries.
39. Moreover, he is the only poet since Milton who has been a public man at a time when his country was involved in a struggle for political liberty.
40. Yeats responded with all his heart to the reality and the romance of Ireland's struggle for independence.

Directions: Arrange each group of five sentences in logical order so that each group makes up a well-organized paragraph. (Scratchwork may be done in the testbook.) Then answer the questions that follow each group of five sentences.

End Of Section II

If you finish before time is called, check your work on this section only.
When time is called, proceed directly to the next section and do not return to this section.

SECTION III—EDITING ABILITY
(20 minutes)

Directions: A sentence is given, of which one part is underlined. Following the sentence are five choices. The first (A) choice simply repeats the underlined part. Then you have four additional choices which suggest other ways to express the underlined part of the original sentence. If you think that the underlined part is correct as it stands, write the answer A. If you believe that the underlined part is incorrect, select from the other choices (B or C or D or E) whichever you think is correct. Grammar, sentence structure, word usage, and punctuation are to be considered in your decision. The original meaning of the sentence must be retained.

41. Crossing the bridge, a glimpse of the islands was caught.
    (A) a glimpse of the islands was caught.
    (B) a glimpse of the islands were caught.
    (C) we caught a glimpse of the islands.
    (D) the islands were caught a glimpse of.
    (E) we caught a glimpse of the islands' view.

42. This book has been laying here for weeks.
    (A) laying here for weeks.
    (B) laying here weeks.
    (C) laying down here for weeks.
    (D) lieing here for weeks.
    (E) lying here for weeks.

43. When my brother will come home, I'll tell him you called.
    (A) will come home,
    (B) will come home
    (C) will have come home,
    (D) comes home,
    (E) has come home,

44. After he graduated school, he entered the army,
    (A) After he graduated school,
    (B) After he was graduated from school,
    (C) When he graduated school,
    (D) After he graduated school
    (E) As he was graduated from school,

45. I think they, as a rule, are much more conniving than us.
    (A) as a rule, are much more conniving than us.
    (B) as a rule are much more conniving than us.
    (C) as a rule, are much more conniving than we.
    (D) as a rule; are much more conniving than us.
    (E) are, as a rule, much more conniving than us.

46. Sitting around the fire, mystery stories were told by each of us.
    (A) mystery stories were told by each of us.
    (B) mystery stories were told by all of us.
    (C) each of us told mystery stories.
    (D) stories of mystery were told by each of us.
    (E) there were told mystery stories by each of us.

47. The loud noise of the subway trains and the trolley cars frighten people from the country.
    (A) frighten people from the country.
    (B) frighten country people.
    (C) frighten persons from the country.
    (D) frightens country people.
    (E) frighten people who come from the country.

48. Inspecting Robert's report card, his mother noted that he had received high ratings in Latin and history.
    (A) his mother noted
    (B) it was noted by his mother
    (C) his mother had noted
    (D) a notation was made by his mother
    (E) Robert's mother noted

49. The old man told Mary and I many stories about Europe.
    (A) Mary and I
    (B) Mary and me
    (C) me and Mary
    (D) I and Mary
    (E) Mary together with me

50. There is no man but would give ten years of his life to accomplish that deed.
    (A) no man but would give
    (B) no man but who would give
    (C) not no man who would not give
    (D) no man who would but give
    (E) not any man would give

51. The wild game hunter stalked the tiger slowly, cautiously, and in a silent manner.
    (A) and in a silent manner.
    (B) and silently.
    (C) and by acting silent.
    (D) and also used silence.
    (E) and in silence.

52. European film distributors originated the art of "dubbing"—the substitution of lip-synchronized translations in foreign languages for the original soundtrack voices.
    (A) —the substitution of lip-synchronized translations
    (B) ; the substitution of lip-synchronized translations
    (C) —the substitutions of translations synchronized by the lips
    (D) , the lip-synchronized substitution of translations
    (E) . The substitution of lip-synchronized translations

53. Every pupil understood the assignment except I.
    (A) except I.
    (B) excepting I.
    (C) outside of me.
    (D) excepting me.
    (E) except me.

54. Of the two candidates, I think he is the best suited.
    (A) he is the best suited.
    (B) that he is the best suited.
    (C) he is suited best.
    (D) he is the better suited.
    (E) he's the best suited.

55. You need not go unless you want to.
    (A) You need not go unless you want to.
    (B) You don't need to go not unless you want to.
    (C) You need go not unless you want to.
    (D) You need not go in case unless you want to.
    (E) You can go not unless you want to.

56. I feel as though I was being borne bodily through the air.
    (A) as though I was being borne
    (B) as though I was being born
    (C) like I was being borne
    (D) like as though I was being borne
    (E) as though I were being borne

57. Honor as well as profit are to be gained by this work.
    (A) Honor as well as profit are to be gained by this work.
    (B) Honor as well as profit is to be gained by this work.
    (C) Honor in addition to profit are to be gained by this work.
    (D) Honor, as well as profit, are to be gained by this work.
    (E) Honor also profit is to be gained by this work.

58. He was neither in favor of or opposed to the plan.
    (A) He was neither in favor of or opposed to the plan.
    (B) He was not in favor of or opposed to the plan.
    (C) He was neither in favor of the plan or opposed to it.
    (D) He was neither in favor of the plan or opposed to the plan.
    (E) He was neither in favor of nor opposed to the plan.

59. I don't do well in those kinds of tests.
    (A) I don't do well in those kinds of tests.
    (B) I don't do well in those kind of tests.
    (C) I don't do good in those kinds of tests.
    (D) I don't do good in those kind of tests.
    (E) I don't do good in tests like those.

60. We were amazed to see the amount of people waiting in line at Macy's.
    (A) amount of people waiting in line at Macy's.
    (B) number of people waiting in line at Macy's.
    (C) amount of persons waiting in line at Macy's.
    (D) amount of people waiting in line at Macys.
    (E) amount of people waiting at Macy's in line.

End Of Section III

If you finish before time is called, check your work on this section only.

When time is called, proceed directly to the next section and do not return to this section.

SECTION IV — HUMANITIES
(30 minutes)

DIRECTIONS: Select the one of the four choices following each item which will correctly answer the question or correctly complete the statement, whichever the case may be.

61. If you know the title of a poem and wish to find out in what anthology it appears, the most complete reference among the following is
    (A) the Reader's Guide
    (B) the vertical file
    (C) library card catalogue
    (D) Granger's Index to Poetry and Recitations.

62. All of the following are characters in Gilbert and Sullivan operettas *except*
    (A) Sir Patrick Spens   (B) Nanki-Poo
    (C) Ralph Rackstraw   (D) Iolanthe.

63. Humperdinck's opera for children is
    (A) "Hansel Und Gretel"
    (B) "The Magic Flute"
    (C) "The Chocolate Soldier"
    (D) "The Pirates of Penzance"
    (E) "Tales of Hoffmann."

64. Of the four lines quoted, those written by Robert Frost are
    a. "Something there is that doesn't love a wall"
    b. "One could do worse than be a swinger of birches"
    c. "Come down to Kew in lilac time"
    d. "I must down to the seas again."
    (A) a, b   (B) a, c
    (C) a, d   (D) c, d.

65. In "The Scarlet Letter," the letter referred to is a
    (A) secret letter detailing a murder plot
    (B) letter imparting special powers to its owner
    (C) symbol of the breaking of a moral code
    (D) little girl's initial.

66. All of the following are quotations from the Bible *except*
    (A) All is not gold that glitters
    (B) Man doth not live by bread alone
    (C) The way of transgressors is hard
    (D) They have sown the wind, and they shall reap the whirlwind.

67. Of the following Roman deities, the one *incorrectly* matched with the epithet is
    (A) Mars — warrior
    (B) Ceres — messenger
    (C) Vulcan — blacksmith
    (D) Diana — huntress.

68. Tom Sawyer discovers Injun Joe's hiding place while he is
    (A) exploring the shore on a raft
    (B) hiding with Huck Finn on Jackson's Island
    (C) lost in a cave with Becky Thatcher
    (D) rummaging for paint in Muff Potter's cellar.

69. Of the following stories, the two written by Bret Harte are
    a. The Outcasts of Poker Flat
    b. Marjorie Daw
    c. The Luck of Roaring Camp
    d. The Celebrated Jumping Frog of Calaveras County.
    (A) a, b   (B) a, c
    (C) a, d   (D) c, d.

70. In *all* of the following the book title is correctly paired with the character it describes *except* in
    (A) The Merchant of Venice — Antonio
    (B) The Hunchback of Notre Dame — Quasimodo
    (C) The Count of Monte Cristo — Edmond Dantes
    (D) A Connecticut Yankee in King Arthur's Court — Pudd'nhead Wilson.

71. "The Blue Boy" is a painting by
    (A) Reynolds   (B) Gainsborough
    (C) Sargent   (D) Raphael.

72. The leader of the French Impressionist school of painting was
    (A) Courbet   (B) Ingres
    (C) Monet   (D) Delacroix.

73. To the group represented by Cass Gilbert and Louis Sullivan, it would be most appropriate to add, of the following names, the name of
    (A) Marc Chagall
    (B) Paul Klee
    (C) Charles Demuth
    (D) Frank Lloyd Wright.

74. A 17th century art movement characterized by strong contrasts and elaborately carved and twisted forms was called
    (A) realism   (B) neo-impressionism
    (C) baroque   (D) dadaism.

75. Albert Ryder's "Death at the Race Track" depicts
    (A) a fatal race-track accident
    (B) a dying horse
    (C) a phantom
    (D) an automobile race.

76. The influence of William Morris was felt most strongly in connection with
    (A) the art nouveau movement
    (B) the crafts movement
    (C) architecture of the 19th Century
    (D) elementary art education.

77. The impressionist school as typified by Monet was chiefly concerned with
    (A) capturing the aspects of light
    (B) geometric arrangement of forms
    (C) abstractions
    (D) portraiture stressing the "impression" of the character.

78. Of the following, the artist frequently characterized as the "universal man" because he was also a philosopher, inventer, and scientist was
    (A) Morris   (B) Da Vinci
    (C) Lorenzo   (D) Michelangelo.

79. A contemporary Mexican muralist whose art is frankly political propaganda is
    (A) Velasquez   (B) Rivera
    (C) Murillo   (D) Sorolla.

80. Which of the following artists was *not* classified as a cubist for any portion of his career?
    (A) Derain   (B) Braque
    (C) Picasso   (D) Van Gogh.

81. Of the following, the one who is correctly identified as founder and financial sponsor of the summer concerts given at Lewisohn Stadium in New York City is
    (A) Marie Alberghetti
    (B) Minnie Guggenheim
    (C) Leonard Bernstein
    (D) Marion Anderson.

82. Of the following terms, the one which is opposite in meaning to "pianissimo" is
    (A) bravissimo   (B) glissando
    (C) fortissimo   (D) prestissimo.

83. The name of Gian-Carlo Menotti has become outstanding in which one of the following fields?
    (A) modern opera

(B) violin making
(C) teaching bel canto
(D) composition of symphonic overtures.

84. The reason underlying the violinist's practice of rubbing resin on the hairs of the violin bow prior to playing the violin is that
    (A) friction between the bow and the string is decreased
    (B) resin particles contribute to the tonal quality
    (C) friction between the bow and the string is increased
    (D) resin particles contribute to the vibrato.

85. The instrument to whose pitch the other instruments of a symphony orchestra are tuned is the
    (A) clarinet   (B) harp
    (C) oboe   (D) trumpet.

86. The song, "Flow Gently, Sweet Afton," refers to a stream in
    (A) Germany   (B) Italy
    (C) Scotland   (D) Louisiana.

87. The song, "Somewhere Over the Rainbow," is from the operetta entitled
    (A) Pinafore   (B) Pirates of Penzance
    (C) Porgy and Bess (D) Wizard of Oz.

88. The tonette is a musical instrument played by
    (A) using a bow
    (B) striking it with a drumstick
    (C) blowing it
    (D) shaking it.

89. All of the following belong to the brass "family" of instruments *except* the
    (A) bassoon   (B) French horn
    (C) trombone   (D) tuba.

90. A cadence is the
    (A) beginning of a phrase
    (B) end of a phrase
    (C) interlude in a song
    (D) introduction to a piece of music.

SECTION V — SCIENCE
(15 minutes)

91. The largest part of the brain is called the
    (A) medulla oblongata   (B) cerebellum
    (C) cerebrum   (D) spinal cord.

92. A weather balloon is never fully inflated on the ground because, as the balloon rises,
    (A) it would lack stability in a storm
    (B) the air inside expands

(C) the outside pressure would be too great
(D) a reserve supply of air is automatically pumped into the balloon.

93. A dry cell is safe for children's experimentation because it
    (A) is small and easily carried
    (B) is leakproof

(C) has a low voltage
(D) is fireproof.

94. People who advocate fluoridation of water do so in the interest of
(A) prevention of the spread of typhus
(B) prevention of dental caries
(C) whitening the teeth of the people in the area
(D) improvement of the potability of the water supply.

95. Sal soda is used as a(n)
(A) aid for digestive disturbance
(B) bubble agent in soft drinks
(C) ingredient in baking
(D) water softener.

96. Evaporation is likely to be greatest on days of
(A) high humidity   (B) low humidity
(C) little or no wind   (D) low pressure.

97. Of the following electrical devices found in the home, the one which develops the highest voltage is the
(A) electric broiler
(B) radio tube
(C) television picture tube
(D) electric steam iron.

98. Most soluble food substances enter the blood stream
(A) through the small intestine
(B) through the duodenum
(C) through the capillaries in the stomach
(D) through the hepatic vein.

99. Of the following, the animal which is *not* a rodent is the
(A) beaver   (B) guinea pig
(C) rabbit   (D) skunk.

100. The "dark" side of the moon refers to the
(A) craters into which no sunlight has ever reached
(B) south pole of the moon's axis
(C) hemisphere which has never reflected the sun's rays on the earth
(D) moon itself, which is symbolically "dark" because no man has reached it.

101. Of the following, the one which is *not* characteristic of poison ivy is that it has
(A) milky juice   (B) shiny leaves
(C) three leaflet clusters (D) white berries.

102. Cholesterol is
(A) a basic part of bone structure
(B) an alcohol formed in the body
(C) a substance found in blood
(D) the cause of colitis.

103. Of the following, the one which most closely approximates the diameter of the moon is
(A) 2,000 miles   (B) 8,000 miles
(C) 186,000 miles   (D) 240,000 miles.

104. A man hears the echo from a mountain wall five seconds after he has shouted. Of the following, the one which most nearly expresses the distance of the man from the mountain is
(A) five miles   (B) one mile
(C) nine hundred yards (D) 1100 feet.

105. Of the following, the one which is present in greatest amounts in the air we breathe is
(A) carbon dioxide   (B) oxygen
(C) water vapor   (D) nitrogen.

106. The vitamin which helps coagulation of the blood is
(A) C   (B) D
(C) E   (D) K.

107. At what season is hail most likely to occur during thunderstorms?
(A) fall   (B) winter
(C) spring   (D) summer.

108. We can see only one side of the moon because the
(A) earth rotates on its own axis
(B) moon makes one rotation as it makes one revolution around the earth
(C) moon has no refractive atmosphere
(D) sun does not shine on the moon's unseen side.

109. Which of the following parts of the ear is partly responsible for maintaining body balance?
(A) the middle ear
(B) the semi-circular canals
(C) the semi-lunar valves
(D) the cochlea.

110. Which of the following birds would most probably *not* be found in a wooded area?
(A) thrush   (B) barred owl
(C) green heron   (D) towhee.

SECTION VI — SOCIAL SCIENCE
(15 minutes)

111. The role of the Cabinet in American Government is
     (A) defined in the Constitution
     (B) based on the ideas of Alexander Hamilton
     (C) an example of a practice that developed through custom
     (D) analogous to the system of government prevailing in England in the 18th century.

112. The "Great Compromise" was finally adopted by the Constitutional Convention because
     (A) the small states threatened to bolt the Convention unless representation was made equal in both houses
     (B) the Southern states would not have ratified the Constitution without it
     (C) the membership of Congress would have been too large and unwieldy to be able to function effectively
     (D) an agreement was also made to include a Bill of Rights in the Constitution.

113. Of the following matched items, the one that is *incorrectly* paired is
     (A) Thomas Jefferson — Louisiana Purchase
     (B) John Marshall — strict interpretation of the Constitution
     (C) John Quincy Adams — Monroe Doctrine
     (D) Roger Taney — Dred Scott Decision.

114. The main purpose of the Truman Doctrine was to
     (A) give economic and technical aid to needy countries outside of the Communist orbit
     (B) develop supremacy over the Soviet Union in the building of atomic weapons
     (C) encourage dissension in the satellite countries of the Soviet Union
     (D) contain communism by aiding Greece and Turkey.

115. The great political leader of Athens during the Golden Age of Greece was
     (A) Phidias   (B) Plato
     (C) Pericles   (D) Aristides.

116. Despite that fact that England is farther north than any point in the United States, its winters are generally warmer than those in northern United States because
     (A) England has a Mediterranean climate
     (B) England's shores are warmed by the Gulf Stream
     (C) England is warmed by breezes that blow from Africa
     (D) the winds that influence England's climate are the prevailing easterlies.

117. The loss of Chicago's claim to the title "Hog Butcher for the World" is due mainly to the
     (A) growth of major cities on the west coast and development of superhighways for trucks
     (B) automation in the meat industry
     (C) increase in importation of meat from other countries
     (D) decrease in the consumption of meat products.

118. When Thoreau advocated passive resistance to the tyranny of government he was anticipating the program of
     (A) Sun Yat Sen
     (B) Jan Masaryk
     (C) Mahatma Gandhi
     (D) Susan B. Anthony.

119. The city which is sometimes described as the "Pittsburgh of the South" because of its high production of steel is
     (A) Birmingham, Alabama
     (B) Nashville, Tennessee
     (C) Richmond Virginia
     (D) Atlanta, Georgia.

120. The term "manifest destiny" would most likely be found in the chapter of an American history textbook dealing with
     (A) immigration
     (B) the Industrial Revolution
     (C) expansion
     (D) foreign affairs.

121. The Mesabi Range is famous for its rich deposits of
     (A) coal   (B) copper
     (C) iron   (D) uranium.

122. The Pendleton Act of 1883 was a long overdue attempt to eliminate the evils of the
     (A) Tariff of Abominations
     (B) Specie Circular
     (C) Squatter sovereignty
     (D) Spoils system.

123. Of the following, the one which had the greatest influence upon the development of the American legal system is the
     (A) Roman law
     (B) judicial system set up in colonies
     (C) British common law.
     (D) ideas of John Locke.

124. The idea of Ptolemy that the sun revolved around the earth was disproved by
    (A) Newton   (B) Copernicus
    (C) Galileo   (D) Roger Bacon.

125. Of the following pairs, the one which *incorrectly* attributes a river system to a country is
    (A) Yellow — China
    (B) Vistula — Italy
    (C) Murray-Darling — Australia
    (D) Loire — France.

126. The Domesday Book was a(n)
    (A) census of population and property
    (B) volume detailing religious practices
    (C) example of the rise of vernacular literature
    (D) manual of court procedure.

127. Of the following, the one which names two countries in the United Arab Republic is
    (A) Egypt and Lebanon
    (B) Egypt and Syria
    (C) Syria and Lebanon
    (D) Egypt and Jordan.

128. In the United States government, one of the powers possessed by the Senate and not the House of Representatives is the power to
    (A) approve the appointment of ambassadors
    (B) override the president's veto
    (C) impeach the president
    (D) originate revenue bills.

129. The prevention of unfair practices in conducting television programs is under the jurisdiction of the
    (A) Public Service Commission
    (B) Federal Trade Commission
    (C) Interstate Commerce Commission
    (D) Federal Communications Commission.

130. Each of the following leaders is correctly matched with a country *except*
    (A) Prime Minister Nehru — India
    (B) President Sukarno — Jordan
    (C) President Nasser — United Arab Republic
    (D) President Nkrumah — Ghana.

End Of Section VI

When time is called, stop work on this section
The Afternoon Session part of the test is now concluded

ANSWER KEY TO LAW SCHOOL ADMISSION TEST [B]
Afternoon Session

1. D	16. D	31. A	46. C	61. D	76. B	91. C	106. D	121. C
2. G	17. G	32. C	47. D	62. A	77. A	92. B	107. D	122. D
3. G	18. O	33. B	48. A	63. C	78. B	93. C	108. B	123. C
4. D	19. G	34. C	49. B	64. A	79. B	94. B	109. B	124. B
5. O	20. V	35. B	50. A	65. C	80. D	95. D	110. C	125. B
6. G	21. B	36. C	51. B	66. A	81. B	96. B	111. C	126. A
7. O	22. C	37. D	52. A	67. B	82. C	97. C	112. A	127. B
8. D	23. D	38. A	53. E	68. C	83. A	98. A	113. B	128. A
9. O	24. B	39. B	54. D	69. B	84. C	99. D	114. D	129. D
10. O	25. C	40. C	55. A	70. D	85. C	100. C	115. C	130. B
11. V	26. A	41. C	56. E	71. B	86. C	101. A	116. B	
12. G	27. B	42. E	57. B	72. C	87. D	102. C	117. A	
13. G	28. C	43. D	58. E	73. D	88. C	103. A	118. C	
14. D	29. C	44. B	59. A	74. C	89. A	104. C	119. A	
15. V	30. C	45. C	60. B	75. C	90. B	105. D	120. C	

SUGGESTION: Refer to the unofficial Percentile Ranking Table on page 52 to determine your comparative rating on the Trial Post-Test.

PART FIVE

Supplementary Practice And Study Material For The LSAT

The candidate may now have need for further study and practice in certain areas of the Law School Admission Test. The purpose of this Supplement is to satisfy that need.

This final part of the book offers practice-study material provided by the following sections:

GUIDE TO GRAMMAR

GUIDE TO ENGLISH USAGE

GRAPH, CHART AND TABLE INTERPRE-
TATION

MATCHING PARTS AND FIGURES (Nonverbal Reasoning)

In addition, you will find here

LAW SCHOOLS APPROVED BY THE
AMERICAN BAR ASSOCIATION

REQUIREMENTS FOR ADMISSION TO
LEGAL PRACTICE IN THE UNITED
STATES

GUIDE TO GRAMMAR

Jimmy: *Teacher, ain't it time for lunch?*

Teacher: *Say, "Isn't it time for lunch."*

> *(After several minutes of teacher explanation and pupil drill on verb forms and conjugations . . .)*

Jimmy: *Isn't it time for lunch? I ain't never been so hungry.*

The Method Is Important

PERHAPS the reason that Jimmy repeated the error in the conversation above is that he didn't care to learn grammar—at least, not the way his teacher taught it.

Grammar, though, is really easy—provided you learn it scientifically.

Research has indicated that a great many errors in grammar may be traced to a lack of understanding of simple grammatical principles —and these principles may be learned thoroughly and conclusively by any person of average intelligence in a surprisingly short period of time. Yet torturous days and weeks and months have been spent in classrooms in the drilling of unnecessary grammatical ideas into the poor heads of little boys like Jimmy. This takes place in spite of the fact that pupils have remembered and used a very small percentage of the abstruse grammar to which they have been subjected.

Nominative absolutes, periphrastic conjugations and the rest of the hoity-toity crowd of grammar nuisances have little or no place in a Good English instruction program unless the student is interested in the technical aspects of the language—and since so very few individuals are so inclined, why torment the great majority of those who wish to learn just plain, good, simple English? Why force them to absorb useless concepts? The simple rules are enough. Here they are.

Note: The best way to learn these rules is by the *felt need* method. Wait till you have a grammar problem—then study the rule which solves that problem. You will learn the rules with thorough understanding by using this procedure.

The Simple Rules of Grammar

PARTS OF SPEECH*

1. A NOUN is a person, place or thing: *teacher, city, desk* or *king*.
2. AN ADJECTIVE describes a noun: *warm* or *cold, blue* or *brown*.
3. PRONOUNS substitute for nouns: *she* for Helen, *those* for gowns.
4. A VERB has action or state of being: they *yell*, you *feel* and all *are seeing*.
5. An ADVERB qualifies the verb: run *fast*, walk *slowly*, *hardly* disturb.
6. CONJUNCTIONS join in many ways: in *and* out, night *or* day.
7. A PREPOSITION has its place before a noun: *in* outerspace.
8. The INTERJECTION notes surprise: *My!* how lovely! "*Help!*" he cries.

*Please forgive us for this simplified presentation of the Parts of Speech. But just about every adult to whom we offer this little poem seems to like it. Now let us take a closer look at the foregoing parts of speech.

Nouns

A noun is a name of anything.

A. There are several kinds of nouns.

COMMON (refers to a general group)— *cat, health, girl, sincerity.*

PROPER (distinguishes one from others)—*Chicago, Jack, Central Park.*

These "name" nouns are always capitalized.

COLLECTIVE (denotes several combined into one)— *team, crowd, organization, Congress.*

Note: A *group* of teachers from England *is visiting* our school. The collective noun, *group,* is singular; therefore, verb, *is visiting,* is singular.

CONCRETE (refers to something material)—*pail, steel, desk.*

ABSTRACT (refers to something that is not material)—*hope, weakness, education.*

B. Nouns have NUMBER. Note the tricky plurals for some nouns:

SINGULAR	PLURAL
alumnus	alumni
analysis	analyses
archipelago	archipelagoes
axis	axes
basis	bases
brother-in-law	brothers-in-law
crisis	crises
embryo	embryos
louse	lice
monkey	monkeys
oasis	oases
phenomenon	pheonomena
portfolio	portfolios
salmon	salmon
spoonful	spoonfuls
swine	swine
tomato	tomatoes
veto	vetoes
r	r's
3	3's

add *'s* to form plural of letters and numbers.

C. Nouns have GENDER

MASCULINE	FEMININE
adventurer	adventuress
bull	cow
cock	hen
czar	czarina
drake	duck
executor	executrix
gander	goose
marquis	marchioness
rajah	ranee
ram	ewe
stallion	mare

Note: There is also a NEUTER GENDER for nouns denoting inanimate objects (example: rocks, chair, silence, street, etc.) and a COMMON GENDER for nouns signifying either sex (example: citizen, pedestrian, customer, cousin, etc.).

D. Nouns have CASE

NOMINATIVE (when the noun is the subject of the thought).

OBJECTIVE (when the noun is the object of the thought).

POSSESSIVE (when the noun shows that it possesses something).

E. A noun is in the NOMINATIVE CASE when it is used as follows:

1. SUBJECT — The name or thing about which an assertion is made: The *girl* powdered her face.
   Note: A subject always answers the question WHAT or WHO.
2. PREDICATE NOUN—The noun that comes after a copulative verb (see COPULATIVE VERB).
   Note: The predicate noun means the same as the subject.
   Babe Ruth was a great *hitter.*
3. DIRECT ADDRESS: *Jack,* please pick up the papers.
4. NOMINATE ABSOLUTE (independent idea): The *plane* having departed, we left the airport.
5. NOMINATIVE BY APPOSITION (explanatory adjunct): My instructor, a learned *man,* is now on leave.

F. A noun is in the OBJECTIVE CASE when it is used as follows:

1. DIRECT OBJECT — A noun which receives the action of a transitive verb (see TRANSITIVE VERB)
   Note: The direct object answers the question WHAT or WHOM: The child ate the *cookie.*

2. OBJECTIVE COMPLEMENT — A noun that explains the direct object: They elected Kennedy *president*.

3. OBJECTIVE BY APPOSITION: We met Jack, an old *friend*.

4. ADVERBIAL OBJECTIVE — A noun that denotes distance, time, manner, etc.): My uncle stayed a *week*.

5. OBJECT OF PREPOSITION — A noun which is introduced by a preposition: They have gone to the *game*.

6. SUBJECT OF THE INFINITIVE: We believed the *boys* to be honest.

7. INDIRECT OBJECT
   1. comes after a verb of "giving."
   2. "to" or "for" is expressed or understood.
   3. Must accompany a DIRECT OBJECT.
      Examples: Please lend *Wilson* a nickel.
      Give my love to your *brother*.

8. RETAINED OBJECT—a noun which was the object of the active verb and is held over as the object of the same verb in the Passive Voice: He was offered some *advice* by me. Sentence formerly: I offered him some *advice*. See ACTIVE and PASSIVE VOICE.

G. A noun is in the POSSESSIVE CASE when it is used to express possession, source or origin.
   Charles' book (not Charle's).
   doctor's visit (one doctor)
   doctors' visit (more than one doctor)
   children's shoes
   baby's bottle
   babies' bottle (hardly a sanitary example)
   mother-in-law's house (apostrophe is placed in last element of hyphenated noun)
   Kenyon and Knott's book (one book by two authors)

Jack's and Sam's cars (one owned by each)

Pronouns

A pronoun is used in place of a noun.

A. EXPLETIVE PRONOUN — *it* or *there*.

An expletive pronoun is followed by the subject.

The subject is *men* in this sentence: *There* were three *men* on the bench.
The subject is *they* in this sentence: *It is they* who are going.

B. ANTECEDENT OF THE PRONOUN — The noun to which a pronoun refers. Picasso is the *artist whom* we all admire. (*artist* is the antecedent of the pronoun *whom*.) See WHO and WHOM.

Note: A pronoun must agree with its antecedent in GENDER, PERSON, and NUMBER. Everyone must have *his* own pen. (*their* is *incorrect*).

C. KINDS OF PRONOUNS
   1. DEMONSTRATIVE PRONOUN — *this* and *that*, *these* and *those*.

   2. INDEFINITE PRONOUN — all, any, nobody, etc.

   3. INTERROGATIVE PRONOUN — who, which, what.
      who refers to persons.
      what refers to animals and things.
      which (selectively used) refers to persons or animals or things.

      Who broke the cup?
      Which of the two children broke the cup?
      Which of the puppies do you want?
      Which of the apples tastes sweetest?
      What is that noise?
      What is that annoying creature?

   4. PERSONAL PRONOUN — No other part of speech has as many forms or changes as the personal pronoun.

		NOMINATIVE CASE	OBJECTIVE CASE	POSSESSIVE CASE
SINGULAR	1st person	I	me	mine
	2nd person	you	you	yours
	3rd person	he, she, it	him, her, it	his, hers
PLURAL	1st person	we	us	ours
	2nd person	you	you	yours
	3rd person	they	them	theirs

Note 1: The apostrophe is *not* used in POS-SESSIVE CASE forms of the personal pronouns. **Don't** write this is *your's*.

Note 2: *It's* means *it is*. *It's* is *not* a personal pronoun.

Note 3: The Nominative form must be used in the following constructions:

It is *I.*
It is *she.* } Underlined pronouns are all
I am *he.* } Predicate Nouns.

She is younger than *we*. This really means . . .
"than we are"; "we" is a subject — therefore *we* is in the Nominative Case.

He likes Joan better than *I*. This means . . .
"better than I like Joan"

He likes Joan better than *me*. This means . . .
"He likes Joan better than he likes me."

Note 4. The objective form must be used in the following constructions:

. . . between you and *me.* }
. . . with John and *her.* } see Object of
. . . from Mary and *us.* } Preposition

5. REFLEXIVE PRONOUN — *myself, yourselves, oneself,* etc.

6. RELATIVE PRONOUN — *who, which, that, what.*
   who refers to persons.
   which refers to animals and things.
   that refers to persons, animals, and things.
   what (that which) refers to things.

   Example: Tell me *what* you know.

   Note 1: Infrequently, *as* and *but* may be used as relative pronouns:
   He gave us such food *as* he had.
   There is no one *but* considers him a genius. (*but* in this case, means *other than the person who*).

   Note 2: **More** errors are made in the use of *who* and *whom* than in the use of any other word pairs in our language. (See WHO —

WHOM in Arco "Guide to English Usage").

Adjectives

An adjective usually modifies a noun

He is a *tall* man.
A *soft* answer turneth away wrath.

A. Do not use an adjective to modify a verb. (See ADVERBS)
She sings *good* is *incorrect*. (SAY, *well*)

B. There are two other adjective uses besides the use of noun modifier.

PREDICATE ADJECTIVE — comes after a copulative verb (see COPULATIVE VERB).

Note: We feel *bad*. (We're troubled) *Bad* is an adjective. *We feel badly*. (There is something wrong with our sense of touch.) *Badly* is an adverb.

OBJECTIVE COMPLEMENT (see Objective Complement under NOUN).
Jack painted the car *pink*.

Note: *AN ARTICLE* is another name for the following three adjectives: *the, a, an*.

DEFINITE ARTICLE — the

INDEFINITE ARTICLE — a, an
a desk (Before a consonant)
an apple (Before a vowel)

C. Adjectives change in form by COMPARISON. There are three degrees of comparison.

POSITIVE DEGREE — no comparison is made. The *sweet* peach.

COMPARATIVE DEGREE — The *sweeter* peach. (one of two peaches)

SUPERLATIVE DEGREE — The *sweetest* peach. (One of three or more peaches).

Verbs

A Verb Usually Expresses Action

A. There are three major types of verbs.

TRANSITIVE	1)	has action and
	2)	takes a direct object He *killed* the cat.
INTRANSI-TIVE	1)	has action but
	2)	takes no direct object. She *fell* down.
COPULATIVE	1)	has no action and
	2)	may take a predicate noun or adjective. Jim *is* captain. (*captain* is predicate noun ... also called predicate nominative)

A COPULATIVE VERB may be:

1) any part of the verb BE (*was, is,* etc.)
2) one of the *sensate* verbs (*smell, feel, taste,* etc.)
3) one of the *"appear"* verbs (*appear, become, seem,* etc.)

Mary *was* ill. (*ill* is predicate adjective)

We *are going.* (*are going* is not a copulative verb — it's intransitive).

The candy *tastes* sweet. (If you say sweetly, you are giving the candy tasting ability).

He *feels* strong about this matter. (*strongly* is incorrect.)

B. A PRINCIPAL verb is that part of a verb combination that expresses the action.

I do *believe.* (*do* is the AUXILIARY verb,...*believe* is the PRINCIPAL verb).

You may *enter.* (*may* is the AUXILIARY verb ... *enter* is the PRINCIPAL verb. In the past tense, say *might have entered*).

We shall *eat.* (*shall* is the AUXILIARY verb ... *eat* is the PRINCIPAL verb).

For SHALL and WILL see "Arco Guide to English Usage."

C.   TENSES — There are six tenses.

	SIMPLE FORM	PROGRESSIVE FORM	EMPHATIC FORM
1. PRESENT	Roger Maris hits	is hitting	does hit (a home run.)
2. PAST	hit	was hitting	did hit (a home run.)
3. PRESENT PERFECT	has hit	has been hitting	
4. FUTURE	will hit	will be hitting	
5. PAST PERFECT	had hit	had been hitting	
6. FUTURE PERFECT	will have hit	will have been hitting	

WHEN TO USE THE PAST PERFECT

Consider the sentence — "The foreman *asked* what *had happened* to my eye."

(Don't say what *happened* in this case.) The action *had happened* and the action *asked* are both *past.* The PAST PERFECT tense (*had happened*) is used because it is "more past" than the action *asked.*

WHEN TO USE THE PRESENT PERFECT.

Consider the sentence — "I'm glad you're here at last — I *have* waited an hour for you to arrive." (Don't say I *waited* in this case.) The action *have waited* began in the *past* and extended to the *present.* In this case we use the PRESENT PERFECT.

WHEN TO USE THE FUTURE PERFECT.

Consider the sentence — "When I reach Chicago tonight, my uncle *will have left* for Los Angeles."

The action *will have left* is going to take place before the action *reach,* although both actions are in the future. When there are two future actions, the action completed first is expressed in the FUTURE PERFECT tense.

D.   PRINCIPAL PARTS — There are three principal parts. From these we get all parts of the verb. The principal parts are the following:

1.   Present
2.   Past
3.   Present perfect

The other three tenses come from the three

Principal Parts:

The FUTURE tense is derived from the Present ... The FUTURE PERFECT tense and the PAST PERFECT tense are both derived from the Present Perfect tense.

Learn the Principal Parts of the following irregular verbs. You will then know every form of each irregular verb.

PRESENT	PAST	PRESENT PERFECT
abide	abode	has abode
arise	arose	has arisen
bear (carry)	bore	has borne
bear (bring forth)	bore	has born
bid	bade	has bid, bidden
bide	bode, bided	has bode, bided
bleed	bled	has bled
broadcast	broadcast	has broadcast
burst	burst	has burst
chide	chid, chidded	has chid, chidded, chidden
choose	chose	has chosen
cleave (adhere)	cleaved	has cleaved
cleave (split)	cleft, cleaved	has cleft, cleaved, cloven
cling	clung	has clung
drown	drowned	has drowned
drink	drank	has drunk
flee	fled	has fled
fling	flung	has flung
fly	flew	has flown
flow	flowed	has flowed
forsake	forsook	has forsaken
freeze	froze	has frozen
grind	ground	has ground
hang (a picture)	hung	has hung
hang (a person)	hanged	has hanged
lay (place)	laid	has laid
lead	led	has led
lend	lent	has lent
lie (rest)	lay	has lain
light	lit, lighted	has lit, lighted
raise	raised	has raised
rid	rid	has rid
ring	rang	has rung
set	set	has set
sew	sewed	has sewed, sewn
shrink	shrank or shrunk	has shrunk, shrunken
sink	sank	has sunk
sit	sat	has sat
ski	skied (rhymes with seed)	has skied
slay	slew	has slain
slide	slid	has slid or slidden
sling	slung	has slung
slink	slunk	has slunk
smite	smote	has smitten
spring	sprang or sprung	has sprung
sting	stung	has stung
stink	stank	has stunk
stride	strode	has stridden
strive	strove	has striven
swim	swam	has swum
swing	swung	has swung
thrust	thrust	has thrust
weave	wove	has woven
wring	wrung	has wrung

E. VOICE . . . **There are two Verb Voices.**

1. ACTIVE VOICE – the *subject* of the sentence is the *doer* of action.
2. PASSIVE VOICE – the *subject* is *acted upon.*

Examples: Pittsburgh *won* the pennant. (ACTIVE VOICE)

The pennant *was won* by Pittsburgh. (PASSIVE VOICE)

Only *transitive* verbs may be converted from the Active Voice to the Passive Voice.

A Passive Verb may sometimes be COPULATIVE.

Examples: He *is considered* a genius. ("genius" here is a predicate nominative . . . see)

The lady *was made* ill by the pill. ("ill" is a predicate adjective . . . see)

F. MOOD (or MODE) . . . is the manner in which the action or the state of the verb is expressed. There are three Moods.

INDICATIVE MOOD is factual.

Example: We *are* going to the concert.
There are six tenses in the Indicative Mood. (see TENSES).

SUBJUNCTIVE MOOD is used for *orders, supposition, contrary to fact* conditions.

Examples: The principal ordered that there *be* a fire drill. (ORDER)

They are frightened lest they be *attacked* on the way home. (SUPPOSITION)

If I *were* rich, I'd be in Paris now. (CONTRARY TO FACT PRESENT CONDITION)

If the student *had studied,* he would have passed. (CONTRARY TO FACT PAST CONDITION)

Note that there are two Contrary to Fact Tenses (Present and Past.)

IMPERATIVE MOOD is used for *commands* and *wishes.*

Examples: *Leave* the premises at once! (COMMAND)

Bless your heart! (WISH)
The Imperative Mood has only one tense . . . **the** *Present.*

G. NUMBER and PERSON . . . A verb **must** agree with its subject in Number and **Person.**

Examples:

He doesn't know. ("don't" is incorrect)

Neither Mary nor Helen *is coming.* ("are coming" is incorrect).

Neither Jim nor we *are going.* ⎫ verb agrees
Neither he or I *am willing.* ⎬ with LAST
                               ⎭ subject

None of them *is* missing. (subject "none" is singular)

He and she *are* going. (subject is plural)

It is I who *am* the most willing. ("who," like its antecedent "I," is in the first person singular)

She as well as I *is* going. ("she" is the subject)

Smith together with Jones and Jackson *is* arriving. ("Smith" is the subject)

Three and three *is* six. ("Three and three" comprise a unit)

That man, not we, *is* guilty. (Second subject "we" is parenthetical. Verb here agrees with the first subject)

Four-fifths of the task *is* accomplished. (Unity of the subject "four-fifths" is conveyed by the object of the preposition "task")

Two-thirds of the straws *have* fallen on the floor. (Plurality of the subject "two-thirds" is conveyed by the object of the preposition "straws")

It *is* the men who count, not the machines. ("It" always takes a singular verb . . . see EXPLETIVE PRONOUN)

Adverbs

An Adverb Usually Modifies A Verb.

A. Adverbs commonly answer questions WHY? HOW? WHERE? WHEN? TO WHAT DEGREE?

Examples: Since it is snowing, I shall stay *here.* (WHERE)

Please do it *now.* (WHEN)

We *wholly* agree with you. (TO WHAT DEGREE)

She played the selection *beautifully.* (HOW)

He dived *for the pearl.* (WHY . . . adverbial phrase)

B. Two special types of adverbs follow:
1. RELATIVE ADVERB . . . introduces

adjective and adverbial clauses (see).

Examples: This is the place where he broke his leg. ("Where" begins the adjective clause) I'll phone you *when* I arrive. ("when" begins the adverbial clause)

2. INTERROGATIVE ADVERB . . . introduces questions.

Examples: *When* do you expect to leave?

How are we to save ourselves?

Prepositions

A preposition shows relationship between the word that follows it and the idea that precedes the preposition.

A. The most common prepositions are *with, to, on, of, in, from, for, by, at.*

B. Do *not* omit prepositions.

Example: Play it *in* this way. (play it this way is *incorrect*).

C. Use no unnecessary prepositions.

Example: It fell *off* the table. ("off of" is incorrect)

D. A preposition may be used at the end of a sentence . . . unless such use is awkward.

Example: Whom did he give the book to? (correct)

She is the nurse whom I was helped by. (awkward)

IDIOMS

English, like other languages, has its own idioms—that is, its own way of saying something. Here, below, is a list of frequently used (or shall we say "misused") idioms in which the correct preposition is important.

IDIOM	EXAMPLE
ABOUND IN (or WITH)	This letter ABOUNDS IN mistakes.
ACCOMPANIED BY (a person)	The salesman was ACCOMPANIED BY the buyer.
ACCOMPANIED WITH (a present)	He ACCOMPANIED the closing of the contract WITH a gift.
IN ACCORDANCE WITH	Act in ACCORDANCE WITH the regulations.
ACQUIESCE IN (ak-wee-ESS)	The executives were compelled to ACQUIESCE IN the director's policy.
ACQUIT OF	The office boy was ACQUITTED OF the charge of stealing pencils.
ADEPT IN (or AT)	The store manager is ADEPT IN typing.
AGREE TO (an offer)	The firm AGREES TO your payment of $100 in settlement of the claim.
AGREE WITH (a person)	I AGREE WITH Mr. Smith on that point.
AGREE UPON-or ON-(a plan)	We must AGREE UPON the best method.
ALLERGIC TO	The patient is ALLERGIC TO chocolate.
ANGRY AT (a situation) ANGRY WITH (a person)	The customer is ANGRY WITH the clerk AT being detained.
APPROPRIATE FOR (meaning *suitable to*)	This gown is also APPROPRIATE FOR a dinner dance.
AVAILABLE FOR (a purpose) AVAILABLE TO (a person)	These typewriters are now AVAILABLE TO offices FOR essential use.

IDIOM	EXAMPLE
AVERSE TO	The President is AVERSE TO increasing his staff.
COGNIZANT OF	He was not COGNIZANT OF dissension among his workers.
COINCIDE WITH	Your wishes in this matter COINCIDE WITH mine.
COMMENSURATE WITH (kum-MEN shure-it).	What you earn will be COMMENSURATE WITH how much effort you put into the job.
COMPARE TO (shows similarity between things that have different forms)	A man's life may be COMPARED TO a play.
COMPARE WITH (shows difference between things of like form)	How can you COMPARE a mink coat WITH a beaver?
COMPATIBLE WITH	The ideas of the section manager should be COMPATIBLE WITH those of the buyer.
COMPLY WITH	If you do not wish to COMPLY WITH our request, please submit your resignation.
CONDUCIVE TO	The employer's kindness is CONDUCIVE TO good work.
CONFORM TO (to adapt oneself to) CONFORM WITH (means to be in harmony with)	The average person CONFORMS TO the will of the majority. It is necessary to CONFORM WITH these rules.
CONVERSANT WITH	A salesman should be fully CONVERSANT WITH the articles he is selling.
DESIROUS OF	Some people are DESIROUS OF a price increase.
DIFFER WITH (an opinion)	I DIFFER WITH you in regard to its quality.
DIFFER FROM (a thing)	This machine DIFFERS FROM the old one in many respects.
DISSUADE FROM	We should DISSUADE him FROM making that investment.
EMPLOYED AT (a definite salary)	Our secretary is EMPLOYED AT $35 a week.
EMPLOYED IN (certain work)	My father is EMPLOYED IN blue-print reading.
ENVIOUS OF	Some of the employees are ENVIOUS OF his promotion.
IDENTICAL WITH	These stockings are IDENTICAL WITH those I showed you last week.
INFER FROM	I INFER FROM his remarks that he is dissatisfied.
OBLIVIOUS OF (or TO)	The typist is OBLIVIOUS OF the construction noise outside.
OPPOSITE TO (or FROM) (meaning contrary)	Your point of view is OPPOSITE TO mine.
PERTINENT TO	This sales talk must be PERTINENT TO the item to be sold.
PREFER TO	I PREFER nylon TO silk.
PRIOR TO	I want a deposit PRIOR TO final settlement.
VIE WITH	The salesmen are VYING WITH one another for this week's prize.

Conjunctions

A conjunction connects words, phrases and clauses.

There are three types of CONJUNCTIONS:

1. CO-ORDINATE CONJUNCTIONS... connect words, phrases, independent (main) clauses of EQUAL VALUE. (see CLAUSES)

    Examples: Mary *and* Jane (WORDS are connected)

    Into the village *or* through the woods (PHRASES are connected)

    You may go to the park *but* wear your rubbers. (INDEPENDENT CLAUSES are connected)

2. SUBORDINATE CONJUNCTIONS... connect dependent clauses to independent clauses. (see CLAUSES)

    Examples: *Although* he felt better, he refused to leave the house.

    (Note that the *Subordinate Conjunction* may start the sentence)

    We shall leave *since* there is nothing for us to do.

3. CORRELATIVE CONJUNCTIONS... are used in pairs.

    Examples: *Both* men *and* women are needed for the job.

    Neither Jim *nor* Jack is going.

Interjections

An interjection expresses strong feeling.

O denotes wishing. It is used in Direct Address (see).

It is not directly followed by a comma or by any other punctuation mark.

Example: O mother of mine!

Oh denotes sorrow, hope, surprise, pain.

It may be followed by a comma or by an exclamation mark.

Example: Oh, I'm in real trouble!

UNITS OF THOUGHT

There are three ways to express a thought:

PHRASE — *has no subject or verb. A phrase is an incomplete thought.*

Example: *in the park*

CLAUSE — *has a subject and a verb. A clause is an incomplete thought.*

Example: *after they had left*

SENTENCE — *has a subject and a verb. A sentence is a complete thought.*

Example: *We saw you.*

KINDS OF SENTENCES

SIMPLE . . . one main clause.

Example: I feel fine.

COMPOUND . . . two or more main clauses.

Example: Symphonic music stimulates some persons to noble thoughts, but others are lulled to sleep by it.

COMPLEX . . . one main and one subordinate clause.

Example: Because snow had closed the airport, the pilot made a forced landing.

COMPOUND – COMPLEX . . . two main clauses and one (or more) subordinate clauses.

Example: You prefer art and I prefer music although I am an art major.

Note: A *main* clause is the same as an *independent* clause.

A *subordinate clause* is the same as a *dependent* clause.

PHRASES AND CLAUSES

. . . There are three kinds of phrases

. . . There are three kinds of clauses

THREE KINDS OF PHRASES
NOUN PHRASE (takes place of noun)
e.g.   *"On to Paris"* was the cry of the enemy.
ADJECTIVE PHRASE (takes place of adjective)
e.g.   The girl *in the red bathing suit* is my sister.
ADVERBIAL PHRASE (takes place of adverb)
e.g.   He ran *into the house.*

Note: All of the foregoing phrases are also PREPOSITIONAL PHRASES. A prepositional phrase is so called because it is introduced by a *preposition.*

Other types of phrases (according to what they are introduced by) are:

INFINITIVE PHRASES (see INFINITIVE)

PARTICIPIAL PHRASES (see PARTICIPLE)

GERUND PHRASES (see GERUND)

THREE KINDS OF CLAUSES
NOUN CLAUSE (takes place of noun)
e.g.   *That he was talented* was obvious.
ADJECTIVE CLAUSE (takes place of adjective)
e.g.   The child *who fell down* is my cousin.
ADVERBIAL CLAUSE (takes place of adverb)
e.g.   He arrived *after I had left.*

VERBALS

A verbal is a form of the verb — it is NOT a verb.

There are THREE VERBALS (Infinitive - Participle - Gerund)

INFINITIVE — to go, to run, to see, etc. . . . may be noun *or* adjective *or* adverb.

e.g.   I like *to swim.* (noun)

e.g.   A book *to read* is what the child wants. (adjective)

e.g.   He went *to play* ball (adverb)

PARTICIPLE

    a.   Present Participle — going, seeing, feeling, etc.

    b.   Past Participle — having gone, having seen, having felt, etc.

    . . . a participle is ALWAYS AN ADJECTIVE.

e.g.   *Going* to the store, Joe slipped.

GERUND — knowing, running, hearing, etc.

    . . . a gerund is ALWAYS A NOUN.

e.g.   He enjoys *running.*

Verbal Phrases

INFINITIVE PHRASE

To study hard is sometimes necessary. (also a *noun phrase*)

He had a job *to do quickly.* (also an *adjective phrase*)

She was too emotional *to drive the car.* (also an *adverbial phrase*)

Note: Avoid the *split infinitive.* This is an infinitive which is "split" by an adverb.

INCORRECT: We decided *TO carefully CONSIDER* the matter.

SAY, we decided *TO CONSIDER* the matter *carefully.*

PARTICIPIAL PHRASE

Running to the store, the boy tripped. (also *adjective phrase*)

Feeling very ill, the party was called off. (This is incorrect because "feeling" has nothing to modify . . . it certainly does not modify. "party." Every participle — since it is an adjective — must have a noun to modify. If the participle does not modify, it is DANGLING. A *dangling participle* is *always wrong.*)

GERUND PHRASE

She likes *dancing in the dark.* (also a *noun phrase*)

MISPLACED MODIFIERS

The modifiers in the English language are:

Adjectives	
Adjective Phrases	} They modify *nouns* or *pronouns.*
Adjective Clauses	

Adverbs	
Adverbial Phrases	} They modify *verbs, adjectives* and other *adverbs.*
Adverbial Clauses	

Occasionally, these modifiers are misplaced. Let us consider the modifying word *only.* It may be an adjective or adverb. Note the various meanings of the following sentence by your placing *only* in the positions indicated by arrows.

I   saw   Jones   shoot   Smith.
↑ ↑   ↑   ↑   ↑

Try this MISPLACED MODIFIER test. Preserve the meaning that was originally intended.

Test On Misplaced Modifiers

1. Does a person live here with one eye named Wilson?
2. The musician played the piano with wooden legs. (three possibilities).
3. Mrs. Jones was injured while preparing her husband's supper in a horrible manner.
4. While enjoying lunch, the gong sounded.
5. A strange man was strolling down Broadway with a red beard.
6. At the age of six, her mother died and left four children.
7. Mrs. McGillicuddy resigned from the Women's League after belonging fifteen years with much disappointment on the part of the members.
8. While eating oats, they took the horse out of the stable.
9. The flames were put out before any damage was done by the Fire Department.
10. While paddling, a huge fish leaped into the canoe.
11. The child watched the St. Patrick's Day Parade sitting in a carriage.
12. Have you read about the girl who was run over in the newspaper?
13. I wish to sell a brand-new house by an expert builder of the best concrete block.
14. He sold the watch to the young lady with the Swiss movement.
15. The girl went to the party with the young man wearing a low-cut gown.
16. We found a description of the crocodile in the dictionary.
17. They read about the arrest of the gangster who had intimidated his victims with relief.
18. I found it pleasant studying about knights in shining armor in the library.
19. The old man went to the barn to milk the cow with a cane.
20. The table was delivered by the driver with the wooden top.

Answers to Misplaced Modifier Test

1. Does a one-eyed person named Wilson live here?
2. A. The musician with wooden legs played the piano.
   B. The musician played the piano which had wooden legs.
   C. The musician played the piano by using wooden legs.
3. Mrs. Jones was injured in a horrible manner while preparing her husband's supper.
4. While we were enjoying lunch, the gong sounded.
5. A strange man with a red beard was strolling down Broadway.
6. When the girl was six, her mother died and left four children.
7. With much disappointment on the part of the members, Mrs. McGillicuddy resigned from the Women's League after belonging fifteen years.
8. They took the horse out of the stable while he was eating his oats.
9. The flames were put out by the Fire Department before any damage was done.
10. While we were paddling, a huge fish leaped into the canoe.
11. Sitting in a carriage, the child watched the St. Patrick's Day Parade.
12. Have you read in the newspaper about the girl who was run over?
13. I wish to sell a brand-new house made by an expert builder who used the finest concrete block.
14. He sold the watch with the Swiss movement to the young lady.
15. Wearing a low-cut gown, the girl went to the party with the young man.
16. In the dictionary, we found a description of the crocodile.
17. With relief, we read about the arrest of the gangster who had intimidated his victims.
18. I found it pleasant studying in the library about knights in shining armor.
19. The old man with the cane went to the barn to milk the cow.
20. The table with the wooden top was delivered by the driver.

GUIDE TO ENGLISH USAGE

This section will teach you Correct English Usage directly and rapidly.

FIRST of all, it is important for you to know the essential difference between two special categories in the study of Correct Usage —

COLLOQUIAL ENGLISH and SLANG.

COLLOQUIAL (or INFORMAL) ENGLISH — This is English customarily used in conversation and informal types of writing (notes, diaries, friendly letters, etc.). It is ACCEPTABLE.

SLANG — This is used by people who are poor in vocabulary and/or lazy. It is generally UNACCEPTABLE.

Note: Certain colloquial expressions are so close to the unacceptable SLANG category that you will sometimes be advised to avoid a colloquialism. On the other hand, a slang word may — in rare cases — fill a specific need and the slang word may, consequently, be allowable for that situation. For example, "Defeat payola!" was used in a recent political campaign. The word, payola, though slang, was temporarily accepted.

Words Often Misused

abbreviate—means *to shorten by omitting*.

abridge—means *to shorten by condensing*.

New York is *abbreviated* to *N. Y.*, Tennesee to *Tenn.*

In order to save time in the reading, the report was *abridged*.

ability—means a *developed, actual* power.

capacity—means an *undeveloped, potential* power.

He now has fair writing *ability*, but additional courses in college will develop his *capacity* beyond the average level.

above—Avoid *above* except in business forms where it may be used in reference to a preceding part of the text. In normal writing use *foregoing* or *preceding*, instead of *above*.

Unacceptable: The *above* books are available in the library.

Acceptable: The *above* prices are subject to change without notice.

accede—means *to agree with*.

concede—means *to yield*, but not necessarily in agreement.

exceed—means *to be more than*.

We shall *accede* to your request for more evidence.

To avoid delay, we shall *concede* that more evidence is necessary.

Federal expenditures now *exceed* federal income.

accept—means *to take when offered*.

except—means *excluding*. (preposition)

except—means *to leave out*. (verb)

The draft board will *accept* all seniors as volunteers before graduation.

All eighteen-year-olds *except* seniors will be called.

The draft board will *except* all seniors until after graduation.

access—means *availability*.

excess—means *too much*.

The lawyer was given *access* to the grand jury records.

The expenditures this month are far in *excess* of income.

accident—means *an unexpected happening* with or without damage or injury.

injury—means *damage, hurt or impairment*.

The *accident* was caused by faulty brakes in both cars.

Fortunately, neither driver sustained any *injury*. (NOT *accident*).

accidently—No such word. The word is *accidentally* (adverb). Pronounce it ak-si-DENT-ally.

in accord with—means *in agreement with a person.*

I am *in accord with* you about this.

in accordance with—means *in agreement with a thing.*

The police officer acted *in accordance with* the law.

acoustics—when used in the *singular* means *the science* of sound.

Acoustics is a subdivision of physics.

acoustics—when used in the *plural* denotes the *qualities* of sound.

The *acoustics* of Carnegie Hall are incomparable.

Note: *Athletics* is an *activity* (or *are activities*) that will aid in weight-reducing.

Politics is a method (or *are methods*) of getting favors.

Physics is a science. (*singular* as a *branch of science*).

Physics are used to relieve sickness. (*plural* as a *medicine*)

Economics is taught in most high schools. (*singular only*)

acquiesce in—means *to accept with or without objection.* Do NOT use *acquiesce* WITH or *acquiesce* TO.

Although there is some doubt about your plan, I shall *acquiesce in* its adoption.

ad—this abbreviation for *advertisement* is colloquial; it is not to be used in formal speech or writing.

Other colloquial words of this type, with the formal word in parentheses, are *exam* (examination) *auto* (automobile); *phone* (telephone); *gym* (gymnasium).

adapt—means *to adjust or change.*

adopt—means *to take as one's own.*

adept—means *skillful.*

Children can *adapt* to changing conditions very easily.

The war orphan was *adopted* by the general and his wife.

Proper instruction makes children *adept* in various games.

NOTE: adapt *to*, adopt *by*, adept *in* or *at*.

adapted to—implies *original or natural suitability.*

The gills of the fish are *adapted to* underwater breathing.

adapted for—implies *created suitability.*

Atomic energy is constantly being *adapted for* new uses.

adapted from—implies *changed to be made suitable.*

Many of Richard Wagner's opera librettos were *adapted from* old Norse sagas.

addicted to—means *accustomed to by strong habit.*

subject to—means *exposed to* or *liable to.*

People *addicted to* drugs or alcohol need constant medical care.

The coast of Wales is *subject* to extremely heavy fogs.

addition—means *the act or process of adding.*

edition—means *a printing of a publication.*

In *addition* to a dictionary, he always used a thesaurus.

The first *edition* of Shakespeare's plays appeared in 1623.

admit—means *to give entrance to* or *to grant as true.*

admit of—means *to allow* or *permit.*

This ticket *admits* one person to the game.

I *admit* the possibility of error in this experiment.

The scope of the experiment will *admit of* not more than four research assistants.

admit—means *to grant the existence of error,* without original intent.

confess—means *to grant the existence of error,* with original intent.

I *admit* that I was mistaken in my calculations.

I *confess* that I am guilty of tax evasion.

admittance—means *permission to enter.*

admission—means *permission to enter, with certain privileges.*

No *admittance* was permitted to the laboratory.

Friendly aliens may secure *admission* to this country.

advantage—means *a superior position.*

benefit—means *a favor conferred* or *earned* (as a profit).

He had an *advantage* in experience over his opponent.

The rules were changed for his *benefit.*

Note: To *take* advantage *of*, to *have* an advantage *over.*

adverse—means *unfavorable.* (pronounced AD-verse)

averse—means *disliking.* (pronounced a-VERSE)

He took the *adverse* decision in poor taste.

Many students are *averse* to criticism by their classmates.

advise—best means *to give advice. Advise* is losing favor as a synonym for *notify.*

Acceptable: The teacher will *advise* the student in habits of study.

Unacceptable: We are *advising* you of a delivery under separate cover. (SAY *notifying*)

affect—means *to influence.* (a verb)

effect—means *an influence.* (a noun)

effect—means *to bring about.* (a verb)

Your education must *affect* your future.

The *effect* of the last war is still being felt.

A diploma *effected* a tremendous change in his attitude.

Note: *affect* also has a meaning of *pretend.*

She had an *affected* manner.

affection—means *feeling.*

affectation—means *pose.*

Alumni develop a strong *affection* for their former school.

The *affectation* of a Harvard accent is no guarantee of success.

affinity—means an *attraction to a person or thing.*

infinity—means an *unlimited time, space* or *quantity.*

She has an *affinity* for men who own Cadillac cars.

That the universe has *infinity* is questionable.

after—is unnecessary with the *past* participle.

SAY: *After* checking the timetable, I left for the station.

DON'T say: *After having checked* (omit *after*) the timetable, I left for the station.

aggravate—means *to make worse.*

exasperate—means *to irritate* or *annoy.*

His cold was *aggravated* by faulty medication.

His inability to make a quick recovery *exasperated* him exceedingly.

agree—means *to be in general accord.*

concur—means *to be in specific agreement.*

The judges *agreed* with the plaintiff who was seeking relief under the law.

Nevertheless, the five judges *concurred* in the verdict for the defendant.

Note: For agree *with*, agree *to*, agree *on* see "Guide to Grammar" (Prepositions).

ain't—is an *unacceptable* contraction for *am not, are not,* or *is not.*

aisle—is *a passageway* between seats.

isle—is *a small island.* (both words rhyme with *pile*)

alibi—is an explanation on the basis of being *in another place.*

excuse—is an *explanation* on *any basis.*

His *alibi* offered at the trial was that he was twenty miles away from the scene of the crime at the time indicated.

His *excuse* for failing on the test was that he was sick.

alimentary—refers to the process of *nutrition.*

elementary—means *primary.*

The *alimentary* canal includes the stomach and the intestines.

Elementary education is the foundation of all human development.

all ready—means *everybody* or *everything ready.*

already—means *previously.*

They were *all ready* to write when the teacher arrived.

They had *already* begun writing when the teacher arrived.

alright—is *unacceptable*.
all right is *acceptable*.

all-round—means *versatile* or *general*.
all around—means *all over a given area*.

Rafer Johnson, decathlon champion, is an *all-round* athlete.

The police were lined up for miles *all around*.

all together—means *everybody* or *everything together*.
altogether—means *completely*.

The boys and girls sang *all together*.

This was *altogether* strange for a person of his type.

all ways—means *in every possible way*.
always—means *at all times*.

He was in *all ways* acceptable to the voters.

His reputation had *always* been spotless.

allege—means *to state without proof*, (same as *assert* or *maintain*)
claim—means *to state ownership by proof*, NOT *to assert* or *maintain*.

He *alleges* that Plato was Aristotle's teacher.

The informant *claimed* the reward for having helped catch the thief.

allow—does NOT mean *to suppose. It* DOES mean *to give permission*.

Acceptable: The teacher *allows* adequate time for study in class.

Unacceptable: I *allow* I haven't ever seen anything like this.

allude—means *to make a reference to*.
elude—means *to escape from*.

Only incidentally does Coleridge *allude* to Shakespeare's puns.

It is almost impossible for one to *elude* tax collectors.

allusion—means *a reference*.
illusion—means *a deception of the eye or mind*.

The student made *allusions* to his teacher's habits.

Illusions of the mind, unlike those of the eye, cannot be corrected with glasses.

alongside of—means *side by side with*.
Bill stood *alongside of* Henry.
alongside—means *parallel to the side*.
Park the car *alongside* the curb.

alot—is *unacceptable*. It should always be written as two words: *a lot*.
allot—means *to apportion*.

We bought *a lot* of land on which to build a small house.

Before the attack, we shall *allot* the ammunition to the troops.

Note: *A lot* should never be used in formal English to signify *very much*, or *a large quantity*.

Unacceptable: I like spinach *a lot*. (SAY *very much*)

altar—means *a platform*.
alter—means *to change*.

The bride and groom approached the *altar*.

The tailor *altered* the old-fashioned suit.

alternate—(the noun) means *a substitute* or *second choice*.
alternative—means *a statement* or *offer of two things, both equally preferable, but only one of which may be accepted*.

He served as an *alternate* to the delegate selected.

Since there was no *alternative*, I had to accept the position.

alumnus—means *a male graduate*.
alumna—means *a female graduate*.

With the granting of the diploma, he became an *alumnus* of the school.

Note: The masculine plural form of *alumnus* is *alumni* (*ni* rhymes with *high*)

She is an *alumna* of Hunter College.

Note: The feminine plural form is *alumnae* (*ae* rhymes with *key*)

amend—means *to correct*.
emend—means *to correct a literary work; to edit*.

Our Constitution, as *amended* by the Bill of Rights, was finally ratified.

Before publication, several chapters of the book had to be *emended.*

among—is used with *more than two persons or things.*

Note: *Amongst should be avoided.*

between—is used with *two persons or things.*

The inheritance was equally divided *among* the four children.

The business, however, was divided *between* the oldest and the youngest one.

amount—applies to quantities *that cannot be counted one by one.*

number—applies to quantities *that can be counted one by one.*

A large *amount* of grain was delivered to the storehouse.

A large *number* of bags of grain was delivered.

and—should NOT be used before *etc.*

etc.—is the Latin expression *et cetera* meaning *and other things, and so forth.* Since the *et* means *and,* a combination of the two would have to be translated "and and so forth."

Acceptable: Oranges, peaches, cherries, *etc.* are healthful.

Unacceptable: Pickles, pizza, frankfurters, *and etc.* should be eaten sparingly.

angel—is *a heavenly creature.*

angle—is *a point at which two sides meet,* also *a corner.*

Lucifer was the most famous of the fallen *angels.*

A line perpendicular to another line forms a right *angle.*

angry at—means *annoyed by a thing.*

angry with—means *annoyed by a person.*

We were *angry at* the gross carelessness of the attendant.

We were *angry with* the careless attendant.

annual—means *yearly.*

biannual—means *twice a year.* (*semiannual* means the same).

biennial—means *once in two years* or *every two years.*

another such—is *acceptable.*

such another—is *unacceptable.*

Another such error may lead to legal prosecution.

After his illness, he seemed *quite another* person *from* what he had been. (NOT *such another*)

ante—is a prefix meaning *before.*

anti—is a prefix meaning *against.*

The *ante*chamber is the room just before the main room.

An *anti*-fascist is one who is opposed to fascists.

anxious—means *worried.*

eager—means *keenly desirous.*

We were *anxious* about our first airplane flight.

We are *eager* to fly again.

any—should not be used for *at all.*

SAY I haven't rested *at all* (NOT *any*) during this Easter vacation.

Note: When a comparison is indicated, say *any other*—NOT *any.*

Acceptable: He likes France better than *any other* country.

anywheres—is *unacceptable.*

anywhere—is *acceptable.*

SAY we can't find it *anywhere.*

Also SAY $\begin{cases} nowhere \text{ (NOT nowheres)} \\ somewhere \text{ (NOT somewheres)} \end{cases}$

appraise—means *to set a value.*

apprise—means *to inform.*

The jeweler *appraised* the diamond at a very high value.

We were *apprised* of their arrival by the honking of the car horn.

apprehend—means *to catch the meaning of something.*

comprehend—means *to understand a thing completely.*

It is fairly simple to *apprehend* the stupidity of war.

It is far more difficult to *comprehend* the Euclidean postulates.

Note: *Apprehend* may also mean *to take into custody.*

The sheriff succeeded in *apprehending* the rustler.

apt—suggests *habitual behavior.*
likely—suggests *probable behavior.*
liable—suggests an exposure to something *harmful.*

Boys are *apt* to be rather lazy in the morning.

A cat, if annoyed, is *likely* to scratch.

Cheating on a test may make one *liable* to expulsion from school.

aren't I—is colloquial. Its use is to be discouraged.

SAY *Am I not* entitled to an explanation? (preferred to *Aren't I . . .*)

argue—means *to prove something by logical methods.*
quarrel—means *to dispute without reason or logic.*

The opposing lawyers *argued* before the judge.

The lawyers became emotional and *quarreled.*

around—meaning *about* or *near* is a poor colloquialism.

It's *about* ten o'clock. (NOT *around*)

We'll be *near* the house. (NOT *around*)

artisan—means *mechanic* or *craftsman.*
artist—means *one who practises the fine arts.*

Many *artisans* participated in the building of the Sistine Chapel.

The basic design, however, was prepared by the *artist* Michelangelo.

as—(used as a conjunction) is followed by a verb.
like—(used as a preposition) is NOT followed by a verb.

Do *as* I do, not *as* I say.

Try not to behave *like* a child.

Unacceptable: He acts *like* I do.

as far as—expresses *distance.*
so far as—indicates *a limitation.*

We hiked *as far as* the next guest house.

So far as we know, the barn was adequate for a night's stay.

as good as—should be used *for comparisons only.*

This motel is *as good as* the next one.

Note: *As good as* does NOT mean *practically.*

Unacceptable: They *as good as* promised us a place in the hall.

Acceptable: They *practically* promised us a place in the hall.

as if—is correctly used in the expression, "He talked *as if* his jaw hurt him."

Unacceptable: "He talked *like* his jaw hurt him."

as much—is *unacceptable* for *so* or *this.*

He thought *so.*

They admitted *this* freely.

NOT He thought *as much,* or They admitted *as much* freely.

as per—is poor usage for *according to* or *in accordance with.*

The secretary typed the letter *in accordance with* the manager's directions. (NOT *as per*)

as regards to—is *unacceptable.* So is *in regards to.*

SAY, *in regard* to or *as regards.*

The teacher would say nothing *in regard to* the student's marks.

ascared—no such word. It is *unacceptable* for *scared.*

The child was *scared* of ghosts. (NOT *ascared*).

as to whether—is *unacceptable. Whether* includes the unnecessary words *as to.*

Acceptable: I don't know *whether* it is going to rain.

ascent—is *the act of rising.*
assent—means *approval.*

The *ascent* to the top of the mountain was perilous.

Congress gave its *assent* to the President's emergency directive.

assay—means *to try* or *experiment.*
essay—means *to make an intellectual effort.*

We shall *assay* the ascent to the mountain tomorrow.

Why not *essay* a description of the mountain in composition?

astonish—means *to strike with sudden wonder.*

surprise—means *to catch unaware.*

The extreme violence of the hurricane *astonished* everybody.

A heat wave in April would *surprise* us.

at—should be avoided where it does not contribute to the meaning.

SAY Where shall I meet you? (DON'T add the word *at*)

at about—should not be used for *about.*

The group will arrive *about* noon.

attend to—means to *take care of.*

tend to—means to *be inclined to.*

One of the clerk's will *attend to* mail in my absence.

Lazy people *tend* to gain weight.

audience—means *a group of listeners.*

spectators—refers to *a group of watchers.*

Leonard Bernstein conducted a concert for the school *audience.*

The slow baseball game bored the *spectators.*

Note: A group that both watches and listens is called an *audience.*

aught—is *the figure* O (zero); it also means *nothing* (same as *naught.*)

ought—expresses *obligation.*

Add a *naught.*

You *ought* to do it.

Note: The expression *had ought* is *unacceptable.*

average—means *conforming to norms or standards.*

ordinary—means *usual, customary,* or *without distinction.*

A book of about 300 pages is of *average* length.

The contents of the book were rather *ordinary.*

avocation—means *a temporary interest* or *employment.*

vocation—means *one's regular employment.*

Fishing and swimming are two of **my** favorite *avocations.*

I am by *vocation* a civil engineer.

award—means *the result of a decision of many; a decision.*

reward—means *pay for good* or *evil done.*

The judge gave him an *award* of $100.00 in damages in the case.

Satisfactory marks are the *reward* for intensive study.

awful—means *inspiring fear or respect.* It is an *unacceptable* synonym for *bad, ugly, shocking, very.*

The *awful* shadow of the bomber's wings threw terror into their hearts.

Unacceptable: I received an *awful* mark in history.

ay, aye—both mean *always* or *ever,* when rhyming with *may.* Both mean *yes,* when rhyming with *my.*

I shall love you *forever and aye.*

Those in favor of the bill, please say "*Aye.*"

back—should NOT be used with such words as *refer* and *return* since the prefix *re* means *back.*

Unacceptable: Refer *back* to the text, if you have difficulty recalling the facts.

backward } Both are *acceptable* and may be
backwards } used interchangeably as an adverb.

We tried to run *backward.* (or *backwards*)

Backward as an adjective means *slow in learning.* (DON'T say *backwards* in this case)

A *backward* pupil should be given every encouragement.

balance—meaning *remainder* is *acceptable* only in commercial usage.

Use *remainder* or *rest* otherwise.

Even after the withdrawal, his bank *balance* was considerable.

Three of the students voted for John; the *rest* voted for Jim.

bazaar—is a *market place* or a *charity sale*.

bizarre—means *odd* or *strange*.

> We are going to the *bazaar* to buy things.
> He dresses in a *bizarre* manner.

being that—is *unacceptable* for *since* or *because*.

> SAY, *Since* (*or Because*) you have come a long way, why not remain here for the night?

berth—is *a resting place*.

birth—means *the beginning of life*.

> The new liner was given a wide *berth* in the harbor.
> He was a fortunate man from *birth*.

beside—means *close to*.

besides—refers *to something that has been added*.

> He lived *beside* the stream.
> He found wild flowers and weeds *besides*.

better—means *recovering*.

well—means *completely recovered*.

> He is *better* now than he was a week ago.
> In a few more weeks, he will be *well*.

better part of—implies *quality*.

greater part of—implies *quantity*.

> The *better part of* his performance came in the first act of the play.
> Fortunately for the audience, the first act took *the greater part of the time*.

biannual—means *twice a year*.

biennial—means *every two years*.

> Most schools have *biannual* promotion, in January and June.
> The *biennial* election of Congressmen is held in the even-numbered years.

blame on—is *unacceptable* for *blame* or *blame for*.

> *Blame* the person who is responsible for the error.
> Don't *blame* me for it.
> *Unacceptable*: Why do you put the *blame on* me?

born—means *brought into existence*.

borne—means *carried*.

> All men are *born* free.

> We have *borne* our burdens with patience.

both—means *two considered together*.

each—means *one of two* or *more*.

> *Both* of the applicants qualified for the position.
> *Each* applicant was given a generous reference.
> Note: Avoid using such expressions as the following:
> *Both* girls had a new typewriter. (Use *each girl* instead).
> *Both* girls tried to outdo the other. (Use *each girl* instead).
> They are *both* alike. (Omit *both*).

bouillon—(pronounced boo-YON) is a *soup*.

bullion—(pronounced BULL-yun) means *gold* or *silver* in the form of bars.

> This restaurant serves tasty *bouillon*.
> A mint makes coins out of *bullion*.

breath—means *an intake of air*.

breathe—means *to draw air in and give it out*.

breadth—means *width*.

> Before you dive in, take a very deep *breath*.
> It is difficult to *breathe* under water.
> In a square, the *breadth* should be equal to the length.

bridal—means *of a wedding*.

bridle—means *to hold back*.

> The *bridal* party was late in arriving at the church.
> You must learn to *bridle* your short temper as you grow older.

bring—means *to carry toward the person who is speaking*.

take—means *to carry away from the speaker*.

> *Bring* the books here.
> *Take* your raincoat with you when you go out.

broach—means to *mention for the first time*.

brooch—(pronounced BROACH) means an *ornament* for clothing.

> At the meeting, one of the speakers *broached* the question of salary increases.

The model was wearing an expensive *brooch*.

broke—is the past tense of *break*.

broke—is *unacceptable* for *without money*.

> He *broke* his arm.
>
> "Go for broke" is a slang expression widely used in gambling circles.

bunch—refers to *things*.

group—refers to *persons* or *things*.

> This looks like a delicious *bunch* of bananas.
>
> What a well-behaved *group* of children!
>
> Note: The colloquial use of bunch applied to *persons* is to be discouraged.
>
> A bunch of the boys were whooping it up. (*number* is preferable)

burgle ⎱ are humorous ways of expressing
burglarize ⎰ the idea of committing burglary.

> SAY, Thieves *broke* into (NOT *burglarized*) the store.

burst—is *acceptable* for *broke*.

bust—is *unacceptable* for *broke* (or broken).

> *Acceptable*: The balloon *burst*.
>
> *Unacceptable*: My pen is *busted*.
>
> *Acceptable*: That is a *bust* of Wagner.

business—is sometimes incorrectly used for work.

> *Unacceptable*: I went to *business* very late today. (SAY, work).
>
> *Acceptable*: He owns a thriving *business*.

but—should NOT be used after the expression *cannot help*.

> *Acceptable*: One *cannot help noticing* the errors he makes in English.
>
> *Unacceptable*: One *cannot help but* notice. . .

byword—is *a pet expression*.

password—is *a secret word uttered to gain passage*.

> In ancient Greece, truth and beauty were *bywords*.
>
> The sentry asked the scout for the *password*.

calculate—means *to determine mathematically*. It does NOT mean *to think*.

Some Chinese still know how to *calculate on* an abacus.

Unacceptable: I *calculate* it's going to rain.

calendar—is *a system of time*.

calender—is *a smoothing and glazing machine*.

colander—is *a kind of sieve*.

> In this part of the world, most people prefer the twelve-month *calendar*.
>
> In ceramic work, the potting wheel and the *calender* are indispensable.
>
> Garden-picked vegetables should be washed in a *colander* before cooking.

Calvary—is *the name of the place of the Crucifixion*.

cavalry—is *a military unit on horseback*.

> *Calvary* and Gethsemane are place-names in the Bible.
>
> Most of our modern *cavalry* is now motorized.

can—means *physically able*.

may—implies *permission*.

> I *can* lift this chair over my head.
>
> You *may* leave after you finish your work.

cannon—is *a gun* for heavy firing.

canon—is *a rule* or *law* of the church.

> Don't remain near the *cannon* when it is being fired.
>
> Churchgoers are expected to observe the *canons*.

cannot help—must be followed by an *ing* form.

> We cannot help *feeling* (NOT *feel*) distressed about this.
>
> Note: cannot help *but* is unacceptable.

can't hardly—is a *double negative*. It is *unacceptable*.

> SAY, The child *can hardly* walk in those shoes.

capital—is *the city*.

capitol—is *the building*

> Paris is the *capital* of France.
>
> The Capitol in Washington is occupied by the Congress. (The Washington *Capitol* is capitalized).
>
> Note: *capital* also means wealth.

catalog—is a *systematic* list. (also **catalogue**)

category—is a *class* of things.

The item is precisely described in the sales *catalog*.

A trowel is included in the *category* of farm tools.

cease—means *to end*.

seize—means *to take hold of*.

Will you please *cease* making those sounds?

Seize him by the collar as he comes around the corner.

celery—is *a vegetable*.

salary—means *payment*. (generally a fixed amount, as opposed to wages)

Celery grows in stalks.

Your starting *salary* may appear low, but bonuses will make up for it.

censor—means *to examine for the purpose of judging moral aspects*.

censure—means *to find fault with*.

The government *censors* films in some countries.

She *censured* her husband for coming home late.

cent—means *a coin*.

scent—means *an odor*.

sent—is the past tense of *send*.

The one-*cent* postal card is a thing of the past.

The *scent* of roses is pleasing.

We were *sent* to the rear of the balcony

center around—is *unacceptable*. Use *center in* or *center on*.

The maximum power was *centered in* the nuclear reactor.

All attention was *centered on* the launching pad.

certainly—(and *surely*) is an *adverb*.

sure—is an *adjective*.

He was *certainly* learning fast.

Unacceptable: He *sure* was learning fast.

cession—means *a yielding*.

session—means *a meeting*.

The *cession* of a piece of territory could have avoided the war.

The legislative *session* lasted three months.

character. Do NOT use for a strange or eccentric person.

Unacceptable: He's as unpredictable as they come—what a *character*! (SAY *eccentric person*).

childish—means *silly, immature*.

childlike—means *innocent, unspoiled*.

Pouting appears *childish* in an adult.

His *childlike* appreciation of art gave him great pleasure.

choice—means *a selection*.

choose—means *to select*.

chose—means *have selected*.

My *choice* for a career is teaching.

We may *choose* our own leader.

I finally *chose* teaching for a career.

cite—means *to quote*.

sight—means *seeing*.

site—means *a place for a building*.

He was fond of *citing* from the Scriptures.

The *sight* of the wreck was appalling.

The Board of Education is seeking a *site* for the new school.

climatic—refers *to climate*.

climactic—refers to *climax*.

New York City has many *climatic* changes.

The *climactic* parts of novels are often the most interesting.

climate—is the average weather *over a period of many years*.

weather—is the *hour by hour or day by day* condition of the atmosphere.

He likes the *climate* of California better than that of Illinois.

The *weather* is sometimes hard to predict.

coarse—means *vulgar* or *harsh*.

course—means a *path* or a *study*.

> He was shunned because of his *coarse* behavior.
>
> The ship took its usual *course*.
>
> Which *course* in English are you taking?

come to be—should NOT be replaced with the expression *become to be*, since *become* means *come to be*.

> True freedom will *come to be* when all tyrants have been overthrown.

comic—means *intentionally funny*.

comical—means *unintentionally funny*.

> A clown is a *comic* figure.
>
> The peculiar hat she wore gave her a *comical* appearance.

comma—is *a mark of punctuation*.

coma—means *a period of prolonged unconsciousness*. (rhymes with *aroma*)

> A *comma* can never separate two complete sentences.
>
> The accident put him into a *coma* lasting three days.

common—means *shared equally by two or more*.

mutual—means *interchanged*.

> The town hall is the *common* pride of every citizen.
>
> We can do business to our *mutual* profit and satisfaction.

compare to—means *to liken to something which has a different form*.

compare with—means *to compare persons or things with each other when they are of the same kind*.

contrast with—means *to show the difference between two things*.

> A minister is sometimes *compared to* a shepherd.
>
> Shakespeare's plays are often *compared with* those of Marlowe.
>
> The writer *contrasted* the sensitivity of the dancer *with* the grossness of the pugilist.

complement—means *a completing part*.

compliment—is *an expression of admiration*.

> His wit was a *complement* to her beauty.

> He received many *compliments* on his valedictory speech.

complected—is *unacceptable* for *complexioned*.

> SAY, Most South Sea Islanders are *dark-complexioned*.

comprehensible—means *understandable*.

comprehensive—means *including a great deal*.

> Under the circumstances, your doubts were *comprehensible*.
>
> Toynbee's *comprehensive* study of history covers many centuries.

comprise—means *to include*.

compose—means *to form the substance of*.

> Toynbee's study of history *comprises* seven volumes.
>
> Some modern symphonies are *composed* of as little as one movement.

concur in—must be followed by *an action*.

concur with—must be followed by *a person*.

> I shall *concur in* the decision reached by the majority.
>
> I cannot *concur with* the chairman, however much I respect his opinion.
>
> Note: See **agree — concur**.

conducive to—means *leading to*.

conducive for—is *unacceptable*.

> Your proposals for compromise are *conducive to* a setttlement of our disagreement.

conform to—means *to adapt one's self to*.

conform with—means *to be in harmony with*.

> Youngsters are inclined to *conform to* a group pattern.
>
> They feel it dangerous not to *conform with* the rules of the group.

conscience—means *sense of right*.

conscientious—means *faithful*.

conscious—means *aware of one's self*.

> Man's *conscience* prevents him from becoming completely selfish.
>
> We all depend on him because he is *conscientious*.
>
> The injured man was completely *conscious*.

considerable—is properly used *only as an adjective*, NOT as a noun.

Acceptable: The fraternal organization invested a *considerable amount* in government bonds.

Unacceptable: He lost *considerable* in the stock market.

consistently—means *in harmony*.

constantly—means *regularly, steadily*.

If you choose to give advice, act *consistently* with that advice.

Doctors *constantly* warn against over-exertion after forty-five.

consul—means *a government representative*.

council—means *an assembly which meets for deliberation*.

counsel—means *advice*.

Americans abroad should keep in touch with their *consuls*.

The City *Council* enacts local laws and regulations.

The defendant heeded the *counsel* of his friends.

contact—meaning *to communicate with a person* should be left for business usage only.

Acceptable: The owner *contacted* his salesmen.

Unacceptable: *Contact* me if you want to play bridge some evening. (say *telephone* me)

contagious—means *catching*.

contiguous—means *adjacent or touching*.

Measles is a *contagious* disease.

The United States and Canada are *contiguous* countries.

contemptible—means *worthy of contempt*.

contemptuous—means *feeling contempt*.

His spying activities were *contemptible*.

It was plain to all that he was *contemptuous* of his co-workers.

continual—means *happening again and again at short intervals*.

continuous—means *without interruption*.

The teacher gave the class *continual* warnings.

Noah experienced *continuous* rain for forty days.

convenient to—should be followed by a *person*.

convenient for—should be followed by a *purpose*.

Will these plans be *convenient to* you?

You must agree that they are *convenient for* the occasion.

copy—is *an imitation of an original work*. (not necessarily an exact imitation)

facsimile—is *an exact imitation of an original work*.

The counterfeiters made a crude *copy* of the hundred-dollar bill.

The official government engraver, however, prepared a *facsimile* of the bill.

core—means *the heart of something*.

corps—(pronounced like *core*) means an *organized military body*.

corpse—means *a dead body*.

The *core* of the apple was rotten.

The *corps* consisted of three full-sized armies.

The *corpse* was quietly slipped overboard after a brief service.

co-respondent—is a *joint defendant* in a divorce case.

correspondent—is *one who communicates*.

The *co-respondent* declared that he loved the other man's wife.

Max Frankel is a special *correspondent* for the New York Times.

corporeal—means *bodily as the opposite of spiritual*.

corporal—means *bodily as it pertains to a person*.

Many believe that our *corporeal* existence changes to a spiritual one after death.

Corporal punishment is not recommended in modern schools.

costumes—are *garments belonging to another period*.

customs—are *habitual practices*.

The company played "*Macbeth*" in Elizabethan *costumes*.

Every country has its own distinctive *customs*.

could of—is *unacceptable*. (*should of* is also *unacceptable*)

could have—is *acceptable*. (*should have* is acceptable)

Acceptable: You *could have* done better with more care.

Unacceptable: I *could of* won.

AVOID ALSO: *must of, would of*.

couple—refers *to two things that are joined*.

pair—refers *to two things that are related, but not necessarily joined*.

Four *couples* remained on the dance floor.

The left shoe in this *pair* is a size seven; the right is a size nine.

Note: *couple* refers to *two*. Do not use couple for more than two or for an undetermined number.

The *couple* has just become engaged.

Phone me in a *few* (NOT *couple of*) days.

credible—means *believable*.

creditable—means *worthy of receiving praise*.

credulous—means *believing too easily*.

The pupil gave a *credible* explanation for his lateness.

Considering all the handicaps, he gave a *creditable* performance.

Politicians prefer to address *credulous* people.

cute—is an abbreviated form of the word *acute*.

It may mean *attractive* in colloquial usage. AVOID IT.

data—has *plural* meaning.

The *data* for the report *are* (NOT *is*) ready.

Note 1: The singular (*datum*) is seldom used.

Note 2: *errata, strata, phenomena* are plural forms of *erratum, stratum, phenomenon*.

deal—is *acceptable* when it means a quantity.

When it means a business transaction it is *unacceptable*.

Acceptable: I have a great *deal* of confidence in you.

Unacceptable: Let's make a *deal* and I'll buy your car.

decease—means *death*.

disease—means *illness*.

The court announced the *decease* of the crown prince.

Leukemia is a deadly *disease*.

decent—means *suitable*.

descent—means *going down*.

dissent—means *disagreement*.

The *decent* thing to do is to admit your fault.

The *descent* into the cave was treacherous.

Two of the nine justices filed a *dissenting* opinion.

decided—means *unmistakable* when used of persons or things.

decisive—means *conclusive*, and is used of things only.

He was a *decided* supporter of the left-wing candidate.

The atom-bomb explosion over Hiroshima was the *decisive* act of World War II.

deduction—means *reasoning from the general (laws or principles) to the particular (facts)*.

induction—means *reasoning from the particular (facts) to the general (laws or principles)*.

All men are mortal. Since John is a man, he is mortal. (*deduction*)

There are 10,000 oranges in this truckload. I have examined 100 from various parts of the load and find them all of the same quality. I conclude that the 10,000 oranges are of this quality. (*induction*)

deference—means *respect*.

difference—means *unlikeness*.

In *deference* to his memory, we did not play yesterday.

The *difference* between the two boys is unmistakable.

definite—means *clear, with set limits.*

definitive—means *final, decisive.*

> We would prefer a *definite* answer to our *definite* question.
>
> The dictionary is the *definitive* authority for word meanings.

delusion—means *a wrong idea* which will probably influence action.

illusion—means *a wrong idea* that will probably *not* influence action.

> People were under the *delusion* that the earth was flat.
>
> It is just an *illusion* that the earth is flat.

deprecate—means *to disapprove.*

depreciate—means *to lower the value.*

> His classmates *deprecated* his discourtesy.
>
> The service station *depreciated* the value of our house.

desirable—means *that which is desired.*

desirous—means *desiring or wanting.*

> It was a most *desirable* position.
>
> He was *desirous* of obtaining it. (Note the preposition *of*)

despise—means *to look down upon.*

detest—means *to hate.*

> Some wealthy persons *despise* the poor.
>
> I *detest* cold weather. (NOT *despise*)

despite—means *notwithstanding, nevertheless.*

in spite of—is a synonym.

> *Despite* the weather, he went on the hike. (*Note:* no preposition)
>
> *In spite of* the weather, he went on the hike.

desert—(pronounced DEZZ-ert) means *an arid area.*

desert—(pronounced di-ZERT) means *to abandon;* also *a reward or punishment.*

dessert—(pronounced di-ZERT) means *the final course of a meal.*

> The Sahara is the world's most famous *desert.*
>
> A husband must not *desert* his wife.

> Execution was a just *desert* for his crime.
>
> We had plum pudding for *dessert.*

device—means *a way to do something.* (a noun)

devise—means *to find the way.* (a verb)

> A hook is a good fishing *device.*
>
> Some fishermen prefer to *devise* other ways for catching fish.
>
> Note: *Advice* (noun), *advise* (verb); *prophecy* (noun), *prophesy* (verb).

differ from—is used when there is a difference *in appearance.*

differ with—is used when there is a difference *in opinion.*

> A coat *differs from* a cape.
>
> You have the right to *differ with* me on public affairs.

different from—is *acceptable.*

different than—is *unacceptable.*

> *Acceptable:* Jack is *different from* his brother.
>
> *Unacceptable:* Florida climate is *different than* New York climate.

discover—means to find something already in existence.

invent—means to create something that never existed before.

> Pasteur *discovered* the germ theory of disease.
>
> Whitney *invented* the cotton gin.

discomfit—means to *upset.* (a verb)

discomfort—means *lack of ease.* (a noun)

> The general's plan was designed to *discomfit* the enemy.
>
> This collar causes *discomfort.*

discreet—means *cautious.*

discrete—means *separate.*

> The employee was *discreet* in her comments about her employer.
>
> Since these two questions are *discrete,* you must provide two separate answers.

disinterested—means *impartial.*

uninterested—means *not interested.*

> The judge must always be a *disinterested* party in a trial.

As an *uninterested* observer, he was inclined to yawn at times.

dissociate } Both mean to *separate one's self.*
disassociate } Although both are *acceptable, use dissociate.*

After graduation, he *dissociated* himself from his former friends.

dissuade from—means *to urge against.* (Note the preposition *from*)

Acceptable: We tried to *dissuade* him *from* his rash scheme.

Unacceptable: He *dissuaded* me *against* going on a trip.

divers—means *several.* (pronounced DIE-vurz)

diverse—means *different.* (pronounced di-VERSE)

The store had *divers* foodstuffs for sale. Many of the items were completely *diverse* from staple foods.

doubt that—is *acceptable.*

doubt whether—is *unacceptable.*

Acceptable: I *doubt that* you will pass this term.

Unacceptable: We *doubt whether* you will succeed.

doubtless—is *acceptable.*

doubtlessly—is *unacceptable.*

Acceptable: You *doubtless* know your work; why, then, don't you pass?

Unacceptable: He *doubtlessly* thinks that you can do the job well.

drouth—(rhymes with MOUTH) and **drought** (rhymes with OUT) are two forms of the same word; the second is preferred.

The lengthy *drought* caused severe damage to the crops.

dual—means *relating to two.*

duel—means *a contest between two persons.*

Dr. Jekyl had a *dual* personality.

Alexander Hamilton was fatally injured in a *duel* with Aaron Burr.

due to—is unacceptable at the beginning of a sentence. Use *because of, on account of,* or some similar expression instead.

Unacceptable: *Due to* the rain, the game was postponed.

Acceptable: *Because of* the rain, the game was postponed.

Acceptable: The postponement was *due to* the rain.

each other—refers to *two persons.*

one another—refers to *more than two persons.*

The two girls have known *each other* for many years.

Several of the girls have known *one another* for many years.

eats—is *unacceptable* as a synonym for *food.*

We enjoyed the *food* (NOT *eats*) at the party.

economic—refers to *the subject of economics.*

economical—means *thrifty.*

An *economic* discussion was held at the United Nations.

A housewife should be *economical.*

either . . . or—is used when referring to choices.

neither . . . nor—is the *negative* form.

Either you *or* I will win the election.

Neither Bill *nor* Henry is expected to have a chance.

elegy—is a *mournful* or *melancholy* poem.

eulogy—is a speech in praise of a deceased person.

Gray's "*Elegy* Written in a Country Churchyard" is one of the greatest poems ever written.

The minister delivered the *eulogy.*

eligible—means *fit to be chosen.*

illegible—means *impossible to read* or *hard to read.*

Not all thirty-five year-old persons are *eligible* to be President.

His childish handwriting was *illegible.*

eliminate—means *to get rid of.*

illuminate—means *to supply with light.*

Let us try to *eliminate* the unnecessary steps.

Several lamps were needed to *illuminate* the corridor.

else—is superfluous in such expressions as the following:

Unacceptable: We want *no one else* but you.

Acceptable: We want *no one* but you.

Note: The possessive form of *else* is else's.

emerge—means *to rise out of*.

immerge—means *to sink into*. (also **immerse**)

The swimmer *emerged* from the pool.

The laundress *immerged* the dress in the tub of water.

emigrate—means *to leave one's country for another*.

immigrate—means *to enter another country*.

The Norwegians *emigrated* to America in mid-1860.

Many of the Norwegian *immigrants* settled in the Middle West.

enclosed herewith—is *unacceptable*.

enclosed—is *acceptable*.

Acceptable: You will find *enclosed* one copy of our brochure.

Unacceptable: *Enclosure herewith* is the book you ordered.

endorse—means *to write on the back of*.

Acceptable: He *endorsed* the check.

Unacceptable: He *endorsed* the check *on the back*.

enormity—means *viciousness*.

enormousness—means *vastness*.

The *enormity* of his crime was appalling.

The *enormousness* of the Sahara exceeds that of any other desert.

enthused—should be avoided.

enthusiastic—is preferred.

Acceptable: We were *enthusiastic* over the performance.

Unacceptable: I am truly *enthused* about my coming vacation.

equally as good—is *unacceptable*.

just as good—is *acceptable*.

Acceptable: This book is *just as good* as that.

Unacceptable: Your marks are *equally as good* as mine.

eruption—means *a breaking out*.

irruption—means *a breaking in*.

The *eruption* of Mt. Vesuvius caused extensive damage.

The *irruption* of the river devasted the coastal town.

everyone—is written as one word when it is a *pronoun*.

every one—(two words) is used when each individual is stressed.

Everyone present voted for the proposal.

Every one of the voters accepted the proposal.

Note: *Everybody* is written as one word.

every bit—is *incorrectly* used for *just as*.

Acceptable: You are *just as* clever as she is.

Unacceptable: He is *every bit* as lazy as his father.

every so often—is *unacceptable*.

ever so often—is *acceptable*.

We go to the ball game *ever so* often. (NOT *every* so often)

everywheres—is *unacceptable*.

everywhere—is *acceptable*.

We searched *everywhere* for the missing book.

Note: *Everyplace* (one word) is likewise *unacceptable*.

every which way—meaning *in all directions* is *unacceptable*.

every way—is *acceptable*.

He tried to solve the problem in *every* (OMIT *which*) *way*.

exceed—means *going beyond the limit*.

excel—refers *to superior quality*.

You have *exceeded* the time allotted to you.

All-round athletes are expected to *excel* in many sports.

except—is *acceptable*.

excepting—is *unacceptable*.

Acceptable: All *except* Joe are going.

Unacceptable: All cities, *excepting* Washington, are in a state.

Note: Don't use *except* for *unless*.

Unacceptable: He won't consent *except* you give him the money. (SAY *unless*)

exceptional—means *extraordinary*.
exceptionable—means *objectionable*.
> *Exceptional* children learn to read before the age of five.
> The behavior of exceptional children is sometimes *exceptionable*.

excessively—means *beyond acceptable limits*.
exceedingly—means *to a very great degree*.
> In view of our recent feud, he was *excessively* friendly.
> The weather in July was *exceedingly* hot.

expand—means *to spread out*.
expend—means *to use up*.
> As the staff increases, we shall have to *expand* our office space.
> Don't *expend* all your energy on one project.

expect—means *to look forward to*.
suspect—means *to imagine to be bad*.
> We *expect* that the girls will come home before New Year's Day.
> They *suspect* that we have a plan to attack them.

factitious—means *unnatural* or *artificial*.
fictitious—means *imaginary*.
> His *factitious* enthusiasm did not deceive us.
> Jim Hawkins is a *fictitious* character.

faint—means *to lose consciousness*.
feint—means *to make a pretended attack*.
> The lack of fresh air caused her to *faint*.
> First he *feinted* his opponent out of position; then he lobbed the ball over the net.

fair—means *light in color, reasonable, pretty*.
fare—means *a set price*.
> Your attitude is not a *fair* one.
> Children may ride the bus for half-*fare*.

farther—is used to describe *concrete distance*.
further—is used to describe *abstract ideas*.
> Chicago is *farther* from New York than Cincinnati is.

I'll explain my point of view *further*.

faze—meaning *to worry* or *disturb* may be used colloquially.
> Don't let his angry look *faze* you.

phase—means *an aspect*.
> A crescent is a *phase* of the moon.

feel bad—means *to feel ill*.
feel badly—means *to have a poor sense of touch*.
> I *feel bad* about the accident I saw.
> The numbness in his limbs caused him to *feel badly*.

feel good—means *to be happy*.
feel well—means to be in *good health*.
> I *feel* very *good* about by recent promotion.
> Spring weather always made him *feel well*.

fellow—means *man* or *person* in the *colloquial* sense only.

fever—refers to an *undue rise of temperature*.
temperature—refers to the *degree of heat* which may be normal.
> We had better call the doctor—he has a *fever*.
> The *temperature* is 80 degrees.

fewer—refers to *persons or things that can be counted*.
less—refers to *something considered as a mass*.
> We have *fewer* customers this week than last week.
> I have *less* money in my pocket than you have.

finalize—is a new word meaning *conclude* or *complete*. The word has not yet received complete acceptance.
> SAY, Labor and management *completed* arrangements for a settlement. (NOT *finalized*)

financial—refers to *money matters in a general sense*.
fiscal—refers to the *public treasury*.
> Scholars are usually not *financial* successes.
> The government's *fiscal year* begins July 1 and ends June 30.

fix—*means to fasten in place*. There are certain senses in which *fix* should *NOT* be used.

Acceptable: He *fixed* the leg to the table.

Unacceptable: The mechanic *fixed* the Buick. (SAY *repaired*)

Unacceptable: How did I ever get into this *fix*? (SAY *predicament*)

flout—*means to insult*.

flaunt—*means to make a display of*.

He *flouted* the authority of the principal.

Hester Prynne *flaunted* her scarlet "A."

flowed—is the past participle of *flow*.

flown—is the past participle of *fly*.

The flood waters had *flowed* over the levee before nightfall.

He had *flown* for 500 hours before he crashed.

folk—means *people in the sense of a group*. It is no longer used alone, but in combination with other words.

folks—is *unacceptable* for *friends, relatives, etc.*

Unacceptable: I'm going to see my *folks* on Sunday.

Acceptable: Anthropologists study *folk*ways, *folk*lore, and *folk*songs.

forbear—*means to refrain from doing something*. (accent on second syllable)

forebear—*means ancestor*. (accent on first syllable)

Forebear seeking vengeance.

Most of our *forebears* came from England.

formally—means *in a formal way*.

formerly—means *at an earlier time*.

The letter of reference was *formally* written.

He was *formerly* a delegate to the convention.

former—means *the first of two*.

latter—means *the second of two*.

The *former* half of the book was in prose.

The *latter* half of the book was in poetry.

fort—means *a fortified place*.

forte—(rhymes with *fort*) means *a strong point*.

A small garrison was able to hold the *fort*.

Conducting Wagner's music was Toscanini's forte.

Note: forte (pronounced FOR-tay) is a musical term meaning *loudly*.

forth—means *forward*.

fourth—*comes after third*.

They went *forth* like warriors of old.

The *Fourth* of July is our Independence Day.

Note: spelling of *forty* (40) and *fourteen* (14).

freeze—means *to turn into ice*.

frieze—is *a decorated band in or on a building*.

As the temperature dropped, the water began to *freeze*.

The *friezes* on the Parthenon are wonders of art.

funny—means *humorous* or *laughable*.

That clown is truly *funny*.

Note: *Funny* meaning *odd* or *strange* is a colloquial use that should be avoided.

SAY I have *queer* feeling in my stomach. (NOT *funny*)

genial—means *cheerful*.

congenial—means *agreeing in spirit*.

Genial landlords are rare today.

A successful party depends on *congenial* guests.

genius—means *extraordinary natural ability*, or *one so gifted*.

genus—means *class* or *kind*.

Mozart showed his *genius* for music at a very early age.

The rose-of-Sharon flower probably does not belong to the *genus* of roses.

Note: A particular member of a genus is called *a species*.

get—is a verb which strictly means *to obtain*.

Please *get* my bag.

There are many slang forms of GET that should be avoided:

AVOID: Do you *get* me? (SAY, Do you *understand* me?)

You can't *get* away with it. (SAY,

You won't *avoid* punishment if you do it.)

Get wise to yourself. (Say, *Use common sense.*)

We didn't *get* to go. (SAY, We didn't *manage* to go.)

get-up—meaning *dress* or *costume* should be *avoided*.

gibe |
jibe | (pronounced alike) – both mean *to scoff*.

We are inclined to *gibe* at awkward speakers.

Jibe also means *to agree*.

The two stories are now beginning to *jibe*.

got—means *obtained*.

He *got* the tickets yesterday.

AVOID: You've *got* to do it. SAY, You *have* to do it.)

We *have got* no sympathy for them. (SAY, We *have* no sympathy for them.)

They have *got* a great deal of property. (SAY, They *have* a great deal of property.)

gourmand—is *one who eats large quantities of food.* (rhymes with POOR-mund)

gourmet—is *one who eats fastidiously; a connoisseur.* (rhymes with POOR-may)

His uncontrollable appetite soon turned him into a *gourmand*.

The *gourmet* chooses the right wine for the right dish.

graduated—is followed by the prep. *from*.

He *graduated* (or *was graduated*) from high school in 1961.

Unacceptable: He *graduated* college.

Note: A *graduated* test tube is one that has markings on it to indicate volume or capacity.

guess—is *unacceptable* for *think* or *suppose*.

SAY, I *think* I'll go downtown. (NOT I *guess*)

habit—means *an individual tendency to repeat a thing.*

custom—means *group habit.*

He had a *habit* of breaking glasses before each ball game.

The *custom* of the country was to betroth girls at the age of ten.

had ought—is *unacceptable*.

SAY, You *ought* not to eat fish if you are allergic to it.

hanged—is used in reference to a *person*.

hung—is used in reference to *a thing*.

The prisoner was *hanged* at dawn.

The picture was *hung* above the fireplace.

happen—means *to take place.*

transpire—means *to come to general knowledge.*

The meeting *happened* last year.

The decisions reached at that meeting did not *transpire* until recently.

healthy—means *having health.*

healthful—means *giving health.*

The man is *healthy*.

Fruit is *healthful*.

heap—means *a pile.*

heaps—is *unacceptable* in the sense of *very much*.

Unacceptable: Thanks *heaps* for the gift.

Note: LOTS is also *unacceptable* for very much.

help—meaning employees is *unacceptable*.

Unacceptable: Some of the *help* are sick. (SAY, *employees*)

him |
his | Use these pronouns correctly:

We saw *him working* from sunup to sunset. (The *object* of saw is *him*.)

We saw *his working* as a means of solving a financial problem.

(The object of saw is *his working*).

Note: The same rule applies to *me — my, you — your, them — their.*

holy—means *sacred.*

holely—means *with holes.*

wholly—means *completely or altogether.*

Easter Week is a *holy* time in many lands.

Old stockings tend to become *holely* after a while.

We are *wholly* in agreement with your decision.

however—means *nevertheless.*
how ever—means *in what possible way.*

We are certain, *however*, that you will like this class.

We are certain that, *how ever* you decide to study, you will succeed.

human—is *unacceptable* in the sense of *human being.*

Love is one of the basic needs of all *human beings.* (not *humans*)

Love is a basic *human* (as adj. only) need.

hypercritical—refers to a person *who finds fault easily.*
hypocritical—refers to a person *who pretends.*

Don't be so *hypercritical* about the meals at such low prices.

It is better to be sincere than to be *hypocritical.*

identical with—means *agreeing exactly in every respect.*
similar to—means *having a general likeness* or *resemblance.*

By coincidence, his plan was *identical with* mine.

He had used methods *similar to* mine.

idle—means *unemployed* or *unoccupied.*
idol—means *image* or *object of worship.*

Idle men, like *idle* machines, are inclined to lose their sharpness.

Some dictators prefer to be looked upon as *idols* by the masses.

if—introduces a *condition.*
whether—introduces *a choice.*

I shall go to Europe *if* I win the prize.

He asked me *whether* I intended to go to Europe. (not *if*)

if it was—implies that *something might have been true in the past.*
if it were—implies *doubt,* or indicates *something that is contrary* to fact.

If your book was there last night, it is there now.

If it were summer now, we would all go swimming.

immunity—implies *resistance to a disease.*
impunity—means *freedom from punishment.*

The Salk vaccine helps develop an *immunity* to poliomyelitis.

Because he was an only child, he frequently misbehaved with *impunity.*

imply—means *to suggest* or *hint at.* (The speaker *implies*)
infer—means *to deduce* or *conclude.* (The listener *infers*)

Are you *implying* that I have disobeyed orders?

From your carefree attitude, what else are we to *infer?*

in—usually refers to *a state of being.* (no motion)
into—is used for *motion from one place to another.*

The records are *in* that drawer.

I put the records *into* that drawer.

Note: "We were walking in the room" is correct even though there is motion. The motion is *not* from one place to another.

in back of—means *behind.*
in the back of—(or *at the back of*) means *in the rear of.*

The shovel is in *back of* (that is, *behind*) the barn.

John is sitting *in the back* of the theatre.

inclement—(pronounced in-CLEM-ent) refers to *severe weather,* such as a heavy rainfall or storm. It does NOT mean threatening.

Because of the *inclement* weather, we were soaked to the skin.

indict—(pronounced *indite*) means *to charge with a crime.*
indite—means *to write.*

The grand jury *indicted* him for embezzlement.

Modern authors prefer the expression *to write,* rather than *indite;* the latter is now a stuffy sort of expression.

infect—means *to contaminate with germs.*

infest—means *to be present in large numbers* (in a *bad sense*)

> The quick application of a germicide can prevent *infection.*
>
> The abandoned barn was *infested* with field mice.

ingenious—means *skillful, imaginative.*

ingenuous—means *naive, frank, candid.*

> The *ingenious* boy created his own rocket.
>
> One must be *ingenuous* to accept the Communist definition of freedom.

inside
inside of } When referring to time, use WITHIN.

> She is arriving *within* two hours. (NOT *inside* or *inside of*)

invite—is *unacceptable* for *invitation.*

> SAY, We received an *invitation* to the party.

irregardless—is *unacceptable.*

regardless—is *acceptable.*

> *Unacceptable*: *Irregardless* of the weather, I am going to the game.
>
> *Acceptable*: *Regardless* of his ability, he is not likely to win.

irresponsible—means *having no sense of responsibility.*

not responsible for—means *not accountable for something.*

> *Irresponsible* people are frequently late for appointments.
>
> Since you came late, we are *not responsible* for your having missed the first act.

its—means *belonging to it.*

it's—means *it is.*

> The house lost *its* roof.
>
> *It's* an exposed house, now.

join together—is incorrect for *connect.* Omit *together.*

> *Acceptable*: I want to *join* these pieces of wood.
>
> *Unacceptable*: All of us should *join together* to fight intolerance.

judicial—means *pertaining to courts* or *to the law.*

judicious—means *wise.*

> The problem required the *judicial* consideration of an expert.
>
> We were certainly in no position to make a *judicious* decision.

jump at—means *to accept eagerly.*

jump to—means *to spring to.*

> We would be foolish not to *jump at* such an opportunity.
>
> At the sound of the bell, they all *jumped to* attention.

just terrible—is barely *acceptable.*

> SAY, The sight of the accident was *simply* (or *quite*) *terrible.*

kid—meaning *child* is colloquial. Don't use it formally.

> My cousin is a clever *kid.* (*acceptable* in the informal use)
>
> Note: *kid* meaning *to make fun of* is *unacceptable.*
>
> SAY, You must be *making fun of me.* (NOT *kidding*)

kind of
sort of } are *unacceptable* for *rather.*

> SAY, We are *rather* disappointed in you.

kinfolks—is *unacceptable* for *kinfolk,* or *kinsfolk.*

> SAY, We now know that the Irish and the Welsh are distant *kinfolk.*

last—refers to *the final member in a series.*

latest—refers to *the most recent in time.*

latter—refers to *the second of two.*

> This is the *last* bulletin. There won't be any other bulletins.
>
> This is the *latest* bulletin. There will be other bulletins.
>
> Of the two most recent bulletins, the *latter* is more encouraging.

later on—is *unacceptable for later.*

> SAY, *Later,* we shall give your request fuller attention.

lay—means *to place.* (**transitive verb**)
lie—means *to recline.* (**intransitive verb**) } see Grammar Section (verbs)

> Note the forms of each verb:

TENSE	LAY (PLACE)	LIE (RECLINE)
PRESENT	The chicken *is laying* an egg.	The child *is lying* down.
PAST	The chicken *laid* an egg.	The child *lay* down.
PRES. PERF.	The chicken *has laid* an egg.	The child *has lain* down.

learn—means *to acquire knowledge.*
teach—means *to give knowledge.*

> We can *learn* many things just by observing carefully.
>
> In technical matters it is better to get someone to *teach* you.

least—means *the smallest.*
less—means *the smaller of two.*

> This was the *least* desirable of all the locations we have seen.
>
> We may finally have to accept the *less* desirable of the two locations we last saw.

leave—means *to go away from.* (A verb is NOT used with *leave*)
let—means *to permit.* (A verb is used with *let*)

> *Leave* this house at once.
> *Let* me remain in peace in my own house.
> (*remain* is the verb used with *let*)

legible—means *able to be read.*
readable—means *able to be read with pleasure.*

> Your themes have become increasingly more *legible.*
>
> In fact, I now find most of them extremely *readable.*

lengthened—means *made longer.*
lengthy—means *annoyingly long.*

> The essay, now *lengthened,* is more readable.
>
> However, try to avoid writing *lengthy* explanations of obvious facts.

levy—(rhymes with *heavy*) means *to impose a tax.*
levee—(pronounced like *levy*) means *an embankment.*

> It is the duty of Congress to *levy* taxes.
> The Mississippi River is held in with massive *levees.*

libel—is *a written and published statement injurious to a person's character.*

slander—is *a spoken statement of the same sort.*

> The unfavorable references to me in your book are *libelous.*
>
> When you say these vicious things about me, you are committing *slander.*

lief—(rhymes with *thief*) means *gladly.*

> He had as *lief* give me the tools as sell them to me.
>
> He would *liefer* (*more gladly*) give me the tools as sell them to me.

lightening—is the present participle of to *lighten.*
lightning—means *the flashes of light accompanied by thunder.*

> Leaving the extra food behind resulted in *lightening* the pack.
>
> Summer thunderstorms produce startling *lightning* bolts.

line—meaning occupation is *unacceptable.*

> He is in the engineering *profession.*
> *Unacceptable*: What *line* are you in? (SAY, *occupation*)

lineament—means *outline* or *contour.*
liniment—is *a medicated liquid.*

> His face had the *lineaments* of a Greek Adonis.
>
> After the football game, we all applied *liniment* to our legs.

loan—is a *noun.*
lend—is a *verb.*

> The bank was willing to grant him a *loan* of $500.00.
>
> The bank was willing to *lend* him $500.00.

locate—means *to discover the position of.*

> We *located* my uncle's whereabouts.
> AVOID these uses of LOCATE:
>> The school is *located* on the north side of the street. (omit *located*)
>> Have you *located* the book? (SAY, *found*)

Note: *locate* meaning *to settle* is colloquial.
Example: We have *located* in Texas. This use is *unacceptable* in formal English.

lonely—means *longing for companionship*.
solitary—means *isolated*.
Some people are forced to live *lonely* lives.
Sometimes *solitary* surroundings are conducive to deep thought.

lots—(or *a lot, a whole lot*) meaning *a great deal, much*, is *unacceptable*.
Unacceptable: He has *lots* of friends. (SAY, *many*)
Unacceptable: I have a *lot* of trouble. (SAY, *a great deal of*)

luxuriant—means *abundant growth*.
luxurious—implies *wealth*.
One expects to see *luxuriant* plants in the tropics.
The *luxurious* surroundings indicated both wealth and good taste.

majority—means *more than half of the total number*.
plurality—means an *excess* of votes received by the leading candidate over *those* received by the next candidate.
Example: A received 251 votes.
B received 127 votes.
C received 123 votes.
A received a *majority*, or 1 vote more than half of the total.
A received a *plurality* of 124 votes over B.

many—refers to *a number*.
much—refers to *a quantity in bulk*.
How *many* inches of rain fell last night? I don't know; but I would say *much* rain fell last night.

material—means *of* or *pertaining to matter*.
materiel—(accent the last syllable, EL) is French, and means *material equipment*, the opposite of *personnel* (*manpower*). His *material* assets included an automobile and two suits of clothing.

The small army was rich in *materiel*, poor in personnel.

may—is used in the *present tense*.
might—is used in the *past tense*.
We are hoping that he *may* come today.
He *might* have done it if you had encouraged him.

it's I—is always *acceptable*.
it's me—is *acceptable* only in colloquial speech or writing.

It's him This is her It was them	always *unacceptable*
It's he This is she It was they	always *acceptable*

my—must be used in such expressions as, Why do you object to *my going* (NOT *me* going)?
SEE HIM — HIS.

measles—is plural in form, singular in meaning.
SAY, *Measles* is now a minor childhood disease.
Note also, *mumps, shingles, chills, etc.* is . . .

medieval—means *of or pertaining to the Middle Ages* (1000-1400 A.D.).
middle-aged—refers to persons *in the middle period of life*.
Serfs and feudal baronies were part of *medieval* times.
According to the Bible, the *middle-aged* man has thirty-five more years of life to look forward to.

memorandum—is *a reminder*. The plural is *memoranda*.
Send me a short *memorandum* of his meeting with you.
The *memoranda* will help me reconstruct the story of the meeting.
Note: *addendum - addenda; bacterium - bacteria; datum-data; dictum - dicta; erratum-errata; medium - media; stratum - strata.*

Messrs.—(rhymes with *guessers*) used instead of "Misters" ("Misters" is *unacceptable*.)

The meeting was attended by *Messrs.* Smith, Jones, Brown, and Swift.

metal—is *the common chemical element*.
mettle—means *spirit*.

Lead is one of the more familiar *metals*.

One had to admire his *mettle* in the face of a crisis.

mighty—means *powerful* or *bulky*. Do NOT use it to mean *very*.

Samson was a *mighty* warrior.

The Philistines were all *very* (NOT *mighty*) unhappy to meet him.

minutiae—(pronounced min-YEW-she-ee) is the plural of *minutia*, and means *minor details*.

A meticulous person spends much time on *minutiae*.

miss out on—is *unacceptable* for *miss*.

SAY, We almost *missed* (not *missed out on*) seeing the game because of the traffic tieup.

Mmes.—is the abbreviation for Mesdames. (pronounced med-DAM)

It introduces a series of names of married women.

The party was attended by the *Mmes.* Jones, Smith, Wilson, and Miss Brown.

Note: The plural of Miss is *Misses*.

moment—is a *brief, indefinite space of time*.
minute—means *the sixtieth part of an hour*.

The lightning flared for a *moment*.

The thunder followed one *minute* afterwards—or so it seemed.

Unacceptable: I'll be there in a *minute* (SAY *moment* if you mean *briefly*.)

moneys—is *the plural of money*.

We shall vote on the disposition of the various *moneys* in the treasury.

Note: *alley - alleys; monkey - monkeys; valley - valleys*.

moral—means *good or ethical*; also, *an ethical lesson to be drawn*.

morale—(pronounced more-AL) means *spirit*.

The *moral* of the story is that it pays to be honest.

The *morale* of the troops rose after the general's inspiring speech.

more than—is correct. Do not add *rather* to this construction.

SAY, I depend *more* on you *than* (NOT *rather than*) on him.

BUT, I depend on you *rather than* on him.

most—is an adjective in the *superlative degree*.
almost—is an adverb, meaning *nearly*.

He is the *most* courteous boy in the class.

It's *almost* time to go to school.

myself—is *unacceptable* for *I* or *me*.

SAY, My son and *I* will play.

He is a better player than *I*.

They gave my son and *me* some berries.

Note: *Myself* may be used if the subject of the verb is I.

Since I know *myself* better, let me try it my way.

nauseous—means *causing sickness*. (NAWSH-us)
nauseated—means *being sick*. (NAW-she-ate-id)

The odor is *nauseous*.

I feel *nauseated*. (NOT *nauseous*)

naval—refers *to ships*.
nautical—refers *to navigation and seamen*.

John Paul Jones was a famous *naval* commander.

A *nautical* mile is a little longer than a land mile.

near—is an adjective meaning *close*.
nearly—is an adverb meaning *almost*.

Before 1933, only *near* beer was available.

Unacceptable: It is *near* a week since you called. (SAY *nearly*)

needless to say—Avoid this expression—it doesn't mean anything.

Unacceptable: *Needless to say*, I refused to go. (omit *needless to say*)

neither—means *not either of two*, and should NOT be used for *none* or *not one*.

Neither of his two books was very popular.

Of the many plays he has written, *not one* (or *none*) was very popular.

never—means *at no time*. Do NOT use it for *not*.

SAY, Shakespeare was *never* in Italy.

Shakespeare was *not* very fond of France.

nevertheless—means *notwithstanding*.

none the less—means *not any the less*, and is always followed by an adjective.

I have often warned you; *nevertheless*, you have persisted in doing the wrong thing.

I am *none the less* willing to give you a second chance.

nice—means *precise* or *exact*.

Your argument makes a *nice*, logical distinction.

Some use *nice* for anything and everything that is *pleasing*.

*Try to be more exact in your descriptive word.

AVOID: This is *nice* weather. (SAY *sunny*, or whatever you really mean)

He is such a *nice* person. (SAY *kind*, or whatever you really mean.)

*Other trite "blanket" expressions to avoid are: *fine, elegant, grand, lovely, splendid, terrific, swell, wonderful*—also, *rotten, lousy, miserable, terrible, awful*.

Note: NICELY is *unacceptable* for *well*.

Considering the seriousness of his illness, he is now doing *well*. (NOT *nicely*)

no-account—(and *no-good* and *no-use*) is *unacceptable* for *worthless*.

of no account—meaning *useless* is *acceptable*.

SAY, He is a *worthless* (NOT *no-account*) painter.

He will always be a painter *of no account*.

no better—(or **no worse**) is *acceptable* in colloquial use.

He is *no better* than this record.

Note: *No different* is *unacceptable*.

SAY, Your proposal is *not different* from mine.

noplace—as a solid word, is *unacceptable* for *no place* or *nowhere*.

Acceptable: You now have *nowhere* to go.

nohow—is *unacceptable* for *regardless*.

Unacceptable: I can't do this *nohow*.

no sooner...than—(NOT *no sooner...when*) is the *acceptable* expression.

SAY, *No sooner* did the rain start *than* (not *when*) the game was called off.

nowhere near—is *unacceptable* for *not nearly*.

SAY, The work was *not nearly* finished by nightfall.

nowheres—is *unacceptable*.

nowhere—is *acceptable*.

The child was *nowhere* (NOT *nowheres*) to be found.

nominate—means *to propose as a candidate*.

denominate—means *to describe*.

Nixon was *nominated* for President in 1960.

He was *denominated* a "favorite son" from the State of California.

notable—means *remarkable*.

notorious—means *of bad reputation*.

December 7, 1941, was a *notable* day.

At that time, the *notorious* Tojo commanded the Japanese forces.

nothing more or less—is *unacceptable* for *nothing more nor less*.

SAY, Correct English is *nothing more nor less* than a matter of careful practice.

number—is singular *when the total is intended*.

The *number* (of pages in the book) is 500.

number—is plural *when the individual units are referred* to.

A *number of pages* (in the book) were printed in italic type.

obligate—implies *a moral or legal responsibility*.

oblige—means *to do a favor to*, or *to accommodate*.

The principal felt *obligated* to disqualify himself in the dispute between the pupils. Please *oblige* me by refraining from discussing this matter with anyone else.

observance—means the *act of complying*.

observation—means the *act of noting*.

In *observance* of the new regulation, we shall omit further tests.

His scientific *observations* became the basis for a new rocket theory.

occupancy—refers to *the mere act of occupying*, usually legally.

occupation—means *the forceful act of occupying*.

According to the lease, the tenant still had *occupancy* of the apartment for another month.

The *occupation* of the enemy worried the townspeople.

oculist—is an M.D. who *treats diseases of the eye*.

optometrist—is a person who *measures the eye* to prescribe glasses.

optician—is a person who *makes the glasses*.

Note: An *oculist* is also called an *ophthalmologist* (ahf-thal- (like pal)- MOLL-ogist)

Note: An *optometrist* may also be an *optician*.

of any—(and *of anyone*) is *unacceptable* for *of all*.

SAY, His was the highest mark *of all*. (NOT *of any* or *of anyone*)

off of—is *unacceptable*.

SAY, He took the book *off* the table.

oftentimes—is *unacceptable* for *often*.

SAY, He *often* went back to the scenes of his childhood.

O.K.—is *acceptable* for *all right* or *approved* in informal business and informal social usage.

AVOID the use of O.K. in formal situations.

Acceptable: This retyped letter is O.K.

on account of—is *unacceptable* for *because*.

SAY, We could not meet you *because* (NOT *on account of*) we did not receive your message in time.

one and the same—is repetitious. Omit *one and*.

Your plan and mine are *the same*.

one ... one—is the acceptable construction in such expressions as:

The more *one* listens to President Kennedy's speeches, the more *one* (NOT *he*) wonders how a young man can be so wise.

SAY, The more a *person* listens to President Kennedy's speeches, the more *he* wonders how a young man can be so wise.

oral—means *spoken*.

verbal—means *expressed in words*, either spoken or written.

In international intrigue, *oral* messages are less risky than written ones.

Shorthand must usually be transcribed into *verbal* form.

ordinance—means *regulation*.

ordnance—refers to *guns, cannon, and the like*.

The local *ordinance* restricted driving speeds to thirty-five miles an hour.

Some rockets and guided missiles are now included in military *ordnance*.

ostensible—means *shown (usually for the purpose of deceiving others)*.

ostentatious—means *showy*.

Although he was known to be ambitious, his *ostensible* motive was civic pride.

His *ostentatious* efforts in behalf of civic improvement impressed no one.

other ... than—is *acceptable*; *other ... but* (or *other ... except*) is *unacceptable*.

SAY, We have no *other* motive *than* friendship in asking you.

other—is an adjective and means *different*.

otherwise—is an adverb and means *in a different way*.

What you did was *other* (NOT *otherwise*) than what you had promised.

I cannot look *otherwise* (NOT *other*) than with delight at the improvement in your work.

SAY, All students, *except* (NOT *other than*) those exempted, should take the examination.

All students, *unless* they have been exempted (NOT *otherwise*), will take the examination.

out loud—is *unacceptable* for *aloud*.

SAY, he read *aloud* to his family every evening.

outdoor—(and *out-of-door*) is an adjective.

outdoors—is an adverb.

We spent most of the summer at an *outdoor* music camp.

Most of the time we played string quartets *outdoors*.

Note: *Out-of-doors* is *acceptable* in either case.

over—is *unacceptable* for *at*.

SAY, We shall be *at* (NOT *over*) your house tonight.

overly—is *unacceptable* for *over*.

SAY, We were *over-anxious* (not *overly anxious*) about the train's delay.

over with—is *unacceptable* for *completed*.

SAY, Thank goodness, that job is now *over!*

packed—means *full*.

pact—means *a treaty*.

The crate is *packed* with mixed fruits.

The peace *pact* between the former enemy nations was signed today.

part—means *a fraction of a whole*.

portion—means *an allotted* or *designated part*.

We had time to read just a *part* of the story.

Tomorrow, each of us will be responsible for reading a *portion* of the story.

part from—*a person*.

part with—*a thing*.

It was difficult for him to *part from* his classmates.

It will be difficult for him to *part with* his memories as well.

partial to—is *unacceptable* for *fond of*.

SAY, I am *fond of* (or *prefer*) bamboo fishing rods. (NOT *partial to*)

party—refers to a *group*, NOT an *individual*.

A *party* of men went on a scouting mission.

I told the woman (NOT *party*) that she was using the phone too long.

Note: *Party* may be used in a legal sense —The *party* of the second part . . .

passed—is the past tense of *to pass*.

past—means *just preceding*.

The week *passed* very slowly.

The *past* week was a very dull one.

patron—means *supporter*.

customer—is a *buyer*.

Mrs. Kennedy is a *patron* of early American art.

The rain kept the *customers* away.

pedal—means *a lever operated by foot*. (AVOID *foot* pedal)

peddle—means *to sell from door to door*.

It is impossible to ride a bicycle without moving the *pedals*.

The traveling salesman today seldom *peddles* from farm door to farm door.

people—comprise *a united* or *collective group of individuals*.

persons—are *individuals that are separate and unrelated*.

Only five *persons* remained in the theater after the first act.

The *people* of New York City have enthusiastically accepted "Shakespeare-in-the-Park" productions.

per—is Latin and is *chiefly commercial*.

per diem (by the day); *per minute*, etc.

AVOID *as per* your instruction, (SAY *according to*)

percent— (also **per cent**) expresses rate of interest.

percentage—means a part or proportion of the *whole*.

The interest rate of some banks is 4 *percent*.

The *percentage* of unmarried people in our community is small.

persecute—means *to make life miserable for someone*. (It's non-legal)

prosecute—means *to conduct a criminal investigation*. (It's legal)

Some racial groups insist upon *persecuting* other groups.

The District Attorney is *prosecuting* the racketeers.

personal—refers *to a person.*

personnel—means *an organized body of individuals.*

> The general took a *personal* interest in every one of his men.
>
> He believed that this was necessary in order to maintain the morale of the *personnel* in his division.

perspicacity—means *keenness in seeing* or *understanding.*

perspicuity—means *clearness to the understanding.*

> The teacher showed *perspicacity* in respect to the needs of his class.
>
> The class, in turn, appreciated the *perspicuity* of his explanations.

physic—means *a drug.*

physics—means *a branch of science.*

physique—means *body structure.*

> A doctor should determine the safe dose of a *physic.*
>
> Nuclear *physics* is the most advanced of the sciences.
>
> Athletes must take care of their *physiques.*

plain—means *simple,* or *a prairie.*

plane—means *a flat surface,* or *a tool.*

> The Great *Plains* are to be found in Western America.
>
> In *plane* geometry, we are concerned with two dimensions: *length* and *width.*

pled—is *unacceptable* as the past tense for *plead* (use *pleaded*).

> All the men who were arrested *pleaded* not guilty.

plenty—is a noun; it means *abundance.*

> America is land of *plenty.*
>
> SAY, There is *plenty of* (NOT *plenty*) room in the compact car for me.
>
> Note: *plenty* as an adverb is *unacceptable.*
>
> Note: *plenty* as an adj. is *unacceptable.*
>
> SAY, The compact car is *quite* (NOT *plenty*) large enough for me.

pole—means *a long stick.*

poll—means *vote.*

> We bought a new *pole* for the flag.

> The seniors took a *poll* to determine the graduate most likely to succeed.

poorly—meaning in poor health is *unacceptable.*

> Grandfather was feeling *in poor health* (NOT *poorly*) all last winter.

pour—is to send flowing *with direction and control.*

spill—is to send flowing *accidentally.*

> Please *pour* some cream into my cup of coffee.
>
> Careless people *spill* things.

posted—meaning informed is *unacceptable.*

> SAY, One can keep *well-informed* (NOT *well-posted*) by reading *The New York Times* daily.

practicable—means *useful, usable,* or *workable,* and is applied only to objects.

practical—means *realistic, having to do with action.* It applies to persons and things.

> There is as yet no *practicable* method for resisting atomic bomb attacks.
>
> *Practical* technicians, nevertheless, are attempting to translate the theories of the atomic scientists into some form of defense.

precede—means *to come before.*

proceed—means *to go ahead.* (*procedure* is the noun)

supersede—means *to replace.*

> What are the circumstances that *preceded* the attack?
>
> We can then *proceed* with our plan for resisting a second attack.
>
> It is then possible that Plan B will *supersede* Plan A.

predominately—is *unacceptable* for *predominantly,* meaning *powerfully* or *influentially.*

> SAY, The *predominantly* rich people in the area resisted all governmental attempts to create adequate power facilities.

prescribe—means *to lay down a course of action.*

proscribe—means *to outlaw* or *forbid.*

> The doctor *prescribed* plenty of rest and good food for the man.

Mark Antony *proscribed* many of Brutus' followers after Brutus' death.

principal—means *chief* or *main* (as an adjective); *a leader* (as a noun).

principle—means *a fundamental truth* or *belief*.

His *principal* supporters came from among the peasants.

The *principal* of the school asked for cooperation from the staff.

Humility was the guiding *principle* of Buddha's life.

Note: *Principal* may also mean *a sum placed at interest.*

Part of his monthly payment was applied as interest on the *principal*.

prodigy—means *a person endowed with extraordinary gifts* or *powers*.

protégé—means *someone under the protection of another*.

Mozart was a musical *prodigy* at the age of three.

For a time, Schumann was the *protege* of Johannes Brahms.

prophecy—(rhymes with *sea*) is the noun meaning *prediction*.

prophesy—(rhymes with *sigh*) is the verb meaning *to predict*.

The *prophecy* of the three witches eventually misled Macbeth.

The witches had *prophesied* that Macbeth would become king.

proposal—means *an offer*.

proposition—means *a statement*.

Lincoln's *proposal* for freeing the slaves through government purchase was unacceptable to the South.

The *proposition* that all men are created equal first appeared in the writings of the French Encyclopedists.

propose—means *to offer*.

purpose—means *to resolve* or *to intend*.

Let the teacher *propose* the subject for our debate.

The teacher *purposed* to announce the subject of the debate next week.

put across—meaning *to get something accepted* is *unacceptable*.

SAY, A good teacher may be defined as one who *succeeds in her purpose*. (NOT *puts it across*)

put in—meaning *to spend, make* or *devote* is *unacceptable*.

SAY, Every good student should *spend* (NOT *put in*) at least four hours a day in studying.

SAY, Be sure to *make* (NOT *put in*) an appearance at the council meeting.

rain—means *water from the clouds*.

reign—means *rule*.

rein—means *a strap for guiding a horse*.

The *rain* in Spain falls mainly on the plain.

A queen now *reigns* over England.

When the *reins* were pulled too tightly, the horse reared.

raise—means *to lift, erect*.

raze—(pronounced like *raise*) means *to tear down*.

The neighbors helped him *raise* a new barn.

The tornado *razed* his barn.

AVOID *raise* in connection with rearing *children*.

SAY, She *brought up* three lovely girls. (NOT *raised*)

rarely or ever—is *unacceptable*.

Say *rarely ever, rarely if ever, rarely or never*.

One *rarely if ever* (NOT *rarely or ever*) sees a trolley car today.

Students today *seldom if ever* (NOT *seldom or ever*) read Thackeray's novels.

real—meaning *very* or *extremely* is *unacceptable*.

SAY, He is a *very* (NOT *real*) handsome young man.

He is *really* handsome.

reason is because—is *unacceptable* for *the reason is that*.

SAY, *The reason* young people do not read Trollope today *is that* his sentences are too involved.

Note: Avoid *due to* after *reason is*.

SAY, *The reason* he refused *was that he was proud* (NOT *due to his pride*).

rebellion—means *open, armed, organized resistance to authority.*

revolt—means *similar resistance on a smaller scale.*

revolution—means *the overthrowing of one government and the setting up of another.*

Bootlegging has sometimes been referred to as a *rebellion* against high whiskey taxes.

An increase in the grain tax caused a peasant's *revolt* agains the landowners.

Castro's Cuban *revolution* is a matter of grave concern to Latin America.

reckon—meaning *suppose* or *think* is *unacceptable.*

SAY, I *think* it may rain this afternoon.

recollect—means *to bring back to memory.*

remember—means *to keep in memory.*

Now I can *recollect* your returning the money to me.

I *remember* the occasion well.

reconciled to—means *resigned to* or *adjusted to.*

reconciled with—means *to become friendly again with someone;* also, *to bring one set of facts into harmony with another one.*

I am now *reconciled to* this chronic ache in my back.

The boy was *reconciled with* his parents after he had promised not to try to run away from home again.

How does one *reconcile* the politician's shabby accomplishments *with* the same politician's noble promises?

regular—meaning *real* or *true* is *unacceptable.*

SAY, He was a *real* (NOT *regular*) tyrant.

respectably—means *in a manner deserving respect.*

respectfully—means *with respect and decency.*

respectively—means *as relating to each, in the order given.*

Young people should conduct themselves *respectably* in school as well as in church.

The students listened *respectfully* to the principal.

John and Bill are the sons *respectively* of Mr. Smith and Mr. Brown.

restive—means *fretting under restraint.*

restless—means *fidgety.*

As the principal continued talking, the students became *restive.*

Spring always makes me feel *restless.*

retaliate—means *to return evil for evil.*

reciprocate—means *to return in kind—usually a favor for a favor.*

The private *retaliated* by putting a snake into the sergeant's bed.

When she received the mink coat, she *reciprocated* by cooking a delicious meal for her husband.

reverend—means *worthy of reverence* or *respect.*

reverent—means *feeling* or *showing respect.*

Shakespeare, the *reverend* master of the drama, still inspires most readers.

Sometimes a too *reverent* attitude toward Shakespeare causes the reader to miss much of the fun in his plays.

Note: *The Reverend* (abbreviated *Rev.*) John W. Smith is pastor of our church.

Reverend—should be used with the full name or the initials of the person.

Acceptable: The Reverend James Wilson will address us. (NOT the *Reverend Wilson*)

Unacceptable: The Reverend will conduct the services.

right along—is *unacceptable* for *continuously.*

SAY, His contemporaries were *continuously* (NOT *right along*) in opposition to Shakespeare.

Note: *Right away* and *right off* are *unacceptable* for *at once.*

SAY, Other of Shakespeare's contemporaries, especially Ben Jonson, *immediately* (NOT *right off* or *right away*) recognized his genius.

rob—one *robs* a *person.*

steal—one *steals* a *thing.*

They *robbed* the blind man of his money.

He *stole* my wallet.

Note: "They *robbed* the First National Bank" is correct because they actually robbed the persons working in the bank.

rout—(rhymes with *stout*) means *a defeat*.

route—(rhymes with *boot*) means *a way of travel*.

The *rout* of the army was near.

The milkman has a steady *route*.

same as—is *unacceptable* for *in the same way* and *just as*.

SAY, The owner's son was treated *in the same way as* any other worker. (NOT *the same as*)

AVOID *same* as a pronoun, except in *legal* usage.

SAY, If the books are available, please send *them* (NOT *same*) by parcel post.

saw—is the past tense of *see*.

seen—is the past participle of *see*.

We *saw* a play yesterday. (NOT *seen*)

I have never *seen* a live play before. (NOT *saw*)

scan—means to *examine carefully*. It does *not* mean to examine *hastily* or *superficially*.

You must *scan* a book on nuclear physics in order to understand it thoroughly.

DON'T SAY When I am in a hurry, I *scan* the headlines. (SAY *glance at*)

seem—as used in the expression *I couldn't seem to* and *I don't seem to* is *unacceptable*.

SAY, *We can't find* (NOT *We can't seem to find*) the address.

self-confessed—is *unacceptable* for *confessed*. Omit *self*.

He was a *confessed* slayer.

sensible of—means *aware of*.

sensitive to—means *affected by*.

I am very *sensible of* my shortcomings in written English.

He is *sensitive to* criticism.

sensual—means *pleasure-loving*.

sensuous—means *influenced through the senses, esthetic*.

The *sensual* man cares little about the salvation of his soul.

A *sensuous* person usually appreciates art and music.

settle—meaning *to pay* is *unacceptable*.

We *paid* all our former bills. (NOT *settled*)

AVOID: We'll *settle* you, We'll *settle* your hash, etc.

sewage—means *waste matter in a sewer*.

sewerage—means *the system* of *sewers*.

The careful disposal of *sewage* is essential to proper public health.

For such disposal, an adequate amount of *sewerage* is necessary.

shall }
will } SAY I *shall*, we *shall* (Otherwise, say *will*—you *will*, he *will*, she *will*, they *will*, it *will*)

Note: In informal speech, I *will* (would) may be used instead of I *shall*.

Note: In cases of determination, reverse the foregoing rule: I certainly *will* insist on full payment.

They *shall* not pass.

shape—meaning *state* or *condition* is *unacceptable*.

SAY, The refugees were in a serious *condition* (NOT *shape*) when they arrived here.

show—meaning *opportunity* or *chance* is *unacceptable*.

The sailors on the torpedoed vessel *didn't have a chance* (NOT *didn't have a show*) of surviving in the wild waters.

show up—meaning *to make an appearance* is *unacceptable*.

SAY, We were all disappointed in **the** star's failure to *appear* (NOT *to show up*).

Note: *Show up* meaning *to expose* is *unacceptable*.

SAY, It is my firm intention to *expose* (NOT *show up*) your hypocrisy.

sign up—meaning *to enlist* or *enroll* is *unacceptable*.

SAY, Many young men hurried *to enlist* (NOT *sign up*) after the President's talk.

simple reason—is *unacceptable* for *reason*. Omit the word *simple* in similar expressions: *simple truth, simple purpose*, etc.

Unacceptable: I refuse to do it for the *simple reason* that I don't like your attitude.

Acceptable: The *truth* (omit *simple*) is that I feel tired.

simply—meaning *absolutely* is *unacceptable*.

SAY, The performance was *absolutely* (NOT *simply*) thrilling.

sit—means *take a seat.* (intransitive verb)

set—means *place.*   (transitive verb)

Note the forms of each verb:

TENSE	SIT (TAKE A SEAT)
PRESENT	He *is sitting* on a chair.
PAST	He *sat* on the chair.
PRES. PERF.	He *has sat* on the chair.

TENSE	SET (PLACE)
PRESENT	He *is setting* the lamp on the table.
PAST	He *set* the lamp on the table.
PRES. PERF.	He *has set* the lamp on the table.

size up—meaning *to estimate* is *unacceptable*.

SAY, The detectives were able *to estimate* (NOT *size up*) the fugitive's remaining ammunition supply from his careless shooting.

so—should be avoided for *very, great,* etc.

SAY, She is *very* (NOT *so*) beautiful! *So* should not be used for *so that* to express purpose.

Unacceptable: He gave up his seat *so* (SAY *so that*) the old lady could sit down.

sociable—means *friendly.*

social—means *relating to people in general.*

Sociable individuals prefer to have plenty of people around them.

The President's *social* program included old age insurance, housing, education, etc.

sole—means *all alone.*

soul—means *man's spirit.*

He was the *sole* owner of the business.

Man's *soul* is unconquerable.

some—meaning *somewhat* is *unacceptable*.

SAY, She is *somewhat* (NOT *some*) better today.

Note: *Some* is *unacceptable* in such expressions as the following:

We had a *very* (NOT *some*) strong scare this morning.

some time—means *a portion of time.*

sometime—means *at an indefinite time in the future.*

sometimes—means *occasionally.*

I'll need *some time* to make a decision.

Let us meet *sometime* after twelve noon. *Sometimes* it is better to hesitate before signing a contract.

somewheres—is *unacceptable.*

somewhere—is *acceptable.*

specie—means *money as coins.* (*Specie* is singular only).

species—means *a class of related things.* (*Species* is singular and plural).

He preferred to be paid in *specie*, rather than in bank notes.

The human *species* is relatively young. (singular)

Several animal *species* existed before man. (plural)

stand—meaning *to tolerate* is *unacceptable*.

SAY, I refuse *to tolerate* (NOT *to stand for*) your nonsense.

start in—is *unacceptable* for *start*.

We shall *start* (NOT *start in*) to read the story in a few minutes.

state—means *to declare formally.*

say—means *to speak generally.*

Our ambassador *stated* the terms for a cease-fire agreement.

We *said* (NOT *stated*) that we would not attend the meeting.

stationary—means *standing still.*

stationery—means *writing materials.*

In ancient times people thought the earth was *stationary*.

We bought writing paper at the *stationery* store.

statue—means *a piece of sculpture.*

stature—means *height.*

statute—is *a law.*

The *Statue* of Liberty stands in New York Harbor.

The athlete was a man of great *stature*.

Compulsory education was established by *statute*.

stay—means *to remain*.

stop—means *to cease*.

We *stayed* (NOT *stopped*) at the hotel for three days.

The power failure caused the clock *to stop*.

Note: *To stop off, to stop over*, and *to stay put* are *unacceptable*.

stayed—means *remained*.

stood—means *remained upright* or *erect*.

The army *stayed* in the trenches for five days.

The soldiers *stood* at attention for one hour.

straight—means *direct* or *not crooked*.

strait—means *narrow, restricted*.

The road led *straight* to the deserted farmhouse.

The violent patient was placed in a *strait*-jacket.

strangled to death—is *unacceptable* for *strangled*. Omit *to death*.

Unacceptable: The girl was found *strangled to death*.

Acceptable: The madman attempted *to strangle* his victim.

summons—is singular; *summonses* is the plural.

We received a *summons* to appear in court.

This was the first of three *summonses* we were to receive that week.

Note: *Summons* is also a verb.

We were *summonsed* to appear in court. (also *summoned*)

sure—for *surely* is *unacceptable*.

SAY, You *surely* (NOT *sure*) are not going to write that!

surround—means *to inclose on all sides*. Do NOT add *on all sides* to it.

The camp was *surrounded* by heavy woods.

suspicioned—is *unacceptable* for *suspected*.

SAY, We *suspected* (NOT *suspicioned*) that he was ready to betray us.

take in—is *unacceptable* in the sense of *deceive* or *attend*.

SAY, We were *deceived* (NOT *taken in*) by his oily manner.

We should like to *attend* (NOT *take in*) a few plays during our vacation.

take stock in—is *unacceptable* for *rely on*.

SAY, We rarely *rely on* (NOT *take stock in*) the advice of younger employees.

tasteful—means *having good taste*.

tasty—means *pleasing to the taste*.

The home of our host was decorated in a *tasteful* manner.

Our host also served us very *tasty* meals.

tenants—are *occupants*.

tenets—are *principles*.

Several *tenants* occupied that apartment during the first month.

His religious *tenets* led him to perform many good deeds.

tender—means *to offer officially* or *formally*.

give—means *to donate* or *surrender something willingly*.

The discredited official decided to *tender* his resignation.

He *gave* testimony readily before the grand jury.

testimony—means *information given orally only*.

evidence—means *information given orally or in writing*.

He gave *testimony* readily to the grand jury.

The defendant presented written *evidence* to prove he was not at the scene of the crime.

that there } are *unacceptable*. Omit *there, here*.
this here }

SAY, *That* (NOT *that there*) person is taller than *this* (NOT *this here*) one.

their—means *belonging to them*.

there—means *in that place*.

they're—means *they are*.

We took *their* books home with us.

You will find your books over *there* on the desk.

They're not as young as we expected them to be.

theirselves—is *unacceptable* for *themselves*.
SAY, Most children of school age are able to care for *themselves* in many ways.

therefor—means *for that*.
therefore—means *because of that*.
One day's detention is the punishment *therefor*.
You will, *therefore*, have to remain in school after dismissal time.

these kind—is *unacceptable*.
this kind—is *acceptable*.
I am fond of *this kind* of apples.
Note: *These kinds* would be also acceptable.

through—meaning *finished* or *completed* is *unacceptable*.
SAY, We'll finish (NOT *be through with*) the work by five o'clock.

thusly—is *unacceptable* for *thus*.
SAY, Speak words *thus*: . . .

to my knowledge—implies *certain knowledge*.
to the best of my knowledge—implies *limited knowledge*.
He is, *to my knowledge*, the brightest boy in the class.
As for his character, he has never, *to the best of my knowledge*, been in trouble with the law.

tortuous—means *twisting*.
torturing—means *causing pain*.
The wagon train followed a *tortuous* trail through the mountains.
The *torturing* memory of his defeat kept him awake all night.
Note: *Torturesome* is unacceptable.

track—means *a path* or *road*.
tract—means *a brief but serious piece of writing; a piece of land*.
The horses raced around the fair grounds *track*.
John Locke wrote a famous *tract* on education.

The heavily wooded *tract* was sold to a lumber company.

treat—means *to deal with*.
treat of—means *to give an explanation of*.
treat with—means *to negotiate with*.
I shall *treat* that subject in our next lesson.
The lesson itself will *treat* of Shakespeare's humor.
I shall *treat* with the delinquent students at some other time.

try to—is *acceptable*.
try and—is *unacceptable*.
Try to come (NOT *try and* come).
Note: *plan on going* is *unacceptable*.
plan to go is *acceptable*.

two—is the *numeral 2*.
to—means *in the direction of*.
too—means *more than* or *also*.
There are *two* sides to every story.
Three *twos* (or 2's) equal six.
We shall go *to* school.
We shall go, *too*.
The weather is *too* hot for school.

type man—(*type book, type game,* etc.) is *unacceptable* for *type of man, type of book, type of game,* etc.
SAY, He is a high *type of man* for this position.

ugly—meaning *unpleasant* or *dangerous* is *unacceptable*.
SAY, This is a very *dangerous* (NOT *ugly*) situation.

ulterior—means *hidden underneath*.
underlying—means *fundamental*.
His noble words were contradicted by his *ulterior* motives.
Shakespeare's *underlying* motive in *Hamlet* was to criticize the moral climate of his own times.

unbeknownst to—is *unacceptable* for *without the knowledge of*.
SAY, The young couple decided to get married *without the knowledge of* (NOT *unbeknownst to*) their parents.

unique—means *the only one of its kind*, and therefore does not take *very, most, extremely* before it.

SAY, The First Folio edition of Shakespeare's works is *unique* (NOT *very unique*)

Note: The same rule applies to *perfect*.

uninterested—means *bored*.

disinterested—means *fair, impartial*.

I am *uninterested* in this slow-moving game.

Let us ask a *disinterested* person to settle this argument.

United States should always have *The* before it.

SAY, *The United States* of America is not the largest land mass in the Western Hemisphere. (Note the singular verb *is*)

The United States of Brazil is also a federal republic.

unmoral—(and *amoral*) means *not involving morality*.

immoral—means *contrary to moral law*.

The principles of science are considered *unmoral*.

The question of beauty is an *amoral* one.

It is *immoral* to steal or to bear false witness.

upwards of—is *unacceptable* for *more than*.

SAY, There are *more than* (NOT *upwards of*) one million people unemployed today.

valuable—means *of great worth*.

valued—means *held in high regard*.

invaluable—means *priceless*.

This is a *valuable* manuscript.

The expert gave him highly *valued* advice.

A good name is an *invaluable* possession.

venal—means *capable of being bribed*.

venial—means *pardonable*.

The *venal* councilman yielded to corruption.

A white lie is a *venial* sin.

veracity—means *truthfulness*.

truth—is *a true statement, a fact*.

Because he had a reputation for *veracity*, we could not doubt his story.

We would have questioned the *truth* of his story otherwise.

via—means *by way of* and should be used in connection with travel or motion only.

SAY, We shipped the merchandise *via* motor express.

I received the information through (NOT *via*) his letter.

virtue—means *goodness*.

virtuosity—means *technical skill*.

We should expect a considerable degree of *virtue* in our public officials.

The young pianist played with amazing *virtuosity* at his debut.

virtually—means *in effect*.

actually—means *in fact*.

A tie in the final game was *virtually* a defeat for us.

We had *actually* won more games than they at that time.

waive—means *to give up*.

wave—means *a swell* or *roll of water*.

As a citizen, I refuse to *waive* my right of free speech.

The *waves* reached the top deck of the ship.

was }
were } If something is contrary to fact (not a fact), use *were* in every instance.

I wish I *were* in Bermuda.

Unacceptable: If he *was* sensible, he wouldn't act like that.

(SAY If he *were* . . .)

way back—(and *way down yonder, way behind us*,) is *unacceptable*.

SAY, We knew him from *early times*. (NOT *way back*)

ways—is *unacceptable* for *way*.

SAY, We climbed a little *way*, (NOT *ways*) up the hill.

went and took—(*went and stole*, etc.) is *unacceptable*.

SAY, They *stole* (NOT *went and stole*) our tools.

what—is *unacceptable* for *that*.

SAY, Everything *that* (NOT *what*) you write displeases me.

when—(and *where*) should NOT be used to introduce a definition of a noun.

> SAY, A tornado *is a* twisting, high wind on land (NOT *is when a twisting, high wind is on land*).
>
> A pool *is a place for swimming.* (NOT *is where people swim*)

whereabouts—is *unacceptable* for *where*.

> SAY, *Where* (NOT *whereabouts*) do you live?
>
> Note: *Whereabouts* as a noun meaning a place is *acceptable*.
> Do you know his *whereabouts?*

whether—should NOT be preceded by *of* or *as to*.

> SAY, The President will consider the question *whether* (NOT *of whether*) it is better to ask for or demand higher taxes now.
>
> He inquired *whether* (NOT *as to whether*) we were going or not.

which—is used *incorrectly* in the following expressions:

> He asked me to stay, *which I did*. (CORRECT: He asked me to stay and I did.)
>
> It has been a severe winter, *which* is unfortunate. (CORRECT: Unfortunately, it has been a severe winter.)
>
> You did not write; besides *which* you have not telephoned. (CORRECT: Omit *which*)

while—is *unacceptable* for *and* or *though*.

> SAY, The library is situated on the south side; (OMIT *while*) the laboratory is on the north side.
>
> *Though* (NOT while) I disagree with you, I shall not interfere with your right to express your opinion.
>
> *Though* (NOT *while*) I am in my office every day, you do not attempt to see me.

who ⎫
whom ⎭ The following is a method (without going into grammar rules) for determining when to use WHO or WHOM.

> "Tell me (*Who, Whom*) you think should represent our company?"
>
> STEP ONE—Change the who—whom part of the sentence to its natural order.

"You think (*who, whom*) should represent our company?"

STEP TWO—Substitute HE for WHO, HIM for WHOM.

"You think (*he, him*) should represent our company?"

You would say *he* in this case.

THEREFORE—"Tell me WHO you think should represent the company?" is correct.

who is ⎫
who am ⎭ Note these constructions:

> It is I who *am* the most experienced.
> It is he who *is* . . .
> It is he or I who *am* . . .
> It is I or he who *is* . . .
> It is he and I who *are* . . .

whose—means *of whom.*
who's—means *who is.*

> *Whose* is this notebook?
> *Who's* in the next office?

win—you *win* a game.
beat—you *beat* another player.

> We *won* the contest.
> He *beat* me in tennis. (NOT *won* me)
> Note: Don't use *beat* for swindle.
> SAY, The peddler *swindled* the customer out of five dollars. (NOT *beat*)

worst kind—(and *worst way*) is *unacceptable* for *very badly* or *extremely*.

> SAY, The school is *greatly in need of more teachers.* (NOT *needs teachers the worst way.*)

would have—is *unacceptable* for *had.*

> SAY, I wish you *had* (NOT *would have*) called earlier.

you all—is *unacceptable* for *you* (plural).

> SAY, We welcome *you*, the delegates from Ethiopia.
>
> *You* are all welcome, delegates of Ethiopia.

GRAPH, CHART AND TABLE INTERPRETATION

The questions presented below on the interpretation of graphs and statistical tables have been compiled from previous examinations, and are designed to help you prepare for test questions which require reasoning and analytical ability.

GRAPH and table interpretation forms an important part of your examination. Many questions require the ability to read graphs and charts, or to make them up from a collection of data. You need a thorough understanding of their forms and meaning.

Wherever a question is based on a map, chart, graph or table, remember that it is important to answer it in the light of the information presented in the particular chart or table, without adding any ideas of your own. You are allowed to use scratch paper for computation while working on questions of this type.

DIRECTIONS FOR ANSWERING QUESTIONS. For each question, decide which is the best answer of the choices given. Note the capital letter preceding the best answer. On machine scored examinations you will be given an answer sheet and told to blacken the proper space on that answer sheet. Near the end of this book we have provided facsimiles of such answer sheets. Tear one out, and mark your answers on it, just as you would do on an actual exam.

A Sample Question Analyzed

CHART NO. I

Look at the two columns of data below:

Time sec.	Velocity ft./sec.
0	2
2	3
4	4
6	5
8	6
10	7

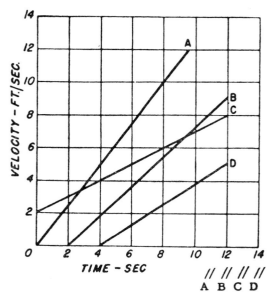

Which one of the lines on the graph at the right most closely represents the data in these two columns?

An examination of the graph shows that time values are indicated along the horizontal scale, and velocity values along the vertical scale. If we observe the velocity value at zero time, we see that the A line has a value of 0 velocity, and the C line a value of 2 ft./sec. No values are shown at 0 time for lines B and D. Hence line C is the only one which shows a velocity of 2 ft./sec. at 0 time.

Similarly at 2 sec. the velocity value for line B is 0, for line A is 2.5, and for line C, 3. Here again C is the only line which corresponds to the data in the table. At 4 sec. the velocity value for line D is 0, for line B is 1.9, for line C is 4, and for line A is 5. Here also line C is the only one that gives the value shown in the table. The same process can be repeated for time values 6, 8, and 10 sec., all of which show that line C is the only one corresponding to the values given in the table.

S-386

CHART NO. II

In the following graph the heavy curve represents postal receipts at St. Louis from 1930 to 1939. The light curve represents postal receipts at Detroit from 1930 to 1939.

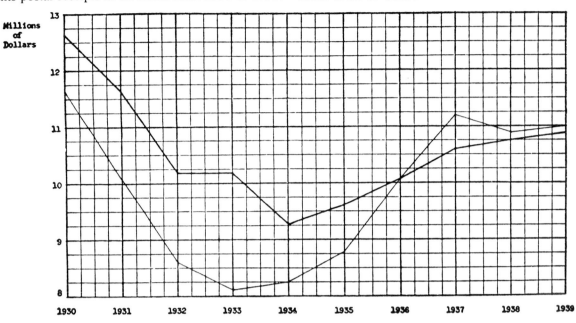

1. In 1937 the value of receipts in St. Louis was
   (A) 10,300,000   (B) 10,600,000
   (C) 11,100,000   (D) 11,200,000

2. Receipts were greatest in Detroit in
   (A) 1930   (B) 1933
   (C) 1937   (D) 1939

3. Detroit's and St. Louis' receipts were equal in
   (A) 1930   (B) 1933
   (C) 1936

4. Receipts in St. Louis were least in
   (A) 1932   (B) 1933
   (C) 1934   (D) 1937

5. In 1935 the ratio of the receipts in St. Louis to those in Detroit was
   (A) 2 to 1   (B) 5 to 3
   (C) 10 to 9   (D) 12 to 11

CHART NO. III

Answer Questions 6 to 10 on the basis of the following table:

VALUE OF PROPERTY STOLEN— 1963 and 1964
LARCENY

CATEGORY	1963		1964	
	Number of Offenses	Value of Stolen Property	Number of Offenses	Value of Stolen Property
Pocket - picking	20	$ 1,950	10	$ 950
Purse - snatching	175	5,750	120	12,050
Shoplifting	155	7,950	225	17,350
Automobile thefts	1040	127,050	860	108,000
Thefts of automobile accessories	1135	34,950	970	24,400
Bicycle thefts	355	8,250	240	6,350
All other thefts	1375	187,150	1300	153,150

6. Of the total number of larcenies reported for 1963, automobile thefts accounted for, most nearly,
   (A) 5%   (B) 15%
   (C) 25%   (D) 50%
   (E) 75%

7. The largest percentage decrease in the value of the stolen property from 1963 to 1964 was in the category of
   (A) bicycle thefts
   (B) automobile thefts
   (C) thefts of automobile accessories
   (D) pocket-picking
   (E) all other thefts

8. In 1964 the average amount of each theft was lowest for the category of
   (A) pocket-picking
   (B) purse-snatching
   (C) thefts of automobile accessories
   (D) shoplifting
   (E) bicycle thefts

9. The category which had the largest numerical reduction in the number of offenses from 1963 to 1964 was
   (A) pocket-picking
   (B) automobile thefts
   (C) thefts of automobile accessories
   (D) bicycle thefts
   (E) all other thefts

10. When the categories are ranked, for each year, according to the number of offenses committed in each category (largest number to rank first), the number of categories which will have the same rank in 1963 as in 1964 is
   (A) 3   (B) 4
   (C) 5   (D) 6
   (E) 7

11. For the two years combined (1963 and 1964), the average value of property stolen by pocket-picking was approximately
   (A) $25   (B) $30
   (C) $150   (D) $97
   (E) $74

Questions 12 through 16 are to be answered on the basis of the following graphs:

CHART NO. IV

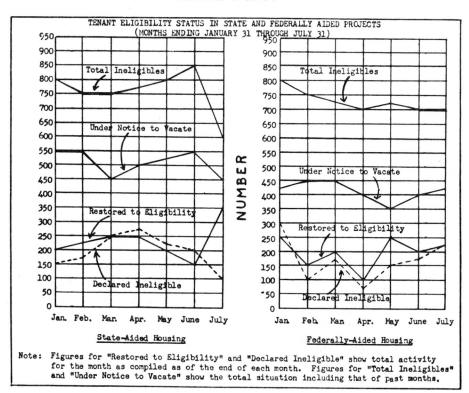

TENANT ELIGIBILITY STATUS IN STATE AND FEDERALLY AIDED PROJECTS
(MONTHS ENDING JANUARY 31 THROUGH JULY 31)

State-Aided Housing   Federally-Aided Housing

Note: Figures for "Restored to Eligibility" and "Declared Ineligible" show total activity for the month as compiled as of the end of each month. Figures for "Total Ineligibles" and "Under Notice to Vacate" show the total situation including that of past months.

12. In Federally-aided housing, the average number of tenants restored to eligibility during the first six months of the year is, most nearly
    (A) 100   (B) 192
    (C) 188   (D) 196
    (E) 200

13. For the months covered by the graphs, in State-aided housing, the ratio of the average number of total ineligibles to the average number under notice to vacate is, most nearly
    (A) 1:2   (B) 2:3
    (C) 3:2   (D) 2:1
    (E) 3:1

14. For State-aided housing, assume that it has been decided to predict figures for the end of August and the end of September on the basis that the number of tenants expected to be declared ineligible in each future month will be 30% less than the average for the previous three months. The number of tenants expected to be declared ineligible during the month of September is expected to be, most nearly,
    (A) 122   (B) 100
    (C) 141   (D) 158
    (E) 175

15. Of the four categories of tenant status in the graph, the number of categories in which, at the end of May as compared with the end of April, there was a greater *numerical* increase in State-aided housing as compared with the same category in Federally-aided housing, is
    (A) 1   (B) 0
    (C) 2   (D) 3
    (E) 4

16. Assume that, at the end of March, in State-aided housing, the total number of ineligibles was 10% greater than shown on the graph, and that this 10% increase was due entirely to a greater number of tenants being declared ineligible in that month than is shown on the graph. Under this assumption, the percentage increase in the number *declared ineligible,* as compared with the figure in the graph, would be, most nearly,
    (A) 3%   (B) 30%
    (C) 17%   (D) 23%
    (E) 10%

Questions 17 to 23 are to be answered on the basis of information contained in the chart and table below. The chart shows the percentage of annual expenditures for equipment, supplies, and salaries. The table shows the annual expenditures for each of the years 1957-1961.

CHART NO. V

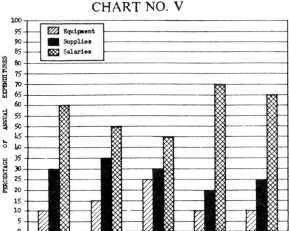

The bureau's annual expenditures for the years 1957-1961 are shown in the following table:

Year	Expenditures
1957	$ 800,000
1958	1,200,000
1959	1,500,000
1960	1,000,000
1961	1,200,000

Equipment, supplies, and salaries were the only three categories for which the bureau spent money.

17. The information contained in the chart and table is sufficient to determine the
    (A) average annual salary of an employee in the bureau in 1958
    (B) decrease in the amount of money spent on supplies in the bureau in 1957 from the amount spent in the preceding year
    (C) changes, between 1959 and 1960, in the prices of supplies bought by the bureau
    (D) increase in the amount of money spent on salaries in the bureau in 1961 over the amount spent in the preceding year

18. If the percentage of expenditures for salaries in one year is added to the percentage of expenditures for equipment in that year, a total of the two percentages for that year is obtained. The two years for which this total is the same are
    (A) 1958 and 1960   (B) 1957 and 1959
    (C) 1957 and 1960   (D) 1958 and 1961

19. On the following, the year in which the bureau spent the greatest amount of money on supplies was
    (A) 1961   (B) 1957
    (C) 1958   (D) 1959

20. Of the following years, the one in which there was the greatest increase over the preceding year in the amount of money spent on salaries is
    (A) 1958   (B) 1961
    (C) 1960   (D) 1959

21. Of the bureau's expenditures for equipment in 1961, one-third was used for the purchase of mailroom equipment and the remainder was spent on miscellaneous office equipment. How much money did the bureau spend on miscellaneous office equipment in 1961?
    (A) $400,000   (B) $40,000
    (C) $800,000   (D) $80,000

22. If there were 120 employees in the bureau in 1960, then the average annual salary paid to the employees in that year was, most nearly,
    (A) $4,345   (B) $4,960
    (C) $5,835   (D) $8,080

23. In 1959 the bureau had 125 employees. If 20 of the employees earned an average annual salary of $8,000, then the average annual salary of the other 105 employees was, most nearly,
    (A) $6,400   (B) $4,900
    (C) $4,100   (D) $5,400

24. Assume that the bureau estimated that the amount of money it would spend on supplies in 1962 would be the same as the amount it spent on that category in 1961. Similarly, the bureau estimated that the amount of money it would spend on equipment in 1962 would be the same as the amount it spent on that category in 1961. However the bureau estimated that in 1962 the amount it would spend on salaries would be 10 per cent higher than the amount it spent on that category in 1961. The percentage of its annual expenditures that the bureau estimated it would spend on supplies in 1962 is most nearly
    (A) 27.5%   (B) 22.5%
    (C) 23.5%   (D) 25%

CHART NO. VI

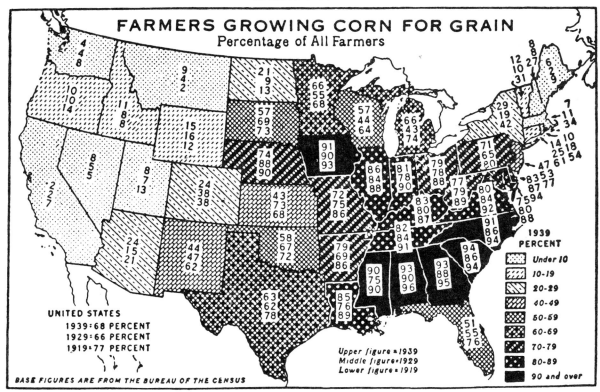

FARMERS GROWING CORN FOR GRAIN
Percentage of All Farmers

UNITED STATES
1939=68 PERCENT
1929=66 PERCENT
1919=77 PERCENT

BASE FIGURES ARE FROM THE BUREAU OF THE CENSUS

1939 PERCENT
Under 10
10-19
20-29
40-49
50-59
60-69
70-79
80-89
90 and over

Upper figure = 1939
Middle figure = 1929
Lower figure = 1919

Answer the following by referring to the map above.

25. In what State(s) west of the Mississippi did 90% or more of the farmers raise corn for grain in 1919?
    (A) Minnesota and Kansas
    (B) Kansas and Nebraska
    (C) Missouri and Kansas
    (D) Nebraska and Iowa
    (E) Iowa

26. In 1939, how many States had the same percentage of farmers growing corn for grain as

Colorado had in 1919?

(A) 0   (B) 1
(C) 2   (D) 3
(E) Not answerable

27. What was the average percentage of Illinois farmers raising corn for grain for the three years referred to on the map?

(A) 77.7   (B) 83.0
(C) 86.0   (D) 91.25
(E) 129.0

28. The quantity of corn produced for grain was the same in Mississippi and Missouri in what year?

(A) 1919   (B) 1929
(C) 1935 (approximately)   (D) 1939
(E) Not answerable

29. What two States had the lowest proportion of farmers growing corn for grain in 1929?

(A) Washington and Montana
(B) Washington and California
(C) Maine and California
(D) Montana and Maine
(E) Montana and Nevada

30. In what two States east of the Missouri River did 60% to 69% of the farmers raise corn for grain in 1939?

(A) Illinois and Wisconsin
(B) Michigan and Minnesota
(C) Texas and Michigan
(D) Wisconsin and Minnesota
(E) Texas and Oklahoma

31. In Washington, Oregon, and California combined, the percentage of farmers growing corn for grain in 1919 exceeded the percentage in 1929 by approximately what percent?

(A) 6   (B) 4
(C) 8   (D) 13
(E) Not answerable

32. The proportion of farmers in New York growing corn for grain in 1919 was what percent greater than the proportion in North Dakota in 1939?

(A) 21   (B) 50
(C) 100   (D) 200
(E) Not answerable

33. The number of farmers in Vermont in 1939 was approximately 24,000 and in 1929 approximately 25,000. The number of farmers growing corn for grain in 1939 was an increase of approximately what percent over those in 1929?

(A) 2.0   (B) 13.3
(C) 15.2   (D) 20.0
(E) Not answerable

34. Based on the map and the table below, in which of the three states given was there an increase in farmers growing corn for grain between the 1929 and 1939 figures?

(A) Oregon
(B) Oregon and New Mexico
(C) Oregon and Texas
(D) Texas and New Mexico
(E) All three

TOTAL NUMBER OF FARMERS

	1929	1939
New Mexico	31, 000	34, 000
Oregon	55, 000	62, 000
Texas	495, 000	418, 000

35. Assuming that the number of farmers in the United States increased by 8% from 1919 to 1929, the number of farmers growing corn for grain decreased by what percent from 1919 to 1929?

(A) 3.0   (B) 7.4
(C) 10.1   (D) 11.9
(E) Not answerable

CHART NO. VII

Answer questions 36 to 40 on the basis of the chart following.

36. The one of the following years for which average employee production was LOWEST was

(A) 1941   (B) 1943
(C) 1945   (D) 1947
(E) 1949

37. The average annual employee production for the ten year period was, in terms of work units, most nearly

(A) 30   (B) 50
(C) 70   (D) 80
(E) 90

38. On the basis of the chart, it can be deduced

that personnel needs for the coming year are budgeted on the basis of

(A) workload for the current year
(B) expected workload for the coming year
(C) no set plan
(D) average workload over the five years immediately preceding the period
(E) expected workload for the five coming years

39. "The chart indicates that the operation is carefully programmed and that the labor force has been used properly."   This opinion is

(A) supported by the chart; the organization has been able to meet emergency situations requiring much additional work without commensurate increases in staff
(B) not supported by the chart; the irregular work load shows a complete absence of planning
(C) supported by the chart; the similar shapes of the "Workload" and "Labor Force" curves show that these important factors are closely related
(D) not supported by the chart; poor planning with respect to labor requirements is obvious from the chart
(E) supported by the chart; the average number of units of work performed in any 5 year period during the 10 years shows sufficient regularity to indicate a definite trend.

40. "The chart indicates that the department may be organized in such a way as to require a permanent minimum staff which is too large for the type of operation indicated."   This opinion is

(A) supported by the chart; there is indication that the operation calls for an irreducible minimum number of employees and application of the most favorable work production records show this to be too high for normal operation

(B) not supported by the chart; the absence of any sort of regularity makes it impossible to express any opinion with any degree of certainty

(C) supported by the chart; the expected close relationship between workload and labor force is displaced somewhat, a phenomenon which usually occurs as a result of a fixed minimum requirement
(D) not supported by the chart; the violent movement of the "Labor Force" curve makes it evident that no minimum requirements are in effect
(E) supported by the chart; calculation shows that the average number of employees was 84 with an average variation of 17.8 thus indicating that the minimum number of 60 persons was too high for efficient operation.

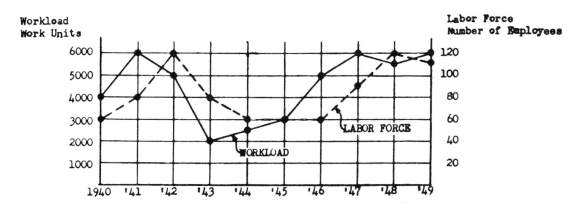

DEPARTMENT X
WORKLOAD AND LABOR FORCE
1940-1949

Questions 41 to 44 are to be answered on the basis of the following graph.

AVERAGE HOURLY INCIDENCE OF ARRESTS AND ACCIDENTS FOR COMMUNITY X FOR 1955

Note: Hourly figures represent total number of occurrences in the immediately preceding hour.

CHART NO. VIII

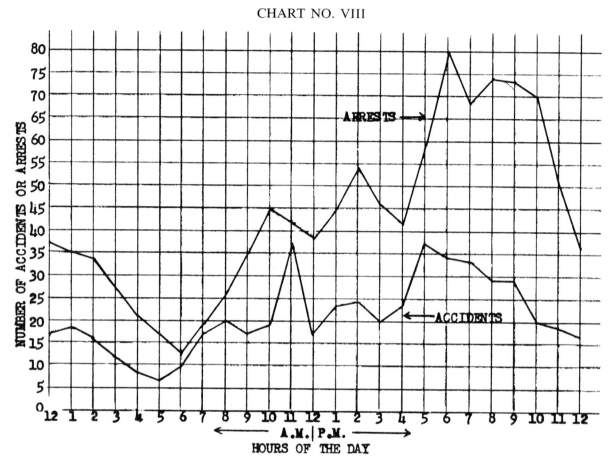

41. According to this graph, of the following hours of the day, the hour which shows the highest ratio of arrests to accidents is
    (A) 2 p.m.   (B) 6 p.m.
    (C) 8 p.m.   (D) 10 p.m.

42. According to the above graph, the *least* average hour-to-hour variation, during the following time periods, was in the number of
    (A) arrests during the 4 p.m. through 8 p.m. period
    (B) accidents during the 12 noon through 4 p.m. period
    (C) arrests during the 8 p.m. through 12 midnight period
    (D) accidents during the 8 a.m. through 12 noon period.

43. According to the above graph, of all the ac-cidents occurring from 12 noon through midnight, the percentage which occurred from 12 noon through 4 p.m. was most nearly
    (A) 26%   (B) 30%
    (C) 34%   (D) 38%.

44. On the basis of the above graph
    (A) an equal number of accidents was recorded daily at 8 a.m. and 3 p.m.
    (B) on any given day, during the year covered, there were more arrests recorded at 2 p.m. than at 10 a.m.
    (C) the number of accidents entered in the first 12 o'clock column must always equal the number of accidents in the last 12 o'clock column
    (D) the wide variation in the number of arrests makes statistical interpretation of the figures unreliable.   (298.2)

Questions 45 through 54 are to be answered on the basis of Chart IX, Immigration.

Select the date which completes each of the following statements.

45. Emigration was 1/4 immigration in:
    (A) 1910   (B) 1913
    (C) 1920   (D) 1924

46. Immigration was 1/2 emigration in:
    (A) 1915   (B) 1921
    (C) 1932   (D) 1934

47. Emigration and immigration were equal in:
    (A) 1919   (B) 1922
    (C) 1931   (D) 1935

48. Emigration rose at the greatest rate between:
    (A) 1914 and 1915 (B) 1919 and 1920
    (C) 1922 and 1923 (D) 1931 and 1932

49. The excess of immigrants over emigrants was greatest in:
    (A) 1910   (B) 1914
    (C) 1921   (D) 1932

50. Immigration fell off at the greatest rate between:

(A) 1914 and 1915
(B) 1919 and 1920
(C) 1924 and 1925
(D) 1931 and 1932

51. There were fewest emigrants in:
    (A) 1917   (B) 1923
    (C) 1933   (D) 1935

52. The rate of change of net immigration and greatest between:
    (A) 1920 and 1921
    (B) 1925 and 1926
    (C) 1930 and 1931
    (D) 1932 and 1933

53. The rates of increase of emigrants and immigrants were most nearly equal between:
    (A) 1932 and 1933
    (B) 1925 and 1926
    (C) 1918 and 1919
    (D) 1913 and 1914

54. Immigration was lowest in:
    (A) 1918   (B) 1931
    (C) 1933   (D) 1935

CHART NO. IX

In the graph below, the heavy curve represents immigration from 1910-1935. The light curve represents emigration from 1910-1935.

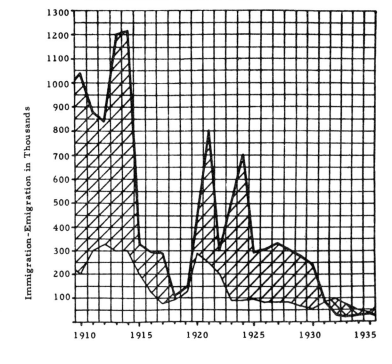

CHART NO. X

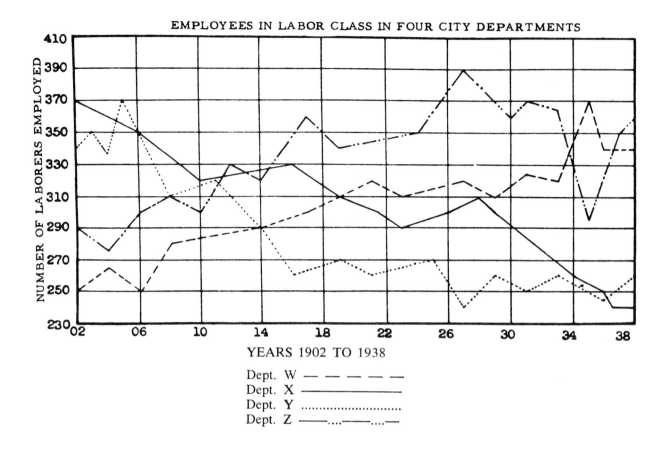

EMPLOYEES IN LABOR CLASS IN FOUR CITY DEPARTMENTS

YEARS 1902 TO 1938

Dept. W — — — — —
Dept. X ——————
Dept. Y ....
Dept. Z ——...——...—

Items 55 to 64 are based on information contained in   chart.   No. X. Choose the letter which is the same as the answer which correctly completes the statement.

55. W had its largest number of laborers in
    (A) 1926   (B) 1914
    (C) 1935   (D) 1906
                (E) 1937

56. In 1919 the same number of laborers were employed in
    (A) W and Z   (B) Y and Z
    (C) X and Y   (D) W and X
                (E) X and Z

57. In the same year that Z reached its greatest peak, the lowest number of laborers was employed in
    (A) W and X   (B) Y
    (C) W   (D) X
                (E) W and Y

58. The department which showed the greatest increase of labor class employees in 1938 as compared to 1902 is
    (A) W   (B) X
    (C) Y   (D) Z
    (E) not determinable from graph

59. In 1930 Z showed a 20% increase over
    (A) 1910   (B) 1926
    (C) 1914   (D) 1934
                (E) 1938

60. W employed the same number of laborers in 1906 as X did in
    (A) 1913   (B) 1931
    (C) 1906   (D)· 1927
                (E) 1936

61. The smallest number of laborers employed in 1914 was in
    (A) Z   (B) Y and Z
    (C) W and Y   (D) W and X
                (E) X and Z

62. Z in 1906 is to X in 1926 as Z in 1910 is to
    (A) Y in 1938   (B) W in 1921
    (C) Z in 1927   (D) Y in 1919
                (E) X in 1929

63. In 1935 W had .... times as many laborers as in 1906
(A) 2   (B) 2.22
(C) 1.48   (D) 1.50
        (E) 1.65

64. Z in 1904 is to Y in 1931 as X in 1916 is to
(A) Y in 1919   (B) W in 1917
(C) Z in 1927   (D) Z in 1919
        (E) W in 1923

CHART NO. XI

Answer questions 65 to 69 solely on the basis of the following table.

Number of Persons Receiving Public Assistance and Cost of Public Assistance in 1961 and 1962

Category of Assistance	Monthly average number receiving assistance during		Total Cost for Year in Millions of Dollars		Cost Paid by New York City for Year in Millions of Dollars	
	1961	1962	1961	1962	1961	1962
H R	36,097	38,263	$19.2	$17.4	$9.7	$8.7
V A	6,632	5,972	2.5	1.6	1.3	.8
O A A	32,545	31,804	33.7	29.7	6.5	5.0
M A A	13,992	11,782	13.2	21.3	3.3	5.3
A D C	212,795	228,795	108.3	121.4	27.5	31.3

65. Assume that the *total* cost of the Home Relief program decreases by 10% each year for the next three years after 1962. Then the total cost of the Home Relief program for 1965 will be, most nearly,
(A) $11.5 million   (C) $12.7 million
(B) $14.1 million   (D) $14.5 million
        (E) $36.0 million

66. The category for which New York City paid the smallest percentage of the total cost was
(A) O A A in 1961   (C) V A in 1961
(B) A D C in 1961   (D) O A A in 1962
        (E) A D C in 1962

67. The *monthly* cost to the city for each person receiving MAA during 1962 was, most nearly,
(A) $18 more than in 1961
(B) $26 less than in 1961
(C) $20 more than in 1961
(D) $67 more than in 1961

(E) $18 less than in 1961

68. Assume that 40% of the number of persons receiving ADC in 1961 were adults caring for minor children, but the city's contribution towards maintaining these adults was only 36% of its total contribution to the ADC program in 1961, then the amount paid by the city for each adult per month in 1961 is, most nearly,
(A) $10   (B) $14   (C) $31   (D) $36
        (E) $107

69. Assume that 10% of the persons receiving OAA in 1962 will be transferred to MAA in 1963, and 6% of the persons receiving MAA in 1962 will no longer need any public assistance in 1963, then the percentage change from 1962 to 1963 in the monthly average number receiving MAA would be, most nearly,
(A) an increase of 4%
(B) an increase of 27%
(C) a decrease of 6%
(D) an increase of 21%

Questions 70 to 79 are to be answered solely on the basis of Chart XII which relates to the Investigation Division of Department X. This chart contains four curves which connect the points that show for each year the variations in percentage deviation from normal in the number of investigators, the number of clerical employees, the cost of personnel, and the number of cases processed for the period 1942-1952 inclusive. The year 1942 was designated as the normal year. The personnel of the Investigation Division consists of investigators and clerical employees only.

CHART NO. XII
INVESTIGATION DIVISION, DEPARTMENT X
VARIATIONS IN NUMBER OF CASES PROCESSED, COST OF PERSONNEL
NUMBER OF CLERICAL EMPLOYEES, AND NUMBER OF INVESTI-
GATORS FOR EACH YEAR FROM 1942 TO 1952 INCLUSIVE
(IN PERCENTAGES FROM NORMAL)

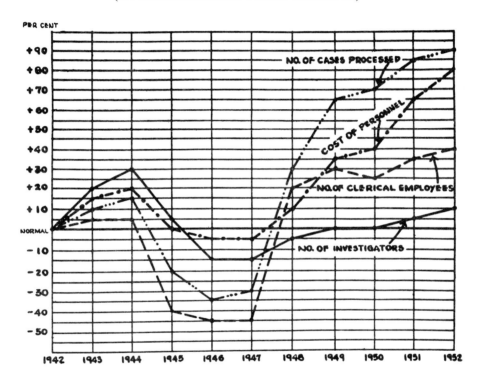

70. If 1300 cases were processed by the division in 1946, then the number of cases processed in 1942 was
(A) 2000   (B) 1755
(C) 2145   (D) 1650.

71. Of the following, the year in which there was no change in the size of the division's total staff from that of the preceding year is
(A) 1945   (B) 1947
(C) 1949   (D) 1951.

72. Of the following, the year in which the size of the division's total staff decreased most sharply from that of the preceding year is
(A) 1945   (B) 1946
(C) 1947   (D) 1948.

73. An inspection of the chart discloses that the curve that fluctuated *least,* as determined by the average deviation from normal, is the curve for the
(A) number of cases processed
(B) cost of personnel
(C) number of clerical employees
(D) number of investigators.

74. A comparison of 1946 with 1942 reveals an increase in 1946 in the
(A) cost of personnel for the division
(B) number of cases processed per investigator
(C) number of cases processed per clerical employee
(D) number of clerical employees per investigator.

75. If the personnel cost per case processed in 1942 was $12.30, then the personnel cost per case processed in 1952 was most nearly
   (A) $ 9.85   (B) $10.95
   (C) $11.65   (D) $13.85.

76. Suppose that there was a total of 108 employees in the division in 1942 and a total of 125 employees in 1950. On the basis of these figures, it is most accurate to state that the number of investigators employed in the division in 1950 was
   (A) 40   (B) 57
   (C) 68   (D) 85.

77. It is predicted that the number of cases processed in 1953 will exceed the number processed in 1952 by exactly the same quantity that the number processed in 1952 exceeded that processed in 1951. It is also predicted that the personnel cost in 1953 will exceed the personnel cost in 1952 by exactly the same amount that that the 1952 personnel cost exceeded that for 1951. On the basis ot these predictions, it is most accurate to state that the personnel cost per case in 1953 will be
   (A) ten per cent less than the personnel cost in 1952
   (B) exactly the same as the personnel cost per case in 1952
   (C) twice as much as the personnel cost per case in 1942
   (D) exactly the same as the personnel cost per case in 1942.   (17)

78. The variation between the per cent of cases processed and the number of investigators of Department X was greatest in
   (A) 1949   (B) 1951
   (C) 1952   (D) 1944.

79. In 1950, the difference between two categories in Department X is equal to a third. The third is the
   (A) number of investigators
   (B) cost of personnel
   (C) number of clerical employees
   (D) number of cases processed.

CHART NO. XIII

NUMBER OF EMPLOYEES IN CIVIL SERVICE BETWEEN YEARS 1902 AND 1937

Year	Total Number (In Thousands)	Competitive Class (In Thousands)	Labor Class (In Thousands)	Non-Competitive Class (In Thousands)
1902	33	18	12	2
1906	43	24	16	2
1910	53	29	18	5
1914	56	31	18	6
1918	54	31	16	6
1922	60	35	17	7
1926	74	44	19	9
1930	90	52	24	12
1933	91	49	25	15
1937	107	63	27	17

Items 80 through 84 relate to the table above.

80.. The greatest percentage increase in the competitive class occurred between the years of

   (A) 1933 and 1937
   (B) 1926 and 1930
   (C) 1922 and 1926
   (D) 1906 and 1910
   (E) 1902 and 1906

81. The smallest percentage of employees in the competitive class is found in the year
   (A) 1902   (B) 1910
   (C) 1914   (D) 1933
            (E) 1937

82. The greatest percentage of employees in the labor class is found in the year
   (A) 1902   (B) 1906
   (C) 1910   (D) 1930
            (E) 1937

83. The approximate ratio of 54%, 27%, and 16% for competitive, labor class and non-competitive employees respectively

   (A) never occurs
   (B) occurs once
   (C) occurs twice
   (D) occurs three times
   (E) occurs five times

84. The most accurate of the following statements regarding the interpretation of the table is that
  (A) the percentage of employees in the non-competitive class has been constantly increasing since the World War
  (B) the percentage of employees in the competitive class has never fallen below 55%
  (C) since 1926, employees in the labor class have been increasing at a faster rate than in the non-competitive class

(D) the average number of employees in the competitive class between the years of 1922 and 1937 inclusive was greater than the average number of total employees between 1902 and 1922 inclusive

(E) between 1933 and 1937, the percentage increase in the competitive class was more than 3 1/2 times the percentage increase in the labor class.

CHART NO. XIV

Carefully study the table below. You are to answer questions 85 through 89 solely on the basis of the data given in the table.

| YEAR | PRIVATELY FINANCED | | | | Total publicly financed | TOTAL |
	1-family	2-family	Multi-family	Total		
1937	267,000	16,000	49,000	332,000	4,000	336,000
1938	316,000	18,000	65,000	399,000	7,000	406,000
1939	373,000	19,000	66,000	458,000	57,000	515,000
1940	448,000	26,000	56,000	530,000	73,000	603,000
1941	533,000	28,000	58,000	619,000	96,000	715,000
1942	252,000	18,000	31,000	301,000	196,000	497,000
1943	136,000	18,000	30,000	184,000	166,000	350,000
1944	115,000	11,000	13,000	139,000	30,000	169,000
1945	184,000	9,000	15,000	208,000	18,000	226,000
1946	590,000	24,000	48,000	662,000	114,000	776,000
1947	745,000	34,000	72,000	851,000	3,000	854,000

85. "Multi-family private dwellings have been built in greater numbers than 2-family private dwellings." For the years covered by the table, this statement
  (A) is true
  (B) is false
  (C) is partly true
  (D) cannot be determined from the table

86. Considering only the last ten years of the table, the number of years in which the number of 1-family private dwellings exceeded the number of publicly-financed dwellings is
  (A) 1   (B) 2
  (C) 9   (D) 10

87. The number of years during which the number

of publicly-financed dwellings was more than half the number of privately-financed dwellings is
  (A) 1   (B) 2
  (C) 3   (D) 4.

88. The number of years during which privately-financed 1-family dwellings was less than half the total number of all dwellings is
  (A) 1   (B) 2
  (C) 3   (D) 4.

89. The number of years during which there was an increase of at least 10% in the number of private 2-family dwellings built is
  (A) 1   (B) 2
  (C) 3   (D) 4.   (838.1)

Questions 90 through 94 are to be answered on the basis of the following graph.

CHART NO. XV

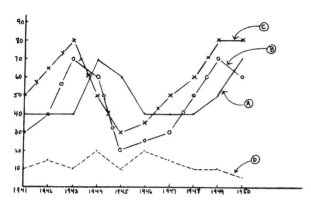

A. _____ total number of examiners employed during year
B. o-o-o-o total number of examinations held during year.
C. x-x-x-x total number of candidates tested during year in thousands.
D. - - - - total number of appeals from candidates who took an examination during year in tens.

90. The number of appeals from candidates who took an examination during any one year is apparently
   (A) directly related to the number of examiners employed during the year
   (B) directly related to the number of examinations held during the year
   (C) inversely related to the number of candidates tested during the year
   (D) unrelated to any of the other curves
   (E) inversely related to the average of the number of candidates tested and examiners employed during each year.

91. The total number of candidates tested during any one year is apparently
   (A) inversely related to the average of the number of tests given and the number of examiners employed during the year
   (B) completely unrelated to any of the other variables
   (C) inversely related to the number of examiners employed during the year
   (D) directly related to the number of appeals received during the year
   (E) directly related to the number of examinations held during that year.

92. It may be inferred that throughout the period covered the number of examinations for the coming year had been assumed to be
   (A) the same as that for the current year

(B) unpredictable
(C) the average of the number of examinations held in each of the past five years
(D) approximately one per cent of the number of candidates in the current year
(E) the average of the number of examinations and one per cent of the number of candidates for the past year.

93. The assumption that the average number of examinations completed by an examiner has remained constant during the ten year period is

   (A) inconsistent with the information given in the graph as the ratio between number of examiners employed during a year and the number of examinations given is not constant

   (B) not inconsistent with the information given in the graph if it is the case that after the examiners have completed the examinations to be given in any year they proceed at once to the preparation of examinations to be given in a future period

   (C) inconsistent with the information given as the sum of the deviations of the ratios between the number of examiners employed during a year and the number of examinations given during a year for all years from the mean of these ratios must be zero

   (D) not inconsistent with the information given as the sum of the deviations of the ratios between number of examiners employed during a year and the number of examinations given during the year for all years from the mean of these ratios is zero

   (E) inconsistent with the information given if we also assume that after the examiners have completed the examination to be given in any year, they proceed at once to the preparation of examinations to be given in a future period.   (5)

94. The one of the following years during which the average number of candidates on an examination was the least is
   (A) 1943   (B) 1944
   (C) 1945   (D) 1948
   (E) 1949.

Questions 95, 96, 97 and 98 are to be answered solely on the basis of the graph below.

CHART NO. XVI

AVERAGE MONTHLY DISTRIBUTION
OF CRIMES AGAINST PROPERTY
FOR COMMUNITY X   1951-1955

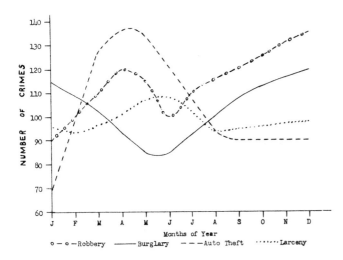

Months of Year

o — o —Robbery   —— Burglary   — — —Auto Theft   ·······Larceny

(A) January   (B) June
(C) July   (D) August
(E) September.

98. According to this graph, of the following crimes, the one which showed the *least* average month-to-month variation in the **number** of occurrences was
   (A) automobile theft during the **January** through June period
   (B) burglary during the January through **June** period
   (C) burglary during the July through December period
   (D) larceny during the July through December period
   (E) robbery during the January through **June** period.   (014.3)

95. The above graph indicates that, during the entire five-year period covered,
   (A) larceny showed the greatest variation
   (B) more crimes against property were being committed at the end of the period than at the beginning
   (C) robbery was becoming an increasingly serious police problem
   (D) specific crimes against property follow no pattern
   (E) there were seasonal variations in the number of burglaries.

96. If the population of this community averaged 150,000 during the period covered by this graph, then the crime rate for burglaries in December, computed in accordance with the F.B.I. method of crime reporting, was most nearly
   (A) 50   (B) 80
   (C) 110   (D) 140
   (E) 170.

97. According to this graph, the month in which all crimes against property (total for the four crimes) were *least* frequently committed is

Key Answers to All Questions

1. B	13. C.	25. D	37. B
2. A	14. B	26. A	38. A
3. C	15. A	27. C	39. C
4. C	16. B	28. B	40. A
5. C	17. D.	29. C	41. D
6. C.	18. B	30. B	42. B
7. D.	19. D	31. B	43. B
8. C.	20. A	32. C	44. C
9. B.	21. D	33. A	45. B
10. C.	22. C	34. B	46. D
11. D.	23. B	35. B	47. C
12. B.	24. C	36. B	48. B

49. B	61. C	73. D	85. A
50. A	62. E	74. C	86. C
51. D	63. C	75. C	87. B
52. A	64. B	76. A	88. A
53. C	65. C	77. D	89. D
54. C	66. D	78. C	90. D
55. C	67. A	79. B	91. E
56. D	68. A	80. E	92. A
57. B	69. D	81. D	93. B
58. A	70. A	82. B	94. B
59. A	71. B	83. B	95. E
60. E	72. A	84. E	96. B
			97. A
			98. D

PATTERN ANALYSIS AND COMPREHENSION

166 practice exercises. Important variations on a significant test theme in spatial relations and aptitude exams.

Visualizing Figures

IN questions like these, which are given on tests like yours, you are required to select one of the drawings of objects (A), (B), (C), or (D) below, that could be made from the flat piece drawn at the left, if this flat piece were folded on the dotted lines shown in the drawing.

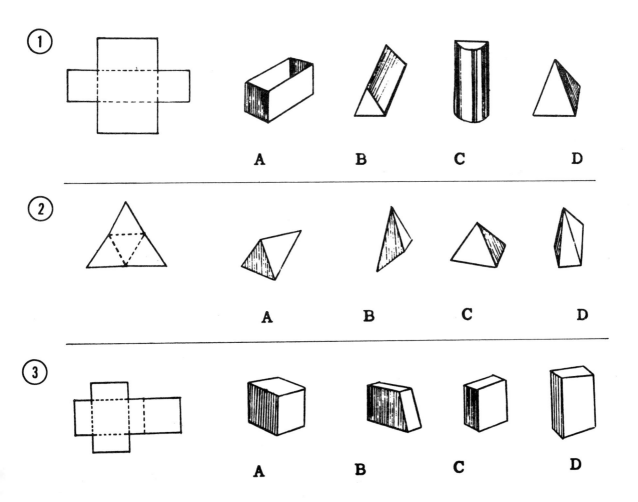

1

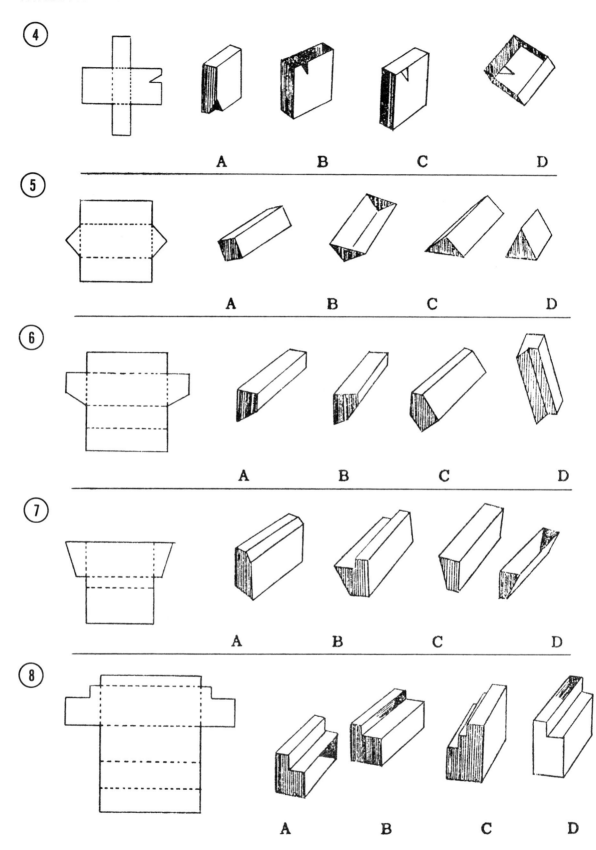

4
    A   B   C   D

5
    A   B   C   D

6
    A   B   C   D

7
    A   B   C   D

8
    A   B   C   D

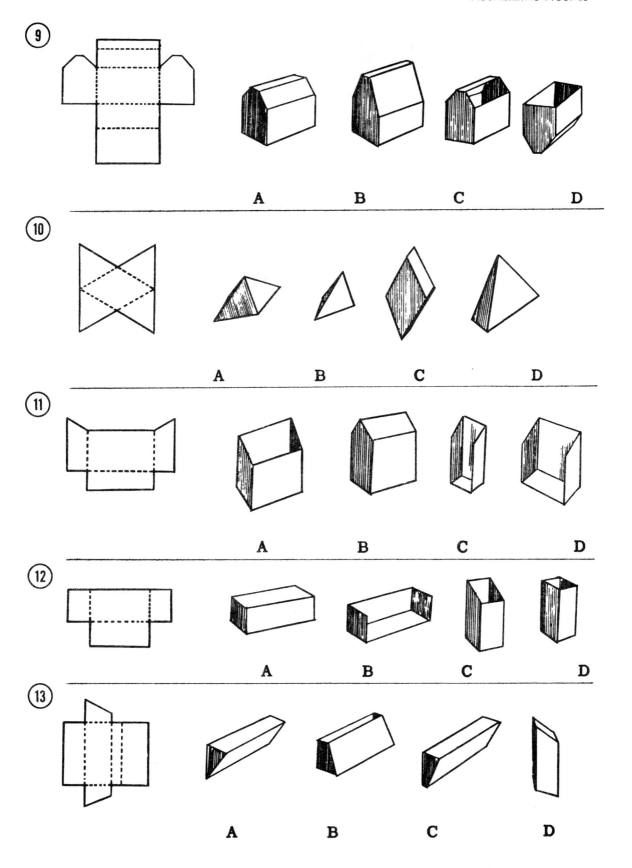

⑨

A   B   C   D

⑩

A   B   C   D

⑪

A   B   C   D

⑫

A   B   C   D

⑬

A   B   C   D

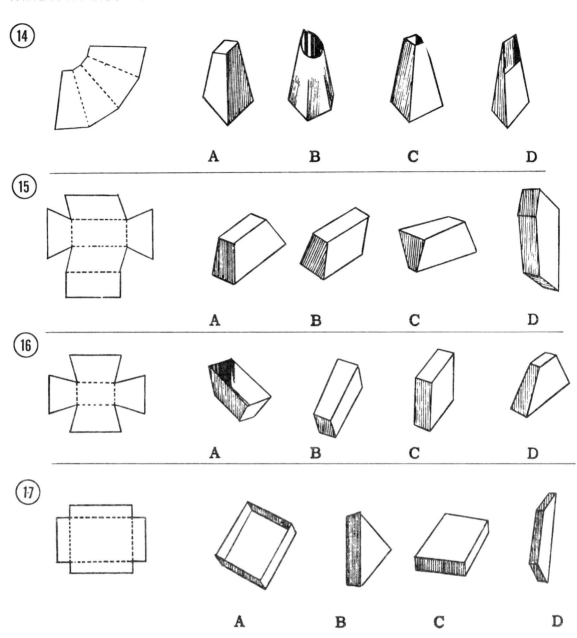

14
A   B   C   D

15
A   B   C   D

16
A   B   C   D

17
A   B   C   D

KEY ANSWERS TO QUESTIONS

1. A	5. C	9. C	13. C	17. A
2. C	6. A	10. A	14. C	
3. C	7. D	11. D	15. B	
4. B	8. B	12. B	16. A	

Practice For View Questions

In View Questions, you are faced again with fairly simple questions which any intelligent person can answer, given sufficient time. But on your test, you probably won't be given sufficient time. That causes you to rush along faster than you are able to do, and as a result, you make errors. By practicing with the scientific selection of questions in this chapter, you will noticeably increase your speed, your skill and your accuracy in answering questions of this type. On your test, you will find that you are familiar with them and that they offer you little difficulty.

DIRECTIONS

In these View Questions, you are asked to select one of the drawings of objects lettered (A), (B), (C), or (D), which would have the top, front and side views as shown in the drawing at the left. For each of the 18 questions that follow, work as quickly and accurately as you can in choosing your answers. Then compare them with those given at the end of the chapter.

EIGHTEEN EXERCISES IN ANALYSIS AND COMPREHENSION

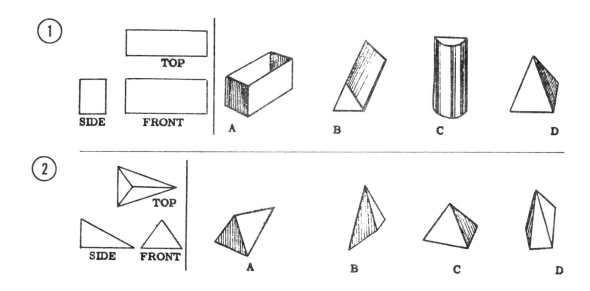

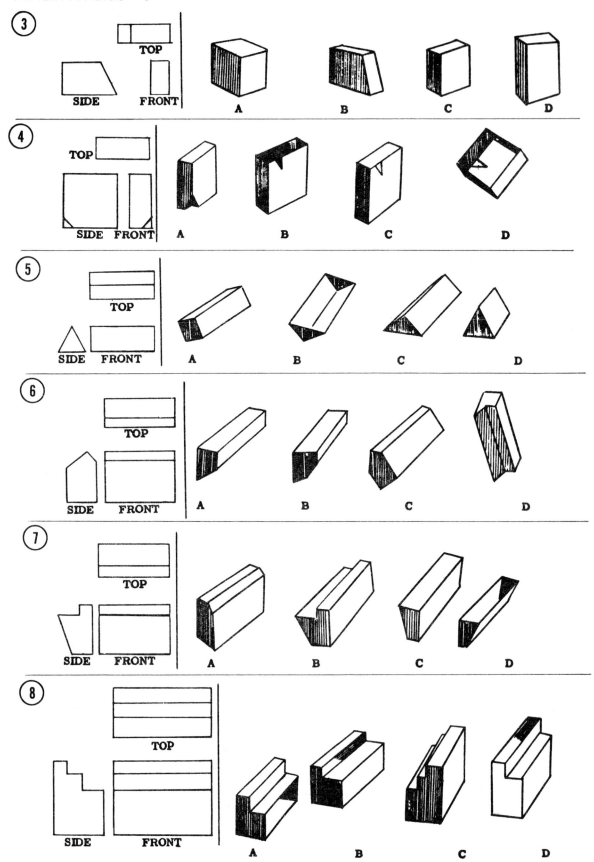

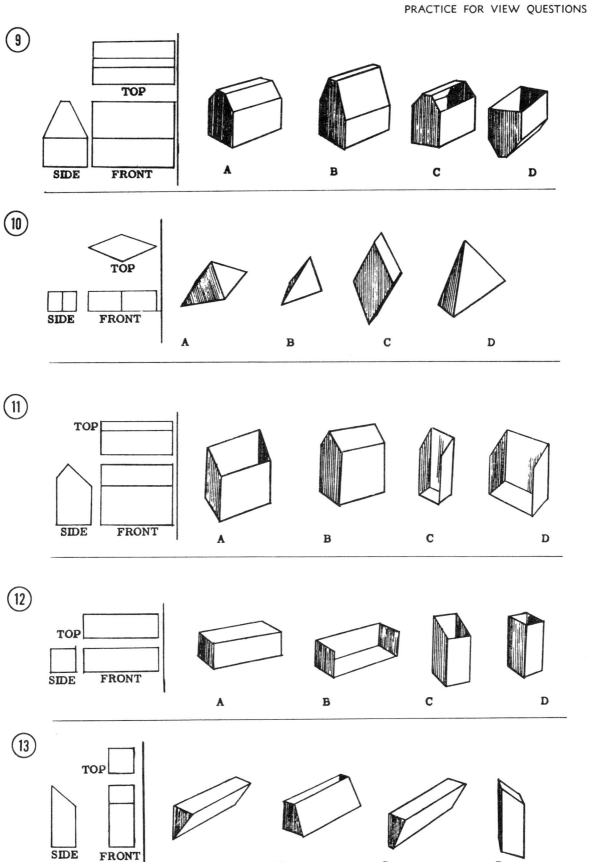

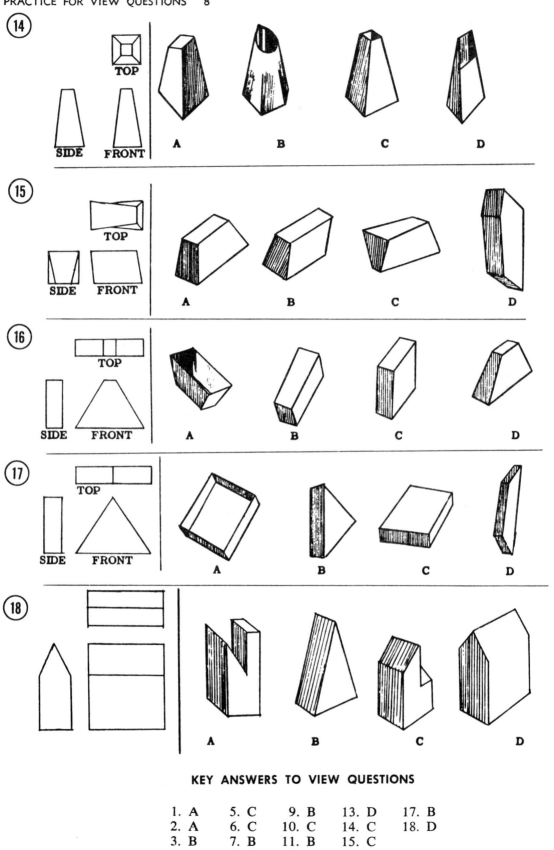

KEY ANSWERS TO VIEW QUESTIONS

1. A	5. C	9. B	13. D	17. B
2. A	6. C	10. C	14. C	18. D
3. B	7. B	11. B	15. C	
4. A	8. C	12. A	16. D	

Matching Parts and Figures

These questions on matching parts and figures test your understanding of spatial relations. They also present the type of problems found in making templates and patterns.

THE first two questions show, at the left side, two or more flat pieces. In each question select the arrangement lettered A, B, C, or D that shows how these pieces can be fitted together without gaps or overlapping. The pieces may be *turned around* or *turned over* in any way to make them fit together.

From these pieces

①

which one of these arrangements can you make?

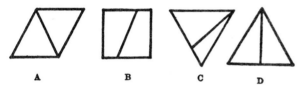

   A   B   C   D

From these pieces

②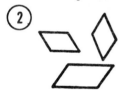

which one of these arrangements can you make?

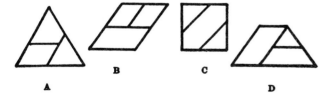

          B   C

A   D

The next questions are based on the four solid patterns shown.

Each of the questions shows *one* of these four patterns cut up into pieces. For each question, decide which one of the four patterns could be made by fitting *all of the pieces* together without having any edges overlap and without leaving any space between pieces. Some of the pieces may need to be *turned around* or *turned over* to make them fit. The pattern must be made in its exact size and shape.

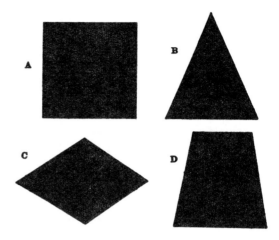

Look at sample question 3. If the two pieces were fitted together they would make pattern D. The piece on the left fits at the bottom of pattern D, and the piece at the right is turned around and over to make the top of the pattern.

③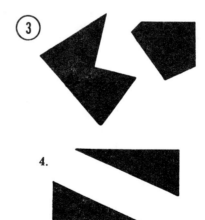

4.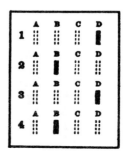

	A	B	C	D
1	∷	∷	∷	▌
2	∷	▌	∷	∷
3	∷	∷	∷	▌
4	∷	▌	∷	∷

9

TEST QUESTIONS FOR PRACTICE

Each of the following items numbered 1 to 46 is followed by a group of five figures lettered A, B, C, D, and E. Two of these lettered figures, when put together, make the drawing marked with the item number. Choose the letters of the two figures, which, when put together, are most nearly the same as the design marked with the item number. In writing answers, place the capital letters in alphabetical order.

Samples: The answer to Item IV is A and D; the answer to Item V is B and C.

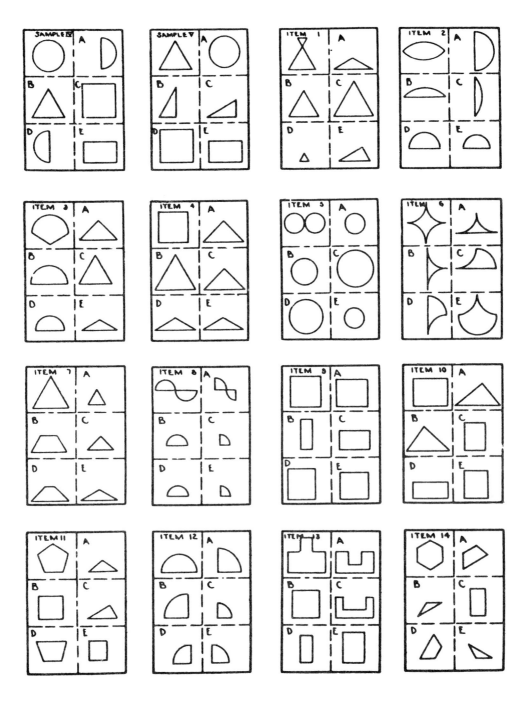

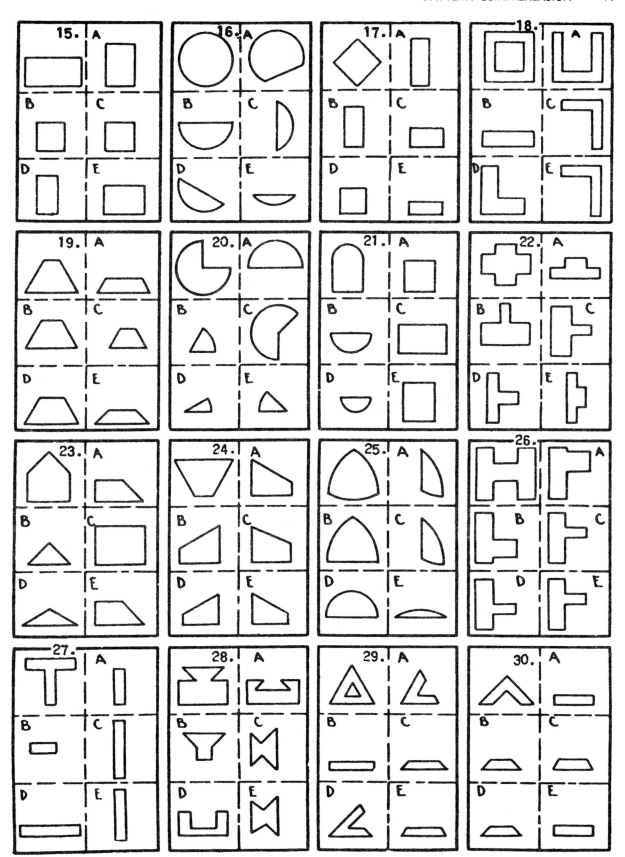

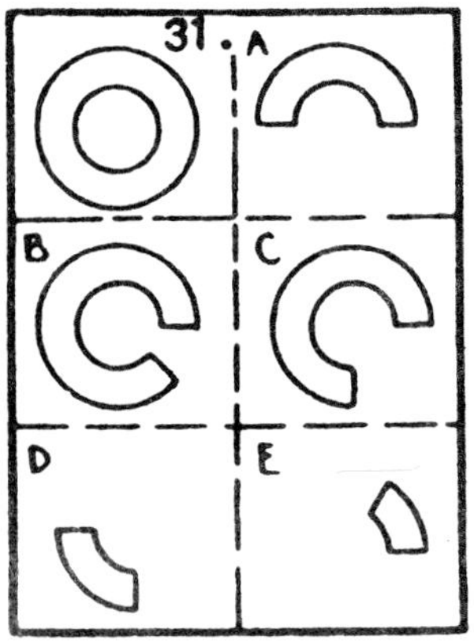
31.
A
B
C
D
E

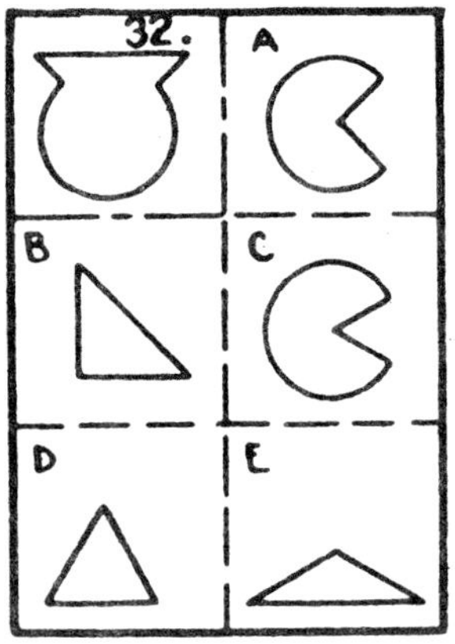
32.
A
B
C
D
E

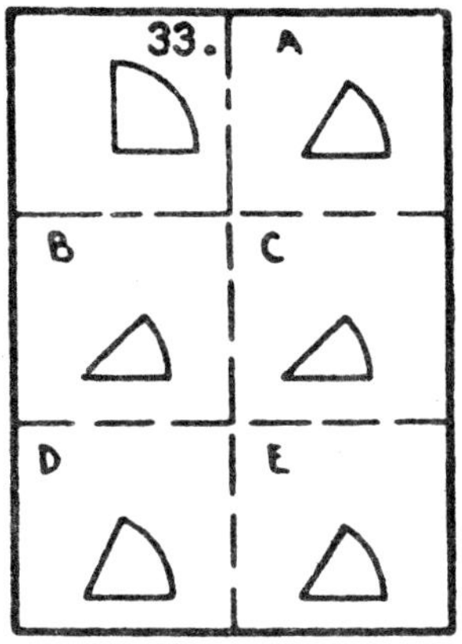
33.
A
B
C
D
E

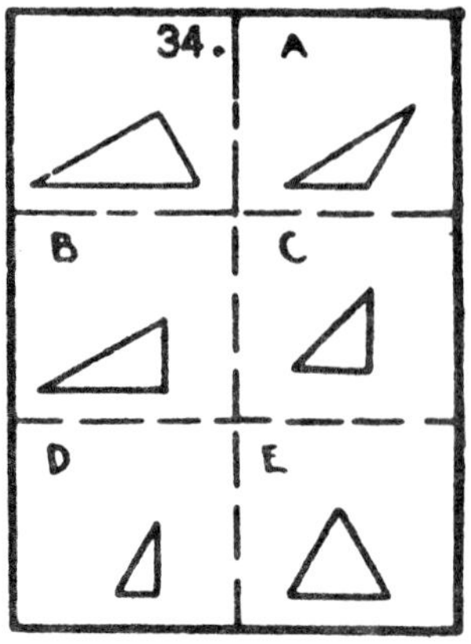
34.
A
B
C
D
E

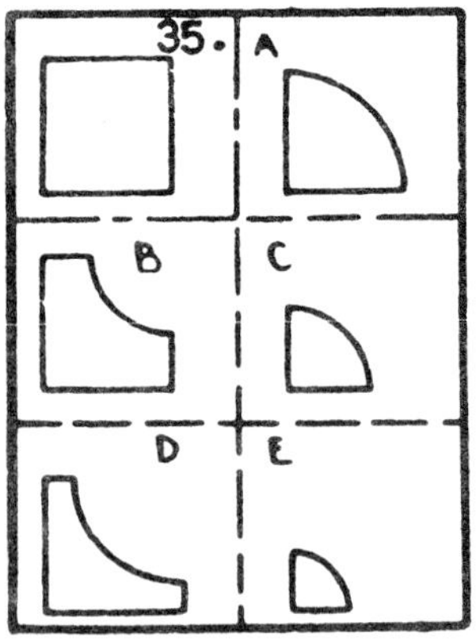
35.
A
B
C
D
E

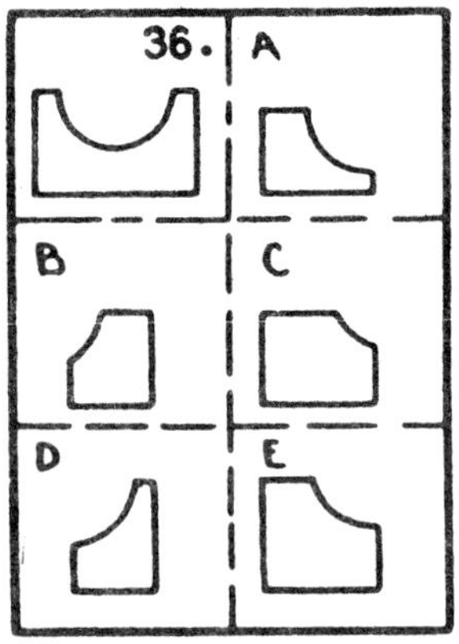
36.
A
B
C
D
E

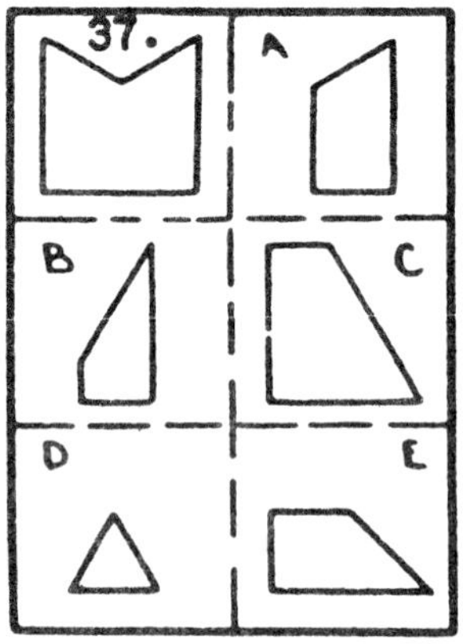
37.
A
B
C
D
E

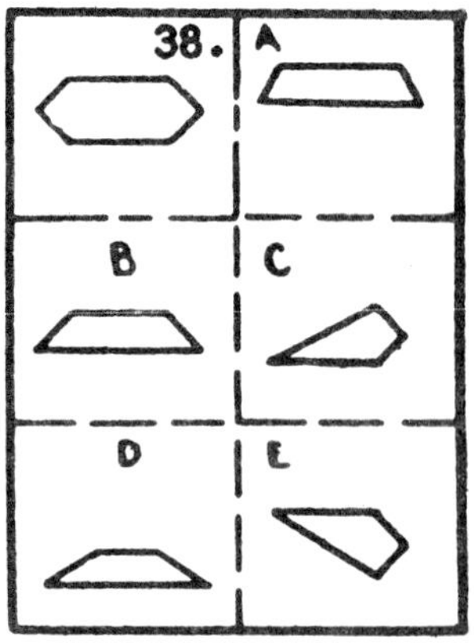
38.
A
B
C
D
E

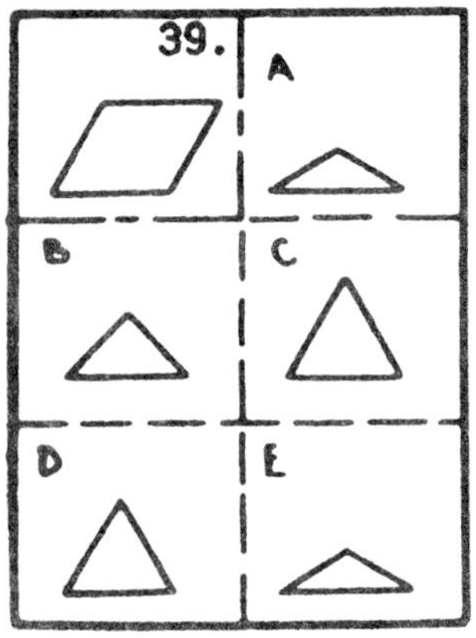
39.
A
B
C
D
E

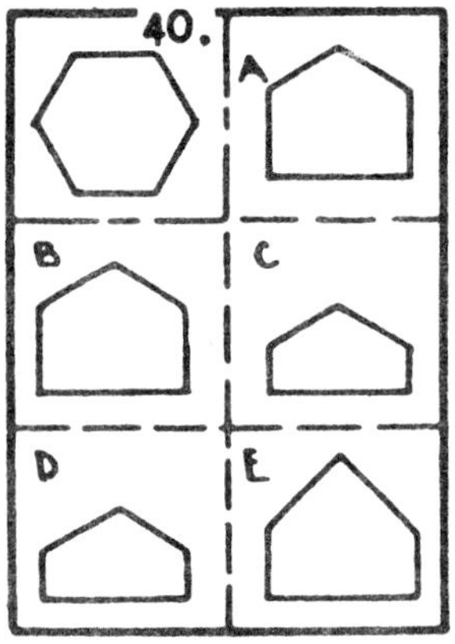
40.
A
B
C
D
E

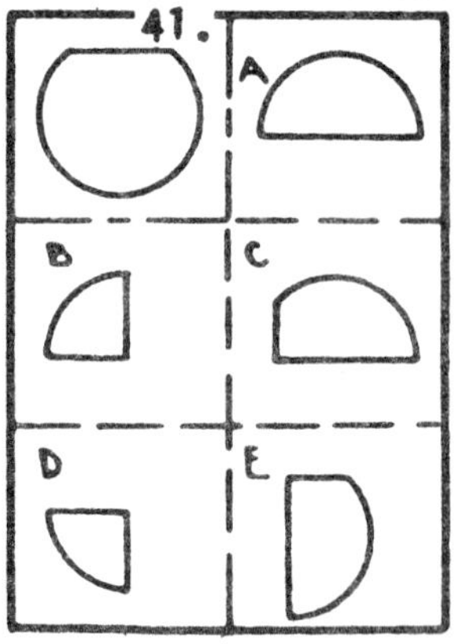
41.
A
B
C
D
E

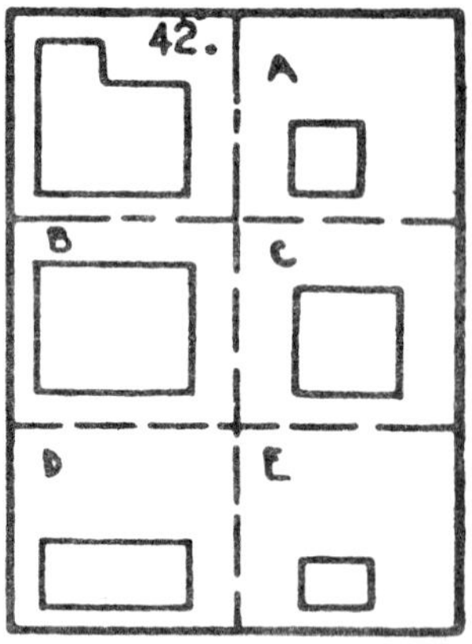
42.
A
B
C
D
E

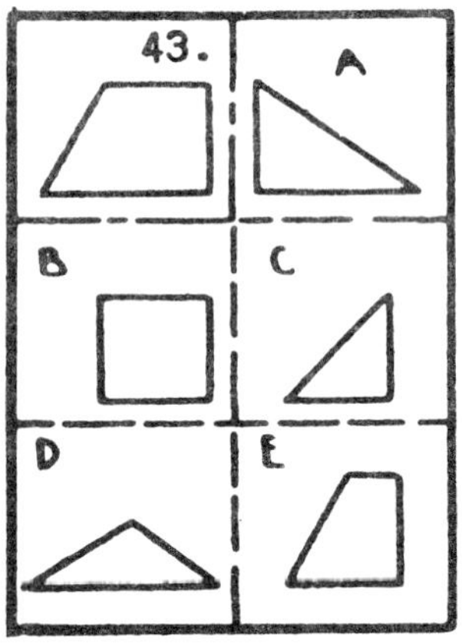
43.
A
B
C
D
E

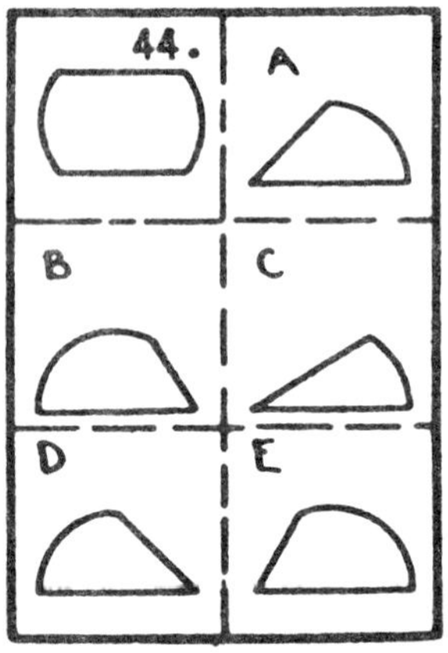
44.
A
B
C
D
E

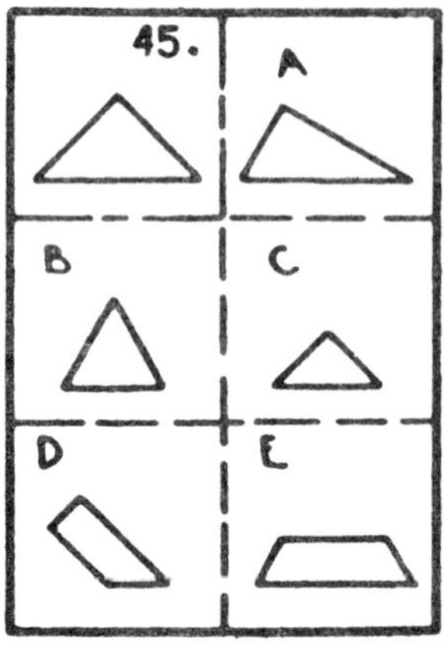
45.
A
B
C
D
E

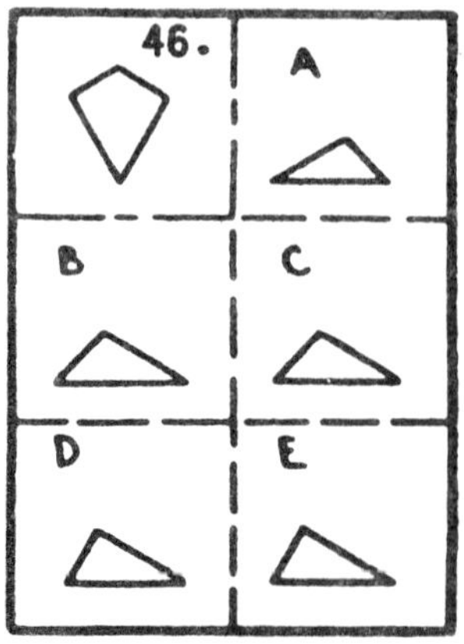
46.
A
B
C
D
E

(47) Fitting Angles (Spatial Relations) :
Which form is made from A?

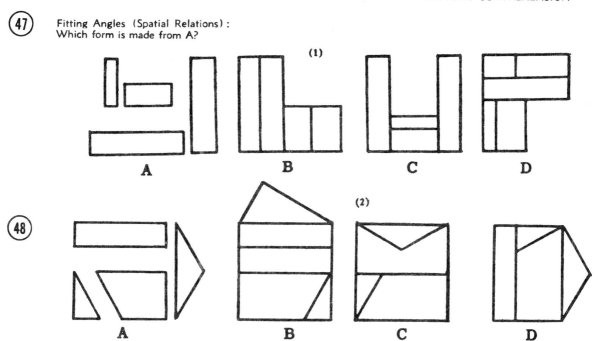

(1)

A   B   C   D

(2)

(48)

A   B   C   D

PAPER FORMS—1ST GROUP

In the diagrams below choose the form B, C, or D, made up only and entirely of the parts shown in A.

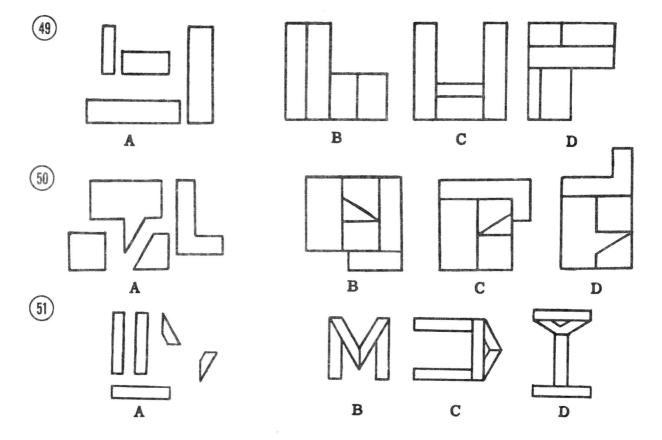

(49)

A   B   C   D

(50)

A   B   C   D

(51)

A   B   C   D

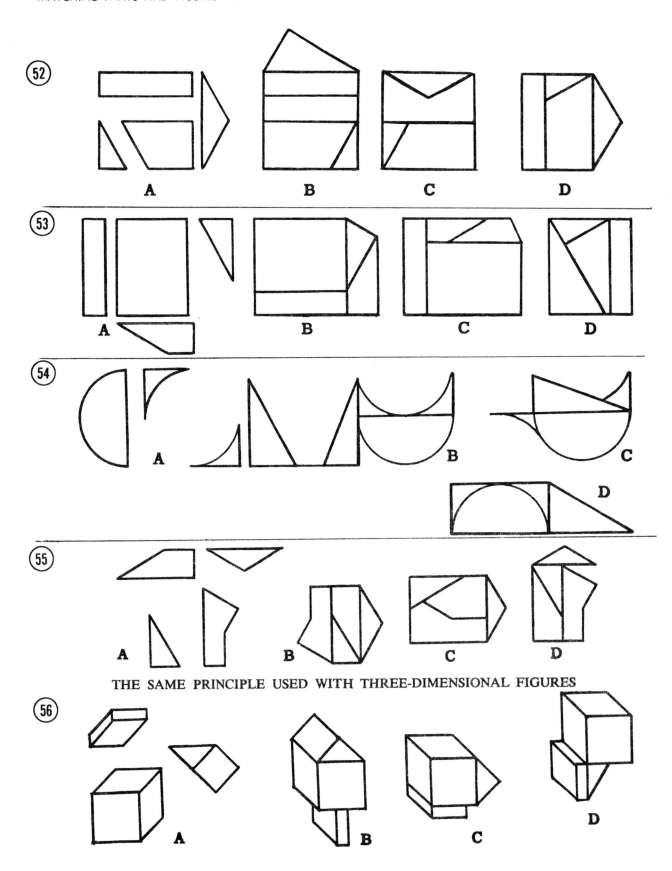

THE SAME PRINCIPLE USED WITH THREE-DIMENSIONAL FIGURES

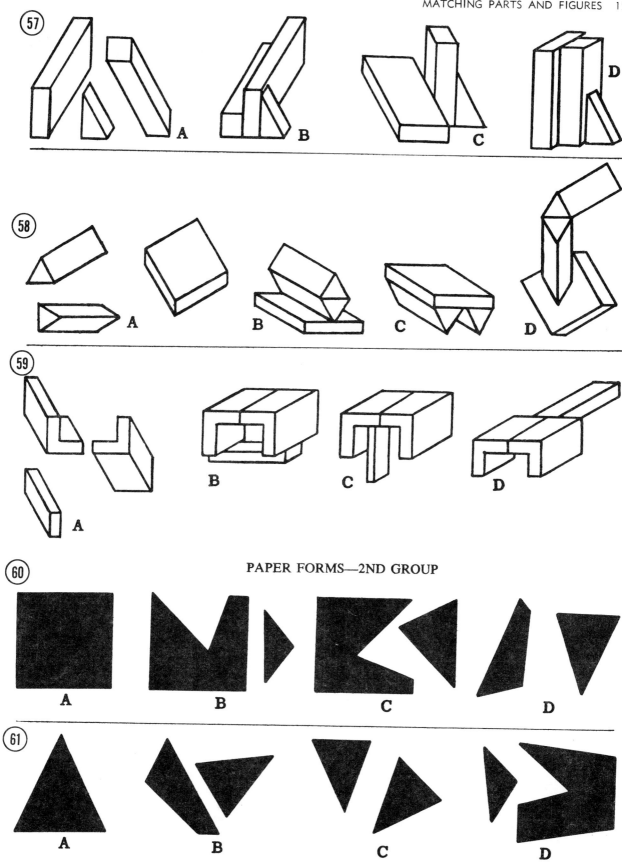

PAPER FORMS—2ND GROUP

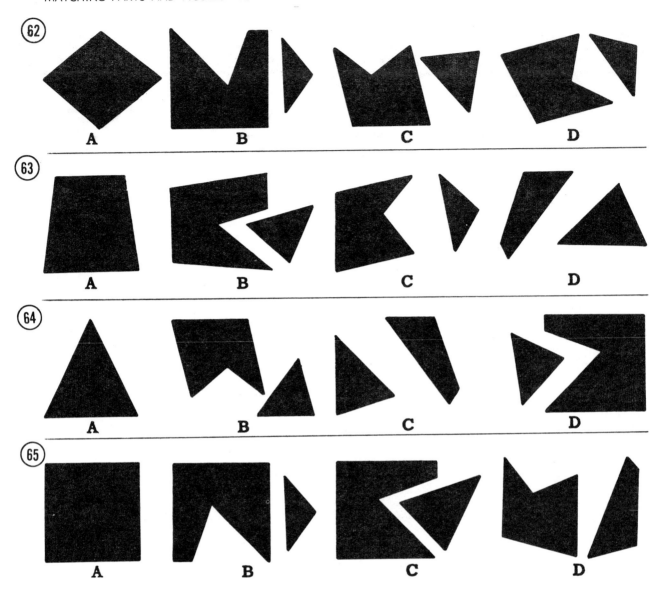

62) A B C D

63) A B C D

64) A B C D

65) A B C D

Answers to matching parts and figures

1. BD	16. AE	31. CD	46. DE	61. B
2. BC	17. CE	32. AB	47. C	62. D
3. BE	18. CE	33. BC	48. D	63. B
4. AC	19. AC	34. BD	49. C	64. C
5. AE	20. CE	35. BC	50. D	65. C
6. AB	21. AD	36. AD	51. C	
7. AB	22. AE	37. CD	52. D	
8. BD	23. AE	38. CE	53. B	
9. BC	24. DE	39. CD	54. D	
10. AB	25. BE	40. CD	55. B	
11. AD	26. CD, DE, CE	41. CE	56. B	
12. DE	27. AE	42. CD	57. B	
13. AD	28. AC	43. AD	58. D	
14. AD	29. AE	44. AD	59. D	
15. BC	30. BD	45. CD	60. C	

LAW SCHOOLS APPROVED BY THE AMERICAN BAR ASSOCIATION

The requirements shown in the following tables are stated in terms of academic years. An academic year in an approved law school consists of not less than thirty weeks if the students devote substantially all of their time to the study of law, or not less than thirty-six weeks in a part-time school.

The figure in parentheses following the name of the law school indicates the year in which the school was approved by the American Bar Association. The figures following M, and E directly beneath the name of the school show the number of students in each class or year, namely, first year, second year, third year, fourth year, graduate, and special or unclassified students. A few of the schools, e. g. University of Washington, have established extended programs for part-time students enrolled in morning classes and the distribution of such part-time students is shown in the figures following M directly beneath E. The figure in parentheses immediately following attendance total is included in the total. It indicates the number of women attending law school classes.

Under the heading "Annual Tuition" the following symbols are used: r stands for resident; n for nonresident; m for morning; e for evening. Tuition given is for two semesters or three-quarters of a school year; tuition for summer sessions is not shown.

Under "Requirements" Roman numeral indicates number of years of college study required for admission as a law student. Capital letter M means full-time morning classes; classes in late afternoon are designated by capital A; capital E denotes part-time classes held in evening (except for Gonzaga University which is a full-time school). Arabic numerals show number of years required to complete course. Parentheses indicate course may be shortened by local summer school work.

LAW SCHOOLS ON THE APPROVED LIST OF A.B.A., 1963

		Total Enrollment Fall 1963	Annual Tuition	Require-ments	No. of Teachers Full-Time	Part-Time
	ALABAMA					
Birming-ham	Howard College, Cumberland School of Law (1949)[1] M 66(1) 32(2) 22(1)	120(4)	$ 24.50 Cr. Hr.	IIIM(3)	7	3
University	University of Alabama, School of Law (1926) M 101 62 56	219	360.00r 710.00n	IIIM(3)	14	3
	ARIZONA					
Tucson	University of Arizona, College of Law (1930) M 232(16) 97(4) 87(2)	416(22)	277.00r 877.00n	IIIM(3)	12	4
	ARKANSAS					
Fayette-ville	University of Arkansas, School of Law (1926) M 102(2) 49(1) 40 1	192(3)	100.00r 235.00n	IIIM(3)	7	6

---

[1]Formerly Cumberland University School of Law at Lebanon, Tenn.

		Enrollment data	Total Enrollment Fall 1963	Annual Tuition	Require-ments	Time	Part-Time

CALIFORNIA

Berkeley	University of California, School of Law (1923)	M 344(15) 226(9) 217(11) .... 16(2)	803(37)	196.50r 796.50n	IVM3	35	7
Los Angeles	University of California, School of Law (1950)	M 264(13) 197(15) 128(6)	589(34)	98.00r 398.00n	IVM(3)	29	2
	Loyola University, School of Law (1935)	M 91(7) 40(1) 47(2) .... 1 E 86(7) 32 38(2) 34(1) 7	376(20)	750.00m 31.25 Cr. Hr.e	IIIM3 IIIE4	10	10
	University of Southern California, School of Law (1924)	M 109(4) 81(4) 64(2) 2 .... M 17(1) 8(1) 12(2) 13(4) .... 5(1) E 74(4) 41(2) 45(2) 42(1) 243(5) 5(2)	761(35)	1200.00m 800.00e	IVM(3) IIM(4) IVE(4½)	15	31
Palo Alto	Stanford University, School of Law (1923)	M 164(9) 117(5) 122(5) 11 1	415(19)	1410.00	IIIM(3)	24	0
San Diego	California Western University, School of Law (1962)[2]	M 60(5) 26(4) 18	104(9)	900.00	IVM3	6	4
	University of San Diego, School of Law (1960)	M 26(4) 12(2) 16(1) .... E 49(2) 25(1) 18 30(1) 2	178(11)	840.00m 600.00e	IVM3 IVE4	6	10
San Francisco	University of California, Hastings College of Law (1939)	M 505(16) 276(8) 203(5) .... 5(2)	989(31)	187.00r 787.00n	IVM3	17	4
	Golden Gate College, School of Law (1956)[3]	E 115(14) 51(3) 30(3) 30 .... 3(1) M 36(3) 10(2) 13(3)	288(29)	23.00 Cr. Hr.	IIIE4 IIIM4	4	13
	University of San Francisco, School of Law (1935)	M 88(1) 48(1) 32(1) .... E 61 34(2) 22 21(2)	306(7)	1620.00mr 720.00mn 1400.00er 500.00en	IIIM3 IIIE4	9	9
Santa Clara	University of Santa Clara, School of Law (1937)	M 20 17 26(2) .... 8(2) E 37(4) 18 2	128(8)	1073.00mr 710.00er	IIIM3 IIIE4	9	7

COLORADO

| Boulder | University of Colorado, School of Law (1923) | M 103(3) 49(5) 51(1) .... 1 | 204(9) | 280.00r 904.00n | IVM(3) | 11 | 0 |
| Denver | University of Denver, College of Law (1928) | M 108(6) 56 51 ....
 E 72(5) 30(3) 25(3) 14 .... 2 | 358(17) | 900.00m 600.00e | IVM(3) IVE(4) | 10 | 22 |

CONNECTICUT

| Hartford | University of Connecticut, School of Law (1933) | M 90(5) 46(3) 43(3) ....
 E 67(6) 38 19 23 .... 3(1) | 329(18) | 315.00m 265.00e | IVM3 IVE4 | 12 | 18 |

[2]Provisionally approved, February, 1962.
[3]Provisionally approved, August, 1956.

		Total Enrollment Fall 1963	Annual Tuition	Requirements	No. of Teachers Full-Time	Part-Time

New Haven — Yale University, School of Law (1923)
M 183(11) 166(7) 165(2)   9(1) 89(3) 7(3) 619(27) | 1350.00 | IVM3 | 37 5

DISTRICT OF COLUMBIA

Washington — American University, Washington College of Law (1940)
M 94(6) 45(1) 22(1) .... | 1012.00m | IIIM(3)
E 95(4) 45(2) 54(2) 42(2) .... 3(1) 400(19) | 36.00 Cr. Hr.e | IIIE(4) | 10 10

Catholic University of America, The Columbus School of Law (1925)
M 47(3) 27(2) 32(1) .... | 812.00m | IVM3
E 50(2) 47 41(1) 12 .... 4(1) 260(10) | 32.00 Cr. Hr.e | IVE(4) | 9 10

Georgetown University, School of Law (1924)
M 239(6) 147(6) 115(4) .... 13 .... | 1120.00m | IVM3
E 109(10) 136(8) 133(6) 90(1) 179(5) 6 1167(46) | 820.00e | IVE(4) | 28 57

George Washington University, Law School (1923)
M 220(11) 100(3) 45(2) .... 13 4(3) | 1000.00m | IVM(3)
E 185(3) 129(2) 112(2) 125 67(3) 48(6)1048(35) | 36.00 Cr. Hr.e | IVE(4) | 31 36

Howard University, School of Law (1931)
M 64(10) 27(1) 47(6) .... 138(17) | 390.00 | IIIM3 | 10 1

FLORIDA

Coral Gables — University of Miami, School of Law (1941)
M 114(5) 65(4) 86(2) .... 7(1) .... | | IVM(3)
E 45(2) 20(2) 17 14 26(2) 10 404(18) | 39.00 Cr. Hr. | IVE(4½) | 18 3

Gainesville — University of Florida, College of Law (1925)
M 293(4) 131(1) 112(3) .... 536(8) | 339.00 | IVM3 | 23 3

St. Petersburg — Stetson University, College of Law (1930)
M 94(1) 52(2) 78(1) .... 224(4) | 1000.00 | IIIM(3) | 8 8

Tallahassee — Florida A. & M. University, College of Law (1955)[4]
M 4 5(1) 5 .... 1 15(1) | 225.00r 755.00n | IVM3 | 6 0

GEORGIA

Athens — University of Georgia, School of Law (1930)
M 74 85 64(1) .... 1 224(1) | 289.50r 634.50n | IIIM(3) | 8 4

Atlanta — Emory University, Lamar School of Law (1923)
M 73(3) 58(2) 34(1) .... | 1095.00m | IIIM(3)
E 75(6) 36(3) 15 14 4 .... 309(15) | 250.00e | IIIE(4) | 12 6

Macon — Mercer University, Walter F. George School of Law (1925)
M 65 39 25(1) .... | | IIIM3
M 10(1) 3(1) 3(1) 3 .... 148(4) | 675.00 | IIM4 | 8 1

---

[4]Provisionally approved, February, 1955.

								Total Enrollment Fall 1963	Annual Tuition	Require-ments	Full-Time	Part-Time

IDAHO

Moscow — University of Idaho, College of Law (1925)

| M 57 | 24 | 21 | .... | .... | .... | 102 | | | 82.00r 237.00n | IIIM3 | 6 | 0 |

ILLINOIS

Chicago — Chicago-Kent, College of Law (1936)

| M 103(6) | 45(2) | 23 | .... | .... | 2(1) | | | | 677.00m | IIIM3 | | |
| E 130(4) | 43(3) | 19(1) | 17 | .... | 5 | | | 387(17) | 457.00e | IIIE(4) | 8 | 11 |

DePaul University, College of Law (1925)

| M 217(8) | 107(5) | 65(1) | .... | .... | 1 | | | | 896.00m | IIIM3 | | |
| E 123(7) | 41(5) | 37(1) | 46(4) | .... | 2 | | | 639(31) | 640.00e | IIIE4 | 12 | 8 |

The John Marshall Law School (1951)

| M 100(3) | 47(3) | 49(1) | .... | .... | 1 | | | | 635.00m | IIIM(3) | | |
| E 182(9) | 57(1) | 52 | 51(3) | 166(3) | 4 | | | 709(23) | 480.00e | IIIE(4) | 6 | 29 |

Loyola University, School of Law (1925)

| M 73(2) | 34 | 31 | .... | .... | .... | | | | 910.00m | IIIM3 | | |
| E 50(4) | 28(2) | 15 | 26(2) | .... | 3 | | | 260(10) | 660.00e | IIIE4 | 8 | 13 |

Northwestern University, School of Law (1923)

| M 164(11) | 151(5) | 128(1) | .... | 15(1) | .... | 458(18) | | | 1270.00 | IVM(3) | 24 | 12 |

University of Chicago, Law School (1923)

| M 144(8) | 137(6) | 129(10) | .... | 40(2) | .... | 450(26) | | | 1350.00 | IVM(3) | 25 | 13 |

Urbana — University of Illinois, College of Law (1923)

| M 191(8) | 131(4) | 87(5) | .... | 15(2) | .... | 424(19) | | | 270.00r 620.00n | IIIM(3) | 20 | 5 |

INDIANA

Bloomington — Indiana University, School of Law (1923) (Includes Indianapolis Division—1932)

| M 181(6) | 106(2) | 78(1) | .... | 6(1) | 1 | | | | 312.00mr 663.00mn | IIIM(3) | | |
| E 194(15) | 75(3) | 70(2) | 38(3) | .... | 4(1) | 753(34) | | | 150.00e | IIIE(4) | 26 | 1 |

Notre Dame — University of Notre Dame, School of Law (1925)

| M 76 | 47 | 47 | .... | .... | 2 | 172 | | | 1000.00 | IVM3 | 12 | 4 |

Valparaiso — Valparaiso University, School of Law (1929)

| M 35 | 25 | 18 | .... | .... | 2 | 80 | | | 1055.00 | IIIM3 | 9 | 1 |

IOWA

Des Moines — Drake University, Law School (1923)

| M 77(9) | 40(3) | 29(2) | .... | .... | 1 | 147(14) | | | 700.00 | IIIM3 | 8 | 4 |

Iowa City — State University of Iowa, College of Law (1923)

| M 190(2) | 125(1) | 103(2) | .... | .... | .... | 418(5) | | | 330.00r 660.00n | IIIM(3½) | 15 | 5 |

KANSAS

Lawrence — University of Kansas, School of Law (1923)

| M 83(3) | 56(2) | 48(2) | .... | .... | 14(2) | 201(9) | | | 244.00r 574.00n | IVM(3) | 11 | 2 |

Topeka — Washburn University of Topeka, School of Law (1923)

| M 108(3) | 66(1) | 41(1) | 2 | .... | .... | 217(5) | | | 12.00 Cr. Hr. | IVM(3) IVM(4) | 6 | 18 |

		Total Enrollment Fall 1963					Annual Tuition	Requirements	No. of Teachers Full-Time	Part-Time

KENTUCKY

Lexington — University of Kentucky, College of Law (1925)
M 102(1) 78 44 .... 224(1) 230.00r 540.00n IIIM(3) 11 0

Louisville — University of Louisville, School of Law (1931)
M 56(1) 26(1) 20 .... 675.00mr 1075.00mn IIIM(3)
E 68(3) 25(1) 14 13 .... 222(6) 506.00er 805.00en IIIE(4) 13 3

LOUISIANA

Baton Rouge — Louisiana State University, Law School (1926)
M 153(2) 87(3) 58 .... 2 300(5) 210.00r 510.00n IIIM(3½) 16 2

Southern University, School of Law (1953)[5]
M 7(1) 3 .... 10(1) 48.00r 648.00n IIIM3 6 0

New Orleans — Loyola University, School of Law (1931)
M 68(4) 44(2) 26(2) 750.00m IIIM3
E 47(2) 32(5) 33(1) 27(1) .... 5 282(17) 580.00e IIIE4 11 11

Tulane University of Louisiana, School of Law (1925)
M 116(5) 104(4) 84(3) .... 8 .... 312(12) 1050.00 IIIM3 12 8

MARYLAND

Baltimore — University of Maryland, School of Law (1930)
M 87(1) 80(9) 55(3) 250.00mr 300.00mn IIIM3
E 100(5) 54(5) 49 52(1) .... 1(1) 478(25) 166.00e IIIE4 13 11

MASSACHUSETTS

Boston — Boston University, School of Law (1925)
M 244(17) 181(4) 113(2) .... 12 ....
E .... 76(2) .... 626(25) 1251.00 IVM3 18 20

Suffolk University, School of Law (1953)
M 110(7) 43(3) 17(1) 4 905.00m IIIM3
E 183(10) 83(1) 73(3) 67 10 12(2) 602(27) 680.00e IIIE4 11 10

Brighton — Boston College, Law School (1932)
M 175(5) 117(6) 72(3) .... 1(1) 1200.00m IVM3
E .... 21(1) 15 27(2) .... 428(18) 900.00e IVE4 17 6

Cambridge — Harvard University, Law School (1923)
M 526(27) 510(22) 511(15) .... 83(3) 21(2) 1651(69) 1324.00 IVM3 53 11

MICHIGAN

Ann Arbor — University of Michigan, Law School (1923)
M 371(12) 290(10) 309(4) 37(4) ....1007(30) 500.00r 1120.00n IVM(3) 41 3

Detroit — Detroit College of Law (1941)
M 76(5) 34(1) 22 .... 570.00m IIIM(3)
E 224(10) 74(3) 72(2) 35(1) .... 6 430.00e IIIE(4)
M 12(1) 7(1) 13(2) .... 575(26) IIIM(4) 10 12

---

[5]Provisionally approved, August, 1953.

Location	School / Class							Total Enrollment Fall 1963	Annual Tuition	Require- ments	Full- Time	Part- Time
	University of Detroit, School of Law (1933)											
	M 45(4)	30	36(4)	....	....	....		870.00r	IIIM3		
	M 40(2)	33(2)	11	16	....	3	214(12)	580.00n	IIIM4	5	22
	Wayne State University, Law School (1936)											
	M 147(6)	72(7)	61(3)	....	....	....		312.00mr 750.00mn	IIIM3		
	E 83(2)	39(3)	37	25	54	4	522(21)	252.00er 567.00en	IIIE4	12	11

MINNESOTA

Location	School / Class							Total Enrollment Fall 1963	Annual Tuition	Require- ments	Full- Time	Part- Time
Minne- apolis	University of Minnesota, Law School (1923)											
	M 256(3)	148(7)	122(4)	1	....	....	527(14)	375.00r 795.00n	IIIM(3⅓)	21	1
St. Paul	William Mitchell College of Law (1938)											
	E 102(2)	79(1)	76(2)	73	....	4	334(5)	500.00	IIIE4	7	22

MISSISSIPPI

Location	School / Class							Total Enrollment Fall 1963	Annual Tuition	Require- ments	Full- Time	Part- Time
University	University of Mississippi, School of Law (1930)											
	M 123(1)	78(1)	50	....	....	1	252(2)	430.00r 830.00n	IVM(3)	9	5

MISSOURI

Location	School / Class							Total Enrollment Fall 1963	Annual Tuition	Require- ments	Full- Time	Part- Time
Columbia	University of Missouri, School of Law (1923)											
	M 131(1)	75(1)	50	....	....	....	256(2)	215.00r 515.00n	IIIM(3)	10	3
Kansas City	University of Missouri at Kansas City, School of Law (1936)[6]											
	M 52(1)	23(2)	16(1)	....	....	....		310.00m	IIIM(3)		
	E 56(4)	30(1)	15(1)	22(2)	8	34(5)		24.00	IIIE(4)		
	M 3	1	3(1)	....	1(1)	....	264(19)	Cr. Hr.	IIIM(4)	12	6
St. Louis	St. Louis University, School of Law (1924)											
	M 76(2)	45	34	....	....	....		960.00m	IIIM(3)		
	E 81(4)	33	20(1)	10	....	....	299(7)	35.00 Cr. Hr.e	IIIE(4½)	13	10
	Washington University, School of Law (1923)											
	M 87(3)	74(3)	57(1)	....	....	1	219(7)	1350.00	IIIM3	12	13

MONTANA

Location	School / Class							Total Enrollment Fall 1963	Annual Tuition	Require- ments	Full- Time	Part- Time
Missoula	Montana State University, School of Law (1923)											
	M 57(2)	26	21	....	....	....	104(2)	262.00r 599.50n	IIIM3	8	2

NEBRASKA

Location	School / Class							Total Enrollment Fall 1963	Annual Tuition	Require- ments	Full- Time	Part- Time
Lincoln	University of Nebraska, College of Law (1923)											
	M 73(1)	42	42	....	....	....		132.00r	IIIM3		
	M	....	....	11	....	....	168(1)	252.00n	IIM4 IVM3	9	3
Omaha	The Creighton University, School of Law (1924)											
	M 49(1)	47(2)	23	....	....	....	119(3)	800.00	IIIM3	8	5

NEW JERSEY

Location	School / Class							Total Enrollment Fall 1963	Annual Tuition	Require- ments	Full- Time	Part- Time
Camden	Rutgers University, The State University of New Jersey, School of Law (1950)											
	M 47(4)	22	15	....	....	1	85(4)	540.00	IIIM3	9	3
Newark	Rutgers University, The State University of New Jersey, School of Law (1941)											
	M 144(10)	120(2)	122(5)	....	....	....	386(17)	540.00	IIIM3	18	7

[6]Formerly the University of Kansas City.

		Enrollment detail						Total Enrollment Fall 1963	Annual Tuition	Requirements	Full-Time	Part-Time
	Seton Hall University, School of Law (1951)	M	66	39(1)	30(2)	....	....	....	30.00 Cr. Hr.	IVM3		
		E	82	58(5)	57	39	....	.... 371(8)		IVE4	12	5

New Mexico

		Enrollment detail						Total Enrollment Fall 1963	Annual Tuition	Requirements	Full-Time	Part-Time
Albuquerque	University of New Mexico, School of Law (1948)	M	53	23(4)	13	....	....	.... 89(4)	276.00r 546.00n	IIIM3	6	2

New York

		Enrollment detail						Total Enrollment Fall 1963	Annual Tuition	Requirements	Full-Time	Part-Time
Albany	Union University, Albany Law School (1930)	M	116(3)	54(1)	42(1)	....	....	2(1) 214(6)	1020.00	IIIM3	9	5
Buffalo	State University of New York at Buffalo* School of Law (1936)	M	85(3)	60(3)	50(2)	....	....	....	861.00r	IIIM3		
		E	....	....	....	....	....	....	1061.00n	IIIM4	12	16
		M	4	7	12(1)	12	....	.... 230(9)				
Ithaca	Cornell University, Law School (1923)	M	148(5)	108(2)	105(1)	....	3	.... 364(8)	1700.00	IVM3	15	5
New York	Brooklyn Law School (1937)	M	307(11)	198(5)	169(6)	....	....	....	810.00m	IIIM(3)		
		E	130(4)	102(9)	66(2)	82(3)	142(6)	..........1196(46)	610.00e	IIIE(4)	17	8
	Columbia University, School of Law (1923)	M	303(25)	266(12)	264(9)	....	47(2)	.... 880(48)	1500.00	IIIM3	27	10
	Fordham University, School of Law (1936)	M	231(12)	159(2)	141(4)	....	....	....	1300.00m	IVM3		
		E	95(7)	75(2)	67(2)	68	1	.... 837(29)	975.00e	IVE4	15	14
	New York Law School (1954)[7]	M	113(6)	98(9)	73(2)	....	....	....	836.00m	IIIM3		
		E	72(3)	84(7)	46(1)	55(2)	24(2)	.... 565(32)	636.00e	IIIE4	11	5
	New York University, School of Law (1930)	M	301(21)	290(13)	231(18)	....	168(5)	....	1340.00m	IVM(3)		
		E	105(10)	73(6)	61(2)	82(4)	724(37)	3 2038(116)	1000.00e	IVE(4)	45	69
	St. John's University, School of Law (1937)	M	274(11)	151(3)	114(3)	....	....	....	850.00m	IIIM3		
		E	110(5)	61(2)	53	41(3)	....	.... 804(27)	650.00e	IIIE4	16	14
Syracuse	Syracuse University, College of Law (1923)	M	96(3)	74(1)	65(2)	....	....	....	1500.00	IIIM3		
		E	....	....	....	....	....	....		IIIM4	11	4
		M	6	3	1	1	....	1 247(6)				

North Carolina

		Enrollment detail						Total Enrollment Fall 1963	Annual Tuition	Requirements	Full-Time	Part-Time
Chapel Hill	University of North Carolina, School of Law (1925)	M	171(5)	107(4)	98	....	....	.... 376(9)	281.06r 706.06n	IIIM(3)	17	2
Durham	Duke University, School of Law (1931)	M	108(1)	87	76	....	....	.... 271(1)	1000.00	IIIM3	15	0

*Formerly University of Buffalo.
[7]Provisionally approved, March, 1954.

								Total Enrollment Fall 1963	Annual Tuition	Require-ments	Full-Time	Part-Time

	North Carolina College at Durham, Law School (1950)											
	M	7	8(1)	6	....	....	2	23(1)	251.50r 601.50n	IIIM3	4	3
Winston-Salem	Wake Forest College, School of Law (1936)											
	M	56(1)	51(1)	54	....	....	....	161(2)	550.00	IIIM(3)	9	0

NORTH DAKOTA

| | University of North Dakota, School of Law (1923) | | | | | | | | | | | |
| Grand Forks | M | 63(1) | 56 | 43 | .... | .... | .... | 162(1) | 165.00r 300.00n | IIIM3 | 7 | 5 |

OHIO

	Ohio Northern University, College of Law (1948)											
Ada	M	58(1)	32(1)	24	....	....	....	114(2)	763.50	IVM3	8	2
Akron	University of Akron, School of Law (1961)[8]											
	E	47(3)	33(3)	31(1)	24	....	7(1)	142(8)	542.00r 642.00n	IVE4	5	5
Cincinnati	University of Cincinnati, College of Law (1923)											
	M	75(3)	38(1)	36(1)	....	....	5(1)	154(6)	490.00r 765.00n	IVM3	10	16
	Salmon P. Chase College, School of Law (1954)											
	E	89(2)	61(1)	34(2)	40(3)	....	1	225(8)	570.00	IVE4¾	5	16
Cleveland	Cleveland-Marshall Law School (1957)											
	E	197(4)	123(5)	106(4)	82(3)	10	....	518(16)	615.00	IVE4	9	18
	Western Reserve University, Franklin Thomas Backus School of Law (1923)											
	M	85(3)	54(1)	61	....	116	2	318(4)	1050.00	IVM(3)	9	13
Columbus	Franklin University, School of Law (1950)											
	E	64	38	15	16(1)	....	....	133(1)	540.00	IVE4	5	8
	Ohio State University, College of Law (1923)											
	M	177(4)	106(1)	87(2)	....	....	....	370(7)	465.00r 960.00n	IVM(3)	18	3
Toledo	University of Toledo, College of Law (1939)									620.00mr 800.00mn	IVM(3)		
	M	53(4)	....	....	....	....	....					
	E	65(3)	28(1)	16	23(3)	....	....	185(11)	371.60er 479.60en	IVE(4½)	9	4

OKLAHOMA

Norman	University of Oklahoma, College of Law (1923)											
	M	192(10)	112(1)	86(4)	....	....	4	394(15)	210.00r 540.00n	IIIM(3)	12	0
Oklahoma City	Oklahoma City University, School of Law (1960)[9]											
	E	81(6)	66	42(2)	40	1	5(2)	235(10)	500.00	IIIE4½	4	5
Tulsa	University of Tulsa, School of Law (1950)									550.00m	IIIM(3)		
	M	28(2)	16	16	....	....	....					
	E	71(3)	46(1)	28(1)	27	....	9(2)	241(9)	20.00 Cr. Hr.e	IIIE4	8	5

[8]Provisionally approved, August, 1961.

[9]Provisionally approved, August, 1960.

		Total Enrollment Fall 1963	Annual Tuition	Require-ments	No. of Teachers Full-Time	Part-Time

OREGON

| Eugene | University of Oregon, School of Law (1923) M 70(4) 47(2) 28 | 145(6) | 330.00r 900.00n | IIIM3 | 8 | 1 |
| Salem | Willamette University, College of Law (1938) M 75(1) 64(1) 49(1) | 188(3) | 875.00 | IIIM3 | 8 | 1 |

PENNSYLVANIA

Carlisle	Dickinson School of Law (1931) M 115(1) 75(3) 59(3) 4(2)	253(9)	723.00	IIIM3	9	8
Phila-delphia	Temple University, School of Law (1933) M 84(4) 67(2) 58(1) 7 E 95(8) 30(3) 33(2) 35(3) 19 3	431(23)	960.00m 720.00e	IVM(3) IVE(4)	13	16
	University of Pennsylvania, School of Law (1923) M 201(9) 146(5) 146(7) 8(1) 3	504(22)	1520.00	IVM3	27	6
Pitts-burgh	Duquesne University, School of Law (1960) M 48 26 13 E 39(2) 22 19(1) 15	182(3)	800.00m 600.00e	IVM3 1VE4	10	9
	University of Pittsburgh, School of Law (1923) M 72(1) 42 33(1) 3	150(2)	1212.00	IVM3	10	8
Villanova	Villanova University, School of Law (1954) M 107(5) 76(1) 49(1)	232(7)	1075.00	IVM3	10	6

PUERTO RICO

| Rio Piedras | University of Puerto Rico, School of Law (1945) M 110(18) 72(9) 58(6) E 100(5) 52(3) 27(4) 20(2) | 439(47) | 160.00 | IVM3 IVE4 | 23 | 15 |

SOUTH CAROLINA

| Columbia | University of South Carolina, School of Law (1925) M 113(4) 72 73(1) | 258(5) | 420.00r 710.00n | IIIM(3) | 8 | 1 |
| Orange-burg | South Carolina State College, School of Law (1950)[10] M 3 7(1) 2 | 12(1) | 320.00r 520.00n | IIIM3 | 5 | 0 |

SOUTH DAKOTA

| Vermillion | State University of South Dakota, School of Law (1923) M 39(1) 24 19(1) 1 | 83(2) | 386.00r 492.00n | IIIM3 | 8 | 0 |

TENNESSEE

| Knoxville | University of Tennessee, College of Law (1925) M 124(7) 85(1) 53(1) 3 | 265(9) | 225.00r 525.00n | IIIM(3) | 8 | 3 |
| Nashville | Vanderbilt University, School of Law (1925) M 127(4) 109(4) 77(3) 2(1) 1 | 316(12) | 800.00 | IIIM(3) | 15 | 7 |

[10]Provisionally approved, February, 1950.

								Total Enrollment Fall 1963	Annual Tuition	Require-ments	No. of Teachers Full-Time	Part-Time

TEXAS

| Austin | University of Texas, School of Law (1923) | | | | | | | | | | | |
| | M 625(22) | 425(10) | 250(3) | .... | 5 | 7 | 1312(35) | 100.00r 400.00n | IIIM(3⅓) | 33 | 6 |

Dallas	Southern Methodist University, School of Law (1927)											
	M 114(5)	94(4)	78(9)	....	28(4)	....		907.00m	IVM3		
	E 77(3)	44(1)	44(1)	49	23	5	556(27)	565.00e	IVE4	20	5

Houston	University of Houston, College of Law (1950)							170.00mr			
	M 154(5)	49(1)	25(2)	....	....	....		320.00mn	IIIM(3)		
	E 174(8)	48(4)	14	19	....	....	483(20)	138.00er 288.00en	IIIE(4)	11	8
	South Texas College Law School (1959)[11]										
	E 192(5)	88(1)	64(2)	19	1	1	365(8)	20.00 Cr. Hr.	IIIE4	3	13
	Texas Southern University, School of Law (1949)										
	M 12(3)	9(1)	4(1)	....	....	1				
	E	....	....	....	....	....		73.00r	IIIM(3)		
	M 5(1)	2	1	....	....	1	35(6)	223.00n	IIIM(4)	5	2

San Antonio	St. Mary's University of San Antonio, School of Law (1948)							25.00	IIIM(3)		
	M 52(2)	32(3)	18	....	....	....		Cr. Hr.	IIIE5		
	E 37(2)	23(1)	18	12	....	....	192(8)			7	16

| Waco | Baylor University, School of Law (1931) | | | | | | | | | | |
| | M 116(4) | 71(2) | 63 | .... | .... | .... | 250(6) | 600.00 | IIIM(3) | 8 | 6 |

UTAH

| Salt Lake City | University of Utah, College of Law (1927) | | | | | | | 345.00r | | | |
| | M 123(4) | 76(3) | 55(1) | .... | .... | .... | 254(8) | 540.00n | IIIM(3) | 13 | 2 |

VIRGINIA

Charlottes-ville	University of Virginia, School of Law (1923)							456.00r			
	M 246(2)	209(3)	211(3)	....	5	....	671(8)	861.00n	IVM(3)	22	22
	Judge Advocate General's School (1955)[12]										
	M									20	1

Lexington	Washington & Lee University, School of Law (1923)										
	M 61	49	42	....	....	....				
	E	....	....	....	....	....				
	M 2	2	....	....	....	1	157	785.00	IIIM(3)	8	2

Richmond	University of Richmond, T. C. Williams School of Law (1928)										
	M 74	63	47	....	1	2				
	E	....	....	....	....	....			IIIM(3)		
	M 1	1	2(1)	....	....	....	191(1)	745.00		8	2

Williams-burg	College of William and Mary, The Marshall-Wythe School of Law (1932)										
	M 57(5)	35(2)	22	....	2	1				
	E	....	....	....	2	....		352.00r	IVM(3)		
	M 1	1	....	....	....	2	121(7)	722.00n	IVM(4)	6	4

---

[11]Provisionally approved, February, 1959.
[12]Graduate program only approved.

						Total Enrollment Fall 1963	Annual Tuition	Require-ments	No. of Teachers	
									Part-Time	Full-Time

WASHINGTON

Seattle	University of Washington, School of Law (1924)									
	M 140(4)	122(3)	68	....	....	....				
	E	....	....	....	....	....		300.00r	IIIM(3)	
	M 10(1)	....	5	....	....	....	345(8)	600.00n	IIIM(4)	19	1

| Spokane | Gonzaga University, School of Law (1951)[13] | | | | | | | | | |
| | E 49(1) | 33 | 24 | 24(1) | .... | 17(1) | 147(3) | 760.00 | IIIE4 | 4 | 19 |

WEST VIRGINIA

| Morgan-town | West Virginia University, College of Law (1924) | | | | | | | 260.00r | | |
| | M 88(4) | 58(2) | 45(1) | .... | .... | 1 | 192(7) | 910.00n | IVM3 | 7 | 1 |

WISCONSIN

| Madison | University of Wisconsin, Law School (1923) | | | | | | | 330.00r | | |
| | M 251(9) | 156(3) | 106(3) | .... | 6 | 2 | 521(15) | 1030.00n | IIIM(3) | 26 | 3 |

| Milwaukee | Marquette University, Law School (1925) | | | | | | | | | |
| | M 80(5) | 62(2) | 60(2) | .... | .... | 3(1) | 205(10) | 850.00 | IIIM3 | 8 | 7 |

WYOMING

Laramie	University of Wyoming, College of Law (1923)									
	M 53(1)	17	18	....	....	6(1)		390.00r		
	E	....	....	....	....	....		590.00n	IIIM3	
	M 1(1)	1	....	2	....	....	98(3)		IIIM4	7	2

---

[13]Full-time program offered in evening.

MINIMUM REQUIREMENTS FOR ADMISSION TO LEGAL PRACTICE IN THE UNITED STATES

This table contains information of educational and residence requirements reported November 1, 1963. Full information and subsequent changes, if any, may be obtained by writing to the Clerk of the Supreme Court or the Secretary of the Bar Board in each state.

	Minimum amount of general education required before:		Duration and distribution of period of law study if pursued:			Residence Requirements (for original applicants only, does not apply to lawyers seeking admission on comity for whom separate requirements are usually laid down)
	Beginning period of law study	Taking final examination	Wholly outside a law school	Partly in a law school	Wholly in a law school	
American Bar Association Recommendations	Three years of resident study in a college	....	Not permitted	At least the law school study recommended in the next column. No recommendation as to supplementary office work	Three years of full-time or "a longer course, equivalent in the number of working hours," of part-time study	
Alabama	3 years college	....	Not permitted	No credit for office work	4 years from school approved by Board or if school is approved by A. B. A., 3 years	Bona fide residence at time of application
Alaska	3 years college	....	Permitted if begun before Jan. 1, 1956	....	Graduate of A.B.A. approved law school	Bona fide resident for 60 days prior to submission of application, which application must be submitted not less than 90 days prior to the date of examination.
Arizona	3 years college	....	Not permitted	Not permitted	Graduate of an A. B. A. approved law school except for one who has practiced in another state at least 5 of last seven years immediately preceding application	Six months and presence in state for 75% of said period. Students of College of Law, Univ. of Arizona, 2 semesters resident attendance immediately prior to examination. Not applicable to Arizona residents attending out-of-state law schools
Arkansas	2 years college	....	Four Years of not less than 48 weeks annually	....	Graduation from law school approved by A.B.A. or Board requiring at least 1250 class room hours.	Bona fide residence at time of application.
California	2 years approved college, or be 23 years of age and pass an educational equivalency examination	....	4 years in California law office or California judge's chambers, or by correspondence. Must study aggregate of 3,456 hours and must take and pass first-year law students' examination at end of first year of law study	4 years. Any combination of study mentioned in preceding column and law school study	3 yrs. full-time and graduation or 4 yrs. part-time in accredited law school. 4 yrs. in unaccredited law school and must take and pass first year students' examination at end of first year of law study	Two months prior to date of bar examination
Colorado	2 years regular college work in approved institution	....	Not permitted	Not permitted	Graduation from a 3 year approved day school; 4 year approved night law school	Bona fide intention to become resident
Connecticut	Three-fourths of the work required for a bachelor's degree at an accredited college or university	Bachelor's degree at an accredited college or university	Not permitted	Not permitted	Pursued the study of law as a regular law student in residence at and obtained a bachelor of laws degree from a law school accredited by the State Bar Examining Committee	Bona fide intention to become resident
Delaware	Degree from college or university in a course approved by the Board of Examiners, or examination in college level work given by Delaware University	Registration required before examination	3 calendar years in office of member of bar of Delaware who has practiced in Delaware at least ten years	Study for at least 3 calendar years partly in a law school and partly in office of a member of bar of Delaware who has practiced in Delaware at least ten years	3 academic years and graduation from A. B. A. approved school or School of Jurisprudence, Oxford University, plus 6 months clerkship	6 months for admission. Bona fide residence at time of application for registration or examination
U. S. District Court for the District of Columbia	3 years college	....	Not permitted	Not permitted	3 years of full-time or "a longer course, equivalent in the number of working hours" of part-time study in a school approved by the Court or its Committee on Admissions and Grievances	None

Jurisdiction						
U. S. Ct. of Appeals for the District of Columbia—(circuit)	3 years college	....	No credit given for office study	....	If admitted in highest court of any state after July 1, 1944, graduation from law school approved by Court of Appeals with 3 years full-time course —not applicable to part-time course —not applicable to members of bar of Supreme Court of U. S. and of U. S. District Court for D. C.	None
Florida	3 years college, or its equivalent	....	Not permitted	Not permitted	Graduate of law school approved by A. B. A. or member of A. A. L. S.	None
Georgia	High school or substantial equivalent	High school or equivalent	2 years of reading law in office of Georgia practitioner	No rule	2 years of successfully completed legal study in a law school	12 months next preceding examination, upon required certification. Graduate of ABA law school who is bona fide resident at time of application need not meet 12 months residence requirement but must meet it before admission.
Hawaii	3 years college	....	Not permitted	Not permitted	Graduate of A.B.A. approved law school except for foreign attorney who is American citizen and has engaged in active practice for ten years immediately preceding application	1 year and qualified and registered voter in the state
Idaho	3 years college or equivalent, in case of registration for law office study, established by examination	....	4 years law office study, 36 weeks per year	4 years law office study, in case of registration for law office study, established by examination	Graduate of law school approved by A.B.A.	Bona fide resident for at least 3 months prior to application or graduation from A.B.A. approved school within 3 months before application deadline and residence established prior to application
Illinois	90 semester hours' college work or 60 semester hours of college work for admission to 4 year full-time law program	....	4 years	Not permitted	Graduate of law school approved by A.B.A.	None
Indiana	....	....	Not permitted	Not permitted	Graduate of law school approved by A.B.A.	Bona fide resident voter
Iowa	3 years college	....	Not permitted	Not permitted	3 full years in an accredited law school and LL.B. or J.D. degree	Bona fide resident at time of application
Kansas	B.A., B.S. or higher degree	....	3 years law office study. Registration required	No provision	After June 1, 1960, applicant must show that his academic and law degrees have been earned during 14 academic semesters in accredited institutions, with not less than 6 semesters in an accredited college and 6 semesters in an accredited law school, and the other 2 semesters in either one or the other of such institutions, as their curricula may provide	Resident of state, provided that non-residents graduating from an accredited school in Kansas may take the first examination held after graduation
Kentucky	Satisfy A. B. A. requirements	....	Not permitted	Not permitted	LL.B. degree from a law school approved by A. B. A. or by Assn. of American Law Schools	Consult their detailed rules
Louisiana	3 years college	....	Permitted if begun prior to Oct. 15, 1959	Law office study and law school study equivalent to 3 years full-time law school study	Graduate of law school approved by A. B. A.	None

MINIMUM REQUIREMENTS FOR ADMISSION TO LEGAL PRACTICE IN THE UNITED STATES

	Minimum amount of general education required before:		Duration and distribution of period of law study if pursued:			Residence Requirements (for original applicants only; does not apply to lawyers seeking admission on comity for whom separate requirements are usually laid down)
	Beginning period of law study	Taking final examination	Wholly outside a law school	Partly in a law school	Wholly in a law school	
Maine	2 years college	....	Not permitted	Successful completion of 2/3 of requirement for graduation from approved law school followed by 1 year of law office study in Maine	3 years approved day law school; 4 years approved night law school; or graduation from an approved law school	6 months
Maryland	2 years college but not less than 60 sem. hrs.	....	Not permitted	Not permitted	3 years resulting in graduation from school approved by Board	Bona fide residence at time of application
Massachusetts	2 years college or equivalent in opinion of Board	....	3 years law office study. Approval in advance	3 to 4 years. Approval of such study in advance	Completion with either graduation therefrom or no more than two failures in a 3 yr. full-time day school; 4 yr. part-time law school	Residence or domicile required
Michigan	2 years college	....	Not permitted	Not permitted	3 years full-time law school; 4 years part-time law school	None
Minnesota	Satisfy A.B.A. requirements	....	Not permitted	Not permitted	LL.B. or equivalent degree from A. B. A. approved school	Residence required but length not specified
Mississippi	2 years college	4 years high school	2 years office study. Approval of such study in advance	No rule	Graduation from A. B. A. approved school or Jackson School of Law	Bona fide residence for one year preceding date of application
Missouri	3 years college	....	Not permitted	Not permitted	Registration required and LL.B. degree from a school approved by A.B.A.	3 months prior to date of filing application
Montana	2 years college or equivalent	....	No provision	No provision	2 successive years in law school	6 months prior to date of filing application and bona fide resident of the state. Declaration of Registration must be filed with the Supreme Court
Nebraska	2 years in a college accredited to University of Nebraska	....	Not permitted	Not permitted	Graduate of law school approved by A. B. A.	Bona fide intention to become resident
Nevada	2 years in accredited college or university and high school graduate	....	Not permitted	Not permitted	Graduate of law school approved by A. B. A.	Bona fide resident for period of 6 months prior to date of bar examination
New Hampshire	3 years college	....	Not permitted	4 years	Graduate A.B.A. approved school	Residence required at time of admission

State	Pre-Legal Education	Law Office Study	Law School and Office Study	Law School Study	Citizenship and Residence
New Jersey	3 years college	Not permitted	The law school study required in next column and at least 9 months of law office clerkship to be served before or after examinations	Graduate of A.B.A. approved law school	Resident of state during his 9 months' clerkship at time of examination, and at time of admission
New Mexico	2 years college	Not permitted	Not permitted	Graduate of a law school approved by A. B. A.	6 months
New York	3 years college	4 years law office study	4 years partly in law school and partly in a law office	Successful completion of 3-year day school or 4-year evening course at an approved law school and graduation with LL.B. degree	6 months
North Carolina	2 years college or equivalent established by examination	3 years. Registration required	3 years partly in law school and partly in a law office. Registration required	3 years in school approved by the Board, completed within a period of six years except as to time spent in armed service. Registration required	Must have been, for the 12 months next preceding the date of examination, a citizen and resident of state, or must have been a non-resident student, for one scholastic year next preceding the filing of his application in an approved N.C. law school
North Dakota	None; 2 years college work of specified character	3 years	3 years	3 years	Resident at time of admission
Ohio	College degree	Not permitted	Not permitted	LL.B. degree from a school approved by A.B.A. or League of Ohio Law Schools	Resident at time of admission
Oklahoma	3 years college work effective Sept. 1, 1965	Not permitted	Not permitted	Registration required and graduation from school approved by A.B.A. or Board of Bar Examiners	60 days
Oregon	2 years college or passing examination demonstrating equivalent	Not permitted	Not permitted	Satisfactory completion of regular course in law school approved by Supreme Court which shall be not less than 3 years' duration	Resident or bona fide intention to become resident, expressed in affidavit at time of filing application but before being admitted; affidavit of residence filed with Clerk of Supreme Court
Pennsylvania	Satisfactory degree from an approved college or education which in the opinion of the Board is equivalent to a college education entitling applicant to a satisfactory college degree, prior to registration	4 years full-time in the office of a practicing attorney	At least 4 years, successively in an approved law school (whether full-time or part-time) and full time in the office of a practicing attorney—duration of law office study governed by regulations of the Board	Successful completion, under regular program, of regular course of study required for the law degree required for a full-time or part-time law school approved by the American Bar Association, including six months of office work, not more than 3 months of which may be interpolated into one law school vacation and at least 3 months must be served after the bar examination	Bona fide residence at time of issuance of admission certificate
Rhode Island	2 years approved college or education equivalent to successful completion of 2 years work at Brown University	4 years full-time law office study. Registration required	4 years	Degree from approved law school plus 6 months office study. If no degree from law school, aggregate of 4 years study including 6 months in law office	6 months
South Carolina	....	Not permitted	Not permitted	Degree from school approved by A.B.A. or Supreme Court of South Carolina	6 months prior to filing application to take examination

MINIMUM REQUIREMENTS FOR ADMISSION TO LEGAL PRACTICE IN THE UNITED STATES

	Minimum amount of general education required before:		Duration and distribution of period of law study if pursued:			Residence Requirements (for original applicants only, does not apply to lawyers seeking admission on comity for whom separate requirements are usually laid down)
	Beginning period of law study	Taking final examination	Wholly outside a law school	Partly in a law school	Wholly in a law school	
South Dakota	3 years college	....	Not permitted	Not permitted	3 years of full-time or 4 years part-time law school study resulting in graduation from law school approved by A. B. A.	Residence at time of application
Tennessee	3 years college with scholastic average equal to that required for graduation	....	Not permitted	Not permitted	Graduation from a school approved by A.B.A. or Board of Law Examiners	Bona fide intention to reside and practice in state
Texas	90 semester hours of college credit with a "C" average	....	36 months law office study. Registration required	36 months. Registration required	27 months full-time, 36 months part-time, study in approved law school	1 year
Utah	2 years resident college study plus 4 years resident law school study or 3 years resident college plus 3 years resident law school study	....	Not permitted	Not permitted	Graduation with LL.B. degree from a resident law school which requires for such degree a minimum of 6 years professional and academic study in an accredited institution	3 months prior to application
Vermont	2 years satisfactory college work embracing one-half the work required for B.A. degree in a college approved by the court; 3 yrs. effective Jan. 1, 1962	....	4 years after registration	4 years after registration. Credit given for law school study toward 4 year requirement	3 years if in a law school approved by Supreme Court	6 months for law school graduates or for out-of-state attorneys to appear for admission on motion or for examinations. Must be citizen of state in addition to 6 months residence
Virginia	3 years college	....	3 years. Prior registration required	3 years	Graduate school approved by A.B.A. or Board of Examiners	6 months residence
Washington	3 years college	....	4 years law office study. Registration required	3 to 4 years law school work, but not yielding a degree, followed by further study in school or in law office in state, in discretion of the board	Graduate from an approved law school	120 days
West Virginia	2 years college or examination by West Virginia University demonstrating possession of equivalent education	....	Not permitted	Not permitted	3 years of full-time study in law school approved by A. B. A. or member of A. A. L. S.	1 year
Wisconsin	3 years college or 2 years college or equivalent if followed by 4 years resident attendance in full-time law school	....	Not permitted	Not permitted	Graduate school approved by A.B.A.	Residence at time of application
Wyoming	None	....	Not permitted	1 year in approved law school, 2 years in law office study	3 years in approved law school	Bona fide residence at time of application